Democracy at Work

One of the greatest challenges in the twenty-first century is to address large, deep, and historic deficits in human development. Democracy at Work explores a crucial question: how does democracy, with all of its messy, contested, and, time-consuming features, advance well-being and improve citizens' lives? Professors Brian Wampler, Natasha Borges Sugiyama, and Michael Touchton argue that differences in the local robustness of three democratic pathways – participatory institutions, rights-based social programs, and inclusive state capacity – best explain the variation in how democratic governments improve well-being. Using novel data from Brazil and innovative analytic techniques, the authors show that participatory institutions permit citizens to express voice and exercise vote, inclusive social programs promote citizenship rights and access to public resources, and more capable local states use public resources according to democratic principles of rights protections and equal access. The analysis uncovers how democracy works to advance capabilities related to poverty, health, women's empowerment, and education.

Brian Wampler is Professor of Political Science at Boise State University. He is the author of *Activating Democracy in Brazil: Popular Participation, Social Justice, and Interlocking Institutions* (2015), and *Participatory Budgeting in Brazil: Contestation, Cooperation and Accountability* (2007).

Natasha Borges Sugiyama is Associate Professor of Political Science at the University of Wisconsin-Milwaukee. She is the author of *Diffusion of Good Government: Social Sector Reforms in Brazil* (2012).

Michael Touchton is Assistant Professor of Political Science at the University of Miami. He is the co-author of *Salvaging Communities: How American Cities Rebuild Closed Military Bases* (Forthcoming) with Amanda Johnson.

Democracy at Work

Pathways
to Well-Being in Brazil

BRIAN WAMPLER
Boise State University

NATASHA BORGES SUGIYAMA
University of Wisconsin – Milwaukee

MICHAEL TOUCHTON
University of Miami

CAMBRIDGE
UNIVERSITY PRESS

CAMBRIDGE
UNIVERSITY PRESS

University Printing House, Cambridge CB2 8BS, United Kingdom

One Liberty Plaza, 20th Floor, New York, NY 10006, USA

477 Williamstown Road, Port Melbourne, VIC 3207, Australia

314-321, 3rd Floor, Plot 3, Splendor Forum, Jasola District Centre, New Delhi - 110025, India

103 Penang Road, #05-06/07, Visioncrest Commercial, Singapore 238467

Cambridge University Press is part of the University of Cambridge.

It furthers the University's mission by disseminating knowledge in the pursuit of education, learning and research at the highest international levels of excellence.

www.cambridge.org
Information on this title: www.cambridge.org/9781108717335
DOI: 10.1017/9781108675949

© Brian Wampler, Natasha Borges Sugiyama, and Michael Touchton 2020

First published 2020
First paperback edition 2022

A catalogue record for this publication is available from the British Library

Library of Congress Cataloging in Publication data
NAMES: Wampler, Brian, author. | Sugiyama, Natasha Borges, author. | Touchton, Michael, 1979– author.
TITLE: Democracy at work : pathways to well-being in Brazil / Brian Wampler, Natasha Borges Sugiyama, Michael Touchton.
DESCRIPTION: Cambridge, United Kingdom ; New York, NY, USA : Cambridge University Press, 2020. | Includes bibliographical references and index.
IDENTIFIERS: LCCN 2019018390 | ISBN 9781108493147 (hardback : alk. paper)
SUBJECTS: LCSH: Democracy – Social aspects – Brazil. | Income distribution – Brazil. | Public health – Brazil. | Women and democracy – Brazil. | Education and state – Brazil. | Brazil – Social policy | Brazil – Social conditions – 21st century.
CLASSIFICATION: LCC JL2481 .W363 2020 | DDC 306.20981–dc23
LC record available at https://lccn.loc.gov/2019018390

ISBN 978-1-108-49314-7 Hardback
ISBN 978-1-108-71733-5 Paperback

Contents

Figures

Tables

TABLES IN APPENDIX

Preface and Acknowledgments

This book is born out of each of our experiences studying Brazilian politics and issues of development. We spent countless hours discussing how Brazil made progress toward human development in the 2000s and early 2010s and saw how our three skill sets could combine to thoroughly address this question in a way that few teams could. We came to this project having previously explored different research questions: Brian had written extensively about Brazil's participatory infrastructure for citizen engagement in local decision-making. Natasha had developed her expertise on municipal-level, pro-poor policy reforms and citizenship development among the poor. Michael brought research experiences related to economic development and an interest in building new datasets to uncover causal processes for Brazil's social, economic, and political transformations. Each of these unique perspectives comes together in our enterprise to understand how local democratic practices contribute to gains in human development in a context with a supportive federal environment and constitutional guarantees for social rights. Where local experiences falter, we wanted to understand why.

Our analysis developed over time and early iterations of our work appeared as conference papers. Together, we have presented versions of chapters at a number of professional conferences organized by the American Political Science Association, the Latin American Studies Association, the International Political Science Association, the Midwest Political Science Association, and the Southern Political Science Association. We thank our panel discussants and audience members for their thoughtful comments and probing questions. Discussants included: Sarah Brooks, Evelyne Huber, James McGuire, Eduardo Moncada, and

Joseph Wong. An early version of our work, which we presented at the LASA Congress in New York, won the best paper award of the subnational politics and society section. That paper, "Democracy at Work: Moving beyond Elections to Improve Well-Being," was later published in the *American Political Science Review* (2017).

Colleagues from various universities have also been kind enough to host us for research presentations, symposia, and colloquia where we refined our ideas. Collectively, we presented portions of our research at the University of Miami's Political Science Department and Institute for Advanced Study of the Americas; Clemson University; the University of Alaska, Southeast; Boise State University; and the World Bank. The Fulbright Foundation supported Michael's engagement with Brazilian scholars at the State University of Campinas (UNICAMP), the Federal University of Rio Grande do Sul, the Federal University of Espirito Santo, the Federal University of Amapá, and the Fundacão Joaquim Nabuco. Wagner Romão was instrumental in helping to make these connections possible.

Our research was supported by a number of institutions, for which we are grateful. The University of Miami also provided generous support for Michael to take a research leave to complete fieldwork on this project. Boise State University and the School of Public Service provided financial support for Brian's research trip to Brazil, sabbatical support, and funding for undergraduate and graduate research assistants. The University of Wisconsin-Milwaukee (UWM) supported Natasha's sabbatical to Brazil. Thanks also go to UWM's Center for Latin American and Caribbean Studies (CLACS) for Natasha's research support in Brazil and to the Office of Undergraduate Research for their Student Undergraduate Research Fellowship program, which connected Natasha to talented undergraduate research assistants.

At the risk of omitting colleagues who offered us helpful comments along away, we also thank the following individuals: Rebecca Abers, Sonia Alvarez, Leonardo Avritzer, Merike Blofield, Joanildo Burity, Maxwell Cameron, Jose Maria Cardoso de Silva, Euzeneia Carlos, Alan Cavalcanti da Cunha, Helenilza Cunha, Zach Elkins, Gustavo Fernandes, Ben Goldfrank, Laura Gomez-Mera, Calla Hummel, Felicia Knaul, Marcelo Kunrath, Luciana Andressa Martins de Souza, Ricardo Mayer, Françoise Montambeault, Carlos Pereira, Tiago Peixoto, Roberto Pires, Lucio Renno, and Kurt Weyland for providing us with their feedback and venues for fruitful dialogue about our ideas. Special thanks go to Wendy

Hunter, with whom Natasha has worked closely on other research related to Bolsa Família.

Several individuals have served as extended team members on this project, including graduate and undergraduate students at our three home institutions. Ana Costa has been an important contributor to our work, assisting with data collection, Freedom of Information requests, graphics, translations, and even accompanying Brian and Mike to conduct research in Pernambuco. In Milwaukee, Luis Mauro Valadão Quiroz Filho and Samuel Orlowski assisted in transcribing focus group interviews. In Brazil, we were aided by Gleiciane Souza, who assisted us in setting up interviews in Camaragibe, Jaboatão dos Guararapes, and Garanhuns.

At the editorial stage, we benefited from advice and copyediting by Jennifer Morales. We are especially grateful to Sara Doskow at Cambridge University Press who provided us with early feedback and guided our manuscript through the review process. Our anonymous reviewers read our manuscripts with great care and offered valuable suggestions, which improved the book tremendously.

It is a terrible custom in academic book publishing to thank family and friends last. We are remiss in doing so here, not because their contributions are any less important, but rather because it is their support that serves as the backbone to our present and future academic enterprise. Our families made the beginnings of this project possible by joining us on research trips and sabbaticals many years ago. Our children, nephews, and nieces motivate us to keep working for a world where social inclusion is a reality for all. So we end with our thanks to them because they inspire our future. In particular, Brian thanks Paula, Sebastian, and Ginger. Natasha thanks Greg, Nina, and Anton. Michael thanks Mom, Dad, and Paul. This book is dedicated to Brazilians who engage with and defend democratic practices to further a more just and inclusive society.

Interviews

Agenilda Ramos Nascimento. Coordinator of the Social Assistance Council, Jaboatão dos Guararapes, Pernambuco; May 22, 2017.

Ana Claudia, Garanhuns, Pernambuco; June 1, 2017.

Ana Paula Oliveira Soares. President of the FUNDEB Council, Garanhuns, Pernambuco; June 1, 2017.

Ana Selma Santos. Former Executive Secretary of Women, Jaboatão dos Guararapes, Pernambuco; June 6, 2017.

Andrea Gomes de Sa. President of the Municipal Education Council, Garanhuns, Pernambuco; June 1, 2017.

Catalina, Garanhuns, Pernambuco; May 28, 2017.

Cynthia Barbosa. Journalist and education activist, Camaragibe, Pernambuco; May 17, 2017.

David, Garanhuns, Pernambuco; May 31, 2017

Debora Tenorio. Police Chief, Garanhuns, Pernambuco; May 31, 2017.

Denivaldo Freire. Secretary of Education, Camaragibe, Pernambuco; May 17, 2017.

Diana Conceição. President of the Municipal Social Assistance Council, Garanhuns, Pernambuco; May 31, 2017.

Dorvalina Maciel de Vasconcelos. Secretary for the Education Councils, Garanhuns, Pernambuco; May 30, 2017.

Edilene Silva. Member of the Municipal Council of Women's Rights and of the *Uniao Brasiliera de Mulher*, Jaboatão dos Guararapes, Pernambuco; May 22, 2017.

Eduardo Gaspar. Public employee – Secretariat of Social Assistance, Camaragibe, Pernambuco; May 19, 2017.

Edvaldo Ferreira, Jr. Secretary of Social Assistance, Camaragibe, Pernambuco; May 17, 2017.

Eliane Alves. CSO leader and women's advocate, Camaragibe, Pernambuco; May 18, 2017.

Eliane Simões Vilar. Secretary of Women, Garanhuns, Pernambuco; May 31, 2017.

Fatima Lacerda. Former Secretary of Planning (2009-2015), Jaboatão dos Guararapes, Pernambuco; May 30, 2017.

Fernando Antonio. Public employee – Secretariat of Education, Camaragibe, Pernambuco; May 17, 2017.

Flavio Eduardo Santos. Executive Secretary of the Health Care Council, Camaragibe, Pernambuco; May 18, 2017.

Gilberta, Garanhuns, Pernambuco; June 3, 2017.

Gilberto Soares Pereira. Health Manager in Caetes (PE), Garanhuns, Pernambuco; May 30, 2017.

Givaldo Nascimento. President of the Municipal Social Assistance Council, Camaragibe, Pernambuco; May 18, 2017.

Humberto Granja Neto. Manager of *Cadastro Único*, Garanhuns, Pernambuco; June 1, 2017.

Janete Tavares. Former public employee - Secretariat of Women, Jaboatão dos Guararapes, Pernambuco; June 5, 2017.

José Juca Melo Filho. Vice President of the Social Assistance Council and Civil Society Councilor, Garanhuns, Pernambuco; May 31, 2017.

Júlio Antão. President of the Municipal Council for Persons with Disability, Camaragibe, Pernambuco; May 17, 2017.

Karina Antunes. Human Rights Manager, Jaboatão dos Guararapes, Pernambuco; May 30, 2017.

Karla Menezes. Former Secretary of Government, Jaboatão dos Guararapes, Pernambuco; May 31, 2017.

Laudicea Oliveira. Journalist and member of Women's and Health Care Councils, Camaragibe, Pernambuco; May 17, 2017.

Leandra Magalhaes dos Santos. Public employee – Secretariat of Health, Garanhuns, Pernambuco; May 31, 2017.

Lubania Barbosa dos Santos. Coordinator of the Municipal Women's Council, Jaboatão dos Guararapes, Pernambuco; May 22, 2017.

Lúcia Teixeira. Lawyer and public employee – Secretariat of Health, Camaragibe, Pernambuco; May 17, 2017.

Marta, Garanhuns, Pernambuco. May 30, 2017.

Maria Selma Melo. Former public employee in the Secretariat of Education in Jaboatão dos Guararapes, – Secretariat of Education, Olinda, Pernambuco; June 5, 2017.

Maria do Carmo Mendes de Oliveira. Former Executive Secretary of Education in Jaboatão dos Guararapes, Olinda, Pernambuco; June 5, 2017.

Moisés Gomes dos Santos. Member of the Municipal Health Care Council and Community Leader, Jaboatão dos Guararapes, Pernambuco; May 22, 2017.

Raquel Miranda. Coordinator of Drug Policies, Jaboatão dos Guararapes, Pernambuco; May 30, 2017.

Renata Cristina Lopes. High school teacher and employee of the *Fundação Joaquim Nabuco*, Jaboatão dos Guararapes, Pernambuco; June 5, 2017.

Ricardo Souza. Tutelary counselor, Garanhuns, Pernambuco; May 29, 2017.

Rosa Rodrigues. Managed federal grants for education in Jaboatão dos Guararapes, Olinda, Pernambuco; June 5, 2017.

Shisneyida Furtado. Acting Secretary of Health, Garanhuns, Pernambuco; June 3, 2017.

Silvia, Garanhuns, Pernambuco; May 30, 2017.

Socorro Araújo. State Executive Secretary of Social Assistance, Recife, Pernambuco; June 8, 2017.

Vera Leão. President of the Municipal Education Council, Camaragibe, Pernambuco; May 16, 2017.

Yacy Novaes. President of the Municipal Council of Children's and Youth's Rights, Garanhuns, Pernambuco; May 31, 2017.

Washington Silva Vieira. President of the Municipal Education Council, Garanhuns, Pernambuco; May 30, 2017.

Abbreviations

BF	Bolsa Família
	Family Grant
BPC	Beneficio de Proteção Continuada
	Social Protection Benefit
CCT	Conditional Cash Transfer
CEDAW	Convention on the Elimination against All Forms of
	Discrimination against Women
CGU	Controladoria Geral da União
	Comptroller General of the Union
CRAS	Centro de Referência da Assistência Social
	Social Assistance Reference Centers
CREAS	Centro de Referência Especializado de Assistência
	Social
	Specialized Social Assistance Reference Centers
CSO	Civil Society Organization
DEM	Democratas
	Democrats
DFID	Department for International Development
ENEM	Exame Nacional do Ensino Médio
	National High School Exam
FIRJAN	Federação das Indústrias do Estado do Rio de Janeiro
	Industry Federation of the State of Rio de Janeiro
FUNDEB	Fundo de Manutenção e Desenvolvimento da
	Educação Básica
	Fund for the Maintenance and Development of Basic
	Education

FUNDEF	Fundo de Manutenção e Desenvolvimento do Ensino Fundamental e de Valorização do Magistério
	Fund for Maintenance and Development of the Fundamental Education and Valorization of Teaching
GDP	Gross Domestic Product
GMM	Generalized method of moments
GNI	Gross National Income
GOBI	Growth monitoring, oral rehydration, breastfeeding, and immunization
HDI	Human Development Index
IBGE	Instituto Brasileiro de Geografia e Estatística
	Brazilian Institute of Geography and Statistics
IBGE MUNIC	Pesquisa de Informações Básicas Municipais
	Survey of Basic Municipal Information
IGD	Índice de Gestão Descentralizada
INAMPS	Instituto Nacional de Assistência Médica da Previdência Social
	National Institute of Medical and Social Services
MDB	Movimento Democrático Brasileiro
	Brazilian Democratic Movement
MDGs	Millennium Development Goals
MDS	Ministério do Desenvolvimento Social e Combate à Fome
	Ministry of Social Development and Fight against Hunger
NGO	Non-governmental organization
NOB	Normas Operacionais Basicas
	Basic Operational Norms
OECD	Organization for Economic Co-operation and Development
OLS	Ordinary least squares
PAHO	Pan American Health Organization
PC do B	Partido Comunista do Brasil
	Communist Party of BrazilPDT Partido Democrático Trabalhista
	Democratic Labor Party
PFL	Partido da Frente Liberal
	Liberal Front Party
PISA	Program for International Student Assessment
PMDB	Partido do Movimento Democrático Brasileiro

	Brazilian Democratic Movement
PSB	Partido Socialista Brasileiro
	Brazilian Socialist Party
PSDB	Partido da Social Democracia Brasileira
	Brazilian Social Democracy Party
PSF	Programa Saúde da Família
	Family Health Program
PT	Partido dos Trabalhadores
	Workers' Party
PTB	Partido Trabalhista Brasileiro
	Brazilian Labour Party
SDGs	Sustainable Development Goals
SERNAM	Servicio Nacional de la Mujer
	National Women's Service
SPM	Secretaria Nacional de Políticas para Mulheres
	National Women's Secretariat
SUS	Sistema Único de Saúde
	Unified Health System
SUAS	Sistema Único de Assistência Social
	System of Unified Social Assistance
TPA	Transparency, Participation, and Accountability
USAID	United States Agency for International Development
UN	United Nations
UNICEF	United Nations International Children's Emergency Fund
UNDP	United Nations Development Program
WHO	World Health Organization

Introduction

One of the greatest challenges in the twenty-first century is to address large, deep, and historic deficits in human development. A crucial question we explore in this book is how democracy – with all of its messy, contested, and time-consuming features – works to advance well-being and improve citizens' lives. Broad evidence demonstrates that democracies provide more public goods and higher standards of living, on average, for citizens than authoritarian countries (Przeworski et al. 1999: 264–265; Lake and Baum 2001; Besley and Kudamatsu 2006; Brown and Mobarak 2009; Acemoglu et al. 2013; Harding and Stasavage 2014; Hodgson 2017; Gerring et al. 2015). We move beyond the conventional explanations – elections, political competition, and partisanship – to develop theory connecting core dimensions of democracy – participation, citizenship, and an inclusive state – to improvements in well-being. In doing so, we illuminate how these dimensions form "pathways" that help citizens and governments achieve better human development outcomes. We argue that differences in the robustness of three democratic pathways – participatory institutions, rights-based social programs, and inclusive state capacity – best explain variation in how democratic governments improve well-being.

Our "pathways" approach uses a much thicker concept of democracy than many previous studies that focus on national elections. The mechanisms we uncover in this analysis link democracy to human development outcomes in novel ways. Participatory institutions permit citizens to express their voice and exercise their vote, which shift basic governance patterns and contribute to well-being. Inclusive social programs based on citizenship rights promote access to public resources that contribute to

well-being. More capable local states, which use public resources according to democratic principles of rights protections and equal access, also
contribute to well-being. Finally, we argue that each of these factors has
independent *and interactive* effects on well-being. These three pathways
create virtuous circles that promote well-being where they are jointly
present, but vicious circles that undermine well-being where they are
not. The book's argument thus moves beyond elections to show how the
ongoing practices associated with democracy provide the most thorough
explanation for local variation in well-being.

We provide a detailed account of how the everyday practices of governing and political contestation are crucial for well-being across four areas
integral to human development – poverty, health, gender empowerment,
and education. The expansion of citizenship rights is a central feature of
political struggles across democracies; there is a long, rich history of
citizens organizing to secure rights that constitutions formally guarantee
as well as demanding to expand those rights (Marshall 1950; Thompson
1964; Dagnino 1998; Yashar 2005; Somers 2008). Citizenship rights are
also a central feature of democratic theory as scholars explore how
democratic regimes restrict, expand, or guarantee the rights that citizens
are able to formally exercise (Marshall 1950; Dahl 1971; Somers 2008).
Our understanding of democratic citizenship rights draws upon
Marshall's three complementary dimensions: civil, political, and social
rights.[1] Democratic regimes provide the foundational ecosystem that
protects citizens as they exercise available rights and struggle to secure
additional rights. Gaining access to basic citizenship rights then also
promotes the expansion of human capabilities, including increased access
to income, employment, health, and education (Sen 1999; Nussbaum
2011). Expanding capabilities leads to greater individual and collective
agency, which then permits citizens to take advantage more fully of the
rights afforded by the democratic regime. Accessing capabilities, agency,
and democratic citizenship rights is not a linear, even process. Rather, it is
an iterative progression that is marked by expansion and contraction.
Advances across capabilities, agency, and democratic citizenship rights
occur at different paces, and short-term backsliding and stagnation are
common in pursuit of long-term gains.

The stakes are high for getting democracy to work for human development. Hundreds of millions of people living in democracies around the

---

[1] A minimal conceptualization of rights comes from the liberal citizenship tradition whereas
a broader civic conceptualization emphasizes citizenship as rights *and* responsibilities.

world struggle to live a decent life. Will their babies live past their first year of life? Will poor women survive childbirth to see their infants thrive and become capable adults? Beyond mere survival, we know that millions languish in destitution, unable to meet their most basic needs, experiencing hunger and homelessness. Additional millions are vulnerable to market changes, lack adequate housing or access to basic health services, and are unable to send their children to decent schools. Those living in poverty need their democracies to lift them out of deprivation and provide them with the tools to live a capable life. Yet, many poor citizens cannot access public goods that will enable them to develop and exercise basic capabilities. Their wealthier counterparts enjoy access to both public goods and private markets. For example, poor citizens lack access to health care or rely on underfunded health clinics where wait times are long and the quality of service is lower than those found at private facilities that cater to the wealthy. Similarly, poor children attending public schools face overcrowding, a limited supply of textbooks, and unprepared teachers, making their prospects for future economic agency through labor markets harder to achieve. All this is to say that poor citizens around the world struggle to gain access to key, basic services, even though democratic regimes offer the promise of rights protection and the creation of opportunities for all citizens.

In this book, we explain how specific democratic practices contribute to well-being. We identify practices, programs, and institutions that help governments to improve the quality of life of their citizens. We find that, at the most extreme, the presence of democratic programs saves lives. Municipalities that adopt more robust participatory democratic institutions and inclusive rights-based social programs have significantly lower levels of infant and maternal mortality. The benefits of democracy are thus not abstract ideals; concrete, democratic practices have meaningful impacts on survival. Although improvements related to infant and maternal mortality offer the starkest life-and-death benefit, we also find that rights-based practices advance other areas crucial to human development; they empower women, encourage school attendance, and raise income. We provide readers with a theoretical framework for how democracy can advance well-being and help to build the necessary capabilities so that individuals can better engage markets, communities, and governments.

The analysis we present draws on a combination of quantitative and qualitative evidence to illuminate how governments, civil servants, and citizens can work together to improve well-being. These processes cannot be taken for granted. Many municipalities are unable to develop the necessary pathways that permit them to significantly improve the lives of their citizens. In the best-case scenario, captured in this book in the Brazilian city of Camaragibe (see Chapter 8), we see the development of a complex participatory system in which citizens and government officials meet in more than twenty-five participatory venues to deliberate over public policies; these cogovernance venues permit the expansion of public debate of public policies and public goods. Government officials also lead efforts to deliver inclusive social policies that enable their residents to exercise the rights formally guaranteed by Brazil's constitution; elected officials and their political appointees support the development of a capable local state that can deliver public services and public goods to poor residents. However, a wealthier city in the same region, Jaboatão dos Guararapes, struggles to provide basic social services and public goods to its citizens. Citizens there lack access to constitutionally guaranteed rights, such as health care, social assistance, and education. Citizens' access to rights and to well-being thus depends greatly on the local configuration of three democratic pathways.

WHAT IS AT STAKE

Brazil is one of the most unequal countries in the world. At the start of the twenty-first century, tens of millions of families had limited income and could only access low-quality public services (e.g., health, education, public safety). Millions of people faced hunger and lived in neighborhoods marred by poor sanitation, substandard housing, and police violence. In sharp contrast, the living standards of a relatively large middle class have been much higher. Brazil's upper-middle class and elite travel internationally on vacations, send children to private primary and secondary schools, use private medical services, and employ private security firms to guard against urban violence. While Brazil made worldwide headlines for its socioeconomic improvements in the early 2000s, much of the inequality described here persists today. Brazil is a rich country overall (the eighth largest economy in world with a population of 210 million), but the benefits of this wealth have not reached many on the lower social rungs.

Social and economic inequality is even starker in Brazil's poor and arid northeast. This region has fared badly when compared to the industrialized south and southeast. Living in poverty in the northeast is simply much worse than being poor elsewhere in the country. Incomes for the poor are lower, the entrenched economic elite are relatively wealthier, and public services are poorly delivered. For example, residents of the metropolitan region around the capital city of Recife, in the state of Pernambuco, experience some of the worst urban poverty in Brazil. There are many preventable infant deaths, mothers die from postnatal complications, and poor young men are victims of waves of homicides. Many children suffer from malnutrition and can only access a low quality of public education as they grow up. Quite simply, lives are not fully developed because millions of residents in the metropolitan region are mired in deep intergenerational poverty. Rural areas are often even worse off, with poor residents unable to travel long distances to access employment, hospitals, and tertiary education which are concentrated in urban centers. While Brazil has made important strides in ameliorating poverty and improving access to social services in recent years, the historical legacies of social exclusion and uneven development remain central problems for equity and human development today.

THEORETICAL AND EMPIRICAL CONTRIBUTIONS

This book makes four important theoretical contributions and three significant empirical and methodological contributions. First, the book demonstrates how key dimensions of democracy – participation, citizenship rights, and an inclusionary state – permit us to conceptualize the multiple venues, strategies, and policy-making processes within democratic environments that influence well-being on a regular basis. We find that there is a "democracy advantage": those places with thicker democracy are more likely to improve well-being than those places with less robust democratic practices. Second, we link debates on citizenship (Marshall 1950; Somers 2008) and human capabilities (Sen 1999; Crocker 2008; Nussbaum 2011) to build a more complete explanation for how the development of agency helps citizens better utilize basic citizenship rights. Our third theoretical contribution is to illuminate how subnational governance units (e.g., municipalities, counties, cities, states) are crucial actors that account for the ability of citizens to exercise rights and improve well-being (Tendler 1997; Grindle 2007; Heller 2017; Snyder 2001).

Our fourth theoretical contribution is to show how the pathways identified above – participatory institutions, inclusive social programs, and state capacity – operate both independently and interactively to influence well-being. Some existing research identifies how participatory institutions (Gonçalves 2014; Touchton and Wampler 2014; Heller

2017), inclusive social programs (Macinko et al. 2006; Rasella et al. 2013; Garay 2017; Touchton et al. 2017; Gibson 2017), or inclusive state capacity (Centeno et al. 2017) generate independent improvements in well-being. However, those studies do not simultaneously incorporate all three components. Our theoretical approach thus includes a fine-grained analysis that incorporates multiple pathways: the importance of participatory institutions, inclusive social policies, and a local state capable of implementing elected governments' policies.

We also make three empirical and methodological contributions to the study of democracy, human development, and, more narrowly, to Brazilian politics. First, we developed one of the largest subnational databases on democracy in the developing world to provide the first broad, deep empirical test of our arguments. This dataset covers 5,570 Brazilian municipalities from 2000 to 2013 across local political institutions, social program delivery, and local state capacity. It also includes extensive indicators for well-being covering income-based poverty, health, women's empowerment, and education. We use this dataset to build quantitative models of well-being and test our hypotheses while controlling for many other potentially relevant factors such as economic conditions, political competition, and local partisanship. The results of our quantitative analysis showcase clear, strong connections between participatory institutions, rights-based social programs, and inclusive state capacity across twelve different indicators for well-being. These results highlight the importance of local democratic governance for well-being over time and across space in a way that had been impossible to evaluate until now.

Our second contribution is to use fieldwork in Brazil to identify causal mechanisms that influence well-being within each pathway and across them. We interviewed more than forty people to better understand how the pathways independently and interactively generated significant variation in outcomes. Finally, we integrate the quantitative and qualitative approaches into a rich mixed-methods approach. Our qualitative analysis thus complements our quantitative models to provide a comprehensive explanation for variation in well-being across all of Brazil's municipalities, while also providing direct illustrations of how these trends operate in individual settings.

Well-Being and Development

Nobel Prize–winning economist Amartya Sen paved the way for research on well-being, by providing the theoretical imperative to move beyond gross domestic product to evaluate the extent to which countries are able to meet their citizens' basic needs (Sen 1999; Drèze and Sen 2013). Sen placed individual-level quality of life at the center of the outcome (well-being) and then argued that enhancing individual-level capabilities helps individuals to develop agency, which would then improve these individuals' ability to engage the market, government, and their communities.

Development, conceived through a human capabilities approach, emphasizes "the crucial role of social opportunities to expand the realm of human agency and freedom, both as an end in itself and as a means of further expansion of freedom" (Drèze and Sen 2002: 8). We use well-being and human development interchangeably in this book because these concepts address similar phenomena, namely, individuals' and communities' ability to harness social and political opportunities to improve their lives. We cover four broad areas of well-being – poverty, health, gender empowerment, and education – to capture the different ways that people's lives may or may not be changing. We assess very specific features of well-being such as infant and maternal mortality, access to basic income, school attendance, etc. We recognize, of course, that these are not the only ways to measure well-being. However, our approach captures essential components, including whether individuals survive birth, live healthy lives, survive childbirth, attend school, and overcome gender discrimination. The breadth of our outcome variables allows us to better identify relationships between inputs, processes, and outcomes as well as when and how different types of outcomes are likely to change.

Democratic regimes provide a broader ecosystem that allows citizens to build capabilities, use agency to place additional claims on governments, and exercise their constitutionally guaranteed civil, political, and social rights (Marshall 1950; Ostrom 1996; Sen 1999; Crocker 2008; Somers 2008). We do not assume that people in democracies can universally develop these capabilities or easily access these rights, but we follow Sen's lead that the full development of capabilities and agency is more likely to take place under democratic regimes because they facilitate exercising agency across a broader range of venues than under authoritarian regimes. These democratic venues provide opportunities to express political voice in formal policy-making venues, to organize protests against policies, to mobilize against the interests of private companies, and to engage markets. Democratic regimes, thus, provide a broader breadth of opportunities for individuals to pursue their individual and collective interests.

Three Pathways to Improving Well-Being

This book focuses on the inner workings of democracy due to our interest in showing how differences in democratic practices lead to variation in levels of well-being. Our focus is on the additional institutions, programs, and policies that are built into democracy as a means to increase opportunities for citizens to participate in public life, to expand citizens' access to a wider range of social policies, and to reorient the state to deliver these policies. A thicker definition of democracy moves beyond elections to better capture the ongoing practice of democracy: citizens exercise political rights to access constitutionally guaranteed social and civil rights; governments implement social programs designed to fulfill social rights; and bureaucrats deliver the services that help to accomplish these goals. Democracy is thus not reducible to biannual elections but is part of the daily lives of elected governments, civil society activists, civil servants, and citizens. We briefly introduce the three pathways here, but they are more fully developed in Chapter 1.

Direct citizen participation within participatory institutions represents one pathway to expanding citizenship rights and improving well-being. Participatory institutions serve as an important mechanism for advancing well-being, as these state-sanctioned institutional processes devolve decision-making authority to venues that incorporate both citizen and government officials (Avritzer 2002; Font 2003; Fung and Wright 2003; Fung 2006; Cornwall and Coelho 2007; Ansell and Gash 2008; Nabatchi 2012; Baiocchi et al. 2011; Pateman 2012; Abers and Keck 2013; Wampler 2015; Heller 2017). These democratic institutions (e.g., participatory budgeting programs, policy councils, town hall meetings, etc.) serve as deliberative decision-making venues that forge new relationships – among citizens, civil society organizations (CSOs), and public officials – and create new policy-making processes. The proliferation of these types of incremental policy-making bodies allows citizens to focus more broadly on public goods provisioning and more narrowly on policy implementation. The adoption of participatory institutions leads to a shift in democratic governance as citizens and government officials are induced to engage each other differently.

Citizenship, which is advanced through the extension of rights-based social policies as part of the state's social rights obligations, constitutes our second pathway to well-being. For many middle-income and developing democratic countries, the extension of social provisioning for the poor has been difficult because of significant and longstanding needs along with limited resources (Huber 1996; Kaufman and Nelson 2004).

In much of Latin America, reformers have also had to overcome political obstacles that result from a corporativist welfare state, where social insurance has primarily benefited the privileged few (e.g., formal sector workers, military, government officials, etc.) while excluding the informal sector and poor (Kaufman and Nelson 2004; Mesa-Lago 1978; Weyland 1996; Hochstetler 2000). In order for countries to fulfill constitutional aspirations to deliver social rights under democracy, governments need to commit to equal treatment for members of the polity and enforce universal citizenship rights. In recent years, governments around the developing world focused on targeting public resources toward the most vulnerable individuals and groups by emphasizing bureaucratic decision-making and well-designed social policies (Fiszbein and Schady 2009; Garay 2017; Rasella et al. 2013; Sugiyama 2012; Teichman 2008). Nondemocratic countries can also pursue social programs that enhance welfare, but often do so to prop up a dominant party or government (e.g., in Diaz-Cayeros, Estévez, and Magaloni 2016). Our focus here is the establishment of social policies that further democratic principles of inclusive citizenship, such as the right to education, health, and social assistance. In practice, this means the government's fulfillment of its citizens' rights as part of its obligation to do so. From the point of view of poor people, this means social programs treat everyone equally and all those who qualify can receive them.

Inclusive state capacity in democracies is our third pathway to well-being. Much contemporary scholarship on the developmental state is rooted in Sen's work on fostering human capabilities as a means to promote productivity, the foundation for economic growth (Evans and Heller 2015; Centeno et al. 2017). A human capabilities approach highlights the state's ability to deliver public goods to a broader range of citizens (Sen 1999). Delivering public goods to the broader citizenry requires states with a competent, trained staff and resources to implement policies. States also benefit from administrative continuity across elected administrations to deliver public goods without elected officials' direct, ongoing influence. Local states embedded in local territorial units (e.g., cities, municipalities, panchayats, etc.) are often charged with implementing policies that national and provincial governments mandate. Low levels of state capacity (e.g., poorly trained personnel, poor access to telecommunications and equipment) can make it difficult to execute even well-designed national public policy. Crucially, local states in the developing world also need to avoid clientelistic practices that undermine local service delivery and performance. The state's capacity to engage citizens and deliver policy reforms is therefore intricately tied to a larger democratic process of inclusion and participation.

In sum, these three pathways offer the opportunity for local governments to initiate a virtuous circle of well-being. There are no guarantees that local governments will support these pathways. Many government officials are unwilling or unable to support reform efforts that expand individual-level capabilities and agency, citizenship rights, and democratic governance. In this book, we develop theory and provide evidence for what happens when municipalities do support these reform efforts.

Brazil: Evaluating Innovation and Well-Being

We turn to Brazil, a middle-income country known for its internal diversity, to test our argument. Brazil offers amazing internal contrasts, whether we consider its historical patterns of colonization, industrial development, internal migration, ecological diversity, or well-being. Profound social differences along gender, race and ethnicity, region, and class now mean that basic access to well-being is unevenly distributed often along these lines. Extreme poverty is highly gendered and racialized, which means that well-being is considerably lower among Afro-Brazilian women. Infant and maternal mortality, for example, are much worse for Afro-Brazilian women (Caldwell 2017). When Afro-Brazilian women live in Brazil's northeast, their problems are compounded. This stark regional, social, and economic inequality found in Brazil is one of the reasons the country is commonly referred to as "Belindia," a term coined by Brazilian economist Edmar Bacha in 1974, to highlight that some parts of the country are similar to modern wealthy Belgium, while other parts are closer to portions of poor underdeveloped India.

Political and policy reformers in Brazil implemented an astounding array of reforms during the 1990s and 2000s, many of which were designed to mitigate the worst effects of Brazil's highly unequal society: universal health programs, local participatory budgeting programs, public policy councils, and conditional cash transfer programs flourished. The international community recognized multiple Brazilian governments for creating innovative policy and institutional solutions to address a wide range of social and political problems such as extreme poverty, poor health, poor education, and a disengaged citizenry (United Nations 1996; Tendler 1997; Macinko et al. 2006; Lindert et al. 2007; Wampler 2007; Fiszbein and Schady 2009; Sugiyama 2012; Hunter and Sugiyama 2014; Fenwick 2015; Hagopian 2016; Arretche 2018). These reform efforts, many of which are operated locally, had to overcome historical practices that could undermine their effectiveness, including patronage, clientelism, administrative malfeasance, corruption, and – on the part of municipalities – a poor track record of providing public goods. Brazil's complex decentralized structure has meant that municipalities can undermine even well-designed programs to improve well-being.

It is not easy to improve well-being through democratic innovations. Building new democratic institutions, inclusive social programs, and a rights-oriented state requires confronting authoritarian legacies directly and reconfiguring political power (O'Donnell 1994; Hochstetler 2000; Power 2010; Wong 2004). Indeed, authoritarian enclaves can be the hardest to dislodge at the local level. We focus on municipal governance because it is the democratic space that most directly impacts citizens' everyday lives. Brazilian municipalities gained greater authority under the 1988 constitution, which means that municipal-level decision-making and local political processes may drive important variations in well-being. Municipal governments have extensive authority to implement nationally designed and funded social programs in crucial areas such as health, education, and public assistance. These local governments have also been home to most participatory institutions, where hundreds of thousands of Brazilians are now elected to hold seats on public policy councils.

Finally, our focus is on Brazil's first decade of the twenty-first century because it represents a period of renewal, hope, and significant social achievements amid an economic boom. Tens of millions escaped extreme poverty, the country enjoyed long, sustained gains in employment through economic growth, and the country elected a leftist president originally from Brazil's socially excluded classes. However, gains were uneven across the country. Some municipalities took advantage of the political and economic moment to generate real improvements in well-being while other municipalities did not. It is important to note that the real advances in well-being did not also result in changes in Brazil's stark inequality. In short, this book explains why citizens' well-being improved in some municipalities while other municipalities made only marginal improvements from 2003 to 2013.

Methodological Approach

Brazil has a decentralized federal system along with an impressive array of data. This permits us to test our hypotheses against the broadest, deepest dataset on local democracy in the developing world. We use mixed-methods research to evaluate connections between local participatory institutions, federal social programs, local state capacity, and outcomes associated with well-being. We draw on an original dataset covering Brazil's 5,570 municipalities that includes measures for our three pathways to well-being and for a wide variety of other factors that may also influence well-being. The outcomes we evaluate fall into four categories of well-being: poverty, health, women's empowerment, and education. Our dataset on local democracy, social policies, state capacity, and well-being represents one of the largest on subnational policies for a developing country and the only one that aligns key local aspects of participation, social programs, and administrative capacity with local human development outcomes. We also collect data on local economic conditions and local electoral democracy to create quantitative models that account for the most prominent explanations for well-being.

We then build statistical models of well-being with a special emphasis on mitigating one of the most common problems in estimating relationships in data like ours, that cover many contexts across time and space: namely, that some municipalities might perform better on both our pathways (independent variables) and outcomes (our dependent variables) for reasons we cannot observe. Furthermore, previous levels of our dependent variables – such as poor or strong performance on infant mortality, for example – may have influenced governments' subsequent choices and the levels of our independent variables when we measure them later. In these cases, relationships we identify in the data could be the result of unobserved variables or reverse causation. We therefore deploy a variety of strategies to avoid mistakenly connecting municipal-level participatory institutions, social programs, and state capacity to outcomes surrounding well-being.

To supplement the quantitative analysis, we also narrow our analytic lens to trace causal processes connecting participatory institutions, social policy, and local state capacity to well-being in three municipalities. We focus on municipalities in Brazil's northeast, the country's poorest region, and capture a period of roughly twelve to fifteen years – from the mid-2000s to 2017, or about three mayoral administrative terms per research site. The case studies allow us to disentangle the complex political processes that appear in general form as "data set observations" in the statistical models. For example, the modeling can point to the importance of civic engagement through participatory venues, but statistics alone cannot explain how and why they matter in practice. This research strategy builds on "nested case" logic (Lieberman 2005), which pairs large-N, quantitative analysis with intensive studies of cases that the quantitative models predict well. The three Brazilian municipalities perform at low, medium, and high levels surrounding well-being and also show different levels of participatory institutions, social program performance, and local state capacity. Process-tracing in these municipalities allows us to establish a causal direction, but also helps us explore whether there is a causal chain to begin with, whether any intervening variables interrupt connections between our pathways and well-being, and to identify any variables that we omitted from previous consideration (Bennett 2010: 209).

We turn briefly to the voices of community members from three north-eastern municipalities to better illuminate the high stakes of local democratic performance. Citizens and government officials shared their experiences with us and conveyed the complex challenges and needs residents face in their communities. As they told us their stories, it became clear that getting democracy to work has never been more important; we incorporate field work into our analysis in Chapter 8, where we assess the causal mechanisms that produce significant differences in how each pathway functions locally.

CAMARAGIBE

Camaragibe is one of the poorest municipalities in Recife's metropolitan region, with a very low per capita income as well as a very low local tax base to pay for additional public services. As one longtime activist explained, the municipality has a long way to go to improve conditions for the poor. Basic social indicators confirm this activist's observations.

We face many social challenges because of low per capita income for a large population in a large city . . . [I]ncomes are low here and we have little purchasing power. Many people here have serious problems and many neighborhoods have pressing needs. Urban transportation networks are terrible, health care is bad, and crime is a big issue (Givaldo José da Silva Nascimento, Camaragibe).

Despite the high poverty, weak economic conditions, and stark inequality, Camaragibe provides much better public services to its citizens when compared with other poor municipalities across Brazil. The municipality thus manages to save lives, educate children, prevent basic diseases, and keep women safe from domestic violence.

Camaragibe achieved these noteworthy gains by investing in rights-based social programs, constructing an extensive system of participatory institutions, and building an inclusive, capable administrative state.

During the 1990s and 2000s, elected governments and their civil society allies built a layered governance system that includes twenty public policy management councils (with more than 200 citizens elected to decision-making positions), expanded rights-based social programs, and bolstered administrative processes to ensure that well-trained professionals were designing and implementing policies.

During the 2000s Camaragibe made notable advances in health and education. For example, the government improved maternal care by implementing a health program that sent community health teams to deliver services to pregnant women in their homes and also to improve access to postnatal care. Community health agents also provide additional support to young mothers and those without access to clean water or adequate sanitation to help them and their babies survive the first year of birth in difficult living situations.

Government officials and civil society leaders also built a complex participatory governance system in which a health council and related councils (e.g., nutrition, sanitation, environment) allowed for an ongoing flow of information among government officials, civil servants, and community leaders. As activist Veronica Leão da Silva declared, "The health council is very strong, because it includes other groups, not just the government. It has workers, service providers, professionals. . . Thus, it is stronger within its context because each group can fight for its rights." Eduardo Santos, another activist, commented, "The politicians don't mess with the health care policies – too many people get upset."

Camaragibe made significant strides in improving peoples' lives. But these advances are fragile and can be swept away if governmental officials and civil society allies do not invest in these processes. As Veronica Leão da Silva stated, "I was a member of the children's council, the social assistance council, the health council, FUNDEB (funding council for basic education), and now the education council. I have also been a substitute for the tutelary council. We feel the fragility of social gains in all of these councils." The challenge for citizens, governments, and civil society is then not only to build these pathways but to strengthen and maintain them over time.

JABOATÃO DOS GUARARAPES

Located in the same metropolitan region as Camaragibe, Jaboatão dos Guararapes (or Jaboatão, for short) made relatively few advances in crafting policies and programs to help its more vulnerable residents, despite having far more wealth. Reflecting on Jabotatão dos Guararapes, Cicera, an older community leader commented:

Jaboatão is a giant. Jaboatão is bigger than Recife. Here we have a seafront, industry, commerce, and a rural area. The municipality collects revenue and is very diversified. So, every mayor who comes here could use Jaboatão's revenue to assist people and still leave a lot of money left over in the municipal budget. All of them leave only debt. . . The municipality has money, there are ways to get these people out of this misery, but no one does it.

Confirming Cicera's comments, Selma, a teacher turned mid-level administrator, described the difficult conditions in Jaboatão when she first started working there in 2003:

At first, I was shocked because I knew Jaboatão was very rich. I interact a lot with the community. In the schools where I work, in the first week I do a field reconnaissance with the class to identify where the school is, who the neighbors are, and find an escape route. . . I always do these things. When I looked at the community, I noticed extreme poverty – Jaboatão never left the [newspaper's] police pages, with stories about robberies and death involving young people . . . everyone kept telling me to be careful. . . The school was frequently robbed, and I kept thinking about what a horrible world it was. Time was passing – that was 2003 – and then, still under the government of Nilton Carneiro, the assembly of teachers started taking place and I used to attend, often in Prazeres. I used to think: "My God, there is no construction work, nothing, in this city." And such terrible schools.

Remarkably, despite its large population of 750,000, the municipality of Jaboatão lacks a public hospital or a sewage treatment plant, provides extremely limited public schooling opportunities, and has high rates of violence. The local government has been unable to provide its poorer residents with basic social services. Despite its relatively high GDP per capita, basic social indicators lag far behind other municipalities with similar levels of economic activity. Great income and wealth disparities within the city mean that a relatively small percentage of the population drives the economy and the majority of the population lives in a vulnerable position. Jaboatão's political history is marked by clientelistic political practices. Tales of local government payoffs by providing monthly food baskets and even coffins to families in exchange for votes are simply part of the local lore.

The inability of the government to provide policies and programs to benefit the municipality's vulnerable residents is rooted in an underperforming administrative state, poorly developed social programs, and weak participatory infrastructure. The municipality hires few well-qualified policy experts and professionals, instead permitting mayors to hire their underqualified cronies. This poorly performing municipal state underperforms in its delivery of such social programs as a conditional cash transfer program (*Bolsa Família*) and a universal health program. Compounding this poorly functioning state is a weak participatory governance system and anemic civil society. The absence of a robust civil society means that there are few groups that strongly advocate on behalf of Jaboatão's more vulnerable residents. This generates a vicious cycle: elected governments hire their cronies, who lack the skills (or interest) to properly implement universal rights-based social programs. The weak participatory system and the absence of an organized civil society to work within this system means that policy debates exclude ordinary citizens' voices.

Jaboatão's inability to provide basic services can be seen most acutely in the areas of health, education, and women's rights. For instance, the poor encounter a badly run community health program and lack access to public hospitals. This makes pregnancy and childbirth unnecessarily precarious for many women. Compounding this problem is the absence of a sewage treatment facility and residents' limited access to waste water management. The lack of an adequate sewage system increases communicable diseases, which then puts infants at increased risk. The educational arena is also poorly organized and particularly underfunded. As Renata, a former school administrator, commented "[The] schools were in unacceptable conditions. They were not schools, they were little rented houses." Schools in Jaboatão ran a revolving door of shifts: morning, midday, late afternoon, and night-classes but shortchanged students on student instruction hours. Jaboatão also suffers from significant gun-related violence as well as domestic violence. Jaboatão took a first step toward advancing women's status in 2010 when the government established a women's rights council and later instituted its first women's center in 2016. Although this women's center was an important advance, it is noteworthy that it was the first center to provide these services in a city of 750,000 residents; demand for these services was much greater than the available supply. As Janette, an activist working in the women's council, explained, Jaboatão has a long way to go toward addressing intimate-partner violence because women do not understand their rights.

Government officials in Jaboatão have been unable or unwilling to establish policies and programs that might help its most vulnerable citizens access their basic social rights, which the 1988 constitution formally guarantees. Officials have made little progress on improving well-being despite the municipality's relatively high levels of wealth. Jaboatão's experience shows how wealth alone is insufficient to produce new institutions and programs that improve well-being. Rather, governments must act to build institutions, policies, and programs that address shortcomings in service delivery and well-being.

GARANHUNS

Garanhuns is situated in the semi-arid interior of Brazil's northeast, a region long known for endemic poverty, clientelism, and low human development. Former President Luis Inácio Lula da Silva was born in an outlying district of Garanhuns; like many others in the 1950s and 1960s, his family left the northeast in search of jobs and a better way of life. Today, Garanhuns is a moderately wealthy municipality in a very poor region; what is particularly noteworthy is that it underperforms on basic well-being indicators. The political elite administering the municipality have invested insufficient resources to tackle poor residents' problems – especially relative to other municipalities with similar economic conditions. Several interviews among professional civil servants suggest that resources are regularly directed to policies and programs that enrich political elites and do not serve the interests of the municipality's poorest residents.

The inability (or unwillingness) of Garanhuns to provide adequate policies and programs is evident in its management of municipal resources. In the area of health, we find that public health clinics and community health teams are frequently located in middle-class neighborhoods as opposed to poor and low-income communities. This allows wealthier residents to pick and choose among private, insurance-covered facilities and public facilities, but it makes it much more difficult for poorer residents to use the services because they must travel by bus to neighborhoods where they do not always feel welcome. In addition, a former municipal health secretary told us that policy reform and innovation was discouraged; the mayor and his close team preferred the status quo over developing new policy solutions to assist their poor and vulnerable residents. This lack of support is compounded by a city administration that closes its offices for the day at 1:30 p.m. every day, thus only providing administrative support for four to five hours. This is hardly enough for a city of 140,000. Health outcomes are worse than in comparable municipalities, which means that poor and vulnerable people are unable to develop their lives to their fullest potential.

In the area of women's rights, we found a dedicated group of police officers working in the "Women's Police Unit." However, these police officers were isolated from City Hall and civil society. In regard to City Hall, there was minimal support for addressing domestic violence and femicide, two major problems facing women in Brazil. In addition, there was no women's council and a weak civil society, which limited the police officers' ability to provide support to women in abusive relationships.

Government officials and civil society leaders in Garanhuns have done less to build key institutions and programs that improve well-being than in comparable Brazilian municipalities. Similar to Jaboatão, the municipality is relatively wealthy, but elected governments have not taken the necessary steps to build institutions, policies, and programs that contribute to well-being.

These examples illustrate the complex interactions of participatory institutions, rights-based social programs, and an inclusive administrative state. We see noteworthy advances in development when governments and their civil society allies promote the use of participatory institutions, rights-based social programs, and inclusive state capacity, as in Camaragibe. A weaker commitment to these institutional reforms translates to fewer opportunities for poorer residents to access their constitutional rights and leads to outcomes first like Jaboatão, where some elements of the pathways are present and outcomes are mediocre, and like Garanhuns, where these features are generally absent and outcomes are poor.

OUTLINE OF THE BOOK

In Chapter 1, we develop our theory surrounding how three pathways – participatory institutions, inclusive social policies, and inclusive state capacity – comprise broader efforts to produce inclusive citizenship, which, in turn, contributes to well-being. We also identify the theoretical interactions among our three pathways to illuminate the multi-faceted ways through which governments construct citizenship and promote well-being. Of course, we place our argument within the larger literature to illuminate how this argument extends and expands the debate surrounding democracy and well-being.

We situate the reader in the Brazilian context in Chapter 2 to lay the foundation for explaining policy reforms, democratic innovations, and local well-being. Brazil witnessed noteworthy improvements in well-being during the timeframe of our study. Our focus in this chapter is on the period immediately preceding these improvements, which includes key processes and reforms that transformed the country's politics in the 1980s and 1990s. Our goal is not to explain these reforms; rather, Chapter 2 prepares the reader to better understand Brazil's general political, historic, and economic context just prior to the 2000s when significant improvements in well-being emerged throughout the country. We therefore describe the more immediate context, from 1975 to 2000, that sets the stage for the 2000–2013 period.

In Chapter 3, we detail our research design, our methodological strategy, and the way we operationalize concepts to test hypotheses connecting local democratic performance to outcomes surrounding well-being. We begin by presenting the rationale for our mixed-methods approach as well as a justification for why Brazil is an excellent case for hypothesis testing. We then describe our unique, broad, deep dataset on Brazil's local participatory institutions, national social program performance at the local level, local state capacity, and well-being.

The heart of the analysis is in the five empirical chapters that cover key topics related to well-being: poverty, health, women's empowerment, and education. We begin with four chapters that rely heavily on statistics and quantitative analysis and then turn to our municipal-level case studies in Chapter 8. Our focus in Chapter 4 is on specific features of poverty: income, employment, and income inequality. Each of these areas connects directly to citizens' living standards, capabilities, and pursuit of their chosen life. Levels of income, employment, and income inequality then serve as a baseline for capabilities, along with health, education, and gender empowerment – all of which combine to impact well-being. Economic conditions occupy the prime position in explanations of poverty because economic growth can create virtuous circles of rising employment, income from wages and investments, consumption, and demand, which provide poor citizens with economic opportunities. However, there is ample evidence that strong economic growth does not necessarily result in concurrent improvements in well-being. We therefore supplement and move beyond a purely economic understanding of poverty by providing a thorough, rigorous accounting of how specific features of democratic regimes complement economic conditions and also influence income, income inequality, and employment in Brazil.

In Chapter 5, our focus is health. Access to health care is at the core of efforts to improve well-being. At the most fundamental level, infants must survive birth and children must survive early childhood in order to benefit from human development programs such as public schooling. Living a dignified life requires that individuals maintain their health, avoid contracting deadly diseases such as malaria and cholera, and receive lifesaving treatment for other chronic diseases, such as HIV/AIDS. This chapter investigates how democratic practices advance health outcomes when coupled with primary health care provisioning. Specifically, we describe the ways that our three pathways improve health service delivery and health outcomes. In this case, the presence of institutional channels for citizens to participate in policy design, implementation, oversight, and evaluation, of inclusive social programs that deliver health services to poor families, of the establishment of a national primary health care system, and of local state capacity all operate independently and interactively to explain variation in health outcomes.

In Chapter 6, our focus is on women's empowerment. Promoting the broader inclusion of women is increasingly recognized as a fundamental criterion to promote human development and well-being (Sen 1999; Nussbaum 2011). Sen's capabilities approach applies to girls and women and includes a large role for gender equity; countries must expand agency for women and girls if they want their population to enjoy greater well-being. In this chapter, we focus on three dimensions of empowerment: women's health, economic agency, and political engagement. We end by discussing the implications for arguments surrounding global efforts to improve women's capabilities.

In Chapter 7, our focus is on education. Basic public education is essential for generating well-being. At the broadest level, education is a means to build basic stocks of human capital and create individual capabilities. Education gives individuals access to new knowledge and skills that enable them to better engage markets, civil society, and politics. We explore how our pathways contribute to certain educational outcomes, while acknowledging that many other outcomes, such as test scores, are slow to change and are less responsive to some of our pathways' influence. We end by discussing the implications for arguments surrounding global efforts to improve governance, education, and well-being.

In Chapter 8, we turn our attention to three Brazilian municipalities to examine how participatory institutions, inclusive social policy, and local state capacity advance well-being on the ground. Brazilian municipalities implemented a wide array of reforms during the 1990s and 2000s, including programs addressing health, local democratic decision-making, and poverty. In this chapter, we highlight examples of government officials and citizens working together within participatory councils to improve policy outcomes, expand access to rights, and deepen the quality of democracy. But we also see instances of policy neglect, in which elected officials promote few policy initiatives to improve the well-being of constituents who are poor. We show how high performance in participation, inclusive social programs, and local administrative capacity contribute to virtuous circles of high human development performance. Of course, this confluence of high performance is difficult to achieve. Many cities have middling or low performance results related to participation, social policy implementation, and state capacity, thus rendering them prone to vicious cycles of underperformance for well-being.

We consider the theoretical and policy implications of our findings in the final chapter. Theoretically, we situate the findings in the broader debates on the quality of democracy, well-being, and democratic citizenship. Our findings demonstrate that there is a "democracy advantage" and not a "democracy penalty" when it comes to improving well-being: the expansion of participatory architecture is associated with improvements in well-being. Similarly, the creation of inclusive social policies based on citizenship rights improves well-being; these programs have a stronger impact when they are adopted in municipalities that also have a more robust participatory architecture and stronger state capacity. Finally, human development improves when a local, capable state delivers social services within a democratic rights-based framework. In sum, the theoretical contribution linking multiple debates marks this as a book that will make an important contribution to political science and development studies. Our policy-related contribution is to better establish the independent and interactive effects of our three pathways. Institutions like the World Bank, United Nations Development Program, USAID, and the Open Government Partnership are currently pursuing the appropriate balance between developing democratic institutions, social policy programs, and state capacity. Moving beyond the fallacy of promoting a single pathway as the "solution," this book demonstrates the vital importance of working across all three pathways to improve well-being around the world.

I

Democracy at Work

INTRODUCTION

Like its practice, democracy is a rich, muddied, and highly contested concept. Many democratic theorists highlight the central role of participation, contestation, and citizenship as core principles (Marshall 1950; Dahl 1971; Pateman 2012).[1] Dryzek reminds us that democracy is "dynamic and open-ended," which allows for formerly excluded citizens to expand their access to rights, public goods, and deliberative policy-making venues (Dryzek 2000: 29). We showcase the ways that multiple features of democracy contribute to well-being by developing theory that connects participation, citizenship rights, and an inclusive state apparatus to well-being.

The core of this book's argument is that three democratic pathways – participatory institutions, rights-based social policies, and an inclusive state apparatus – help explain local variation in well-being. Each pathway directly connects core features of democracy to local governance and public goods provision, which in turn contribute to performance surrounding poverty reduction, health care, women's empowerment, and education. This chapter provides the theoretical reasoning behind how these three pathways independently and interactively influence well-being. We argue that well-being is greatest when citizens, civil society organizations (CSOs), representatives, and public officials participate and deliberate in formal, state-sanctioned participatory institutions; when

[1] For example, core democratic principles also include representation, majority rule, and minority rights (Pitkin 1967; Przeworski et al. 1999). We acknowledge the importance of these principles, but focus on contestation, participation, and citizenship because our data allows us to contribute most effectively to these areas.

governments implement rights-based social programs; and when local states use their administrative capacity to promote inclusive social programs.

There are strong theoretical reasons why we expect each of these factors to have an independent effect on well-being. These pathways also interact, such that the presence of stronger results in one area (e.g., participatory institutions) will buttress performance in a second area (e.g., inclusive state capacity or rights-based social programs) and produce more robust outcomes. A virtuous circle of positive social development becomes more likely when all three pathways function well. It is important to note that we do not necessarily expect all pathways to be present or operate at high levels in all places where well-being is strong. Of course, many municipalities may have only the most rudimentary beginnings of these pathways, which we argue helps to explain their poor performance on basic well-being.

Amartya Sen's pioneering "capabilities" or "human development" approach focuses on individuals' and communities' ability to secure basic, minimal levels of well-being (e.g., surviving birth, food security), and to exercise agency to pursue their best lives (Sen 1999; Nussbaum 2011). This approach is based on the normative assertion that the goal of development should be to improve peoples' general well-being and allow them to live dignified lives. The debate surrounding what development can and should do, and for whom, is of central importance within the Global South. It is becoming increasingly important in older, wealthier democracies, too, because of high poverty levels and great disparities between economic classes. The Human Development Index, the UN's Millennium Development Goals, and Sustainable Development Goals are inspired by the capabilities approach and have clear criteria for what outcomes countries should pursue to improve well-being.

The capabilities approach provides the theoretical tools to better understand the process through which individuals gain and exercise agency over their lives. Sen's work identifies the importance of establishing a minimum threshold for a dignified life, which we interpret as having access to incomes above the poverty line. Once citizens escape extreme poverty, it becomes more likely that they will develop basic skills that permit them to exercise agency. An expansion of agency, in turn, increases the likelihood that citizens will be able to use formally guaranteed rights that are often inaccessible to poor, politically marginalized individuals.

Our overarching argument here is that political struggles to expand human capabilities and promote human development take place in the context of a "thicker democracy." Citizens now use multiple channels to express their demands, including the use of campaigns and elections, participatory channels, community mobilization, and organized protests. In addition, political and policy reformers working inside the state seek to use their influence to implement inclusive social programs that enable citizens to access these rights. Democracy is not a one-dimensional game in which voters only go to the polls on a semi-regular basis. Rather, it is an ongoing, iterative political process that involves a variety of public officials (elected, appointed, civil servants), organizations (parties, civil society organizations), state institutions (agencies, departments), and democratic institutions (participatory, oversight, electoral). Efforts to actively create meaningful citizenship rights are based on the interactions of citizens, civil society organizations, and governments. In turn, we expect the strengthening of our three democratic pathways to improve government performance and, subsequently, well-being.

COMPETING EXPLANATIONS: THE ECONOMY AND DEMOCRATIC ELECTIONS

The question of how to achieve well-being has been of central concern to fields such as political science, sociology, economics, and development studies. Conventional approaches have largely focused on two explanations: the positive effects of economic growth and the centrality of elections. We begin with a focus on two competing explanations for improvements in well-being: economic growth and democratic elections.

The Role of the Economy

The potential connections between economic growth and well-being occupy a central role in recent debates in economics (Rodrik 2000; Dollar and Kraay 2001; Stiglitz 2012; Bhagwati and Panagariya 2013). A general argument, which theoretically applies to all countries, regardless of regime type, is that – from a broad theoretical perspective – the size of a country's economy relates directly to economic opportunities in that country. Most economists and policymakers agree, in a general, theoretical sense, on the potential for reducing poverty by expanding economic activity. Yet, whether economic growth tends to benefit the poor in practice and precisely how it does so has spurred considerable disagreement.

Theoretically, economic growth creates a self-sustaining process, where firms hire new employees to meet new demand, new employees increase their consumption based on new income, and new consumption completes the hiring circle by increasing demand again. In this scenario, opportunities for employment would rise, thus producing gains in wages for rural and urban populations. Increases in income then raise populations above the poverty line and improve their standards of living by allowing them to purchase goods and services. Moreover, economic growth theoretically allows for increases in government revenue without the government having to raise tax rates or sell assets. Greater revenue then provides opportunities for more spending on health care and education in pursuit of human capital, which should also increase wages and productivity while simultaneously reducing poverty. Optimally, poverty falls as growth attacks it from multiple angles.

Proponents of the growth thesis acknowledge that redistribution of income alone is not enough to reduce poverty in countries with a large, poor underclass because there is simply not enough money to redistribute in the first place. Financing expanded health and education is expensive and impossible without economic growth as a foundation. In this sense, the size of the pie must expand dramatically before billions of poor citizens in the developing world can eat a meaningful piece (Collier 2008). Thus, reforms to promote growth should take precedence over reforms designed to redistribute the benefits of growth in sequencing and intensity (Bhagwati and Panagariya 2013).

The operative argument for the growth thesis is that economic expansion offers opportunities to reduce poverty. Many scholars tie increases in economic growth to decreases in poverty (Dollar and Kraay 2002; Ferreira 2010; Bhagwati and Panagariya 2013) and argue that liberalizing markets will generate that growth. Yet, other scholars argue that growth certainly provides opportunities for poverty reduction, but that it is not sufficient to reduce poverty on its own because governments do not necessarily distribute the spoils of economic growth to poor individuals and communities (Xue 2012; Centeno et al. 2017).

Instead of focusing primarily on economic conditions, many scholars highlight the central role of a developmental state for reducing poverty. Under this framework, development policy is designed to foster industrialization, generate mass employment, increase citizens' income, produce human capital, and reduce poverty (Dos Santos 1970; Johnson 1982; Wade 1990; Kohli 2004; Centeno et al. 2017). Centeno, Kohli, and Yashar capture recent thinking on this topic when they argue that "capable states are essential for promoting broad-based development; states must perform certain roles for any society to function" (2017: 1). Evans, Huber, and Stephens complement this claim, stating that "one of the most robust findings of the empirical analyses of the determinants of economic growth is support for the endogenous growth theory hypothesis that human capital has a strong effect on growth" (2017: 382). In this line of reasoning, the state is a central actor that affects the extent to which countries achieve social inclusion and well-being. Growth is a necessary but insufficient condition for poverty reduction because there are no guarantees that high economic growth will reach poor citizens' incomes and expand pro-poor policies that reduce poverty. Rather, particular economic and social policy choices are necessary to channel the benefits of growth toward the poor (Moore and Donaldson 2016).

Finally, we note that many studies of economic growth and well-being are unable to account for confounding variables because of their broad, cross-national research designs. However, focusing on a subset of countries or on one country in particular goes far to resolve this issue (Ravallion and Chen 2007). Many studies of individual countries provide strong evidence for connections between economic growth and poverty reduction. For example, studies in India (Bhagwati and Panagariya 2013), China (Fan et al. 2002; Montalvo and Ravallion 2010), Taiwan (Wade 1990; Tsai and Huang 2007), Singapore (Quibria 2002), and South Korea (Amsden 1992; Booth 1999) all connect economic conditions with poverty and economic growth with poverty reduction.

It is important to note that not all of the countries that have experienced strong economic growth and large reductions in poverty are democratic. Moreover, much of the economic growth and poverty reduction in other countries that are now democracies occurred before these countries' democratic transitions (e.g., South Korea and Taiwan). Pro-market, liberalizing reforms are designed to spur growth regardless of regime type (e.g., authoritarian, democratic, semi-democratic). However, variation in regime type places different pressures on government officials to address poverty-related issues. Importantly, theory and evidence surrounding democracy describe how the system places pressure on elected officials that facilitates spending on public goods, such as education and health care (Lake and Baum 2001; Brown and Hunter 2004; Brown and Mobarak 2009). Subsequently, these secondary social policy choices improve well-being as they foster human capabilities (Sen 1999). But pro-market policies, economic growth, and massive expansion of public goods are not limited to democracies. Furthermore, poverty has fallen rapidly in many nondemocracies as well. This is in part because secondary reforms designed to redistribute the benefits of growth to broad populations are increasingly common in nondemocracies, particularly in East and Southeast Asia.

Thus, there are significant disagreements among scholars regarding whether the presence of a developmental state, economic reforms that spur growth, or regime type offers the strongest explanation for variation in well-being. In this book, we contribute to some aspects of this debate while sidestepping others. We contribute to this debate by exploring how local state capacity, democratic institutions, and inclusive social programs affect well-being. We also harness the power of substantial local variation within one country to evaluate these arguments. This means we do not compare across national regime type (authoritarian vs. democratic), type of developmental state (active, weak, etc.) or sources of national economic growth (regulatory regime, taxation policy, natural resources) to explain variation in human development outcomes. Nevertheless, our research design provides a powerful examination of potential connections among the ongoing practice of democracy, economic conditions, and well-being.

The Role of Democratic Elections

A second conventional explanation for differences in well-being focuses on the role that democratic elections play to bring about social change. Political scientists have devoted the lion's share of their attention to the role of national-level elections to explain democratic achievements in well-being (Huber and Stephens 2001; Wong 2004; McGuire 2010; Gerring et al. 2015; Garay 2017). Most of the democratic canon begins with the fundamental role of "free and fair" elections, for without them democratic politics is absent (Dahl 1971). Democratic theorists argue that elections play a crucial role for inducing elected officials to respond to citizens' needs (Madison 1788; Dahl 1971; Schmitter and Karl 1991; O'Donnell 1998; Cheibub and Przeworski 1999; Przeworski et al. 1999; Kitschelt 2000). The fear of losing elections is the key to democratic accountability because politicians make promises to citizens in exchange for prospective electoral support and citizens retrospectively evaluate whether politicians delivered while in office. Elections are thus often celebrated as a high point in modern representative democracy because citizens have the opportunity to select their leaders and hold them accountable. From an empirical standpoint, election data is publicly available, measurable, and comparable, which enables cross-national research. Yet, a focus on elections obscures the diverse ways that public contestation and participation help to construct citizenship and promote citizens' ongoing involvement in quotidian democratic activities. The focus on elections also has the potential to hang too much on one representative mechanism, suggesting that if competitive elections do not produce better outcomes for citizens, democracy itself may be at fault.

Proponents of the electoral framework argue that electoral competition is not just necessary for democracy to exist, but it is a necessary component that then allows citizens to expand their rights in other areas. This is because multiparty competition may improve governance, efficiency, and policy credibility (Stigler 1972; Barro 1973; Geddes 1994; Brown et al. 2011; Weitz-Shapiro 2012; Touchton 2016). Competition can also foster ideological diversity and thus, policy deliberation (Dahl 1989). Contestation can promote electoral participation and engagement through turnout (Blais and Logo 2009), which could enhance participation through nonelectoral means. In turn, advancement in all of these areas leads to more responsive government in support of marginalized populations.

Voting in free and fair elections is essential for democratic accountability. Some scholars, such as Przeworski, Stokes, and Manin, argue that the vote is the central feature of modern democratic life. "Governments make thousands of decisions that affect individual welfare; citizens only have one instrument to control these decisions: the vote" (Przeworski et al. 1999: 18). This approach highlights the important role of voting but misses the myriad opportunities that citizens and civil society organizations (CSOs) have to influence decision-making over the course of an annual policy cycle. Peter Lindert's influential work follows a similar line of argument in that he shows how the number of eligible voters is associated with a government's interest in producing policies that are beneficial to larger numbers of citizens; Lindert demonstrates that increases in the number of voters led to greater spending on education (2004). Keefer and Khemani (2003) employ the median voter theorem to argue that elected officials have theoretical incentives to craft pro-poor policies in democracies with large numbers of poor voters.

Building on these insights, there is an extensive body of empirical work that demonstrates how electoral democracy improves well-being. Recently, the Varieties of Democracy project compiled the largest cross-national dataset to date on national-level democracy (www.v-dem.net). Their analysis demonstrates the important role of national elections for improving well-being around the world (Gerring et al. 2015). Gerring and his coauthors argue that civil society and composite democracy indices, such as Polity or Freedom House, have a "tenuous relationship to human development" and that electoral factors are much more relevant to explaining human development performance (2015:2).

We agree with the broad thrust of these arguments: elections give voters an opportunity to signal their preferences at the ballot box and help to hold government officials accountable. But there are a number of noteworthy limitations to electoral arguments that suggest that elections may not be the only important factor, or even the primary mechanisms, connecting modern representative democracy to well-being. We first turn our attention to voters and parties and then to modern policy-making processes.

Voters often lack basic information that limits their ability to reward or punish specific candidates or parties. This is particularly true in the context of new democracies, where low levels of education are common (Cleary 2010). Voters have low party identification/partisan identification in many new democracies, which increases the cost of gathering information and makes it more difficult to select candidates or parties that best represent citizens' core interests (Drèze and Sen 1995; Robinson and Verdier 2002; Keefer and Khemani 2003; Samuels and Zucco 2018). Part of the challenge is that political parties in the developing world are often nonideological, nonprogrammatic, personalistic, clientelistic, and fleeting, which makes it hard for voters to differentiate among parties and their policy priorities (Mainwaring 1999; Power and Zucco 2009; Kitschelt et al. 2010; Lupu and Riedl 2013). Further, party systems in new democracies are often inchoate, which increases the disjuncture between voters' low information base and policy outcomes (Mozzafar and Scarrit 2005; Mainwaring and Zoco 2007; Riedl 2014). All to say, the electoral connection between voters, political parties, and candidates for office are quite weak in nascent democracies.

When it comes to voting for the interests of the poor, there are even more barriers to be overcome. The organizational costs of marshaling large numbers of poor voters into a coherent party that advocates on behalf of poor citizens' economic and social interests are very high (Schattschneider 1960; Olson 1965). For instance, Schattschneider's (1960) identification of a middle and upper middle-class bias in representative democracy references the organizational costs of democratic mobilization, which are weighted in favor of those with more information, larger networks, more income, and more free time. More recently, scholars have found that the poor in particular face challenges in using elections to improve well-being (Schattschneider 1960; O'Donnell 1994; Hochstetler 2000; Keefer and Khemani 2003). This problem is especially notable in the developing world, where instability and future uncertainty are present (Diamond 1999; Lupu and Riedl 2013). Politicians can pursue distinct policies counter to their constituents' long-term preferences because of various short-term incentives, even when voters are able to navigate through these challenges to vote according to their preferences (Haggard 1990; McGuire 2006; Keefer 2007; Ross 2006). These difficulties often combine to limit new, democratically elected governments' ability to address basic well-being (Weyland 1996; O'Donnell 1998; Ross 2006; Cleary 2007; Gibson 2013). For these reasons, elections are imperfect mechanisms for aggregating the interests of broad swaths of poor voters in general, but especially in new, less-affluent democracies.

The process of governing within democracies further complicates the electoral connection among voters and their representatives, as public goods provisioning is directly related to ongoing policy-making processes and state capacity. Politicians' ability to act is frequently contingent on state capacity and the availability of resources. It is also contingent on functioning institutions where executives and legislators can make laws and reach agreements or hold one another accountable. Separation of power and separation of purpose makes it hard for voters to hold elected officials accountable because it is difficult to identify the source of either public goods, on one hand, or inaction, on the other (Cox and McCubbins 1986). The inability to identify the source of beneficial or detrimental policies then makes it difficult for voters to reward or punish politicians appropriately. For example, public spending may generate great support for an incumbent government because voters want governments to spend more resources in their areas (Mayhew 1974; Keefer 1999; Pereira and Renno 2003). This prospect may then decrease support for other candidates who are more likely to promote good governance and perhaps deliver universal public goods that improve well-being more broadly. Elections' role for promoting accountability is thus strongly conditioned by state capacity and the availability of public resources, which may be independent of elected officials' influence (Boulding and Brown 2013).

Although elections matter, they are too distant from ongoing, regular policy-making processes to have a direct effect on the specific features of legislation, budgeting, and implementation. Citizens may vote every two or four years, but policy making is ongoing throughout annual budget and policy cycles. This creates a disconnect between the electoral cycle and policy making. Most citizens lack the interest, time, and knowledge regarding how and when they should more directly engage incremental policy-making processes to best pursue their interests. As a result, policy experts, special interests, and entrenched technocrats are theoretically more likely to capture ongoing policy-making processes, as described in scholarship on "Iron Triangles" in US policy making (Adams 1981). A key challenge of modern, representative democracy has thus been to devise alternative mechanisms to permit citizens and CSOs to surpass these challenges and secure benefits for poor populations.

DEMOCRACY AND ITS VARIANTS

We focus on the inner workings of democracy due to our interest in evaluating how democratic practices explain variation in well-being. We begin here with Sartori's work on concept formation, which proposes a "ladder of abstraction" whereby the highest level corresponds to the most "universal conceptualization," allowing for broad, abstract comparison across contexts (1970). For example, the broadest conceptualization of democracy identifies participation, citizenship, and a "usable" state as key features that distinguish democracies from other regime types (Marshall 1950; Dahl 1971; Schmitter and Karl 1991; Linz and Stepan 1996). Participation includes the ability of citizens to organize themselves and press their claims on government officials and other powerholders through electoral competition, protest, and direct engagement in participatory and deliberative venues (Dahl 1971; Tarrow 1994; Fung and Wright 2003). Citizenship includes the ability of individual citizens to exercise civil, political, and social rights (Marshall 1950; Somers 2008); when citizens are able to access and use these rights, they are more likely to be included as full members of the polity. Finally, a "usable" state indicates the elected officials and civil servants can use state authority and resources (e.g., personnel, budgets, force of law) to ensure citizens are able to access formally guaranteed rights (Linz and Stepan 1996). Moving down the ladder of abstraction allows for differentiation of multiple types of democracy while also avoiding conceptual stretching, as all subtypes share the same overarching attributes (Collier and Levitsky 1997). For example, parliamentary and presidential democracy represent two subtypes of democracy, the difference being how contestation is structured institutionally.

Democracies share the same broad characteristics, including the requirement for participation, citizenship, and a usable state (Marshall 1950; Dahl 1971; Linz and Stepan 1996). Scholars of democratization have largely focused on a set of procedures for determining whether regimes are democratic; these procedures entail: "fully contested elections with suffrage and the absence of massive fraud, combined with effective guarantees of civil liberties, including freedom of speech, assembly, and association" (see Collier and Levitsky 1997: 434). In this way, the focus has been on a "procedural minimum" approach for classifying national governments (Schmitter and Karl 1991; Diamond 1999). International development agencies and research programs, such as Freedom House and Polity, largely measure democracies based on whether countries hold free and fair elections and protect civil and political liberties. Scholars often evaluate the variation in countries' quality of democratic practices based on those rankings (Levine and Molina 2011). This broad categorization of democracy is most useful for distinguishing between democratic and nondemocratic regimes, determining when countries have met the minimum requirements for classification as democracies, and comparing countries across time. However, democracy measures based on procedural minimums do not adequately account for the more complex and admittedly messy features of democratic practice. Our analytic task is therefore to differentiate the key components and processes in democracy that can bring about human development.

We begin by highlighting the importance of three key dimensions of democratic practice – participation, citizenship, and a usable state apparatus – and disentangle their component parts. Like most democracy scholars, we view participation as a key foundational concept that is part of the overarching definition (Dahl 1971; Pateman 2012). We include other forms of participation, beyond elections, including formal institutional venues such as town hall meetings, policy councils, and referenda as well as extra-institutional activities such as protests, boycotts, and social audits.

Our framework highlights citizenship rights as a second key dimension because all democracies must include all adults within the polity. A robust set of citizenship rights is necessary for meaningful political contestation to occur. Without citizenship and its corresponding protections, states and elected governments can infringe upon citizens' rights, on the rights of minorities or already politically marginalized communities. For this reason, democratic theorists rightly highlight the need to protect civil and political rights (Madison 1788; Schumpeter 1950; Downs 1957; Diamond 1999; Przeworski et al. 1999; Moller and Skanning 2012). Marshall goes further to highlight the ways that civil and political rights also lead to protections of social rights; citizens use civil and political rights to seek out public policies that promote and protect social rights (1950). Of course, democracies around the world face different underlying challenges in guaranteeing citizenship for their members. Some with centuries-long histories with the slave trade will need to address the incorporation of slaves' descendants. Others with ethno-linguistic fractionalization, for example, will need to address cleavages across language. The key is that meaningful extension of citizenship rights to individuals and vulnerable groups is a requirement for democracy.

We advance theory building on democracy by including a third key dimension to our conceptualization of democracy: a usable state (Linz and Stepan 1996). Democracies need to have a state apparatus that supports the extension of core democratic values. All democratic countries have legal systems that define the appropriate use of public authority and resources. By following rule of law, often embodied in national constitutions and other legislation, the state has a crucial role in actively guaranteeing and protecting rights. By elevating the key role of the state, we seek to "bring the state back" into analytic focus (Evans et al. 1985). When the state embodies inclusionary principles of citizenship, state resources are directed to mechanisms that further democratic obligations for political, civic, and social rights (Linz and Stepan 1996: Heller 2017). The graphic below thus visually represents the three key dimensions we identify in democracy. Of course, democracies around the world will differ substantially in how these dimensions and their related mechanisms operate. We detail those differences below.

Pathways for Human Development

We use the concept of *pathways* to evoke the causal chain connecting democracy to well-being as we move down the ladder of abstraction. All democracies include core attributes of participation, citizenship, and a usable state, although not all democracies will allow citizens to fully exercise the rights formally guaranteed to them under their constitutions (sub-dimension, level 3 in Figure 1.1). We thus recognize that there is considerable variation regarding how democracies allow citizens to participate in public life, exercise citizenship rights, and access policies provided by the state.

Given the variation across democracies, we would also expect democracies to have different "mechanisms" that link democratic goals to well-being (Falleti and Lynch 2009). We argue that the relative strength of each pathway helps explain variation in well-being. For example, participatory

Level 1: Regime Type	Non-Democracy	Democracy		
Level 2: Dimensions	–	Participation	Citizenship	Usable state
Level 3: Sub-Dimensions	–	Formal participatory opportunities	Rights-based social policies	Inclusionary state apparatus
Level 4: Mechanisms	–	Elections Town Hall meetings Policy councils Participatory budgeting Social audits Referenda	Universal social programs Rights-based social programs	Meritocratic hiring Civil service protections Quality of management
Level 5: Operationalization	–	Women's rights councils Environmental-focused public hearings Planning and zoning committees School boards	Conditional Cash Transfer programs (Bolsa Família) Universal health care GI Bill Maternity leave	Index of Decentralized Management Performance-based budgeting Audit agencies Transparency evaluations Civil service exams

FIGURE I.I: Democratic ladders of abstraction

institutions promote citizen participation, which then improves account-ability, public goods provision, and citizens' outcomes. The expansion of citizenship informs democratic commitments to rights-based social pro-visioning, which also changes basic governance and policy relationships and improves citizens' well-being. Inclusive state capacity redirects state action to focus on expansion of public goods and rights protection for greater numbers of citizens, especially those who were previously excluded by the state.

Importantly, we note that these pathways are absent in nondemocratic countries. The democratic dimensions and mechanisms we underscore – participation and participatory institutions, citizenship rights and inclu-sive social programs, and a usable state with inclusive state capacity – may appear to exist in nondemocracies. However, they are not comparable to those we highlight in our study because they are not embedded within a democratic ecosystem that promotes political competition and the pro-tection of political, social, and civil rights.

Thick versus Thin Variants

Our pathways framework accounts for why democracies have varied outcomes when it comes to human development. "Thin" democracies will have minimal levels of participation and citizenship, and a weakly constituted, usable state apparatus; in those settings, participation is largely restricted to campaigns and elections. For instance, some democ-racies will have achieved the "procedural minimum" of free and fair elections, but will not have broadened meaningful citizen participation through other participatory democratic venues. Other democracies may have well-established mechanisms for participation and citizenship pro-tections, but nevertheless have some features of a predatory state appara-tus that otherwise works to disenfranchise historically disadvantaged populations. In this way, democracies display important differences among the three main democratic dimensions – participation, citizenship, and a usable state – with implications for their potential to advance well-being.

Variation in the ability to participate is a key feature to distinguish among democracies. "Thicker" democracies will allow for greater engagement across a wide number of access points, allow for mean-ingful deliberation, and promote egalitarian elements; these are exam-ples of how countries promote participation (Barber 1984; Dryzek 2000; Avritzer 2001; APSA Task Force report 2012; Pateman 2012;

Lindberg et al. 2014; Gerring et al. 2015; Coppedge et al. 2015, 2016). Citizens' ability to access these basic rights is another key marker that allows us to distinguish among democracies; those that do not protect citizens' access to rights are closer to the "thin" form of democracy, whereas those that actively promote citizenship rights are more robust democracies. Finally, differences in the state apparatus can result in weak oversight of state resources, allowing for the persistence of authoritarian enclaves, clientelism, and uneven expressions of democratic norms (O'Donnell 1998; Auyero 2007). In these settings, political machines and personalism can persist in ways that hinder the ability of the government to fulfill its inclusionary democratic commitments.

When democracies have more robust mechanisms in place to advance participation and citizenship, and have an inclusionary state apparatus, we expect to see advances in human development that Amartya Sen identifies as possible under democracy. Democracies that have advanced may have moved, or be attempting to move, beyond procedural minimums for what constitutes democracy. Countries that build greater participatory opportunities, citizenship rights, and an accompanying state to protect these rights, will have a "thicker" version of democracy. When countries or subnational units develop more robust versions of these three key dimensions of democracy, they will then also produce greater improvements in well-being.

There is no single blueprint for how countries should establish their pathways to produce well-being. In our broader argument, we operationalize causal mechanisms in terms of specific institutions and policies. (See level 5 in Figure 1.2). As we describe in greater detail in Chapter 2, we operationalize participatory institutions as: Brazil's local public policy councils; inclusive social policies as a conditional cash transfer program and a universal health program designed to guarantee a dignified life for marginalized populations; and a usable state as an inclusive state that delivers specific, inclusive social programs that extend citizenship rights to the population. In Chapters 4 through 8 of this book, we then evaluate these institutions and policy programs and show how they contribute directly to well-being.

THREE PATHWAYS TO WELL-BEING: PARTICIPATION, CITIZENSHIP, AND USABLE STATE APPARATUS

In this section, we expand on our theoretical rationale for why we expect each of the three main pathways to impact well-being independently. We

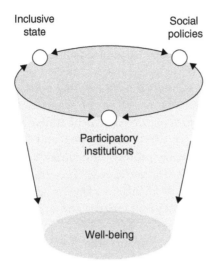

FIGURE I.2: Interaction of pathways

also explain how each pathway interacts with the other two; when two or more pathways are present, we expect that there will be greater performance surrounding well-being than when just one pathway is well represented. These pathways are key features of some democracies, but they also contain within them the mechanisms that produce variations in well-being.

Participation

Citizens' ability to actively participate in public life is the first pathway to promoting human development and improving well-being; participation includes citizens' ability to engage in political competition, vote for government representatives, mobilize for public demonstrations, express voice in formal policy-making processes, and deliberate in the public sphere. Political contestation in new democracies often centers on which rights will be extended to whom – the right to protest, the right to freedom from police harassment, the right to free and fair elections, as well as the right to high-quality public goods and resources. Citizens and organized groups participate to contest existing policies; to promote new ideas, programs, and policies that they believe will allow them to achieve their goals; and to implement, monitor, and evaluate these policies.

Analytically, we identify four distinct areas of participation: (a) engagement in campaigns and elections (Madison 1788; Dahl 1971; Schmitter and Karl 1991; Ferraz and Finan 2011; Huber and Stephens 2012; Gerring et al. 2015); (b) lobbying elected officials (executive and legislative) and civil servants during ongoing policy-making and implementation processes (Adams 1981); (c) engagement in policy-making processes through participatory and deliberative institutions (Fishkin 1991; Dryzek 2000; Avritzer 2002; Fung and Wright 2003; Santos 2005); and (d) organizing protests and direct actions (Alvarez 1990; McAdam et al. 1996; Tarrow 1994; Teixeira and Tatagiba 2005; Mische 2008; Alvarez et al. 2017). These four major areas capture the wide range of activities that citizens and organized groups now use in pursuit of their interests.

Our focus is on the third category, the direct engagement of citizens in participatory and deliberative institutions. Participation and deliberation tread on similar terrain but have important differences. Deliberative institutions theoretically focus more on promoting dialogue to alter participants' attitudes (e.g., reaching consensus) in contrast to participatory institutions, which do not necessarily emphasize extensive deliberation for those ends (Fishkin 1991; Dryzek 2000). Optimally, deliberation creates informed, respectful dialogues that expand participants' understanding of others' attitudes and the issues at hand. In contrast, participation in policy-making processes can occur in many different ways and does not necessarily require a deliberative component to improve policy outcomes. Participatory institutions often incorporate deliberative components, but as one institutional design feature among many (e.g., open vs. closed participation; secret vote vs. consensual decision-making). Another key difference between deliberative and participatory institutions is that the latter are often directly embedded within ongoing local policy-making processes; these institutions empower participants to express voice and exercise their vote to engage public policy-making processes directly (Fung and Wright 2003; Santos 2005). Citizens who engage with these participatory bodies are often granted specific types of decision-making authority over public resources.

In this book, we focus on participatory institutions that incorporate citizens into actual, existing processes that produce local, specific policy changes. As such, participatory institutions directly influence governments' adoption and delivery of programs designed to improve citizens' lives. Ultimately, this translates into influence on outcomes surrounding well-being as well.

Participatory Institutions

Participatory institutions are cogovernance decision-making processes that allow both citizens and government officials to make decisions within them (Pateman 1970, 2012; Avritzer 2002; Fung and Wright 2003; Fung 2006; Cornwall and Coelho 2007; Ansell and Gash 2008; Smith 2009; Baiocchi et al. 2011; Nabatachi 2012; Abers and Keck 2013; Wampler 2015; Falletti and Cunial 2018; Font et al. 2017; Heller 2017). Participatory venues reform existing policy-making processes by forging new relationships among citizens, civil society leaders, and government officials as well as by inducing government officials to use new processes and systems to design and implement policies.

We conceptualize participatory institutions as both politicized democratic institutions and incremental policy-making institutions, a combination that advances efforts to deepen democracy and to improve citizens' well-being. Governments and their civil society allies often adopt participatory institutions in pursuit of democratic goals, such as the incorporation of citizens' voices into deliberative processes (Ostrom 1990; Sen 1999; Dryzek 2000; Avritzer 2002; Fung and Wright 2003; Santos 2005; Smith 2009; Wampler 2012). There is extensive political competition within participatory processes as citizens, organized groups, and elected governments use these new institutions to expand access to civil, political, and social rights (Marshall 1950; Sen 1999; Yashar 2005; Somers 2008). Recent scholarship on participation and deliberation identifies a broad range of processes and institutions necessary to incorporate citizens into policy-making processes (Warren 1996; Dryzek 2000; Fung and Wright 2001; Santos 2005; Fung 2006; Smith 2009; Baiocchi et al 2011; Heller 2017). These include extensive experimentation with how and when citizens participate and deliberate as well as an increased emphasis on transparency (Pateman 2012; Fox 2015). Such approaches allow citizens and government officials to overcome democratic deficits (e.g., low participation, minimal voter knowledge, unresponsive bureaucracies) associated with new, representative democracies.

Participatory institutions focus citizens' attention on all stages of the policy cycle, with special influence over agenda setting and the formulation, adoption, and implementation of policy (Avritzer 2002; Baiocchi

2005; Font 2005; Fung 2006; Wampler 2007; Sintomer et al. 2010; Hartz-Karp 2012). Citizens are induced to participate because they have the potential to directly affect the selection and implementation of public policies; their voice and participation often direct how public resources are spent. There is, of course, variation in the degree of authority that participatory institutions extend to citizens: some institutions allow citizen-participants to propose new policies; others then hold binding votes, while others use nonbinding deliberations and project recommendations.[2] Oversight is part of an ongoing process in which citizens and CSOs monitor the continual delivery of public services, such as health care or education; citizens are then involved in the constant monitoring of politicians', civil servants', and private contractors' actions (Smulovitz and Perruzzoti 2000; Gaventa and McGee 2013; Fox 2015). Thus, participatory institutions allow citizens to engage in the entire policy cycle of implementation, evaluation, and oversight stages of policy-making (Sabatier and Weible 2014).

In practice, participatory venues are designed to alter basic state-society relations. They serve as sites that promote an ongoing dialogue between citizens and elected officials. Citizens and governments exchange information as government officials provide information about the state and policy-making processes; citizens provide information about their needs and demands. This exchange then strengthens bonds and improves trust between citizens and governments and eases the cost of future political interactions (see Wampler 2015; Evans et al. 2017). Citizens, especially those living in underserved communities or with poor access to formal social rights, pursue close involvement with government officials during the policy-formulation stage. This is because these citizens expect the infusion of knowledge, resources, and state authority to help provide individuals living in their neighborhoods and communities with better access social rights.

Finally, these institutions are politicized venues that help community organizations, CSOs, and social movements demonstrate the worthiness of their claims and the strength of their numbers to elected officials (McAdam et al. 1996). Participatory spaces provide the means to support civil society mobilization, which can buttress policy-making processes because the spaces allow CSOs to place pressure on government officials

---

[2] Non-binding votes should be thought of as consultative suggestions from the public to the government. Binding votes are present when representatives working in participatory institutions are required by law to vote to approve new policies or policy changes.

to adopt policies that meet their needs. In addition, elected officials use the venues to identify new leaders, changes in the saliency of policy and political issues, and shifts in mobilization.

The above description highlights the positive impact that participatory institutions may have in political and policy environments, but there are also clear limitations regarding the political and policy impacts that these institutions have on governing and state-society relationships. Participatory institutions still work within a broader democratic ecosystem framed by representative democracy. As such, decision-making authority rests largely with elected officials and civil servants, who often determine participatory institutions' resources and authority (Wampler 2007; Goldfrank 2011; Baiocchi and Ganuza 2017). In the best-case scenario, these venues foster a "cogovernance" process, but there exists a real risk that elected officials will use the participatory institutions to serve their own political agenda (Wampler 2007; McNulty 2011). A further concern relates to the population represented in participatory spaces, often a small subset of the population; this concern leads to fears that the institutions can be captured by the best-organized community organizations or interest groups ("elite capture"). Policy discussions can be complicated by the need to balance specialized knowledge of well-trained civil servants and general knowledge of many participants, most of whom lack the expertise to contribute to in-depth policy discussions. Community members may add new types of knowledge that expand the policy discussion, such as context-specific information or experience with the intensity of problems. But many otherwise struggle to master the intricacies of the policy discussion and therefore cannot contribute at a high level. The policy-making responsibilities within these participatory venues can be quite contradictory: Citizens are expected to work closely with government officials to propose new policy solutions, but they are also supposed to aggressively monitor implementing agencies. Obviously, the balance between working closely with, or in opposition to, strong executive governments is something that legislators around the world have struggled to achieve; citizens working within participatory institutions face even greater challenges to hold executives accountable because their authority is often less clear than that held by elected legislators. For these reasons, the many theoretical benefits associated with citizen engagement can be difficult to fully realize in practice.

Improving Well-Being

Participatory institutions contribute to well-being by creating opportunities for citizens, CSO activists, government officials, and civil servants to directly engage each other in the process of designing, implementing, monitoring, and evaluating new policies. The direct participation of citizens and community leaders in these new venues allows them to advance their demands in deliberative forums that are directly linked to policy selection and implementation. Within these venues, citizens can propose new policies, react to governmental proposals, and oversee implementation of public policies; the exchange of information inside of and parallel to participatory institutions builds knowledge among both citizens and government officials. Building a shared knowledge base generates better policies because citizens can propose policies and reforms that align with existing public resources and authority; governments can alter policies to more effectively address pressing problems.

Building a shared base of knowledge is beneficial for underserved communities that often lack public infrastructure and public goods provision. Community leaders take information back into their communities, thus helping ordinary citizens better understand what types of policy programs or public goods are available. For example, a community leader in the health field first gathers information about the types of prenatal services available or about the nutritional programs for young children. The community leader then provides this information in a targeted fashion to specific individuals and families. In addition, government officials may use the knowledge they gain from community leaders to reallocate resources in order to assess pressing problems. For example, when government officials are informed about the lack of prenatal support of an underserved community, they may be able to provide additional resources.

Participatory institutions also improve well-being when governments adopt and implement public policies that expand citizens' access to basic services. When governments willingly enter into cogovernance relationships, there is then a greater likelihood that the formation of new accountability relationships will encourage them to adopt policies that better meet the needs of citizens and of those communities that lack services. Thus, these institutions create opportunities for new types of political actors – often poor citizens or organizations representing them – to directly influence policy-making processes. Governments respond within these venues, but their growing accountability also encourages them to move beyond the new institutions to craft policies and programs that better meet the needs of poorly served citizens. When governments adopt these policies, there are notable improvements in health, education, poverty, and gender relations. Thus, the adoption of participatory institutions is a key step toward a larger process of crafting policies and programs that can directly influence outcomes.

Participatory institutions also help build citizenship because they encourage citizens to use an expanded set of political rights to advocate for their social and civil rights. In this sense, participatory institutions act as "Schools of Democracy," which permit participants to better understand their rights (Baiocchi 2005). When the "Schools of Democracy" are functioning well, rights-based capabilities are built, which then lead to greater individual and collective agency. Participatory institutions thus serve as a foundational building block that fosters the growth of collective understandings about individual rights and governments' needs to fulfill their democratic obligations: governance and accountability. The ongoing engagement of citizens and government officials in these forums creates the opportunity to generate democratic accountability. Well-being then improves because governments adopt rights-based policies that are designed to address glaring social problems.

Citizenship

The expansion of citizenship through the development of inclusive social policies designed to empower citizens serves as our second pathway to well-being. The extension of citizenship rights is a central feature of political struggles across democracies; there is a long, rich history of citizens organizing themselves to secure access to rights that constitutions formally guarantee, as well as to present claims to expand those rights (Marshall 1950; Thompson 1964; Dagnino 1998; Tarrow 1994; Yashar 2005; Somers 2008). Citizenship rights are also a central feature of democratic theory as scholars have sought to understand how democratic regimes restrict, expand, or guarantee the rights that citizens are able to formally exercise (Marshall 1950; Dahl 1971; Somers 2008).

Our understanding of democratic citizenship rights draws upon Marshall's three complementary dimensions: civil, political, and social rights.[3] Ensuring access to these rights is central to democratic politics

---

[3] A minimal conceptualization of rights comes from the liberal citizenship tradition whereas a broader civic conceptualization emphasizes citizenship as rights *and* responsibilities.

because citizens must have relatively unimpaired opportunities to formulate preferences, engage in individual and collective action, and participate in deliberative processes in pursuit of their interests (Dahl 1971; Dryzek 2000; Avritzer 2002; Fung and Wright 2003; Somers 2008). Marshall's seminal work on citizenship highlights wide variation in citizens' ability to effectively exercise rights; variation occurs across the three dimensions he identifies as well as across different social groups and over time. This is not easy, nor immediate, as the extension of full citizenship must overcome decades or even centuries of practices that have left vulnerable groups subject to semi-feudal and authoritarian social relations in countries that are formally democratic (O'Donnell 1998).

Meaningful access to social rights includes "the right to a modicum of economic welfare and security to the right to share to the full in the social heritage and to live the life of a civilised being according to the standards prevailing in society" (Marshall 1950: 8). The expansion of inclusive social citizenship rights permits poor citizens to access basic public and private goods that wealthier citizens already enjoy. Poor citizens often rely on direct state support to gain access to education, health care, public security, and social assistance because they do not have personal income to purchase these services in the market (Sen 1999). Scholars have noted that the expansion of citizenship rights is often linked to civil society mobilization as well as to purposeful state action directed by elected governments committed to social change (Marshall 1950; Evans and Heller 2015; Heller 2017; Friedman and Hochstetler 2002). Thus, it is the interaction of civil society, elected officials, and a capable state committed to constitutional and legislative acts that produces the conditions most conducive to expanding citizenship rights.

As T. H. Marshall (1950) notes, the expansion of citizenship is not automatic under democracy; in Britain, it took place in sequential order, with civil rights emerging prior to the realization of political and social rights. For much of Europe, the development of the welfare state emerged after the establishment of cross-class voting rights and resulted from political organizing, party politics, and their engagement with democratic political institutions (Huber and Stephens 2001; Esping-Andersen 1990; 2017). In this way, the establishment of the welfare state in many advanced, industrialized countries is not only deeply rooted in a democratic process, but also reflects the adoption of universalistic principles of meaningful social citizenship. We acknowledge that democratic and nondemocratic countries alike can pursue social programs that enhance welfare. But our focus is on social provisioning that furthers the democratic principle of inclusive citizenship. In practice, this means the government's commitment to equal treatment for members in the polity as well as equal enforcement of citizenship rights (Garay 2017).

Rights-Based Social Policies

Rights-based social policies are predicated on the understanding that citizens must be able to access public resources and services to exercise their legal rights. Social rights depend, first and foremost, on citizens surpassing minimum thresholds of health and material conditions to live a dignified life. The second step is for citizens to develop their basic capabilities, which then allows them to exercise individual agency. This, in turn, allows them to take advantage of political and policy opportunities to improve their well-being. Debates on capabilities and citizenship offer a way forward in this area (Marshall 1950 and Sen 1999). Accessing social citizenship rights then increases the probability of achieving greater well-being by overcoming resignation to one's station in life and seeking a better future (Hunter and Sugiyama 2014). For example, exercising rights empowers citizens to work within civil society, engage government and state officials, and participate more effectively in markets. Of course, building capabilities and exercising agency and rights is not necessarily a linear process; we conceptualize this as more of an iterative process, through which citizens slowly accumulate skills and knowledge to advance their well-being by taking advantage of state, market, and societal opportunities.

A rights-based approach to social policy builds citizens' capabilities and agency through universal access to improved public goods. Scholarship on the developing world reveals that public goods provisioning is particularly important for well-being because of its transformative effects at the individual level. Development, conceived through a human capabilities approach, emphasizes "the crucial role of social opportunities to expand the realm of human agency and freedom, both as an end in itself and as a means of further expansion of freedom" (Drèze and Sen 2002: 8). For the most destitute and marginalized populations, minimum social conditions are necessary to even attempt to build capabilities, employ agency, and exercise one's political rights. After all, exercising one's political rights (e.g., through voting, protests, and community engagement) may be impossible when faced with uncertain daily survival that occupies one's total energies (e.g., finding shelter, food, medicine, and clothing). Feelings of powerlessness and despair can paralyze individuals in marginalized circumstances and prevent them from exercising their rights, which further restricts their ability to activate their citizenship. Social policies that advance agency and inclusion, particularly among the poor and historically marginalized groups, thus become an important prescription for finding one's "voice" and demanding social, economic, and political empowerment. Feelings of agency or the notion that individuals "effectively shape their own destiny" are often lacking among the poor, but are essential for building human capabilities (Sen 1999: 11; Narayan et al. 2000).

Scholars acknowledge that social policies are not only ends for transformation, but also become mechanisms for subsequent change that restructures politics, at the state, group, and individual levels (De la O 2015; Pierson 1993; Skocpol 1992; Zucco 2013). Positive feelings of self-worth can emerge from a realization that governments respect their citizenship rights and offer programs to assist them and confer those rights (Mettler 2007). Mettler's 2007 work on the GI Bill in the United States demonstrates how social policies create feelings of inclusion to construct citizens. Within less-developed countries, social policy can be a pathway for deepening feelings of citizenship among groups that had been previously marginalized (Freeland 2007; Hunter and Sugiyama 2014). In short, expanded social provisioning can create a sense of belonging that is vital for full citizenship.

Individual beneficiaries' responses to social policy matter, in part, because of their aggregated effects for creating new groups and political actors. Research on older democracies reveals how expanded social provisioning alongside citizens' engagement work together to create "policy feedback" effects (Pierson 1993). Theda Skocpol's (1992) seminal work on the development of social welfare in the United States shows the post–Civil War expansion of benefits for veterans and widows, known as "mothers' pensions," structured maternalist social welfare in the Progressive Era and beyond. Importantly, Skocpol reveals how policy was linked to women's voluntary organizations that took shape prior to the expansion of women's suffrage. Thus, in the context of a new democracy in the Global South, social policies carry the potential to create rights-bearing individuals, who will exercise agency both individually and collectively.

Improving Well-Being

Rights-based social policies improve well-being through policy design that delivers policies to underserved individuals and communities while also empowering them. Universal education and health programs expand access to services, thus allowing citizens to better exercise constitutionally guaranteed rights. Fewer babies and women die when state programs deliver better health services and, as such, well-being improves. Similarly, children stay in school longer and acquire the skills necessary to secure jobs and engage the broader world when state programs deliver better education services. Thus, well-being improves in these areas as well.

Beginning in the late 1980s and continuing into the beginning of the twenty-first century, many Third Wave democracies grappled with dual pressures: delivering constitutionally guaranteed rights while facing fiscal constraints associated with neoliberal economic reforms (Huber 1996). Even in settings with organized and vocal demands for expanded access to state resources, the extension of universal social provisioning similar to that found in Europe would be infeasible amid a recessionary backdrop. Throughout much of the 1990s, governments reduced state spending in key social areas (e.g., education and health) and mounted minimalist safety net programs designed as temporary measures to offset the labor disruptions associated with neoliberal economic reforms (Graham 1994; Birdsall et al. 1996; Kaufman and Nelson 2004). Rather than expand social welfare through inclusive citizenship principles, as was the case in Europe, new democracies in developing contexts focused instead on more modest and piecemeal efforts (Graham 1994). In the education sector, for example, policymakers encountered unfavorable political conditions for reform. Reforms had highly concentrated costs with diffuse benefits, enabling well-organized interest groups in the form of organized teachers' unions, bureaucrats, and university students to serve as veto points for change (Corrales 1999). Rather than fundamentally reorganize the sector, policymakers would make incremental changes. The challenge would be to do more with fewer resources. The solution for many Latin American economists was technical: to address inclusion through targeted programs, aiming for greater efficiency and effectiveness (Teichman 2004).

During the mid-to-late 1990s, governments around the developing world focused on targeting public resources toward the most vulnerable individuals and groups by emphasizing bureaucratic decision-making and well-designed social policies. For example, Conditional Cash Transfer (CCT) programs are one mechanism through which democracy works to improve well-being. CCTs are emblematic of the strategy to address immediate poverty alleviation, while also advancing human development by improving low levels of well-being and disrupting the intergenerational transmission of poverty. These programs exemplify this approach by linking monthly payments to behavioral changes thought to promote human development (Fiszbein and Schady 2009). The conditional part of the grant means that families can lose access to monthly benefits if they fail to comply with stipulated requirements. This approach is broadly recognized as having positive impacts on short-term behaviors. For example, Mexico's *Oportunidades* (Opportunity), a nationwide CCT program, includes conditionality requirements for children to attend school and receive health monitoring. CCTs were first implemented in Mexico and Brazil in the mid-1990s but have since spread throughout the Americas (Sugiyama 2012; De la O 2015). Many countries that adopted CCTs also restructured the health sector by focusing on universal and preventive health care (Garay 2017).

Reforms to establish rights-based social policies show that governments need not spend large sums of money to achieve marked improvements in poverty relief, education, and health (Hunter and Sugiyama 2009). There is even some evidence that policy design and progressive investment in areas that affect the poor, such as primary school and preventive health care, are more important than absolute spending levels (McGuire 2010; Sugiyama 2012). This is particularly true for developing countries that have historically prioritized expensive services such as hospitals and universities, rather than more basic services that the poor depend upon. The key is to deliver well-designed and targeted social policies in ways that advance social rights, while insulating resources from political capture.

Social policies also extend beyond increasing income to secure a dignified life. Many countries have experimented with inclusive, community-based health programs to improve well-being. Many of these programs are predicated on the argument that health outcomes, such as infant mortality and maternal mortality, depend more on low-cost preventive care and having a skilled attendant at birth (McGuire 2010). Spending on expensive curative care (e.g., specialized doctors and hospital procedures), rather than on primary care, can undermine treatment for common problems that impact broad swaths of the population (e.g., mosquito-borne illnesses, infant mortality, and maternal mortality). Instead, reaching vulnerable groups, such as the poor, women, the disabled, and the elderly, requires expanding access to high-quality care. Public health advocates therefore promote preventive primary care over costly, curative-care models. Thus, how governments spend money on health care may impact health outcomes more than how much they spend. In practice, community-based health care programs serve as direct mechanisms to improve well-being.

Usable State

A usable state with corresponding inclusionary state apparatus constitutes our third pathway to improving well-being. By an inclusionary state, we mean governments' ability to direct state action to deliver public goods, services, and policies to a broad range of citizens. Building inclusive state capacity increases the likelihood that citizens can access formally guaranteed rights, especially social rights. As James C. Scott argues, "[t]he state ... is the vexed institution that is the ground of both our freedoms and our unfreedoms" (Scott 1998: 7). Our focus is on the vital role that states often play in delivering public goods that increase the likelihood that individuals and groups can develop capabilities and access citizenship rights, thus expanding their freedoms. States can play a vital role in allocating public goods to those sectors that have been traditionally excluded from access to basic public goods.

The task of establishing a democratic state is not easy and scholars have noted that features of liberal democratic participation can coincide with more exclusionary state action that serves as instruments of repression, exclusion, and extraction (Somers 2008; Soss and Weaver 2017). States can systematically violate many citizens' basic rights, generating what Scott (2008) refers to as "unfreedoms." For instance, the state can be used to control specific segments of populations, often leading to internal "statelessness" where individuals are formal citizens of a country but are unable to exercise basic rights available to others (Somers 2008). Policing serves as a clear demonstration of these phenomena, where direct police control over poor communities is often much more brutal than policing methods employed among wealthier citizens. As Soss and Weaver argue in the contemporary United States context, policing has taken on a controlling face as "race-class subjected communities" are governed through coercion, containment, repression, surveillance, regulation, predation, discipline, and violence (2017). Low revenue-raising capacity among local governments creates a vicious cycle of predation, as local governments utilize the state's coercive power to extract resources from subjugated communities. For these reasons, we acknowledge that democratic norms of equality before the law along with increased state capacity are crucial for countries to develop states capable of overcoming historic legacies of social, political, and economic exclusion to become instruments of inclusion. This process is not linear or easy to undertake, but crucial if citizens are to enjoy meaningful citizenship.

Much contemporary scholarship on the developmental state is rooted in Sen's work on fostering human capabilities as a means to promote productivity, the foundation for economic growth (Evans and Heller 2015; Fox 2015; Centeno et al. 2017). A human capabilities approach broadens the scope of action to all citizens and highlights the state's ability to deliver public goods (Sen 1999), rather than using collaboration with a narrow group of potential industrialists to incentivize industrial investment (Kohli 2004). Low levels of state capacity (e.g., poorly trained personnel and poor access to telecommunications and equipment) can make it difficult to execute even well-designed public policy. The state's capacity to engage citizens and deliver policy reforms is therefore intricately tied to a larger democratic process of inclusion and participation.

State capacity is notoriously fragmented across the Global South, as middle-income countries often have high levels of capacity in some areas (e.g., oil extraction, ports) but lack the ability to provide other services (e.g., birth registries, sanitation, housing). We acknowledge that authoritarian regimes may be able to establish strong states. However, creating more capable *inclusive* states promotes the expansion of citizens' constitutional rights through social accountability mechanisms (Fox 2015). Thus, capable, democratic states are better situated to deliver inclusive, rights-based social programs, protect civil liberties, and improve well-being.

Inclusionary State Apparatus

Centeno, Kohli, and Yashar (2017) argue that active state involvement is crucial for generating human capital and is a fundamental part of establishing sustainable human development and well-being. Specifically, they identify a central role for state bureaucrats to design and deliver social policies that will enhance citizens' capabilities. Two chapters in Centeno, Kohli, and Yashar's edited volume illuminate directly how building state capacity intimately links local states and civil society. Heller argues, "[i]n order to be effective, the local state must enjoy bureaucratic, fiscal, and coordination capacity" (Heller 2017: 313). Further, Heller argues that "development, both in terms of growth and inclusion, also calls for collective power. This coordination function depends critically on how and with whom the state is embedded. In the democratic ideal, it is embedded in civil society through both representational mechanisms of electoral politics and more direct forms of accountability and coproduction with its citizens" (Heller 2017: 313). Importantly, Heller links democratic politics to state capacity; we should therefore expect local states to act differently depending on how they are linked to civil society. The belief that access to public goods is a social right, rather than a personal favor, needs to be reinforced through federal policy design and enacted locally (Hunter and Sugiyama 2014). We argue that embedding state capacity in a broader democratic ecosystem allows for greater influence of citizens in policy formulation as well as in oversight processes, thereby increasing the likelihood that state capacity will be used to advance the rights formally established in constitutional law.

Building an inclusionary state apparatus encompasses the degree to which states are able and willing to support inclusive social policies. These can take the form of nationally led programs, whereby the line ministries and local states implement centrally coordinated policies. It can also take the form of local initiatives in which elected officials and civil servants adopt new policies to expand access to democratic rights.

Decentralization was designed to address gaps in state capacity among large, Third Wave democracies (Campbell 2003). Decentralized local governance would theoretically improve local service provision by rendering local authorities more responsive to voters and corruption more visible and thus easier to control (Tendler 1997; Faguet 2008; Grindle 2007: 7–8). Yet decentralization has not lived up to expectations in many settings (Gibson 2013; Giraudy 2013) and entrenched clientelism often distorts governing in ways that perpetuate poverty and harm the poor (Weyland 1996; Diaz-Cayeros et al. 2016). Subnational authoritarian enclaves continue to hinder governance and impede the construction of meaningful citizenship in many federal democracies.

Improving Well-Being

An inclusionary state apparatus improves well-being through sufficient administrative staffing, administrative continuity, local resources, and meritocratic hiring. All of these areas directly influence the quality of service delivery across the entire range of government programs. Raising the local administration's capacity to deliver services will extend these services to areas where they are desperately needed and also improve their quality. In turn, well-being stems from delivering high-quality services to vulnerable populations across many sectors, including health, poverty, education, and women's empowerment.

Sufficient administrative staffing is a clear indicator of a capable state. Local states must hire employees with appropriate professional training and experience for their jobs. For instance, creating a professional civil service requires employees in the health sector to be trained in medicine or to have a public health background. Those hired in sanitation should be familiar with that area. Properly trained staff make programs more successful through their competence in regular operations. Competent, trained staff contextualize their work within federal regulations, and understand their roles as part of a larger administrative context. Professional training is not only important for low- and mid-level bureaucrats, but is also critical for high-level political appointees to help them make overall policy decisions and justify spending strategies.

Continuity in administrative staffing is critical to program design and implementation in health, education, and social assistance. In Brazil, for example, many state agencies and elected governments suffer from major turnover among personnel over each four-year electoral cycle. Each reshuffling of qualified personnel then requires reestablishing administrative ties to policy councils, reconfiguring federal program administration, and renegotiating contracts. Moreover, high administrative turnover can even lead to canceling local social programs or, at a minimum, rebuilding programs and redoing much of the previous administrations' work, which then undermines vulnerable populations' access to these programs. Municipalities and vulnerable populations are thus theoretically better off in several important areas when municipalities maintain administrative continuity across mayoral administrations.

Program administration also requires a minimum amount of resources. This condition may be the most difficult to meet because a large percentage of municipal governments across the developing world have limited funding, limited revenue-raising ability, and face general fiscal shortfalls. The biggest challenge for municipalities in this area is then how to maximize services and administrative performance with scarce resources. Municipalities where administrators more effectively prioritize resources for programs that improve well-being and identify fiscal opportunities to improve those programs' performance are likely to advance citizens' well-being relative to those that do not.

Finally, having trained staff who are hired based on their expertise and not their political connections helps programs operate effectively and impartially. Technocratic, nonpolitical allocation of resources protects social programs from being used as political patronage and improves their performance. We expect to see greater well-being in areas where local states hire professionals, commit to assist citizens in accessing constitutionally defined citizenship rights, and commit to enhancing their capabilities. Citizens' and nationally elected governments' ability to harness state capacity and use it to deliver services is therefore a crucial third pathway to improving well-being – especially in new democracies where the local state faces myriad problems with coordination, oversight, and accountability.

Interactive Effects

We theorize potential interactive relationships across participatory institutions, rights-based social policies, and an inclusionary state apparatus. These pathways are independent, as argued above, but they also interact, which amplifies their potential effects on well-being. The relationships comprise interactions that operate as illustrated in Figure 1.2.

Participatory institutions influence the performance of social policies by expanding policy debates and discussing communities' needs. Although these venues vary in their design, they generally work to bring together citizens and government officials to discuss pressing social needs. For instance, participatory budgeting programs focus on the distribution of public resources and allow community members to weigh the relevant social investments that are necessary for human development; whereas public policy councils allow citizens to track current government commitments as well as engage in policy implementation and oversight (Baiocchi et al. 2011; Pogrebinschi and Samuels 2014; Almeida et al. 2015; Gurza et al. 2015). Participatory venues also permit citizens to bring local knowledge to bear on intricate policy discussions (Gaventa and McGee 2013; Fox 2015; Wampler 2015). Within participatory institutions, citizens often deliberate over and vote on a combination of broad thematic issues (e.g., more funding for education) as well as more specific issues (e.g., agency-level budgets and year-end reports). The communication channels are thus multidirectional. For example, community service organizations can use the knowledge they gain through participatory institutions to encourage the community's use of available services. State-society engagement can be crucial to advance service uptake in instances where government services are underutilized for lack of familiarity.

Participatory institutions can also advance inclusionary state capacity because they promote interaction among citizens and state officials.

Providing better information to state officials increases the likelihood that it will inform policy and improve outcomes. Additionally, enhanced transparency may be one of the clearest mechanisms associated with participatory processes, as regular meetings require public officials and the community to share information. The act of making information available represents an advance for nascent democracies, which tend to be less practiced with freedom of information norms. Participatory institutions therefore have the potential to spur government responses for reform when they disseminate information about poor municipal performance in social program administration (Abers and Keck 2013). Participatory venues constitute part of a new web of "interlocking institutions" through which participatory institutions, state agencies, and government bodies interact and buttress one another through formal and informal connections (Wampler 2015). Once made aware of problems, participants in these institutions can pressure local officials to improve service delivery (Gaventa and McGee 2013; Fox 2015). Community leaders also forge new connections to civil servants responsible for implementing specific projects, which permits them to gather information about these programs for their communities as well as to inform these civil servants of their community's needs.

Rights-based social policies also promote the expansion and effectiveness of participatory institutions, as previously vulnerable groups gain political agency. As Pierson (1993) notes, public policies can create feedback effects by creating new groups of actors and redefining the political space for contestation. Progressive and inclusionary social policies, such as the GI Bill in the United States and the Bolsa Família program in Brazil, can empower citizens as they become agents who see themselves as meriting state investment. As Hunter and Sugiyama (2014) argue, Bolsa Família contributes to citizenship as beneficiaries express a sense of agency and claim rights to state benefits. Conditional cash transfer programs also have the potential to generate cross-sectoral demands for improved quality of services as the conditionality requirements for benefits include regular use of health and education services. As active users of social services, the poor have the potential to demand that the government fulfill its obligation to provide education and health services. For instance, the poor have good reason to complain if teachers have high absenteeism or medical facilities lack doctors. Interactions between rights-based social policies and inclusionary state capacity also illuminate the importance of Sen's capabilities approach because individuals and communities must begin to exercise agency in order to pursue their rights.

Finally, experts' concerns for delivering rights-based social policies can expose deficiencies in inclusionary state capacity in ways that ultimately strengthen it. Federal bureaucrats in many developing countries have long been concerned about the capture of public goods through clientelism and patronage practices. In large federal countries, the solution has been to tighten national oversight and design public policies in ways that minimize the transfer of resources to subnational governments (Lindert 2005; Fenwick 2009). Mechanisms such as direct payment of grants to beneficiaries via bankcards or cell phones are just one such mechanism (Garcia and Saavedra 2017).

National policy can also require local transparency and accounting practices that reinforce good governance practices. Tight fiscal controls and reporting requirements theoretically constrain local political patrons' ability to manipulate access to public resources, thereby undermining clientelistic practices such as vote buying. Yet such measures are insufficient when local governments fail to effectively oversee local implementation of national programs. For this reason, national governments can and do use policy design to improve inclusionary state capacity. One such way is to dedicate resources to local governments as part of an overall policy package, by allocating special funding for local infrastructure (e.g., computer upgrades and training personnel). Another is to create inducements for local investments that prioritize social priorities (e.g., matching grants) and fiscal rewards for effective program implementation. As inclusionary state capacity improves, we would expect mutually reinforcing effects with public policy delivery. Technocratic provisioning of constitutionally guaranteed social services thus has the power to elevate poor people's living standards and transform them into full citizens.

Finally, participatory institutions and inclusionary state capacity can work together to produce mutually beneficial results. Participatory channels for community engagement require that government officials provide a minimal investment in personnel and information to stimulate meaningful discussion. The local administration's ability to implement policies and engage with participatory institutions is then critical for their credibility and sustainability, since participatory institutions will have less influence if their chosen policies are never implemented. However, the rewards that come with participation can go both ways, with government officials also gaining insights into the needs and experiences of the poor.

CONCLUSION

The theoretical approach developed in this chapter provides a more nuanced understanding of how democratic practices influence well-being. We rely on a thicker version of democracy that includes liberal, participatory, deliberative, and egalitarian strands to make connections among participatory institutions, rights-based social policies, and an inclusionary state apparatus. Elections still matter for well-being, but we argue that they are often flawed instruments for capturing voters' preferences and that they are distant from day-to-day governance. Expanding our concept of democracy permits us to incorporate a focus on citizenship rights – those rights that ordinary citizens can exercise. The emphasis on citizenship rights then links our argument to Sen's capabilities or human development approach. Very low incomes and high inequality in many democracies, especially those in the Global South, mean that hundreds of millions of citizens live in poverty. The capabilities approach establishes a useful point of departure – humans require minimum capabilities, beyond simply overcoming poverty, to live dignified lives. Once individuals are beyond this threshold, it then becomes more likely that they will develop the necessary agency to demand and exercise political, civil, and social citizenship rights.

In this chapter we developed three pathways to well-being that incorporate features of the citizenship and capabilities approaches. Participatory institutions provide venues where citizens exercise political, civil, and social rights to influence and improve policy throughout the policy cycle. Targeted rights-based social programs raise capabilities in the present and build a foundation for future capabilities. In so doing, they also inform citizens of their rights, increase the prospects that citizens will exercise these rights, and raise the possibility of demanding additional rights. A local inclusionary state apparatus administers programs and delivers services that also promote citizenship rights and well-being through effective, impartial, distribution of resources. Finally, these three pathways interact, forming virtuous circles that promote citizenship rights, good governance, improved service provision, and well-being when all three pathways operate at high levels.

The book now turns to Brazil, the focus of our empirical analysis. Brazil offers unique opportunities to test our hypotheses surrounding well-being. The country has wide local variation in well-being as well as wide variation across the many factors that theoretically influence well-being, such as political competition, all three of our pathways, and economic conditions (Snyder 2001). We present a brief political history of Brazil in Chapter 2, to show how Brazil's political development in the last twenty-five years of the twentieth century helped to set the stage for an expansion of citizenship rights and an extensive, innovative group of institutions and social programs, and construction of an inclusionary state. This history thus bridges our theoretical contribution and empirical evaluations in the remainder of the book.

2

Building Pathways for Change

Brazil experienced significant social, political, and economic transformations during the second half of the twentieth century. The country weathered multiple political regimes, with democratic periods (1946–1964, 1985–present) interrupted by a military dictatorship (1964–1985). Rapid industrialization generated jobs, wealth, and a new national capital (Brasília), and led to massive urbanization as rural residents streamed into cities seeking employment and a better quality of life. Tens of millions of Brazilian citizens gained access to formal employment during this era, which provided the necessary public and private wealth to expand access to health care, education, and basic infrastructure. But Brazil also remained a highly unequal country throughout its impressive economic expansion. The majority of the population lacked access to essential services and resources, including decent housing, clean water, sewage, and a basic income. In this chapter, we explore how Brazil built the foundations for the democratic pathways that would prove fundamental for improving well-being in the twenty-first century.

Brazil serves as a classic example in which the use of Gross Domestic Product (GDP) as a measure of a country's development fails to capture the wide internal variation in citizens' access to public and private goods. The economic miracle of the 1960s and 1970s expanded the country's GDP but did not necessarily improve living standards for tens of millions of citizens. We therefore use Sen and Nussbaum's work on human development, rather than total economic output, as our primary framework to better capture the profound differences in how people live across Brazilian communities – even in wealthy regions and cities. In this area we emphasize developing "capabilities," which include exercising individual agency and engaging markets, states, and communities, to account for Brazil's wide variation in citizens' ability to live dignified lives. The return to democracy in the 1980s was essential for building the foundation for a dignified life. The democratization movement, its emphasis on rights, and the 1988 constitution then set the stage for the emergence of three democratic pathways to well-being.

Brazil dramatically improved basic human development in the first ten to fifteen years of the twenty-first century, which is this book's primary focus. This chapter first contextualizes the challenges at the onset of the twenty-first century by addressing the political and economic context that immediately preceded this era. We limit our discussion to the period of Brazil's transition from military rule to the turn of the twenty-first century because of the important political, economic, and social changes that occurred in this era. These include the renewal of civil society, expansion and fragmentation of the party system, promulgation of the 1988 Constitution, stabilization of the economy, decentralization, and the creation of innovative social policies. Each of these serves as a backdrop for the three democratic pathways (participatory institutions, social programs, and local state capacity) analyzed in other chapters to help account for local variation in outcomes surrounding poverty, health, women's empowerment, and education. In the final section, we identify the contours of how the three pathways were developed in practice during the 1990s and 2000s.

The chapter is separated into four key chronological periods to allow the reader to follow the progression of change across forty years: (a) the Democratic Transition (1974–1985); (b) the Refounding of Democracy (1985–1994); (c) the Plano Real and Cardoso Era (1994–2002); and (d) the Workers' Party and Lula Era (2003–2013). In each section, we briefly analyze the changing role of civil society, the party system, the broader economy, state capacity, federalism, and social policy provision in opening political space and facilitating twenty-first century reforms. The chapter ends with an explicit analysis of how Brazil constructed each pathway to well-being.

MILITARY RULE (1964–1985) AND DEMOCRATIC TRANSITION (1974–1985)

In 1964, Brazil's military led a coup against the democratically elected government. Several factors account for the coup d'état. Brazil had experienced a prolonged period of economic growth as a result of rising internal consumption and capital from international loans. Yet by the early 1960s the country faced a severe economic recession and high inflation. Conservatives became increasingly worried about Brazil's political left, which included progressive church groups, peasants, and labor unions who were inspired by the Cuban revolution and were becoming increasingly radicalized. Some members of congress also grew fearful of President Goulart's left-leaning tendencies. These forces combined to create an alliance between the military, the country's traditional agricultural oligarchy, a growing class of industrial capitalists, and a small but politically important middle class, who increasingly saw a coup as the best mechanism to depose President Goulart.[1] The ensuing 1964 coup ushered in the longest military regime (1964–1985) in South America.

Like its neighbors Argentina and Chile, the Brazilian government displayed characteristics of "bureaucratic authoritarianism" (O'Donnell 1973) by emphasizing modernization, technocratic decision-making, and security as key rationales for military rule. Activated segments of the opposition, including industrial labor and rural peasants, were placed under tight political control. The years 1968 to 1974 brought the most severe restrictions to political and civil liberties. Yet Brazil's military regime allowed elections, parties, and congress to function for most of the 1964–1985 period, unlike military regimes in the Southern Cone during the same era (Mainwaring 1999). Brazilian elections were restricted to federal senators and deputies, state and municipal legislators, and mayors of towns under 200,000, but they did occur regularly. Crucially, the government filled the most important offices through appointments. The military selected the president, the central government selected governors, and governors appointed mayors in capital cities and other cities of national interest. Limited electoral politics took place through two parties: the ARENA party (the National Renewal Alliance, or *Aliança Renovadora Nacional*), affiliated with the government, and the MDB (the Brazilian Democratic Movement, or *Movimento Democrático Brasileiro*), the opposition forced into a single party.

Under the military dictatorship, the late 1960s and early 1970s were known as the Brazilian Miracle. The country witnessed a massive increase in its GDP, the creation of a unionized working class, and the expansion of the middle class. Yet this period is an excellent example of how economic growth does not necessarily produce improvements in well-being (Kohli

---

[1] Jânio Quadros was elected president in 1960; Goulart was his vice-president. President Quadros resigned from office unexpectedly in 1963.

2004). Brazil's poor majority could not access most public goods, such as health care, education, sanitation, and public security, and income inequality did not improve during this period (Arretche 2015). The military regime initiated a prolonged political opening that began with liberalization in 1974. This *abertura* (opening) period is particularly noteworthy because the country's prolonged liberalization period coincided with the emergence of a vibrant civil society that would later press for democratization.

Civil Society

The renewal of civil society in the 1970s and 1980s followed three distinct tracks. First, the labor movement fought to improve working conditions, increase control over unions' internal affairs, extend social rights to the working class, and redemocratize Brazil (Wolfe 1993). The labor movement advocated for narrow interests (e.g., higher wages, fewer hours, more internal control) as well as for interests that appealed to a broader range of citizens, such as democracy and social rights.

Liberation theology and the teachings of Paulo Freire represented a second motivating factor for the resurgence of civil society. Paulo Freire was a world-renowned educator who combined adult literacy campaigns with politicized interpretations of citizens' socioeconomic status. Catholic priests associated with liberation theology founded Christian Base Communities that emphasized improving social conditions and often utilized Freire's methods of adult education for their parishioners (Mainwaring 1986; Burdick 1993).

The proliferation of social movements broadly organized around the concept of citizenship (*cidadania*) represented a third element expanding civil society. Evelina Dagnino argues that the promotion of the "right to have rights" inculcated a belief among ordinary citizens in their rights and responsibilities to engage in public life (Arendt 1958; Dagnino 1998). Furthermore, political reformers and political outsiders made a deliberate effort to work with poor individuals and communities to educate them on their rights (Weffort 1984; Jacobi 1989; Villas Boas and Telles 1995; Holston 2008). Civil society, with a broad focus on citizenship and democratic values, thus served as an incubator for the expansion of new political and social demands. Importantly, many of these efforts crossed class lines. For instance, doctors and nurses led the *sanitarista* movement, but they also connected with community-based organizations to create larger social movements. Lawyers and urban planners led the housing movement, but they, too, expanded their networks and influence through connections with community-based movements (Holston 2008).

Advocates within these social movements were instrumental in pressing for a new constitutional and democratic system that would fulfill social rights; the right to health care, education, and decent housing were at the top of the list (Dagnino 1998; Holston 2008). In addition, social movement leaders began to call for the expansion of participatory venues to move beyond the confines of representative democracy (Avritzer 2002; Wampler and Avritzer 2004). These social movements all engaged in public demonstrations against the military regime, the high point of which was the "direct elections now" (*direitas já*) campaign in 1984. Movement leaders demanded that the population elect Brazil's next president directly rather than through the national legislature. The government did not meet this specific demand, but the broad mobilization of millions of citizens altered the political leaders' calculations, especially among the opposition who had previously been uncertain about their degree of support for direct presidential elections.

Party System

Brazil's military tightly controlled political opposition during their rule by regulating the formal political party system. The military regime instituted a two-party system in which all opposition groups worked with the MDB party and all regime supporters fell under the ARENA party (Hagopian 1996). The Brazilian military eased the restrictions on the party system in 1979 as part of the country's gradual democratic transition. This period's legacy is relevant today partially because the original opposition party, the MDB, later morphed into a centrist, catchall party, the PMDB (Brazilian Democratic Movement Party or *Partido do Movimento Democrático Brasileiro*). Yet, this era is also relevant because the opening of the party system allowed for the creation of numerous opposition parties that represented citizens' interests and preferences more directly.

The Workers' Party (*Partido dos Trabalhadores* or PT) was the most important new political party to emerge during the latter part of the military dictatorship. Union leaders (from both public and private sectors), progressive middle-class intellectuals, and social movement activists founded the PT in 1979 (Couto 1995; Keck 1995; Hunter 2010). The PT represented an assertion of a new type of politics, combining contentious politics with unions and social movements. The Workers' Party competed in national elections beginning in the early 1980s, but had very limited electoral success until the 1988 and 1989 elections. The *Partido da Social Democracia Brasileira* (PSDB or the Brazilian Social Democratic Party) was founded in 1988, with many of its leaders coming from the centrist, catchall PMDB (which was an outgrowth of the MDB). Middle-class intellectuals and policy reformers initially led the PSDB; a centrist middle class situated in the São Paulo metropolitan area constituted their base. The PSDB initially positioned itself as a center-left party that was more centrist than the PT, but with a more progressive social agenda than the PMDB. Alongside the PT and PSDB, multiple parties were resurrected from the previous democratic period (1946–1964) and new, nonprogrammatic parties were also established. Subsequently, the low barriers to entry for new political parties led to the development of a fragmented party system (Mainwaring 1999).

REFOUNDING DEMOCRACY AMID ECONOMIC UPHEAVAL: 1985–1994

The national senate elected a civilian president in 1985, but the drafting and promulgation of a new constitution is largely viewed as the crucial institutional and political shift that ushered in Brazil's democratic era, known as the New Republic (1985–present). The Constitutional Assembly of 1986–1987 was held at a moment of political change; representatives elected to the national congress (lower and upper houses) were charged with drafting a new constitution. The composition of the assembly thus included a wide range of political actors, including supporters of the military government, catchall centrists interested in governing, and opponents of the military regime. Citizens' groups were also allowed to formally enter amendments for consideration if they collected 50,000 signatures. The constitution (1988) formally established the expansion of rights, allocated greater responsibilities to municipalities and states, and broadened political participation (expanding the franchise to include illiterate citizens and permitting the establishment of participatory venues).

The 1988 Constitution, which is still in place to date, is simultaneously an aspirational and unwieldy document. The constitution is aspirational because it guarantees Brazilians a series of rights, such as the rights to education, health care, and housing, which the government has not been fully able to provide. The constitution is also an unwieldy document because of its length – hundreds of pages long with extensive amendments, including these and other "aspirational rights" – without clear mechanisms for their establishment. For instance, the constitution guarantees a "right to health" and specifies that municipalities have a role in delivering health services. Yet important details on how the government would achieve these objectives were left unspecified by constitutional framers, who would leave details on decentralization of health services to future legislation (Weyland 1996). Further, the constitution serves as a political document that, at times, includes opposing ideological tendencies, with numerous amendments that appeal to conservative and leftist political actors. For example, the adoption of a socially progressive "right to health" has not resulted in a single, universal public health care system. Instead, Brazil has a dual system with a free universal health system (SUS) alongside a private health insurance market with private providers.

For the purposes of this book, the 1988 Constitution and accompanying legislation creates three noteworthy shifts from previous political moments. First, the "municipalization" of service delivery elevates municipalities' responsibilities in the federal system. The three-tiered federal system established in the constitution gives municipal governments political and administrative autonomy. Municipalities are responsible for providing a wide range of services – including sanitation, health, education, and social assistance – for the first time. In practice, this has meant that local governments are largely responsible for implementing the policies that allow people to exercise newly established social rights. It also means that municipalities are a vital part of the policy-making process, allowing citizens to secure access to the social rights the constitution guarantees. The federal government supports municipal governments by collecting most taxes and then transferring these revenues to states and municipalities to carry out their responsibilities.

A second significant element of the 1988 Constitution is the provision that permits municipalities and states to adopt new participatory venues without the federal government's additional consent (Avritzer 2002). This change provides an avenue for greater municipal flexibility as governments can experiment with new forms of citizen engagement. A third significant political shift in the 1988 Constitution is the inclusion of a wide range of social rights, such as the rights to health care, education, and housing. Political movements successfully mobilized in the 1980s in support of formally including these rights. Once included in the constitution, these rights created a "policy frame" that many social movements, policy experts, and local governments would utilize to fulfill rights in the future.

However, it is important to note that Brazil was plagued by economic uncertainty and stagnation during its democratic transition. The 1980s are known as the "Lost Decade" across Latin America due to economic contraction, high inflation, and widespread unemployment (Haggard and Kaufman 1997; Baer 2001; Madrid 2003). Brazil's experience was no different and its return to democracy coincided with its worst economic crisis since the 1930s. The formal promulgation of the 1988 Constitution occurred in a broader context of high unemployment, corporate bankruptcies, high interest rates, and lower tax revenue (Schneider 2016). As a result, the general economic stagnation made it difficult for governments to assume responsibility for delivering the goods and services that new voters demanded.

Civil Society

The 1988–1994 period marked the beginning of the institutionalization of a broader participatory architecture. Although there were massive student protests motivated by allegations of corruption against President Collor de Mello in 1990 and 1991, the most significant change during the 1988–1994 period was the institutionalization of new participatory democratic institutions; these institutions would ultimately have greater influence on well-being in the 2000s (Dagnino 1994; Avritzer 2002). Social movements and civil society organizations (CSOs) adjusted their strategies to more closely align themselves with elected governments during this time frame as well as to work within new participatory institutions (Dagnino 1998; Avritzer 2001; Wampler 2007; Holston 2008; Wolford 2010). These actors shifted away from an emphasis on "autonomy" and to a closer alliance between civil society activists and democratic policy-making institutions; CSO activists saw an opportunity to align themselves with government officials and their new conceptualizations of democracy included ongoing participation (Avritzer 2002; Wampler and Avritzer 2004; Holston 2008).

Local governments experimented more extensively with participatory democracy from 1988 to 1994. Civil society activists worked with elected officials and bureaucrats to establish formal processes encouraging citizens' direct involvement in policy making. Governments took two important institutional approaches to participatory democracy during this period: the creation of participatory budgeting programs and public policy management councils (Abers 2000; Avritzer 2002). Public policy councils first gained political and policy space during the early 1980s as reformist mayors brought citizens, CSOs, unions, and government officials into new policy-making venues. A rapid expansion of public policy management councils followed the promulgation of the 1988 Constitution, which created the legal basis for municipal, state, and federal governments to adopt councils. These councils were relatively new, but their existence and rapid proliferation empowered civil society organizations and initiated positive feedback loops, wherein CSOs participated in council activities, strengthened the institutions, and requested additional venues. New venues created space for new CSOs and increased existing CSOs' influence as they also strengthened the new councils.

Party System

The fragmentation of the party system produced a wide range of governing strategies at the local level. The municipalization of resources and responsibilities created opportunities for mayors to experiment with new institutions and programs (Spink and Clemente 1997; Wampler 2007). Perhaps most famously, the southern city of Porto Alegre created a type of participatory democracy called participatory budgeting (Abers 2000; Baiocchi 2005; Wampler 2007). However, other municipalities were led by politicians uninterested in investing scarce resources to activate the social and political rights associated with the 1988 constitution (Gay 1990 and 2010; Arias 2009).

Across many of Brazil's municipalities, personalism, clientelism, and corruption remained important features of local campaigns and governance; policy reforms often were not voters' primary considerations in choosing a candidate. Four nonprogrammatic parties – the PMDB, PFL (Liberal Front Party, or *Partido da Frente Liberal*), PTB (Brazilian Labor Party, or *Partido Trabalhista Brasileiro*), and PDT (Democratic Labor Party, or *Partido Democrático Trabalhista*) – captured 68 percent of the mayoral offices in 1992, demonstrating the power of traditional catchall political parties (Fleischer 2002). Thus, part of the variation in the quality of democratic governance and well-being across Brazilian municipalities is related to the extent to which political and policy reformers were elected to office. Mayors who sought to promote rights-based social programs and democratic practices laid the groundwork for improvements in well-being, while others did not (Spink and Clemente 1997). These rights-based practices then fed into later performance in program administration and service delivery – especially for the Bolsa Família. Political reformers also promoted meritocratic hiring, effective training, and accountable administration, raising the prospects for inclusive state capacity in many municipalities.

Decentralization

The 1988 Constitution ushered in a new federal arrangement and delegated responsibility for service delivery to states and municipalities. The 1988 Constitution granted municipalities much greater responsibility for social service provision than they had ever had before. For example, the constitution established all Brazilians' rights to universal, free health care *and* determined that municipal governments would be responsible for providing these services. Montero and Samuels estimated that the federal government became responsible for allocating roughly 50 percent of all public funds; states allocated 35 percent, and municipalities spent 15 percent (2004).

Although service delivery was decentralized, most revenue collection continued to occur at the federal level. The federal government collected revenues and then initiated a complex transfer system to distribute the resources to municipal governments (Pereira and Spink 2015). Municipal governments retained the right to collect two types of taxes: property taxes and a portion of the sales tax. However, it is important to note that most municipalities are unable to collect taxes due to low property values, unclear property titles, and weak retail sales. Some local governments are also unwilling to raise local revenue because elected officials are allied with property owners.

The 1988 Constitution's decentralization of service delivery highlights the basic contradictions "municipalization" would produce. On one hand, decentralization produced a tremendous number of opportunities for municipal governments to experiment with new policy approaches (Avritzer 2002 and 2009; Abers and Keck 2013). These experiments produced innovations that other municipalities, states, and the federal government would adopt (see Sugiyama 2012; see also Chapter 4). Decentralization also brought government closer to beneficiaries of social services, facilitating their direct engagement in policy making and oversight through nascent participatory institutions (Pires 2011). On the other hand, decentralization created serious challenges. The majority of municipalities lacked the basic capacity to deliver public services, despite their legal responsibility to do so. Second, the federal government had few fiscal, administrative, and regulatory policy controls over how municipal governments used resources. Not surprisingly, many public officials misused their power over spending, sometimes for corrupt purposes. Third, decentralization permitted states and large municipalities to issue bonds to fund infrastructure projects. Although this financial tool can be very useful for growing cities and states, corrupt governments can also redirect the funds to suit their own political and financial needs.

Brazil's initial decentralization produced mixed results. Some cities adopted innovative policies that permitted local governments to experiment with social policy design and delivery. These municipalities created new programs in many new arenas, including housing, poverty relief, job training, and recycling, among others (see Farah 1997). However, many other municipalities remained mired in traditional, clientelistic politics and policy arrangements. Nevertheless, decentralization served as a necessary condition for local autonomy, policy experimentation, and the emergence of pathways to well-being across many of Brazil's municipalities.

THE PLANO REAL AND CARDOSO ERA (1994–2002)

The successful implementation of a new currency, the real, marked the beginning of the 1994–2002 period. The *Plano Real* (Real Plan) effectively tamed Brazil's dramatic, high inflation and ushered in an era of economic stability. As the previous section explained, Brazil's high inflation sowed sufficient economic uncertainty to plunge the economy into a deep recession. Then-Finance Minister Fernando Henrique Cardoso orchestrated the currency stabilization plan, which helped launch his candidacy for president of Brazil. Cardoso won the 1994 election in the first round, soundly defeating Lula da Silva who had also been the runner-up in the 1989 election. Cardoso subsequently won his bid for reelection in 1998, making the 1994–2002 period best conceptualized as the "Cardoso Era."

Building on the perceived successes of the Plano Real, the Cardoso government initiated a process of privatization of state-owned companies. The sell-off was not as extreme as in Argentina, but Cardoso successfully privatized the national mining company and the national banks (Madrid 2003) and also allowed for increased foreign competition in areas of the economy that had previously been protected. The implementation of neoliberal reforms in the government ministries was relatively modest, but did produce a general layoff of public sector workers that decreased government spending and improved Brazil's credit rating. State capacity expanded during the Cardoso Era (1995–2002) despite neoliberal cost-cutting because there was a focus on increasing the professionalism among existing public sector employees. Moreover, ministerial reform and stabilization along several different dimensions laid part of the foundation for good governance and effective service delivery in subsequent decades. Similarly, establishing laws governing subnational governments' fiscal responsibilities and providing external oversight improved transparency and accountability from 2000 on.

Civil Society

Civil society had a weaker "public" presence under the Cardoso administrations than during the 1988 Constitutional period or the 1992 impeachment protests against President Collor de Mello. Social movements and civil society organizations changed their strategies during the 1990s in response to the shifting institutional and political environment. More centrist CSOs and NGOs positioned themselves as "third sector" service providers, contracting with governments to deliver social services (Bresser Perreira 1998; Alvarez 1999). CSOs affiliated with the PSDB, President Cardoso's party, worked closely with the administration as well as with state governments in wealthy states such as São Paulo and Minas Gerais. Thus, the PSDB drew their CSOs into direct relationships with executives to deliver public services. The newly founded relationships between the PSDB and ideologically centrist NGOs then facilitated the creation of social policies that fit within the emerging neoliberal social reform agenda.

Left-wing social movements affiliated with the Workers Party (PT) used different strategies. CSOs worked with PT governments when PT candidates were elected at the municipal level; it was rare for the PT to win governorships during this era. Importantly, the PT's social-movement base invested in innovative participatory and social policy programs. For example, municipal governments almost always adopted participatory budgeting (PB) when the PT won mayoral contests during the 1994–2002 period (Wampler and Avritzer 2005). This strategy had two important impacts for the purposes of our argument. First, the PT actively created new decision-making venues to bring citizens directly into decision-making spaces with specific legal, financial, and technical constraints. This meant that PT officials developed new institutional arrangements to link different types of actors to achieve the PT's broader political and policy agendas. Second, CSOs and social movements were induced to participate so that they could influence policy decisions. This was a significant transition for many CSOs and social movements as they moved away from a politics of protest and contestation to a politics of direct government engagement. For our purposes, the important aspect of this shift was that leftist social movements as well as nonpartisan – but left-leaning – CSOs secured benefits by actively coordinating with government officials.

Left-leaning social movements and CSOs often worked to expand public policy management councils when the PT did not win mayoral elections. The council system, which has its roots in the health field, proliferated across Brazil as civil society activists advocated for its expansion. Policy councils generally had equal representation between civil society (CSOs, NGOs, unions) and public officials. There were over 30,000 municipal-level councils by the beginning of the twenty-first century (Santos 2011; Wampler 2015). Thus, venues for participatory cogovernance existed throughout the country and offered CSOs common points of entry into the policy-making arena. These venues served as a platform for incorporating citizens into policy-making processes, improving services, and ultimately advancing well-being.

Party System

Brazil's party system consolidated in the 1990s, with four major parties at the center of Brazilian politics: the PSDB, the PT, the PMDB, and the PFL/DEM; in 2007 PFL became the Democrats, or *Democratas* (DEM). Beyond the four major parties, there were also a handful of other parties with strong regional followings and more than a dozen smaller parties with congressional representation. In effect, there were eight political parties in the national legislature in the 1990s. Given that at least six of these eight parties were nonprogrammatic, there was wide variation in municipal-level governance; thus there is no simple relationship between party identification and governing platforms (Mainwaring 1999; Power and Zucco 2009). Party switching among members of congress has been a common feature of legislative politics as deputies seek to align with shifting majorities. Further, only the Workers' Party has been regarded has having clear partisan identification among the electorate (Samuels 1999). However, there is also considerable variation among the Workers' Party mayors, which suggests that party affiliation is not a good proxy for mayoral strategies (Couto 1995; Wampler 2007). For these reasons, the country's party system is generally regarded as poorly institutionalized and fragmented (Mainwaring 1999).

President Cardoso (1994–2002) of the centrist PSDB party governed pragmatically through "coalition politics," whereby the executive branch used a combination of pork-barrel politics, clientelism, and distribution of key ministerial positions to govern through a majority coalition in congress (Raile, Pereira, and Power 2011). Presidential coalitions have not displayed ideological coherence among party members. Rather, Brazil's parties showcase politicians' pragmatic goals, either to serve in government and have access to "pork" or to serve in the opposition for future electoral advantage. The Cardoso administration aligned with the conservative PFL and the catchall PMDB to create a stable voting majority in congress.

At the municipal level, the PMDB continued to elect mayors in the greatest number of municipalities. However, the number of mayors elected from the nonprogrammatic parties dropped to 56 percent (1996) and 53 percent (2000), largely due to the increase in support for the PSDB and, secondarily, for the PT (Fleischer 2002). Thus, a key lesson from the 1990s is that reform-oriented political parties, namely the PSDB and PT, began to win more mayoral races, but still only won 19 percent and 21 percent of mayors' offices in 1996 and 2000, respectively. Mayors on the political left were strong proponents of participatory institutions and rights-based social policies. But growing multiparty competition created new incentives for local politicians to deliver services and new mechanisms for citizens to hold local governments accountable. Ultimately, an expanded party system promoted advancement along all three of our democratic pathways: through the adoption of new policy councils; the expansion and execution of rights-based social programs, such as Bolsa Família and the Family Health Program; and administrative improvements through meritocratic hiring, sensible spending, and transparent governance.

Decentralization

The most significant change surrounding decentralization during the 1994–2002 period was the recentralization of policy-making power in the hands of the federal government (Eaton and Dickovick 2004). The Cardoso administration passed landmark legislation giving the federal government increased control over how states and municipalities managed their fiscal affairs. The core of their efforts was the Fiscal Responsibility Law (*Lei de Responsabilidade Fiscal*), which increased federal control over municipal and state finances (Pereira and Spink

2015). The law greatly increased the prospects for clean, subnational government and provided a platform for better local administration of health, education, and other services.

The first important step toward increased federal control was the removal of states' and municipalities' ability to issue bonds. From a budgetary standpoint, the federal government was trying to ensure that states and municipalities could no longer issue bonds, then subsequently default on payments and force the financial burden of repaying the debt on the federal government. Moreover, the Plano Real was based on curbing government spending and tight currency controls, which meant that uncontrolled state and municipal bonds could potentially undermine the financial balance. From a macro-fiscal standpoint, then, large state and municipal bonds had the potential to increase the inflationary pressures on the national currency.

Beyond regulating the ways municipalities raised revenue, the Fiscal Responsibility Law also included stipulations regarding expenditures. Municipalities were required to spend 25 percent of their entire budget on education and 30 percent on health care. In addition, municipalities were forbidden from spending more than 60 percent of their entire budget on personnel. These fiscal guidelines were put in place to ensure local governments were fiscally compliant with their constitutional mandate to provide core services in areas such as education and health care. In turn, ensuring minimum spending levels on critical services advanced the local state's capacity to deliver those services, which were designed to be universal and inclusive.

Social Policies

The 1990s were an extraordinary period of local policy experimentation as municipal and state officials created inclusive social policies intended to enhance citizenship, address poverty, and expand access to public good provisions (Spink 2000; Farah and Spink 2009; Sugiyama 2012). Decentralization of service delivery, the election of policy reformers, and economic stabilization created an environment supportive of local experimentation and innovation. For example, two local governments initiated Brazil's first conditional cash transfer programs in 1995; the Federal District of Brasília created the *Bolsa Escola* (School Grant) program and Campinas created the *Renda Mínima* (Minimum Income) program. Both programs transferred cash to poor families on the condition that school-age children attend school (Sugiyama 2012). Other municipalities, such as

Londrina and Niterói, enacted a Cuba-inspired program, *Médico de Família* (Family Doctor Program), to expand access to primary health care. Municipalities also created new, innovative avenues for citizens to engage in the policy process. For instance, nearly 30,000 public policy councils had been formally established by 2002 (Santos 2011); over 200 participatory budgeting programs were adopted in major cities, thus allowing more than 50 percent of the population to directly engage in budgeting processes (Wampler and Avritzer 2005).

The emergence of the municipality as the locus for innovative social policy was important because federal action along these lines was limited in design and scope. Cardoso's administrations (1995–1998; 1999–2002) focused largely on effecting decentralization, including regulations surrounding fiscal autonomy. For example, in the education arena Minister Paulo Renato Souza emphasized the need to address uneven fiscal resources for education by implementing FUNDEF, a funding formula designed to address fiscal inequality across local governments and to encourage local school districts to enroll students (Sugiyama 2012). The Ministry of Health focused extensively on the operationalization of the Unified Health System (*Sistema Único da Saúde*, or SUS), establishing rules and regulations for the gradual municipalization of health services across Brazil (Arretche 2015). In this way, the Cardoso Era provided some of the institutional and administrative structures for future federal poverty-alleviation efforts.

The Cardoso administration's attempts to reduce poverty reflected both continuity and change. On one hand, there were signs of change as federal officials drew inspiration from local policy innovations by creating national initiatives. Brazil's first national conditional cash transfer program, *Bolsa Escola Federal* (Federal School Grant) was enacted in 2001 under the auspices of the Ministry of Education. The Ministry of Health scaled up the Family Health Program in 1998, contributing to its eventual adoption across the country (Sugiyama 2012). On the other hand, the federal government continued to offer smaller-scale subsidies and vouchers to assist targeted groups. Depending on the composition and size of a family, they might be eligible to receive several federal supports. These included: *Auxílio Gas*, an unconditional grant for cooking gas; *Bolsa Alimentação* (Health and Nutrition Grant), a grant to alleviate health and nutritional deficiencies of pregnant and breastfeeding women and of children under the age of seven; and the *Bolsa Escola Federal* (see Lindert et al. 2007, 11–12). These disparate programs generally targeted the same population but lacked coordination and oversight to avoid duplication of benefits. This was a problem that Lula's administration would later address by consolidating these programs to create the Bolsa Família and expanding its reach in pursuit of well-being through rights-based social policies.

MECHANISMS FOR WELL-BEING IN PRACTICE

We ground the theoretical argument surrounding our pathways in specific mechanisms in Brazil; these mechanisms are specific policies, programs, and institutions that represent/capture the core ideas of the pathway. We describe the construction of specific mechanisms promoting well-being in greater detail in the following section.

Participatory Institutions

Public policy management councils are a key participatory mechanism through which Brazilian citizens engage in the policy-making process. Policy councils are organized thematically along specific issue areas (e.g., health, education, women's rights) at municipal, state, and federal levels. The 1988 Constitution establishes the formal authority that permits municipalities, states, and the federal government to create councils (Avritzer 2009). Municipalities and states then adopt legislation that formally establishes the councils' legal attributes, authority, and responsibilities. Policy councils are based on the principle of cogovernance, whereby government officials (appointed and civil servants) and civil society representatives interact to deliberate over policies and budgets. Although policy councils are not as well-known beyond Brazil as the more famous participatory budgeting programs, there are roughly 60,000 municipal-level councils throughout the country.

Municipalities and states can choose to adopt policy councils at the behest of local political forces; there are now more than twenty thematic areas in which municipalities have adopted councils. The federal government also strongly induces municipalities to adopt policy councils in several high priority areas: health, education, social assistance, youth and adolescents, and child protection. Municipalities and states receive federal funding to induce municipalities to adopt and maintain these councils. Almost all municipalities adopted councils in five key areas, resulting in more than 25,000 councils; many of these were adopted in response to federal incentives. We estimate that municipalities have adopted another 35,000 councils of their own volition, without any federal strings attached to them. The rest of this section reviews the councils' basic design and operational rules with a focus on three areas: representation, decision-making authority, and oversight to connect councils to well-being.

Each issue area has a specific policy council with budgetary and oversight authority. The rules of most councils are similar, although there is some variation. (See Wampler 2015, chapter 5 for an in-depth discussion of councils.) Members have the authority to propose new policies and programs. These proposals can be approved by a majority vote, but they must fall within the normal parameters of municipal, state, and federal legislation. For example, council members can propose new programs to support neonatal care by expanding a maternity wing at the hospital, or they can advocate for increasing spending on community-health teams. The adoption and subsequent implementation of these policies and programs directly supports medical personnel as they provide health services to improve well-being. Councils must approve new policies and programs proposed by governments, thus giving councils members a potential check on a government's agenda. "A council has the potential to act as a veto point in the policy-making process because council members can refuse to approve the adoption of new policies and programs proposed by the government" (Wampler 2015: 135). For example, in 2010 the municipal government in Belo Horizonte proposed to build a new public hospital. Council members rejected the proposal at the first presentation because the government provided only the most basic information about the proposed hospital. The government was forced to spend several additional meetings explaining the funding mechanism, the types of services that the new hospital would provide, and how the hospital fit into the larger public health system. The council approved the hospital proposal but the extensive deliberations and information-sharing increased the quality of the council members' knowledge.

Policy councils are required to approve their area's annual budget as well as mid-year budget modifications. The mayor or governor must first secure the council's approval of the department budget prior to sending the budget to the municipal or state legislature. Thus, the government must work first within the policy council system before they work with municipal legislators. When administrators want to shift money from one line item to another, they must receive approval by the relevant council, but they do not need to get the approval of the municipal legislature. Thus, issue-specific councils are much more involved in policy making than in the municipal legislature. These institutions are now an integral part of the policy formulation and approval process. By bringing together policy experts, interested community and CSO leaders, and union representatives, local governments are able to craft better policies and programs that improve well-being. Councils also have basic oversight through two different processes. "The ongoing process consists of council members' requests for information (e.g., budgetary and personnel data; outcomes indicators) to help them monitor government agencies' activities throughout the year. By having access to information, council members can engage in spirited policy discussions with each other and with government officials. This information gathering and ongoing debates over existing program implementation are part of a larger process of creating a policy network and expanding policy debates" (Wampler 2015: 137). Having access to information improves well-being because council members are better able to alert government officials and civil servants where services are inadequate. For example, civil society representatives can identify which clinics do not have enough basic medical supplies or which facilities are understaffed; civil servants can use this information to reallocate resources, which then improves health care and well-being.

Second, the budget offers council members another key oversight role. Councils must approve the previous year's financial statements. For the "induced councils," members must approve the relevant department's budget to allow the federal governments to transfer resources to the municipality legally. This then gives the council greater authority than that held by the municipal legislature; the legislature focuses more on approving the entire municipal budget rather than on specific departments. The councils' budgetary oversight authority thereby induces government officials to provide necessary documentation on the previous year's spending (Wampler 2015, chapter 5). Monitoring budget spending improves well-being because it decreases the probability that public resources will be diverted illegally for private gain; civil servants and service providers will be less likely to steal resources or misuse resources because there is a greater likelihood of being caught. This helps to improve well-being because resources are spent as they were designed to be spent. More broadly, a focus on the budget allows council members to hold government officials accountable for how they allocate resources.

Finally, the distribution of council seats is typically divided evenly between government officials (with 50 percent of seats) and civil society representatives (remaining 50 percent).[2] The elected government (mayor's office) nominates a combination of political appointees and civil servants to serve on the councils. The distribution of the civil society seats is typically divided between representatives from the general community, issue-specific community organizations (e.g., parents of disabled children), and union representatives (e.g., nurses' union). In addition, some councils may have a seat reserved for a municipal legislator or for a representative of a private lobby (e.g., insurance lobby). Council members typically serve two-year terms and are not paid for their service. The number of seats on public policy councils range from nine to twelve in smaller municipalities to twenty to thirty in larger municipalities.

In sum, policy councils are key participatory venues that permit ongoing, public deliberations and decision-making among citizens and government officials. These councils are a veto point in the policy-making process because council members must approve new policies and programs as well as annual budgets and year-end reports. When governments voluntarily adopt policy councils, they are signaling to civil society and the broader population that citizens have the right and responsibility to be involved in policy-making processes. Policy councils improve well-being because they broaden the scope and content of deliberations around policy formulation and implementation. The presence of councils in the policy cycle thus changes which policies are adopted and how they are implemented. In this book, we argue that these changes are a crucial part of the process that leads to improvements in well-being.

Social Programs

Brazilian politicians transformed social policy during the 1990–2000s to incorporate previously excluded, marginalized groups into the country's social welfare system. Informal workers and the poor had less access to Brazil's Bismarckian welfare state than did formal sector workers, government employees, and members of the military (Malloy 1977 and 1979). Brazil's welfare state was established in the 1930s under the Estado Novo and privileged these formal workers with generous social insurance coverage along with other services and benefits that the working poor could not access (Mesa-Lago 1978; Draibe 2003). However, informal workers and

---

[2] The health policy councils typically increase the participation by civil society representatives to 75–80 percent of the seats, leaving the government with just 20–25 percent of the seats.

poor citizens began to benefit from the welfare state in the 1990s. The Lula Administration (2003–2010) then extended eligibility for existing social programs and developed new and more inclusive social policies in areas such as health and poverty relief (Hunter and Sugiyama 2009).

Brazilian policymakers faced the challenge of fulfilling the government's obligation to extend universal health care following the constitutional declaration of health as a social right. The government addressed this issue by creating the Unified Health System (*Sistema Único da Saúde*, SUS) in 1989, which established a universal public health care system throughout the country. In practice, the SUS would take years to implement as the national Ministry of Health developed federal regulations to oversee implementation of a decentralized health system. Nevertheless, municipalization of health services represented an important transformation of the Brazilian health system (Arretche and Marques 2002). Program redesign also consumed reformist health policy experts' efforts. For instance, early advocates for primary health care lobbied for the Family Health Program (*Programa Saúde da Família* or PSF). Inspired by Cuba's community-based Family Doctor Program (Médico de Família) and similar community primary health programs established in some of Brazil's northeastern municipalities, Brazil's PSF began offering integrated primary health services in 1994 (Viana and Poz 1998). Teams of health professionals (doctors, nurses, and nurse's aides) worked alongside resident community-health agents. The program could then provide targeted community services through detailed neighborhood mapping of residents' health care needs. This strategy allowed for preventive care with in-home visits, monitoring of chronic illnesses, and regular check-ups for prenatal and postnatal care, including childhood vaccinations.

The expansion of the Family Health Program occurred over roughly a decade as the program emerged from the poor, rural northeast and eventually spread to nearly every Brazilian municipality (Sugiyama 2012). Local governments began receiving federal transfers for implementing the program according to federal programmatic regulations. Yet local governments had considerable discretion over the timing of the PSF implementation and its scope of coverage. Beginning in 2006, the national Ministry of Health framed the PSF as part of a larger "strategy," reflecting the ministry's vision that community-based integrative care should serve as a broad organizing strategy for primary health care and serve as a critical point of entry into Brazil's health system.

The Lula administration also transformed poverty-reduction policy. Disparate poverty-relief programs, such as *Auxilio Gas, Bolsa*

Alimentação (Health and Nutrition Grant), and the *Bolsa Escola Federal* (Federal School Grant), were combined into a flagship anti-poverty program known as Bolsa Família. The Bolsa Família carried the full weight of Lula's presidency as it represented his commitment to end hunger and extend dignity to the poor. The Bolsa Família, a conditional cash transfer program, represented the first time the federal government made poverty relief a central policy priority. The program offered poor and indigent families cash grants so long as they complied with behavioral requirements thought to enhance long-term human development. Grant amounts have varied according to household characteristics, such as the number of children in the household. The average nominal benefit and its constant inflation-adjusted value has varied from 2004 to 2018; in January 2018, the average nominal benefit peaked at R$178 (USD $45) (Layton 2019: 475). Conditionality requirements first focused on children's school enrollment and regular attendance and later extended to regular health check-ups for pregnant women and their children. Families applied to the program with their municipal government's assistance; applicants declared their income and provided identity documents for household members; then, the information was entered into a national database called the Cadastro Único (Unified Registry). The new Ministry of Social Development was the agency in charge of the program, and established municipal enrollment targets based on census poverty data. The Bolsa Família started small, enrolling only 3.6 million households when it began its full national roll-out in January 2004. Yet it quickly grew to include nearly a quarter of Brazil's population by 2011.

The Bolsa Família represents a significant departure from how local governments previously provided poverty relief. This "rational" policy instrument aims to address immediate poverty relief while also addressing intergenerational transmission of poverty. The tightly controlled program requires local coordination and cooperation for enrollment and monitoring. Yet federal program designers created the Unified Registry with the goal of tight control over who was formally enrolled Bolsa Família (Lindert et al., 2007). Their multiple objectives included eliminating problems associated with duplication of benefits and avoiding errors of inclusion. The massive database of program applicants also fostered improved program evaluation and tracking of outcomes across multiple program areas. At the same time, federal policy makers sought to eliminate resource leakage by circumventing direct municipal transfers. Instead, beneficiaries receive cash grants directly from the federal government through personalized bankcards with unique pin numbers.

This bureaucratic approach to social assistance is a far cry from Brazil's traditional practice of poverty relief, where municipal assistance to the poor was often framed in terms of private charity (Jaccoud et al. 2010). The distribution of local poverty relief was often left to "first ladies" who oversaw nonprofessionalized services. The implication is that charity, unlike a highly regulated, bureaucratic, federal program, is fleeting, uncertain, and dependent on the good will of local officials. Moreover, poverty assistance at the municipal level – in the form of monthly food baskets, refrigerators, and other household goods – has a history of serving as grist for political patronage and vote buying rather than as a social right. In this way, modernization of poverty policy represents a significant departure from politics as usual. For this reason, it is notable that program administrators embedded rights-based language into program literature and defended the program as such (Sugiyama and Hunter 2013). Research suggests that such framing made important contributions toward beneficiaries' increased sense of agency and political belonging (Hunter and Sugiyama 2014).

State Capacity

State capacity to administer inclusive programs and deliver services is essential for human development in Brazil. This capacity developed over time along several distinct, parallel tracks that connect the concept of inclusive state capacity to human development through specific mechanisms. As discussed previously in this chapter, the 1988 Constitution decentralized authority and endowed Brazilian municipalities with responsibility for service delivery. This set the stage to develop mechanisms that connect state capacity to governance and well-being. The *Lei de Responsabilidade Fiscal* (Fiscal Responsibility Law), the transition toward a professionalized civil service using merit-based hiring, and a variety of ministerial reforms all contributed to Brazil's inclusive state capacity. However, we want to be clear that not every municipality follows laws fully, uses merit-based hiring, or makes appropriate information available. For some municipalities, inclusive state capacity has improved dramatically since the 1988 Constitution, but the rate of improvement is not constant within or across municipalities. Some municipalities comply with national laws immediately, while others lurch forward in fits and starts, and some improve only marginally, if at all. All municipalities have the potential to develop these mechanisms, but the extent to which they actually do so explains differences in subsequent service delivery and human development performance in this area.

Brazil's effort to professionalize the civil service also improved state capacity. This consisted primarily of requiring minimum performance on a civil service exam for all government hires. The idea behind this approach was to create a professional civil service where employees have earned university degrees and are competent administrators based on the results of standardized entrance exams. The use of a standard, merit-based approach to hiring then limits elected officials' ability to distribute government jobs as political patronage or favors to friends. The result, at the municipal level, is a broad trend of hiring well-trained, competent employees that administer programs impartially, as opposed to using programs to advance the careers of mayors and other politicians. Merit-based hiring with reasonable salaries insulates public employees from the pressure of elected officials and theoretically limits the possibilities of elite capture and the misuse of federal resources transferred to municipalities to fund a wide variety of programs.

Advances in information transparency act as the next mechanism improving the capacity to administer inclusive social programs. Brazil's national Transparency Law, passed in 2009, requires real-time spending disclosures for all governments. Similarly, the law requires governments to create a transparent online portal to report and publicize considerable information on local finances, spending, and hiring. This means municipalities must not only build the capacity to meet these requirements but must also face sanctions if they do not comply with the law. Information transparency offers watchdog groups in civil society, journalists, and individual citizens a much greater ability to monitor government activities and theoretically to prevent financial misbehavior by voting out of office those politicians who misappropriate resources. The result is government that is theoretically accountable, where politicians and civil servants face serious incentives to report spending accurately and to allocate funds appropriately. Finally, the Access to Information Act, passed in 2012, requires governments to respond to any requests for information for all public policies and government actions. Again, the goal is accountability through the monitoring of government behavior by the public, press, and civil society.

The creation of the Ministry of Social Development and Fight against Hunger (MDS) in 2004 was also critically important for inclusive state capacity. The MDS oversees a group of inter-ministerial programs to reduce poverty. In this case, the capacity to deliver inclusive social programs stems from the expansion and empowerment of the MDS to act as a network hub for interconnected issue areas and to oversee such programs (Gomide and Pires 2014). For example, the MDS administers Bolsa Família and coordinates with the ministries of health and education to ensure that the program's conditionality requirements are being met by beneficiaries. Moreover, the MDS coordinates the collection and use of information from the *Cadastro Único*. The Cadastro Único serves as a massive database of Brazil's poor families and is necessary for program evaluation in multiple sectors. One of the most important administrative innovations undertaken by the MDS was the creation of the Index of Decentralized Management (IGD), which monitors and incentivizes high-quality local program management (Modesto 2014). The creation and expansion of new ministries and new capacities in pursuit of social inclusion is thus a highlight of the Lula era. Greater capacity to administer programs in support of inclusion results in more efficient, less corrupt, higher quality service delivery that reaches a broad swath of Brazil's poor – much more so than under the military dictatorship or even in the 1990s, after democratization.

Finally, general ministerial reforms also connect the concept of inclusive state capacity to the quality of program administration. In particular, the creation of the Comptroller General's Office (*Controladoria Geral da União* or CGU) provided background conditions that promoted clean government. The Lula administration created the Comptroller General's Office in 2003 to establish a central, national anti-corruption institution that oversees Brazilian governments' budget expenditures and monitors compliance with Brazil's transparency laws. The CGU is responsible for monitoring the spending of subnational governments and administering random audits of municipal finances. Since its founding, the CGU has audited roughly 35 percent of Brazilian municipalities (1,949 of 5,570) regarding expenses totaling R$22 billion (US$7.8 billion) of federal funding transferred to the municipalities (Avis et al. 2016). Several studies find that these audits increase local accountability and reduce future corruption (Ferraz and Finan 2008; Ferraz and Finan 2011; Avis et al. 2016; Aranha 2017). Again, the result is a foundation for clean program administration and an inclusive local state.

MOVING FORWARD IN THE TWENTY-FIRST CENTURY, THE
WORKERS' PARTY AND LULA ERA (2003–2013)

The 2003–2013 period – the subject of the empirical chapters, Chapters
4–8 – coincided with a long-term economic boom and the Workers'
Party's hold on the presidency. The PT won the four presidential elections
during this timeframe: in 2002, 2006, 2010, and 2014. The 2002 election
season marked a pragmatic turning point for both Lula as a candidate and
the Workers' Party. A clear front-runner in opinion polls, Lula issued
a "Letter to the Brazilian People" in the early months of the campaign,
reinforcing his support for the Cardoso administration's economic policies. The statement was quickly derided as a "Letter to the Foreign
Bankers" because Lula pledged to maintain the basic contours of
Cardoso's neoliberal economic program. This shift from Lula's previous,
socialist platform was significant not only because of the economic stability that the Plano Real established, but also because it demonstrated the
party's pragmatic resolve to win elections (Hunter 2010). Subsequent
reelections benefited from a widening of the party's electoral base beyond
its early bastions of support in the southeast.

Lula made programs associated with poverty alleviation, such as *Fome
Zero* (Zero Hunger) and Bolsa Família, hallmarks of his administration's
commitment to social inclusion (Hall 2006). His successor, Dilma
Rouseff, followed suit by expanding on the Bolsa Família program
through her signature initiative, *Brasil sem Miséria* (Brazil without
Extreme Poverty). These programs showed great success in reducing
poverty and raising standards of living across Brazil with up to a quarter
of the population enrolled in the Bolsa Família program. Concurrently,
the relatively modest federal expenditures associated with these programs
reflected their administrations' fiscal restraint, which pleased domestic
and international investors.

The ascension of the Workers' Party to Brazil's presidency shifted how
CSOs engaged the federal government. Most importantly, leftist social
movements and CSOs were much more aggressively incorporated into
public policy making. As a consequence of being in federal power, the PT
downplayed the role of municipal-based programs like participatory budgeting and turned to national public policy management conferences,
national-level councils, and new national-level forums to foster broader
public participation. Hundreds of CSOs participated in these forums and
contribute to policy in a vertically and horizontally integrated network of
public officials, advocacy groups, and citizen representatives.

Finally, Brazil experienced a major economic boom during the first decade of the twenty-first century. The boom stemmed from high international demand for commodities, pent-up domestic demand from twenty years of economic stagnation, easier access to credit, and a much more expansive state investment in public goods. Importantly, the twenty-first-century boom improved basic well-being among Brazil's poor majority, unlike the 1960s "Brazilian Miracle" that did not lead to significant changes in most citizens' quality of life. The economic boom ended in 2013, along with our study timeframe. However, the influx of revenue and resources offered municipalities greater opportunities to promote well-being through expanded social programs, public participation in policy making, and greater capacity to deliver services.

The remainder of this book explains three pathways to well-being at the municipal level. Some municipal governments embraced these pathways and crafted policies to improve well-being. However, not all municipalities adopted the policies or administered programs in a way that generated similar improvements. Our aim in Chapters 4–8 is to evaluate the ways that participatory councils, innovative social programs, and local state capacity independently and interactively influence well-being.

3

Research Design, Methods, and Variables

To better capture the varied institutions, programs, and policies associated with a thicker description of democracy, we use mixed-methods research to evaluate connections between local participatory institutions, federal social programs, local state capacity, and outcomes associated with well-being. Our complementary, mixed-methods research provides a thorough evaluation of the connections between democratic performance and well-being. Our quantitative analysis identifies general relationships within data covering an unusually large number of observations at a remarkably granular level. These trends lay the foundation for qualitative work, which unpacks the local, specific causal mechanisms driving relationships between democracy and well-being across Brazil. Our research thus leverages very rich data, considerable variation across Brazil's municipalities, and decades of in-country experience among the coauthors to build theory and test hypotheses in ways that would be impossible in other contexts. The result is thorough analysis that improves our understanding of democracy and human development in Brazil, and a platform to improve local democratic performance around the world.

We draw on an original dataset covering Brazil's 5,570 municipalities that includes indicators for our three pathways to well-being as well as a series of control variables that may also influence well-being. Our dependent variables fall into four categories of well-being: poverty, health, women's empowerment, and education. Our dataset on local democracy, social policies, state capacity, and well-being represents one of the largest repositories of information on subnational policies in the developing world and the only one aligning key local aspects of participation, social programs, and administrative capacity with local outcomes.

Our data cover all Brazilian municipalities from 2006 to 2013 on all measures and extend back to 2000 for many others. This translates to models with up to 65,000 municipal-year observations.[1]

Limiting our study to Brazil leverages the benefits that come from a subnational, single-country study, which holds national institutions and electoral politics constant (King et al. 1994; Snyder 2001). Brazilian municipalities (N = 5,570) are responsible for delivering many services and there is remarkable variation in local experiences with participatory institutions, coverage of new social programs, and local administrative performance – meaning that local quality of life and individuals' potential to access rights, secure public goods, and develop individual capabilities also vary.

Wide municipal variation also makes our research applicable across broader contexts beyond Brazil. Brazil's poor, rural municipalities face challenges resembling those in less-affluent countries around the world, whereas richer municipalities more closely resemble environments in older, wealthier democracies. Brazilian federalism renders municipalities independent and politically autonomous units that represent ideal laboratories for examining the role of democratic mechanisms on human development outcomes. But municipalities also rely on the federal government for financial transfers, thus allowing the federal government significant opportunities to induce municipalities to adopt new policies and institutions.

We first build statistical models of outcomes surrounding well-being to explain variation in local human development performance. Our goal is to estimate the impact of local participatory institutions, social program performance, and state capacity on well-being. We do not explain municipal variation across our independent variables, e.g., why some municipalities have greater capacity, stronger economies, better administration of social programs, or participatory institutions. Modeling these inputs connecting local democracy to well-being would be very difficult because data surrounding institutional and economic development do not go back far enough at the municipal level to build thorough models of municipal adoption of participatory institutions or social program performance. Furthermore, covering those areas would alter our research question entirely and change the focus of the book from human development outcomes to those in very different areas. Therefore, our point of departure is

---

[1] Not all indicators have full coverage for all municipalities in each year.

to describe the variation in local democratic performance and map its influence on well-being.

Our analyses follow previous scholarship in each issue area and reflect the challenges associated with estimating relationships using many different types of data, measured in different ways and stemming from different sources in the Brazilian government (Brazilian Institute for Geography and Statistics; Brazilian Institute for Applied Economic Research or IPEA; Brazilian Ministry of Social Development; Brazilian Ministry of Health; Brazilian Ministry of Education). We did not collect any of the quantitative data ourselves: all of it is technically public and compiled from official government sources.[2] It is important to note that we use a variety of techniques to account for potentially endogenous relationships in our data. Specifically, it is possible that previous levels of our indicators for well-being influence municipalities' future choices surrounding institutional adoption, policy choices, spending, and service provision. For example, a municipality struggling with poor educational performance might adopt education-related policy councils and increase education spending to address this problem. We first use fixed effects models to address any unobserved, time-invariant characteristics that might drive municipal performance on both independent and dependent variables. We also supplement these models with Arellano-Bond dynamic panel estimation and a series of matching algorithms to estimate average treatment effects of specific independent variables on outcomes surrounding well-being. This combination of strategies has the advantage of explaining broad variation in our dependent variables while also generating precise estimates of the influence of independent variables on indicators for well-being.

The quantitative models create a detailed view of processes connecting local democratic performance to well-being over time and across space. We focus on this "birds-eye" view of human development in the first portion of the book. However, the models we build reflect general trends in the data that may not map onto causal relationships in practice. We therefore supplement our large-N chapters by narrowing our analytic lens to trace causal processes connecting participatory institutions, social policy, and local state capacity to well-being in three municipalities.

---

[2] While technically public, much of the data we use is not consistently available on government websites, much less available in a useful format. Compiling these data therefore required extensive cleaning and contact with Brazilian government officials to compile and analyze appropriately.

Three case studies disentangle the complex political processes that appear in general form as "data set observations" in the statistical models. For example, the modeling can point to the importance of civic engagement through participatory venues, but statistics alone cannot explain how and why they matter in practice. This research strategy builds on the "nested case" logic (Lieberman 2005), which uses mixed-method research strategies pairing large-N quantitative analysis with intensive case studies. In Chapter 8, we use process tracing to analyze specific characteristics of three Brazilian municipalities. Process tracing is a method that "provides information about mechanism and context" by meticulously tracing the steps in causal processes that connect inputs to outcomes (Collier, Brady, and Seawright 2004: 253). Like a detective seeking to solve a crime, process tracing uses fine-grained evidence to piece together causal processes (Collier 2011). This approach therefore focuses on intervening steps in a hypothesized causal chain, which can be difficult to establish through statistics alone (Bennett 2010: 208). As Bennett (2010) explains, this method not only allows us to establish a causal direction but also helps us to explore whether there is a causal chain to begin with, whether there are any intervening variables, and to identify any variables that were not previously considered (209).

In our case, process tracing allows us to build analytic narratives of how and why participatory venues, inclusive social policies, and local state capacity shape outcomes surrounding well-being. The analysis broadly captures a period of roughly fifteen years – from the early 2000s to 2017 – covering about three mayoral administrative terms per municipality. This kind of temporal microanalysis insulates the research from "degrees of freedom" problems commonly associated with a small-N analysis, where many factors could explain outcomes and not enough variation exists within and across cases to determine which factors map onto what outcomes (King, Keohane, and Verba 1994). In sum, our mixed-methods approach allows us to better identify causal processes and move beyond quantitative analysis to further examine the robustness of the findings in Chapters 4–7.

We selected our three municipal cases (Camaragibe, Jaboatão dos Guararapes, and Garanhuns, all in the northeastern state of Pernambuco) because our large-N models of poverty, health, gender empowerment, and education, predict these cases well based on their high, medium, and low performance: Our estimates accurately conform to the reality of Camaragibe's strong commitment to participatory institutions, its well-run national social programs, and its capable administrative state – all of which contribute to strong human development outcomes. Similarly, Jaboatão reflects middling inputs for our three pathways and middling outcomes. Finally, Garanhuns reflects low performance for our three pathways and relatively poor well-being outcomes. Although Camaragibe and Jaboatão neighbor the state capital, Recife, they share few similarities otherwise. Proximity to Recife has not significantly and systematically advantaged these cities when they are compared to Garanhuns.

All cities were selected based on the logic of a nested analysis (Lieberman 2005). This strategy is distinct from selecting cases that are broadly similar across all other dimensions that might influence outcomes in question. For example, Jaboatão is wealthier than the other two municipalities but our quantitative models incorporate this difference and still accurately predict all three cities' levels of well-being. Nested analysis thus leverages our quantitative work to identify strong candidates that might illuminate causal mechanisms driving broader relationships across all 5,570 municipal cases. Exploring these cities in greater depth then allows us to trace the causal processes connecting the democratic inputs to outcomes surrounding well-being in a way that we cannot accomplish through quantitative analysis alone.

We selected cases in the same state to ensure similarity across the three local experiences vis-a-vis state investment that might also influence human development outcomes. The northeast is a particularly important area to study because it is one of the most challenged regions when it comes to human development. Like the rest of Brazil, the state of Pernambuco is known for its internal socioeconomic diversity. Economic development and wealth are relatively high along Pernambuco's beautiful coastline. The state's capital, Recife, lies on the coast and acts as a major political and economic engine for the state. By contrast, the state's interior – largely agricultural, arid, and poor – is under-resourced and has some of the lowest overall social indicators within the state. Choosing the northeast allows us to understand where and when one can achieve "good government" despite serious structural hurdles.

Field research in the municipalities of Camaragibe, Jaboatão dos Guararapes, and Garanhuns allows us to analyze where and how some municipal governments produce relatively high, middling, and low rates of human development. Our analysis of these cities draws on more than forty interviews and participant observations conducted between May and June 2017 with civic leaders, municipal civil servants, and politically appointed municipal heads of departments. In each municipality, we first mapped the relevant institutions, including public policy councils, administrative offices, and elected officials. We then used a combination of public records and information requests to identify key individuals within each institution. In each municipality, we interviewed individuals on our original lists; we then used a snowballing technique to interview additional informants. A review of documentation and secondary literature for each municipality complements the small-N analysis.

Overall, the case studies show how high performance in participation, national social programs, and local administrative capacity contribute to virtuous circles of high human development performance. Of course, this confluence of high performance is difficult to achieve and many cities have middling or low performance results related to participation, social policy implementation, and state capacity, thus rendering them prone to vicious cycles of underperformance on human development. Ultimately, our qualitative process tracing complements our quantitative analysis to provide a full explanation of well-being in Brazil.

The remainder of the chapter proceeds as follows. We first describe our quantitative modeling strategy and address common challenges in estimating relationships between democracy and well-being. Then we describe our independent variables, which are largely consistent across the quantitative, issue-oriented chapters.

QUANTITATIVE ESTIMATION STRATEGY

We base our quantitative estimation strategy on previous efforts to explain variation in well-being across our different issue areas. The types of data surrounding each indicator for well-being change from chapter to chapter. Our dependent variables range from count and rate data to continuous measures such as percentages, percentiles, and indices of aggregated components. These data carry different estimation challenges with them and therefore merit different techniques to carry out the initial analyses. For example, both Rasella et al. (2013) and Macinko et al. (2006) use conditional negative binomial models with municipal fixed effects to test hypotheses connecting Brazil's Bolsa Família and Family Health Program to infant mortality at the municipal level. This is because infant mortality is widely dispersed as a rate outcome, where its variance is larger than the unconditional mean (Hilbe 2007; Cameron and Trivedi 2009). Negative binomial regression models account for this particular distribution to improve estimates – of infant mortality, in this case.

Many of our dependent variables surrounding poverty, women's empowerment, and education do not follow negative binomial distributions. We therefore use other techniques to estimate these variables' relationships with local democratic performance. For example, school attendance indicators reflect the percentage of school-age students that attend classes and are much closer to the ideal normal distribution underlying OLS regression assumptions. We use time-series, cross-sectional regressions with municipal and year fixed effects for our primary models of school attendance to reflect this difference across indicators and similarly alter our estimation techniques throughout the book, where appropriate.

Hausman tests and arguments in Wooldridge (2014) and Khandker et al. (2009) direct us toward fixed effects over random effects to account for unobserved, time-invariant characteristics in the panel that could undermine our ability to estimate relationships between local democratic performance and well-being. The municipal characteristics that we cannot identify directly, but need to address, include their historical, political, or sociocultural experiences that remain fixed over the course of our study. These unobserved aspects of local environments could drive levels of our independent variables, for example, of municipalities' service provision, Family Health Program performance, or municipalities' propensity to adopt participatory institutions. For instance, municipalities may have put a lot of resources behind Family Health Program administration in areas with lower infant mortality rates that were already committed to reducing infant mortality in the first place. Including fixed effects in our models adds a term to control for this potential selection bias, where some municipalities may have simply been predisposed to try harder to reduce infant mortality, regardless of the policies they adopted to do so.

The Challenge of Reliable, Accurate Estimation

Estimating relationships between variables within complex political, economic, and social systems presents many challenges. We address these challenges in each chapter and include a variety of models to check the robustness of our central results. Most importantly, we also account for endogeneity in our models in several different ways. Specifically, it is possible that previous levels of our indicators for well-being influence municipalities' future choices surrounding spending and service provision. For example, a municipality struggling with infant mortality might adopt education-related policy councils and increase education spending to address this problem. We first use fixed effects models to address any unobserved, time-invariant characteristics that might drive municipal performance on both independent and dependent variables. However, we supplement this strategy with two additional techniques to account for this potential concern. First, we deploy Arellano-Bond dynamic panel models using the "system" generalized method of moments (GMM) with one lag of the dependent variable.[3] We then use the policy council variables, Bolsa Família and PSF coverage, Bolsa Família management, public goods spending, local economic conditions, and low-income wages as instruments, beginning with the second lag and going back as far in time as the data exists for each variable.

We also address a similar concern, namely that certain municipalities might be predisposed to target well-being more than other municipalities for some unobserved reason. These municipalities might then promote participatory governance and strong management of federal programs as means to welfare-improving ends, along with many other unobserved programs or policies. Any relationships between participatory governance and indicators for well-being may therefore only reflect municipal predispositions, as opposed to any impact from the specific institutions or programs. We therefore use treatment-effects matching with voluntary councils as the primary independent variable as well as difference-in-difference estimation.

By using a variety of matching models, we estimate average treatment effects for independent variables that we identify as relevant for well-being using fixed effects models. Matching lets us use specific levels of our independent variables as experimental "treatments" on our dependent variables in municipalities that are otherwise very similar to one another on dimensions that might also influence outcomes surrounding well-being. For example, matching lets us test whether municipalities using voluntary policy councils surrounding health (one treatment) are associated with different infant mortality rates than municipalities that lack such councils (the control), but are similar regarding per capita GDP, PSF coverage, the mayor's party, the mayor's vote share, and IGD score. Ho et al. (2007) argue that this strategy imparts potential causal leverage to an evaluation of treatment effects because it allows for more direct statistical controls that increase the likelihood that the

---

[3] See Roodman (2014) and Arellano and Bond (1988) for more information on this method.

difference in treatment and control is one of the only differences among the observations.

We find statistically significant results using Arellano-Bond estimation and using different matching algorithms to estimate treatment effects. We also find little evidence to support the idea that some municipalities are simply predisposed to perform better in our three pathways to well-being. Moreover, municipalities do not tend to excel in all three areas simultaneously; there are only low correlations among municipalities with voluntary policy councils in each issue area, social program coverage, and management of these social programs. For instance, voluntary policy councils related to health care are correlated with Bolsa Família coverage at 0.14. The combination of this evidence suggests that commitments to participatory governance, social program coverage, and social program management do not stem from an unobserved penchant for improving well-being. Nevertheless, we use the more sophisticated techniques described above to address the endogeneity question lurking behind common statistical modeling strategies and time-series, cross-sectional data.

We also use a variety of model specifications to address concerns for the influence of model specifications on our results. In our case, in each chapter we specify models with different lags in the dependent variables, with different variables, and without outliers. For example, our Index of Decentralized Management (IGD) for the Bolsa Família variable does not exist before 2006. Dropping this variable extends our coverage back to 2000 and increases the number of observations in each model. We therefore estimate complementary models using specifications that exclude this variable to assess the robustness of our results.

Next, we address the potential for nonlinear relationships between our central explanatory variables and outcomes associated with well-being. Simple measures to improve health care, education, poverty, and even women's empowerment may quickly improve outcomes in municipalities where performance is very low. However, services surrounding these areas may already exist in municipalities with stronger performance and superior outcomes. New efforts targeting well-being further may therefore produce diminishing marginal returns in these contexts. We therefore split our sample into municipalities with low, medium, and high performance in each issue area to address these possibilities and present new models of each dependent variable in the extended, online appendix.

INDEPENDENT VARIABLES

Adoption of Voluntary Policy Councils

We use the Brazilian Institute of Geography and Statistics' survey data on the presence of seventeen different local policy councils among Brazil's municipalities (Brazilian Institute of Geography and Statistics 2016). These councils include health councils, women's councils, housing councils, and education councils, among others.[4] Municipalities adopt some councils, such as health and education councils, at very high rates due to federal program regulations and financial incentives. For example, the mean health council adoption rate in our data is 80 percent and adoption rates approach 100 percent by 2013. Education councils are similarly ubiquitous across Brazilian

TABLE 3.1 *Key independent variables across models in Chapters 4–7*

Voluntary Policy Councils in areas related to poverty, health, women's empowerment, and education
Bolsa Família coverage as a percentage of the eligible population
Family health plan coverage as a percentage of the eligible population
Decentralized management index scores for administration of Bolsa Família program
Municipal GDP per capita (in constant Brazilian reais)
Municipal public goods spending (per capita, in constant Brazilian reais)
PT mayors
Mayoral vote share in the previous election
Presidents Lula's/Dilma's municipal vote share in the previous election (2002, 2006, 2010)

Independent variables appearing in individual chapters:

Wages among lowest income brackets (Chapter 4: Reducing Poverty)
Percentage of the population receiving noncontributory pension benefits (BPC)
Per capita municipal health care spending
Women's median education levels, measured at the municipality
Per capita enrollment in public daycare centers

---

[4] The source surveys we use do not always include the same question for each year. We assume municipalities maintained their policy councils through the mayoral administration when the survey question was originally asked, in the absence of countervailing evidence. This assumption aligns with survey responses in our dataset where only 3 percent of municipalities eliminated a policy council during the same mayoral administration.

TABLE 3.2 *Summary statistics for key independent variables*

Variable	2001	2006	2009	2013
Bolsa Família coverage	N/A	83%	96%	64%
Family health plan coverage	68%	77%	86%	88%
Decentralized management index	N/A	0.67	0.75	0.80
Municipal GDP per capita (in constant Brazilian reais)	4,269	5,163	5,519	5,931
PT mayors	223	390	557	670
Mayoral vote share (2000, 2004, 2008, 2012)	55.93%	54.24%	57.17%	55.55%
Lula/Dilma municipal vote share (2002, 2006, 2010)	53.65%	58.67%	58.67	52.14%

municipalities. Thus, the presence of health or education councils are inappropriate measures for testing our arguments due to their very low variation across municipalities. However, many other councils do not carry federal funds to support their adoption and municipalities therefore adopt them at widely varying rates. Councils that do not carry federal funding are thus more "voluntary" than those for which there is a clear financial benefit for municipal adoption. We hypothesize that adopting these more voluntary councils represents a greater municipal and civil society commitment to democratic participation than does adopting councils with federal inducements. This argument is consistent with scholarship connecting the growth of a stronger civil society and an interested mayoral administration with the voluntary adoption of additional councils (Pires and Vaz 2012; Gurza Lavalle et al. 2015). Finally, voluntary council adoption signals that CSOs and public officials also seek collaborative relationships to improve policy outputs.

We hypothesize that many of the seventeen voluntary policy councils in the data could relate to our indicators for well-being in different ways across different issue areas of poverty, health, education, and women's empowerment. Therefore we identify the voluntary councils that could plausibly relate to our dependent variables in each thematic chapter. Then we create a series of variables based on the presence or absence of these councils to reflect municipal commitments to participatory institutions in each issue area. For example, we use infant mortality as an indicator for well-being surrounding health. Eight of the voluntary councils in our dataset (women's rights, food security, nutrition, tutelary [which monitors child abuse], sanitation, sanitary health, environmental sanitation, and urban policy) focus on areas related to the causes of infant mortality. In this issue area, this means that participants deliberate over issues that directly affect infant mortality, such as sewage, mosquito abatement, prenatal and neonatal nutrition, as well as education surrounding pregnancy and childbirth. We follow this model and identify similar voluntary councils that could plausibly relate to our dependent variables in each thematic chapter. Then we create indicators reflecting the presence or absence of these councils to estimate the influence of a targeted commitment to participatory institutions on different indicators for well-being.

Our primary models use dummy variables for public policy management councils rather than continuous variables, such as the total number of councils. Dummy variables allow us to incorporate our understanding of commitment based on structural breaks in the data: municipalities overwhelmingly have either zero or one voluntary council in an issue area, or all of them. For example, 13 percent of municipalities have all policy councils related to women's empowerment, while 80 percent have none. Just 7 percent have two, three, or four of these councils. Those municipalities with all of the potential voluntary policy councils, based on those that are included in the Brazilian government's annual surveys, have made a much clearer commitment to participatory institutions than have those that have adopted only one of these councils. A dummy variable for this concept allows us to capture the full or empty nature of municipal commitment to policy councils. However, we also use the number of voluntary councils in each issue area as a robustness check on our results.

Table 3.3 presents summary statistics on the policy councils related to public health that carry federal funds with them and are nationally mandated, as well as on the voluntary councils described previously.

Bolsa Família Coverage

We use the percentage of eligible families that receive benefits from the Bolsa Família program as an indicator for the program's reach at the municipal level. Poor Brazilian families do not automatically receive benefits; they must apply by completing an application as part of the Unified Registry. The program is funded at the federal level but

TABLE 3.3 *Brazil's policy management councils*

Type of council	2001	2005/2006	2009	2013
Federally induced				
Health	5,426	5,541	5,417	5,389
School nutrition	N/A	5,375	5,466	5,032
Children's rights	4,306	5,201	5,084	4,623
Education	4,072	5,037	4,403	4,258
Education fund*	N/A	5,372	5,267	5,119
Children's protective services	3,798	4,857	5,472	5,423
Total	17,602	31,383	31,109	29,844
Voluntary				
Urban policy	334	731	981	1,280
Women's rights councils	N/A	438	594	640
Food security	N/A	2,038	786	1,503
Nutrition council	N/A	950	1,067	1,570
Tutelary council	N/A	255	284	290
Health sanitation	N/A	N/A	306	349
Environmental sanitation	N/A	N/A	1,577	2,036
Urban development	N/A	N/A	2,493	3,142
School councils	N/A	3,867	4,290	4,007
School transportation	N/A	2,165	2,201	2,238
Environmental	1,615	**2,039	3,124	3,945
Total	1,949	10,444	17,703	17,055

Sources: Instituto Brasileiro de Geografia e Estatistica (2016), *Survey of Basic Municipal Information (MUNIC)*; Santos 2011.
* The education fund was FUNDEF in 2006 and then switched names to FUNDEB.
** This is from 2004 as data was not collected in 2005 or 2006.

administered locally. This puts the onus on municipalities to identify eligible families, enroll them in the program, and make sure that they receive benefits. We argue that the extent to which benefits actually reach eligible families will explain variation in well-being because of the direct gains associated with receiving cash transfers. Moreover, many of the conditions surrounding the cash transfers, such as attending school or getting medical checkups while pregnant, will also influence well-being in terms of health and education outcomes. The mean coverage level in our data is 83 percent and the standard deviation is 31. This is the same variable used in Rasella et al. (2013) and Macinko et al. (2006) to estimate the program's influence on infant mortality and other health outcomes.[5]

Bolsa Família Management Quality

We use a measure of the quality of local administration surrounding the Bolsa Família program as an indicator for local state capacity. State capacity is difficult to measure. However, the indicator we use reflects the considerable variation in municipal management of Bolsa Família, and, we argue, in the quality of local administration in general. We use operational data from the Ministry of Social Development (MDS), called the Index of Decentralized Management (IGD), to capture this variation. The MDS rates each municipality on how well it administers program elements, such as the quality of data entry in the Unified Registry (Cadastro Único) and tracking of beneficiaries' compliance with conditionality requirements. The MDS created the IGD to promote good administration of the Bolsa Família program and address gaps in local state capacity. To incentivize good performance, the MDS established higher fiscal transfers for cities that perform better on the IGD, with rules stipulating that IGD funds could only go toward strengthening related program operations. The index primarily measures a municipality's ability to collect and report data and to offer related educational and health services, with no penalties for failing to deliver program benefits to the population. This, we argue, provides municipalities with incentives to improve their IGD score and thus capture more resources; small improvements in the IGD performance yield resource gains. Over time, municipalities will therefore report data if they can and to demonstrate improvement. The corollary here is that municipalities that fail to report these data do so because they lack administrative capacity, not political will.

Quality of local management of the Bolsa Família program should reflect existing municipal state capacity. Furthermore, the quality of local management is likely to influence local outcomes surrounding well-being independently from the broad Bolsa Família coverage, which is often high in municipalities where management is poor, such as settings with dense poverty. The IGD measure is thus a distinct indicator from the Bolsa Família Coverage measure above and is only correlated at 0.11 in

[5] Source: www.MDS.gov.br/assuntos/bolsa-familia.

our data. The IGD variable is continuous from zero to one and each municipality receives a monthly score. We use this score to create an annual average: better management results in scores closer to one and worse management closer to zero. The mean score is 0.76 and the standard deviation is 0.15.[6]

Low-Income Wages

Perhaps most obviously, wages influence poor citizens' absolute income and purchasing power as well as their income and assets relative to other classes. Wages are therefore also likely to influence poverty and inequality directly. Economic trends could also influence outcomes surrounding well-being through several channels at the individual level. For example, higher income expands citizens' access to clean water, formula, and food, which combat two chief causes of infant mortality: malnutrition and poor sanitation (Rasella et al. 2013). Thus, higher wages among low-income citizens may be associated with lower levels of infant mortality. Similarly, citizens' wages influence their ability to delay children's entry into the workforce and to send them to school instead, as well as to purchase extra services to improve school performance. We include a measure of median municipal wages for the lowest quintile of earners in our models to account for this prospect; the measure is in constant reais.[7]

Competitive Elections

Elections represent one of the central alternative explanations for how democracy influences well-being. Elections, so the arguments go, provide opportunities for citizens to express their preferences and to hold politicians accountable. In turn, politicians have incentives to provide public goods in exchange for electoral support and to fulfill their campaign promises in order to remain in office. Highly competitive elections are theoretically likely to provide politicians with even greater incentives to keep their promises and provide public goods because winning becomes more difficult, reelection is uncertain, and every vote counts. We therefore code data on the relative competitiveness of municipal elections and include it in our models of well-being in several different

---

[6] Source: Ministry of Social Development (2018).
[7] Source: Brazilian Institute of Geography and Statistics (2017).

ways. We record data on the mayor's share of the overall vote in the previous election's first round.[8] This is a continuous measure that includes mayors from those who ultimately gain office with a small minority of the first-round vote to those mayors who gain 100 percent of the vote.[9]

PT and Left-Leaning Mayors

Previous studies connected mayors from Brazil's Workers' Party (PT) to greater well-being at the municipal level in some circumstances (Touchton and Wampler 2014). PT mayors have historically supported local political participation; subnational research on health and education reforms finds that left and center-left parties are also more likely to adopt progressive social policies (Sugiyama 2012). We therefore include indicators for the mayor's political party and that party's ideological orientation in our models of well-being. First, we code a dummy variable as "1" if municipalities have a PT mayor in a given year, with mayors from all other parties receiving a score of "0" to account for this prospect.[10]

Next, we code a dummy variable for mayors on the political left based on the assessment in the Database of Political Institutions (Beck et al. 2016) of Brazil's political parties. Mayors from leftist and center-left parties receive a score of "1," while those from other parties receive a score of "0."[11]

Presidential Vote

Our models include the percentage of municipal support in the first round for PT presidential candidates who were elected in 2002, 2006, and 2010.[12] These PT presidents promoted participatory institutions and social programs; we therefore control for the possibility that some municipalities and their residents are more committed to specific programs and institutions associated with these presidents.[13]

---

[8] Brazilian municipalities with fewer than 200,000 residents use single-round mayoral elections. These municipalities represent the overwhelming majority of our dataset.

[9] Source: Brazil's Superior Electoral Tribunal: www.tse.jus.br/.

[10] Source: Brazil's Superior Electoral Tribunal: www.tse.jus.br/.

[11] Source: Beck et al. (2016).

[12] President Dilma Rouseff, of the PT, was reelected in 2014 but our data ends in 2013.

[13] Source: Brazil's Superior Electoral Tribunal: www.tse.jus.br/.

Municipal Public Goods Spending

We evaluate the extent to which public spending contributes to well-being. We follow previous literature on public goods spending and well-being to assess whether local health care, education, and general public goods spending, as a percentage of the local budget, have at least some connection to service provision and outcomes at the municipal level (McGuire 2010). In each chapter we separate spending in each issue area depending on its connection to the dependent variables (e.g., we use education spending as a percentage of the municipal budget in models of education performance). Brazil spends a comparatively high level of resources on public goods provision, but has not consistently produced high-quality outcomes related to human development indicators (McGuire 2010; Sugiyama 2012). These measures are distinct from broader economic conditions because they use the percentage of the local budget devoted to public goods in each issue area, rather than per capita spending, which is almost always higher in wealthier places.[14] In this case, wealthier cities do not necessarily spend a greater percentage of their budget on public goods, which is the type of commitment to well-being, or lack thereof, we hope to capture with this measure.[15]

Economic Conditions

Considerable evidence connects local economic conditions to well-being. A strong economy theoretically increases local revenue, which can be spent on public goods and increases economic opportunities, which raise wages, consumption, and living standards. There is a noted disparity in underlying economic conditions between wealthier cities and poorer cities in Brazil, which we expect to help explain variance in well-being in these

---

[14] We do not include an independent measure of municipal population in our models of well-being because many of our control variables are per capita measures, and, thus, already have a population component in their design. These indicators tend to be multicollinear with population measures. For example, GDP grows as municipal populations grow. Most small cities are poor, on an absolute and per capita basis, while most larger cities have more economic activity and more job opportunities for residents. Some wealthy cities have a smaller population than poor municipalities, but these tend to be exceptions. Thus, population is highly correlated with economic conditions and per capita public goods spending. We therefore omit municipal population from our models to avoid mistaken inferences due to multicollinearity. In practice, including population in the models does not substantially change our results, but we prefer greater parsimony and less collinearity in the models we build without municipal population.

[15] Source: Brazilian Institute for Geography and Statistics.

cities. Local economic conditions may also reflect a variety of other, unobserved local factors that also influence well-being, such as the local property rights regime, infrastructure, proximity to other cities, etc. We therefore include an indicator for per capita local GDP to capture these possibilities and account for economic variation among Brazil's cities. This measure also lets us account for increasing revenue and greater general spending throughout the time frame of our study. The measure is in constant Brazilian reais.[16]

CONCLUSION

Our empirical strategy allows us to estimate statistical relationships between the independent variables described above and indicators for well-being surrounding poverty, health, women's empowerment, and education. The relationships we identify in the data provide a broad overview of the recent Brazilian experience in each area. These quantitative findings are important, but we cannot rely exclusively on our statistical models to draw inferences because our data does not necessarily lead us to the appropriate causal mechanisms driving the relationships evident in the data. We therefore complement our quantitative strategy with qualitative case studies that highlight the causal pathways underlying the statistical correlates for poverty, health, women's empowerment, and education. This mixed-methods approach maximizes leverage on our central question and helps to build knowledge surrounding democracy and well-being. Chapter 4 begins this process with a focus on poverty, a critical first area for evaluating well-being.

[16] Source: Brazilian Institute for Geography and Statistics.

4

Reducing Poverty: Broadening Access to Income

The fundamental objectives of the Federative Republic of Brazil are . . . to eradicate poverty and substandard living conditions and to reduce social and regional inequalities.

Brazil's 1988 Constitution, Article 3

INTRODUCTION

Income, employment, and income equality are critical components that help individuals and communities improve their well-being. Individuals need access to resources such as cash to purchase goods and services like food, housing, and health care. Governments around the world seek to expand access to income and employment, with many also citing the importance of reducing income inequality. The current global diffusion of cash transfer programs illustrates the central importance of providing a basic income to better enable individuals and families to live their chosen, dignified life. Each of these areas connects directly to citizens' living standards and capabilities, and to their ability to exercise agency. In this chapter, we focus on the direct, economic aspects of well-being when we discuss poverty; this complements our emphasis on health, education, and gender empowerment in subsequent chapters.

Nearly one billion people in the developing world experience poverty every day (World Bank 2017). We have a long way to go to eradicate poverty worldwide. Some consequences of deprivation are well-known. At the most immediate level, we know income poverty contributes to hunger and malnutrition. We live on a planet where food is abundant, but more than 800 million people consume too few calories to meet their needs (Food and Agriculture Organization of the United Nations 2018). The effects of hunger on overall health are serious for everyone, but especially for children who will suffer lifelong consequences of stunted growth and decreased cognition for learning. The poor also face vulnerabilities related to homelessness and precarious housing as well as unsafe drinking water. Those living in extreme poverty simply cannot extricate themselves from an intergenerational cycle of social and economic exclusion.

We are only beginning to appreciate other consequences of poverty. For instance, *Voices of the Poor* highlights the psychosocial effects of poverty, highlighting how poverty contributes to feelings of powerlessness and hopelessness (Narayan et al. 2000). The feeling of resignation is the antithesis of the kind of agency individuals need to live their chosen lives. More recent research reveals how experiencing scarcity creates "tunneling" behaviors, which means that individuals invest in short-term needs at the expense of planning for medium- and long-term goals (Mullainathan and Shafir 2013). All this is to say, poverty is the condition that detrimentally shapes the corporal, social, and psychological well-being for millions of people.

Efforts to explain variation in poverty and to provide policy solutions that reduce poverty have been central to recent research in development economics and comparative politics (Przeworski et al. 1999; De Soto 2000; Sen 1999; Stiglitz 2002; Grindle 2004; Easterly 2006; Sachs 2008; Bhagwati and Panagariya 2013; Rakodi 2014; Rodrik 2014; Dollar et al. 2016). Economic conditions occupy the prime position in explanations of poverty. Economic growth theoretically creates a virtuous circle of rising employment, income from wages and investments, consumption, and demand that provides economic opportunities to poor citizens and improves their living standards. Empirical support for connections between economic expansion and poverty reduction is strong, but many studies also address the ways differences in political institutions and policies influence economic development and poverty (Acemoglu et al. 2000; Centeno et al. 2017). For example, evaluating general connections between democracy and economic development has also been a hallmark of scholarship on comparative politics since the 1990s (Przeworski et al. 1999; Baum and Lake 2003; McGuire 2010; Gerring et al. 2012; Gerring et al. 2015).

Some new democracies are able to improve and expand public goods provision, which enhances citizens' basic well-being and helps them to develop basic capabilities (Sen 1999; Gerring et al. 2015). In this chapter, we analyze how variation in the institutional and policy terrain at subnational (municipal) levels helps to build a more robust explanation of the factors that increase income and employment and begin to address income inequality. We argue that the combination of establishing national social programs that place cash directly in the hands of poor citizens, improving local state capacity and creating participatory institutions, contribute to additional improvements in well-being. Stated a bit differently: we demonstrate that municipalities with similar economic growth patterns exhibit variation in poverty-related well-being, which we attribute to municipalities' varying capacity to invest in our three local pathways. This framework is particularly significant because research on income-based poverty underemphasizes the role of local governance, as municipalities are thought to have minimal influence over the economy. In contrast, we develop theory and provide evidence to show how the active involvement of municipal governments in implementing inclusive social programs, improving their own state capacity, and promoting participatory institutions is associated with poverty reduction.

The results of our analysis corroborate considerable scholarship connecting economic growth to poverty reduction, which represents the dominant explanation for poverty reduction in Brazil and around the world (Rodrik 2000; Dollar and Kraay 2001; Bhagwati and Panagariya 2013; Rakodi 2014; Rodrik 2014; Olsson et al. 2014; Cruz et al. 2015; Dollar et al. 2016). Economic growth often creates a virtuous circle of increased demand and increased employment, which increases production to meet that demand. The newly employed increase their own consumption, which increases demand further and increases employment and/or wages anew, which continues the circle.

However, we move beyond an economic growth explanation because there is ample evidence that strong economic growth does not necessarily result in concurrent improvements in well-being. Examples of this disconnect include South Africa under apartheid; Brazil and Mexico in the economic booms of the late 1960s and 1970s; and South Korea and Taiwan under authoritarian regimes (Fields 1977; Maddison 1992; Azzoni 2001; Terreblanche 2002). We provide a thorough accounting of how specific features of democratic regimes influence income, income inequality, and employment. (See North and Weingast 1989 as well as Acemoglu and Robinson 2013 for a comprehensive analysis of the importance of institutional rules.) Importantly, we also explore how extending inclusive social programs reduces income-based poverty. We also control for the potential influence of elections on local poverty rates. However, we argue that elections are too distant from ongoing policy cycles to impact poverty directly. Instead, we present evidence for the roles of specific institutions and policies for reducing local poverty in Brazil.

We find, in keeping with many studies of economic conditions and poverty around the world, that growth in Brazil reduces poverty. However, growth alone is not always enough to improve well-being, particularly when the benefits of growth do not reach the poor or when growth exacerbates inequality. Moreover, it is difficult for local governments to produce economic growth: local governments are poorly positioned in terms of expertise, policy tools, and power relative to national governments and thus cannot be expected to generate growth alone in most cases. We therefore move beyond economic conditions as a one-dimensional explanation to draw attention to other factors that we link to well-being.

Ultimately, we provide evidence that participatory institutions, federal social programs, and public goods spending have independent and interactive influences on immediate aspects of poverty such as income, employment, and inequality.

PATHWAYS OUT OF POVERTY

Eradicating poverty is now a central aspect of multilateral, international cooperation and activity. Actors like the United Nations, the World Bank, and national development agencies (USAID, DFID) have made poverty eradication one of their main policy goals. In this section, we highlight the ways rights-based social policies, inclusive state capacity, and participatory institutions reduce poverty.

Rights-Based Social Policies

The 1948 UN Declaration of Human Rights established the right of an individual to a "standard of living adequate for the health and well-being of himself and of his family, including food, clothing, housing, and medical care and necessary social services" (United Nations 1948, Article 25). The concept of freedom from deprivation as a human right was slow to be incorporated into international policy making, but expanded from the 1970s to the present. The World Bank's first World Development Report, in 1978, marked a shift to an emphasis on poverty alleviation and human development and away from an emphasis on large infrastructure projects and macro-economic development. This shift was slow to take root outside of many development circles, but gradually became a broad, multilateral focus by the 1990s. In 1995 the UN defined extreme poverty as a "condition characterized by severe deprivation of basic human needs, including food, safe drinking water, sanitation facilities, health, shelter, education and information" (United Nations 1995a).

The UN also held a series of human development conferences throughout the 1990s, with the purpose of developing a broader policy strategy for improving well-being. The Millennium Declaration of 2000 and the Millennium Development Goals (MDGs) represent the culmination of these efforts, along with parallel developments in the World Bank and the OECD. The Millennium Declaration enshrines a basic standard of living that includes freedom from hunger as a basic human right. The UN then set specific targets for human capital, infrastructure, and human rights in pursuit of achieving this standard, along with other goals.

The international development community focused on designing and implementing programs to achieve the MDGs in the 2000s. For example, the World Bank encouraged governments to focus on programmatic efficiency and resource-targeting to serve the neediest populations (Teichman 2004; World Bank 2004). Universal social welfare policy emblematic of the Nordic welfare state was an unrealistic goal for Latin American countries. Instead, countries throughout the region embraced more targeted poverty alleviation strategies, such as microfinance, efforts to extend property rights, and large public employment projects. The United Nations Development Programme created the Sustainable Development Goals (SDGs) in 2015 to update and expand the MDGs and set new poverty-reduction targets for 2030. The new goals address poverty's many dimensions, but also recognize the overlapping nature of many challenges associated with poverty, such as interactions between income, education, and health. Moreover, the SDGs set expectations for a concerted global effort to reduce poverty. The SDGs thus shift the UN's development focus from single, isolated problems to collective work to address multiple, overlapping problems.

Conditional cash transfers (CCTs) represent one of the largest recent innovations in social policies designed to reduce income-based poverty while also addressing overlapping dimensions of poverty, such as lack of education and healthcare. CCTs provide direct income for families to decrease income pressure, increase consumption, and improve living conditions in the present. This support is conditional upon families' participation in activities – such as attending school or getting regular medical check-ups – that are designed to break the poverty cycle for the future. Considerable scholarship demonstrates the immediate poverty and inequality-reducing effects of these programs in diverse contexts, such as Brazil (Fiszbein and Schady 2009), Mexico (Soares et al. 2009), Chile (Soares et al. 2009), India (Lim et al. 2010), Turkey (Fiszbein and Schady 2009), Colombia (Attanasio et al. 2010), and Ecuador (Araujo et al. 2017).[1]

Distributing cash to marginalized groups reduces poverty directly, in terms of increasing income and allowing the poor to purchase goods and services to fulfill their basic needs. Cash transfers also reduce poverty through multiplier effects. New income from cash transfers leads to greater consumption, greater local production to meet market demand, and broader local employment to produce goods and services.

Inclusive State Capacity

Development specialists acknowledge that private interests can capture even well-intentioned and designed public programs and use them for political ends. As observers of politics in developing countries note, entrenched clientelism and patron-client relationships often distort governing in ways that perpetuate poverty and harm the poor (Weyland 1996; Przeworski, Stokes, and Manin 1999; Diaz-Cayeros, Estévez, and Magaloni 2012). Inclusive state capacity requires trained personnel and resources to deliver services in ways that raise living standards for marginalized populations. Lacking personnel and resources in these areas can make it difficult to execute even well-designed public policy. Decentralization was thought to be part of the solution to this problem in large federal countries where public policy implementation takes place at the subnational level because it would render local authorities more responsive to voters, making corruption more visible and thus easier to control, and would improve the quality of services (Campbell 2003; Grindle 2007: 7–8). Yet, decentralization has not lived up to expectations in practice in many settings and has not proven to be the panacea its advocates had imagined (Bardhan 2002). In part, this is due to the distinction between general and inclusive state capacity. Local governments in the developing world may have the technical ability and the material resources to administer programs and deliver services. However, their commitment to

---

[1] See also Bastagli et al. (2016, chapter 6) for an overview of research on the effects of cash transfers to reduce poverty.

inclusion and training in that area is often lacking. The result is a performance gap between contexts where general state capacity may be present and those where that capacity is explicitly harnessed to include marginalized populations.

Participatory Institutions

Participatory institutions have an indirect relationship with poverty. Conceived broadly, participatory institutions may reduce poverty by helping to forge new relationships among citizens, civil society organizations (CSOs), and public officials. These new relationships induce local governments to increase public good spending in poor communities or to invest greater resources in areas that serve poor citizens' interests. Broadly, these institutions are designed to improve governance and policy performance, but they often contain several elements expressly designed to reduce poverty. For instance, participatory institutions are designed to extend *voice* to marginalized populations, most of whom are poorer than average, from an economic perspective. Including the poor in the policy cycle increases the knowledge that governments and CSOs have surrounding poor citizens' needs and offers the poor venues they can use to learn about their rights, to organize, and to make demands of public officials. In addition, participatory institutions may be associated with increased local tax collection, which increases the resource base available to governments (Touchton, Wampler and Peixoto 2018; Frey 1994; Feld et al. 2010). Expanding public goods provision can also create a multiplier effect, wherein companies winning contracts for service provision purchase material and hire new workers to deliver the goods in the short term. In the long term, public goods provision stimulates the economy and leads to increased productivity because it fosters a healthier, better educated workforce.

Conceived more narrowly, very few studies evaluate direct connections between participatory institutions and material well-being. Participatory institutions often incorporate the poor and alter spending in a way that brings new projects, programs, and resources to poor communities. However, living standards may be slow to change based on these new benefits, particularly in terms of income and assets. This is partially because connections between municipal institutions and individuals' income are diffuse and difficult to identify using common analytic techniques, and partially because public policy impacts through participation may take considerable time to appear as income gains.

Challenges for Poverty Reduction in Brazil

Brazil has experienced high but varying rates of poverty, like other developing and middle-income countries at the start of democratization (World Bank 2015). Brazilian governments in the 1990s and 2000s faced serious challenges surrounding extreme poverty, with few economic opportunities, pervasive inequality, and low-quality public goods despite high state spending. Economic crises in the 1980s and early 1990s featured high debt hyperinflation, liquidity problems, and a "lost decade" of economic growth at the national level. Loss of revenue followed and the Brazilian government cut many social programs, such as education, during this era. Brazil returned to growth following the government's *Real* plan to issue a new currency, combat inflation, and stabilize the economy in 1994. The Cardoso administration's subsequent efforts promoted national growth, but tens of millions of citizens remained impoverished and bereft of economic opportunities.

Extreme poverty and a lack of economic opportunities marked the Brazilian experience for a large percentage of citizens, translating to tens of millions of people. In 1990 twenty percent of the population was mired in extreme poverty (indigence; with incomes less than $2 a day) and an additional 17 percent fell below or at the poverty line (World Bank 2015). Poor Brazilians experienced a life of deprivation from hunger, lack of adequate shelter and inadequate clothing, and other essential basic needs. A lack of economic opportunities extended across the formal and informal sector, but formal employment opportunities were exceptionally scarce, leading to great difficulties in escaping poverty even as many poor people began to gain an education and skills. This economic landscape also led to high rates of child and adolescent labor as families could not forgo the opportunity costs of their labor for school. Children's low-wage work could help support entire families. Additionally, families would not need to divert very limited financial resources to properly clothe children and purchase school supplies.

Brazilian poverty has intergenerational components as well as age-based, racial, gendered, and regional elements that were very strong in the 1990s and 2000s. Brazilian youth, women, Afro-Brazilians and those with indigenous heritage, citizens in rural areas, and those in the north and northeast were all much poorer than average, with some average incomes approaching those in Honduras, a country with a per capita GDP that was 27 percent of Brazil's in 2000 (Gradin 2007). In practice, this meant that the average woman of Afro-Brazilian heritage in the rural northeast experienced deep, intergenerational poverty with very few opportunities to escape.

High economic inequality also plagues Brazil. Brazil has had one of the highest rates of income inequality in the world since long before our study begins. The Gini coefficient for income inequality of 53.2 in 1990 placed Brazil as the country with the tenth least equal income distribution in the world, a mark that changed little by 2000. Income inequality is more persistent than poverty in Brazil, which creates misleading economic indicators for the country. Gross National Income (GNI) and per capita GNI placed Brazil in the upper-middle-income range, but the average citizen was still very poor because of the unequal distribution of that income. Income inequality remained very high despite reductions in extreme poverty and general poverty leading up to the 2000s. Thus, absolute levels of poverty fell some between Brazil's promulgation of the 1988 democratic constitution, and the beginning of some of our indicators in 2000, but poor Brazilians' relative economic position remained just as imbalanced as during earlier timeframes.

Finally, Brazil's governments provided low-quality public goods after the return to democracy, which created additional barriers to lifting citizens out of poverty in the present and to breaking the intergenerational poverty cycle for the future. For example, only 35 percent of Brazil's working population had completed elementary school in 1995 (Brazilian Institute of Geography and Statistics 1995). Doubly challenging from a reform and governance perspective is that Brazil's governments spent high amounts, as a percentage of GDP relative to other countries, to provide these public goods. This means that additional resources are often not available to improve services because of tight budgets. We also must keep in mind that additional resources might not improve services even if they were available because Brazilian governments had long since reached the point of diminishing marginal returns on pure levels of public goods spending.

Subnational governments have experimented with different approaches to poverty-reducing social programs and have met with different levels of success (Sugiyama 2012; Brazilian Ministry of Social Development 2015). For instance, locally administered conditional cash transfer programs, job training programs, and micro-enterprise loans are often packaged as poverty-reducing strategies (De Soto 2000; Avritzer 2009; Sugiyama 2012). However, scholars and practitioners have not explored the extent to which new participatory

TABLE 4.1 *Poverty across Brazil*

	Regions	1990	2000	2010
GINI index	North	0.63	0.66	0.63
	Northeast	0.66	0.67	0.63
	Center-West	0.62	0.64	0.60
	South	0.59	0.59	0.53
	Southeast	0.60	0.61	0.59
	National average	0.61	0.59	0.54
Percentage of residents below poverty line	North	78.6%	67.0%	52.8%
	Northeast	86.1%	73.1%	56.1%
	Center-West	64.8%	44.3%	25.92%
	South	62.1%	36.8%	19.2%
	Southeast	53.2%	35.1%	23.7%
	National average	58.4%	37.2%	25.3%
Human development index	North	0.42	0.53	0.67
	Northeast	0.40	0.52	0.66
	Center-West	0.51	0.64	0.76
	South	0.53	0.66	0.75
	Southeast	0.55	0.68	0.77
	National average	0.61	0.68	0.73

Source: Brazilian Institute for Geography and Statistics (2017).

institutions or rights-based social programs are responsible for Brazil's local reductions in poverty, especially in the context of rapid economic growth that should account for a large proportion of reductions in poverty.

Table 4.1 presents descriptive statistics on poverty across Brazil from 1990 to 2010. The Gini Index measures the degree of income inequality. A score of "0" indicates a perfectly equal income distribution, whereas a score of "1" reflects a scenario of highly concentrated income. The poverty level measure reflects the percentage of the population making less than half of the minimum wage, which is one of the few consistent measures available across all three time periods and available by region. Finally, the Human Development Index (HDI) is an aggregate measure that incorporates health, education, and income – all of which influence human capabilities. All data come from the Brazilian Institute for Geography and Statistics (2017).

Pathways out of Poverty in Brazil

Brazil's Economic Growth

Brazil experienced economic crises and a "lost decade" of growth during the 1980s and early 1990s. The economy stabilized during the mid-1990s and entered an economic "boom" phase in the 2000s as global commodity markets expanded and Brazil's industries in agriculture, forest products, and extractives responded. First, the state downsized and privatized key industries following then-Finance Minister Fernando Henrique Cardoso's 1994 economic stabilization package (Madrid 2003; Montero 2014). Then, Brazil experienced rapid economic growth during the 2000s with a global commodities boom expanding economic opportunities in agriculture (soy, corn, and cattle), logging, mining, and oil and natural gas.

The return of a neodevelopmentalist state also injected new capital across the country and spread it among the population (Schneider 2015). The infusion of cash into the economy brought new jobs, increased the country's revenue base, and infused cash into poor households as it created new opportunities. Household consumption increased throughout this time period, which also drove demand for new products, subsequent job creation, rising wages, and still more opportunities for poor citizens. The result was a direct reduction in Brazilian poverty as economic conditions improved (Lopez-Calva and Rocha 2012; Lustig et al. 2013).

National Social Programs

Brazilian social sector reforms mirror efforts across the developing world to design social programs that serve the poor. Since the mid-1990s, social policy reforms have spread across the country as public officials and citizens developed creative solutions to address enduring social problems (Tendler 1997; Avelino et al. 2005; Sugiyama 2007, 2012).

The national government's most notable effort to address poverty came in the form of President Lula's flagship poverty-alleviation program, the Bolsa Família (Family Grant). Established in 2003, Bolsa Família is the world's largest conditional cash transfer (CCT) program. It is the government's most visible and far-reaching poverty-alleviation program, and serves about a quarter of Brazil's population. The Bolsa Família program provides poor and indigent families with cash grants on the condition they meet behavioral requirements that are thought to enhance well-being.[2] Namely, beneficiaries must ensure their children attend school regularly, receive vaccinations and regular check-ups, and mothers must receive prenatal and postnatal care. Although the Bolsa Família program includes conditionality requirements, the government's discourse surrounding the program focused on rights-based access to incomes that cover basic human needs, health care, and education (Hunter and Sugiyama 2014). Research demonstrates that Bolsa Família has contributed directly to poverty reduction through its transfer of cash to poor households (Soares et al. 2010; Sánchez-Ancochea and Mattei 2011; Soares 2012; Bither-Terry 2014). It has also contributed to well-being, primarily in health care and education. For instance, scholars have identified enrollment in Bolsa Família with significant improvements in school enrollment (Soares et al. 2010), performance in school (Batista de Oliveira and Soares 2013), nutrition (Gilligan and Fruttero 2011), and declines in infant mortality (Rasella et al. 2013).

Much of the scholarship on the Bolsa Família program and poverty highlights the program's small but consistent influence on different, purely economic, poverty measures such as income and consumption (Bither-Terry 2014). Yet, in addition to fostering short-term economic development, federal social programs such as Bolsa Família are designed to increase long-term human development as well. For instance, the conditions attached to the Bolsa Família payments are intended to increase the likelihood that citizens would fulfill their rights to health care and education, which we also expect to increase income and employment and to reduce inequality in the longer term. This is because a better educated, healthier labor pool translates into a more productive workforce. Higher productivity per worker, in turn, leads to greater profits, the potential for higher wages, and the possibility of a virtuous circle: greater income through new jobs and/or increased productivity leads to greater consumption. Greater consumption brings the need for greater production to meet higher consumer demand, which necessitates hiring more workers. These workers then increase their own consumption and drive the continuation of the productivity-consumption-employment circle.

---

[2] The Ministry of Social Development (*Ministerio de Desenvolvimento Social*, MDS) periodically updates its formulas and adjusts values for the cash grants. Amounts vary according to the composition of the family – age and number of household members – and their monthly income per capita. The payments can range from R$32 to R$242 depending on family profiles; in 2010 the average benefit was R$96.97 (MDS Bolsa Família website; Ministry of Planning, Budget, and Management 2011). This translates to USD $55 per month at 2010 exchange rates.

Brazil's *Benefício de Prestação Continuada* (BPC), the country's non-contributory pension for elderly poor and disabled, is another federal program that also injects cash directly into citizens' hands, with redistributive effects. The program was created in 1993 to address the pervasive challenge of poverty among vulnerable, disabled, and elderly populations. The BPC is administered by the federal government and municipal governments do not have a role in its management. The magnitude of federal transfers through this program is large, as beneficiaries receive the equivalent of the Brazilian minimum wage, which is approximately six times greater than the mean Bolsa Família benefit (Medeiros et al. 2015). Several studies provide evidence of this program's positive impact on income and consumption (Medeiros et al. 2008, 2015; de Souza 2012). We also expect benefits from this program to influence income directly, to increase consumption, improve living standards, and reduce poverty.

Inclusive State Capacity

Brazil's municipalities feature uneven economic development and varying experiences with local clientelism. Decentralized governance therefore poses serious challenges for standardized and universal delivery of social benefits.[3] For this reason, during the 1990s and 2000s federal authorities tightened administrative oversight of state and municipal governments simultaneously to diminish clientelism and corruption (Eaton and Dickovick 2004; Sugiyama 2012). The result is a merger of the principles of the 1988 Constitution (universal access to public goods provided by the state) with those of new public management (Barzelay 2001; Grindle 2007).

Several changes contributed to improving the quality of service delivery across many policy areas over the timeframe of our study. First, the federal government began to require greater fiscal transparency and responsibility. For example, the *Lei de Responsabilidade Fiscal* (Fiscal Responsibility Law), enacted in 2000, requires municipalities to spend 50 percent of their annual budget on health care and education and to provide year-end fiscal information to the federal government. Second, the federal government established an independent Supreme Audit Institution to ensure that other

---

[3] Brazil's state is characterized by "islands of excellence" associated with regionally concentrated industrialization that contributed to rapid economic growth in the 1960s. For most of the twentieth century, the state did a poor job providing basic public goods (education, public security, transportation) to vast sectors of the population (Eakin 1997).

public officials are more actively involved in the ongoing monitoring of policy implementation. Third, the federal state created more stringent rules that promoted hiring civil servants through tests rather than through nepotism or political patronage; the best example is the introduction of a professional management career (*gestor de políticas públicas*) at the federal level. Municipal governments now face strict limits on the amount of their budget that they can spend on personnel as these requirements are extended throughout the country.

The changes described in this section theoretically reduce mismanagement, waste, and fraud. In turn, these changes theoretically improve program performance, attract investment, and increase revenue – all of which contribute to income and employment (Baud et al. 2015; Bockstael 2017; Salles and Viera 2017). Improvements in programs that target the poor also likely reduce economic inequality, another important element of poverty in Brazil.

Brazil's Participatory Institutions

Brazil's policy councils may influence poverty in several different ways. Poor citizens constitute a majority of Brazil's population, though most no longer suffer from extreme poverty. Voluntary policy councils tend to focus on areas of municipal service delivery that primarily affect the poor, as poor citizens are unable to opt out of public services in favor of private ones. Participatory venues offer these citizens opportunities to influence policy-making processes and voice their preferences for policies that redistribute income, support employment, and increase standards of living. Similarly, participatory institutions provide a platform for poor citizens, and for the CSOs that advocate for them, to improve national, poverty-reducing policies that are administrated locally, such as the Bolsa Família program. For instance, some cities created Bolsa Família councils early in the program. Later the Ministry of Social Development mandated the establishment of a Social Assistance Council as part of its System of Unified Social Assistance (SUAS) reforms. SUAS councils are now charged with addressing a wider range of social programs – disability, mental health, Bolsa Família, etc. However, the focus is still on programs that primarily affect the poor. Participatory institutions may also offer poor citizens and their advocates points of entry to more broadly influence governance and local administrative performance by familiarizing them with general policy-making processes and providing mechanisms to denounce mismanagement, waste, and fraud. Finally, there is some evidence that participatory institutions increase local tax compliance in Brazil, arguably by increasing social accountability (Touchton, Wampler, and Peixoto 2018). Increasing local government revenue then increases the prospects for improving existing services, attracting investment, and potentially adding programs that improve standards of living.

VARIABLES AND METHODOLOGY

Dependent Variables

There are many ways to measure poverty in Brazil and around the world. We use income, employment, and income inequality because of their direct connection to standards of living and well-being. Extreme poverty and general poverty have fallen far over the timeframe of our study. Yet Brazil remains one of the most economically unequal countries in the world, despite a decade of economic growth between 2003 and 2013. FIRJAN, the Industrial Federation for the State of Rio de Janeiro, captures these nuances of Brazilian poverty by collecting data to code a municipal development index for each of Brazil's 5,570 municipalities from 2005 to 2014.

Economic Development Index

We use the economic component of FIRJAN's index, which includes income, employment, and income inequality. The measure is constructed similarly to the UNDP's Human Development Index, where municipalities receive an annual score between 0 and 1 based on annual median income levels, mean employment levels, and local income GINI – all from IBGE. Municipal development scores between 0 and 0.4 reflect low development and those between 0.4 and 0.6 reflect median levels of development. Scores between 0.6 and 0.8 translate to moderate levels of development, and those between 0.8 and 1.0 to high levels of development (FIRJAN 2015). The mean score is 0.39 and the standard deviation is 0.15.

FIRJAN's data-collection process is standardized across municipalities and therefore allows for comparisons between different municipalities across space and within the same municipalities over time. We can then use this data to evaluate the extent to which municipal-level participatory institutions, federal social programs that are administered at the municipal level, and local economic conditions influence municipal-level poverty indicators. Any connections between economic growth, federal social programs, state capacity, participatory institutions, elections, service delivery, and poverty should emerge in these data. The data is available from FIRJAN's website: www.firjan.com.br/ifdm/

INDEPENDENT VARIABLES

We provide very brief descriptions of the independent variables we use in each thematic chapter. Full descriptions of each variable appear in Chapter 3.

Local Per Capita GDP

This is an annual measure of per capita municipal Gross Domestic Product in constant reais.

Bolsa Família Coverage

Our indicator for Bolsa Família coverage is the percentage of the eligible municipal population that receives program benefits each year.

Bolsa Família Management Quality

We use municipal scores on the *Índice de Gestão Descentralizada* (Index of Decentralized Management, or IGD) to reflect inclusive state capacity.

Percentage of Per Capita Municipal Spending on Public Goods

We use the annual percentage of per capita municipal spending devoted to health care, sanitation, and education to test connections between commitment to public goods that help the poor and reduce poverty.

Policy Councils

Our indicator for participatory governance is the municipal adoption of policy councils that are related to poverty, including women's councils, tutelary councils, food security councils, sanitation councils, women's health councils, and urban policy councils.

Benefício de Prestação Continuada (BPC) Benefits

We also test connections between federal transfers from a large pension program for the elderly and the disabled and poverty. This program, the *Benefício de Prestação Continuada* (BPC), has a strong potential impact on municipal poverty because of direct financial transfers to local residents and is measured by the percentage of the eligible population receiving benefits.

Competitive Elections

We measure electoral competition as the winning mayoral candidate's vote share in the previous municipal election.

Left-Leaning and PT Mayors

This indicator is a dummy variable coded "1" for mayors from the Workers' Party (PT) and "0" for all other mayors. We recode this variable to distinguish between parties on the political left "1" and others ("0") as a robustness check.

ESTIMATION STRATEGY

We use several different estimation techniques to model poverty outcomes. First, we use fixed-effects models to estimate relationships between our independent variables and poverty scores. We use municipal and year fixed effects to account for correlations between unobserved, time-invariant characteristics of the panel and our independent variables.[4]

For our data, the time-invariant characteristics include those of the municipality, such as its historical or socio-political experience, that remained fixed over the timeframe of our study. These fixed, unobserved, elements could influence municipal adoption of voluntary policy councils as well as local coverage for federal social programs such as Bolsa Família. For instance, policy councils may have emerged first in areas with lower poverty rates that were already committed to reducing poverty before we recorded data on their efforts. The estimates of policy councils' impact on

---

[4] We choose fixed effects over random effects based on the results of Hausman tests and on the arguments in Wooldridge (2014), Shahidur et al. (2010), and Frees (2004) surrounding fixed-effects models and impact evaluations.

poverty rates could thus suffer from selection bias if our models failed to account for fixed, unobserved characteristics that might influence our independent variables. Using fixed, not random, effects adds a term to our models that allows us to control for this potential selection bias (Shahidur et al. 2010).

RESULTS AND DISCUSSION

The first model in Table 4.2 provides several important findings. Our first finding surrounds the role of local economic conditions for poverty. Higher local GDP is systematically associated with higher municipal income, employment, and inequality scores in our data, as expected. Our estimate for economic growth's impact on poverty is large: moving from mean local GDP to one standard deviation above the mean results in a 29 percent improvement in poverty scores over other municipalities, on average. This represents the largest estimated impact of any variable in our models, which is also consistent with scholarship on economic growth and poverty.

Our second finding showcases the importance of top-down, federal social programs representing expert-led approaches to service delivery and poverty reduction. Measures of municipal Bolsa Família coverage as a percentage of eligible families are associated with higher municipal scores on the income, employment, and inequality index. These results replicate prominent findings in the literature on Bolsa Família such as Soares et al. (2010), Rocha (2008), Soares (2012), Bither-Terry (2014), and Sugiyama and Hunter (2013). Our results also corroborate recent evidence that Bolsa Família's direct impact on poverty is much smaller than that of economic productivity (Bither-Terry 2014). We estimate a 7 percent improvement in poverty scores, on average, for movement from mean-level Bolsa Família coverage to coverage that is one standard deviation above the mean, all else equal. *This translates to roughly 400,000 additional residents raised above the poverty line per year in municipalities with high-level Bolsa Família coverage and 3.2 million over the course of our study.*

Next, evidence on the relevance of local management of the Bolsa Família program for poverty also supports our argument. The federal indicator for the quality of local Bolsa Família management, "IGD," is a statistically significant determinant of the municipal development score, as expected from literature on the local state's ability to create a regulatory environment conducive to investment, employment, and growth (Heller 2017). Improving Bolsa Família management and state capacity in general are also associated with improvements in health care and education

TABLE 4.2 *Explaining poverty outcomes, 2006–2013: Federal social programs, policy councils, and local state capacity*
This model uses cross-sectional time series estimation with fixed effects.

Variable	Coefficient (SE)
Voluntary council commitment	0.05**
	(0.01)
Incentivized council commitment Bolsa Família coverage	0.003*
	(0.0004)
Bolsa Família management	0.03**
	(0.006)
Per capita municipal public goods spending (% of total spending)	0.10**
	(0.03)
Per capita gross municipal product	0.0003**
	(0.0004)
Percentage of population receiving BPC benefits	0.004**
	(0.001)
Competitive elections	0.04
	(0.06)
Left-leaning mayor	0.02
	(0.02)
Constant	0.31
	(0.52)
N	18,362
Wald Chi^2 (6)	161.86
Prob> Chi^2	0.000

* indicates significance at better than 0.05 (two-tailed test).
** indicates significance at better than 0.01 (two-tailed test).

service delivery, which could increase labor productivity and also influence income and poverty. We estimate an 11 percent improvement in poverty scores, on average, for movement from mean-level IGD scores to scores that are one standard deviation above mean, all else equal.

The percentage of municipal spending devoted to health care, sanitation, and education is positively associated with municipal scores on our central poverty indicator. Given Brazil's federal spending requirements, most municipalities spend very similar percentages of their budgets on health care and education. This means that any municipality that devotes a slightly larger percentage of its budget to public goods compared to other municipalities may see an outsize impact on poverty. Moving from the mean percentage devoted to certain public goods spending to one standard deviation above the mean results in an estimated 21 percent improvement in municipal income, employment, and inequality scores. This relationship is in the expected direction and is independent from the influence of voluntary policy councils, which are only correlated with the percentage of municipal spending that is devoted to health care, sanitation, and education at the 0.18 level.

Local policy councils are also connected to lower poverty levels. The presence of voluntary policy councils that are related to poverty have a negative, statistically significant connection to poverty outcomes in Brazil. We estimate that moving from a municipality with no voluntary councils related to poverty to one with all of the councils would generate a 5 percent improvement in municipal income, employment, and inequality score, on average. Of course, there are many differences between Brazilian municipalities beyond the presence of local policy councils. Our results suggest these councils are relevant for reducing poverty while holding all other observed influences on poverty constant at their mean. By extension, our results also highlight the importance of committing to local, demand-side participatory institutions for improving well-being as Putnam et al. proposed for civic engagement (1994) and Sen for human capabilities (1999).

We do not identify connections between competitive elections and poverty in our data. Importantly, neither the mayors' vote share nor their margin of victory is a statistically significant determinant of our central poverty indicator. This contradicts many expectations based on the literature on the role of parties and elections for poverty. Furthermore, the local presidential vote share is not significant, nor is the mayor's party nor the mayor's ideological orientation. The only significant relationship we identify between electoral variables and poverty is a negative connection between mayors who run unopposed and poverty rates, which is consistent with arguments connecting a total lack of political competition with clientelism and poor government performance.[5] As discussed above, these results do not impugn previous scholarship on elections, democracy, and well-being in a cross-national context. Instead, our results highlight the importance of more proximate aspects of electoral democracy, namely citizen participation, social policy reform efforts, and municipal administration at the local level.

The point here is that reducing poverty is not only a matter of how much municipalities spend, but of how they spend their own money (as

[5] This model appears in the extended, online appendix.

monitored by policy councils) and of how much federal support they have through the Bolsa Família program. We argue that these areas are connected: local monitoring and local program spending choices interact with one another through connections between citizen participation in local politics, the presence of civil society organizations, and the presence of motivated municipal officials to spend on public goods. Thus Bolsa Família is much more than a simple cash transfer to the poorest households; these programs work well when the local administration is able to allocate the necessary resources to ensure that recipients are being embedded into a larger network of policy support programs.

The results in Table 4.3 show how the presence of voluntary policy councils surrounding poverty interact with public goods provision to influence municipal development scores in our data. We argue that policy councils can monitor public goods spending and improve its quality. For example, women's rights councils might provide better oversight of women's health care in a way that improves maternal health. Municipalities in the top quintile of per capita public goods spending as a percentage of total spending and with a commitment to voluntary policy councils related to poverty are associated with a 0.19 improvement in income, employment, and inequality scores. This corresponds to an estimated improvement in municipal development scores of 38 percent, based on mean scores in our data.

Interactions among our three central pathways and public goods provisioning all influence municipal poverty scores. High levels of public goods coupled with high scores on each pathway are associated with low levels of poverty, all else equal. Table 4.4 showcases these relationships beyond what we report in Table 4.3.

In sum, participatory institutions, federal social programs, public goods spending, and economic growth act independently to reduce poverty in Brazil. Additionally, participatory institutions interact with public goods spending to provide an extra boost to Brazilian municipalities' poverty-reduction efforts. We argue that these interactive results reflect the importance of both the quantity and the quality of public goods provision and relate to scholarship on transparency, participation, and accountability (TPA). (See Gaventa and McGee 2013; Fox 2015; Wampler, McNulty and Touchton 2018.) Participatory institutions promote transparency, in this argument, and also provide opportunities for citizens and civil society organizations to pressure officials and hold them accountable for service provision. Improving accountability then increases government responsiveness, which increases the quantity of money spent on public goods. The presence of voluntary policy councils

TABLE 4.3 *Policy councils, federal social programs, and public goods spending, 2006–2013*
These models use cross-sectional time series estimation with fixed effects.

Variable	Councils, top 20 percent spending Coeff (SE)	No councils, top 20 percent spending Coeff (SE)	Councils, bottom 20 percent spending Coeff (SE)	No councils, bottom 20 percent spending Coeff (SE)
Councils*public goods	0.19** (0.04)			
Per capita public goods spending	-0.004 (0.004)	0.001* (0.0005)	-0.001 (0.003)	-0.0003 (0.0004)
Bolsa Família coverage	0.003* (0.001)	0.005 (0.004)	0.005** (0.001)	0.006** (0.001)
Voluntary councils	-0.003 (0.003)	Dropped	0.002 (0.003)	Dropped
Bolsa Família management	-0.006 (0.005)	-0.003 (0.006)	Dropped	Dropped
Percentage of population receiving BPC benefits	0.0003 (0.0002)	0.0004 (0.0004)	0.0002* (0.0001)	0.0004** (0.0001)
Competitive elections	0.02 (0.03)	0.01 (0.01)	0.02* (0.01)	0.02 (0.02)
Left-leaning mayor	0.02 (0.04)	-0.06 (0.04)	0.02 (0.02)	0.03 (0.02)

Per capita gross municipal product	0.04**	0.04**	0.05*	0.03**
	(0.01)	(0.01)	(0.02)	(0.01)
Constant	0.36	0.31	0.38	0.25
	(0.54)	(0.44)	(0.46)	(0.33)
N	4,658	5,320	5,772	4,639
Wald Chi²	251.36	259.79	224.90	312.74
Prob> Chi²	0.00	0.00	0.00	0.00

* indicates significance at better than 0.05 (two-tailed test).
** indicates significance at better than 0.01 (two-tailed test).

TABLE 4.4 *Explaining poverty scores through interactions among policy councils, Bolsa Família coverage, and local state capacity*

	Poverty
All pathways and public goods	Reduce poverty
Councils and Bolsa Família	Reduce poverty
Councils and state capacity	Reduce poverty
Bolsa Família and state capacity	Reduce poverty

also helps to improve the quality of services, through oversight functions that rely on and increase transparency as well.

ROBUSTNESS CHECKS

We perform a variety of tests to assess the robustness of our results. First, our results in supplemental negative binomial regressions with lagged dependent variables are similar to those in Table 4.2. This check addresses the prospect of serial autocorrelation driving the results in our models; in this case, the lagged dependent variables are statistically significant determinants of municipal development scores, but the central variables of interest all retain their approximate magnitudes, directions, and levels of statistical significance.[6] Next, we use several different specifications in our models. For example, models that include per capita municipal spending instead of per capita gross municipal product produce results that are broadly similar to those in Tables 4.2 and 4.3. Replacing the "left-leaning mayor" variable with a dummy variable for a PT mayor also produces similar results. Geographic dummy variables are sometimes significant determinants of poverty rates, especially for the north and the northeast compared to the south. However, the primary explanatory variables retain their significance, magnitude, and direction in models with geographic dummies, too.

Next, we employ different poverty measures to assess the stability of our findings across different indicators. We use interpolated/extrapolated census data on the percentage of each municipality's population in the lowest quintile of national income distribution, the percentage that lives below the national poverty line, and the percentage below the

---

[6] The models we describe in this section all appear in the appendix, in Tables A4.2a–A42.c. Models with geographic dummy variables appear in the extended, online appendix.

extreme poverty line.[7] The results of estimation using these data demonstrate consistent connections between voluntary policy councils and poverty in Brazil. The presence of voluntary policy councils is associated with decreases in all three measures of poverty, as is greater Bolsa Família coverage. The administrative quality of Bolsa Família management is not connected statistically to any of the alternative poverty measures.

We also account for endogeneity in our models in several different ways. Specifically, it is possible that previous levels of poverty influence municipalities' future choices surrounding institutional adoption, public goods spending, and service provision. For example, a municipality struggling with poverty due, in part, to a lack of job training, might have committed to education-related policy councils, expanded Bolsa Família coverage to promote education, and subsequently increased education spending to address this problem. Macinko et al. (2006) address a similar endogeneity issue surrounding infant mortality and federal social programs through instrumental variable regression using the mayor's party as an instrument for Bolsa Família coverage. However, previous scholarship connects the mayor's party directly to health care outcomes in Brazil (Touchton and Wampler 2014), which suggests that this variable violates the exclusion restriction for instrumental variables and would therefore be inappropriate to include as an instrument in our models (Wooldridge 2014).

Instead, we use Arellano-Bond dynamic panel models to account for this potential concern surrounding our estimates.[8] The Arellano-Bond models use the "system" generalized method of moments (GMM) with one lag of the dependent variable. The instruments used are the policy council variables, Bolsa Família coverage, Bolsa Família management, and the percentage of per capita municipal spending devoted to public goods, beginning with the second lag and going back as far in time as the data exists for each variable. The direction of the coefficients and the

---

[7] Many studies exploring poverty in Brazil and tying the Bolsa Família program to poverty reduction use census data, which is collected at ten-year intervals. These studies interpolate data for the intervening years between each census and/or extrapolate data beyond these years based on trends within the census timeframe (Rocha 2008; Soares 2012). This approximation is potentially suspect because poverty is likely to rise and fall in nonlinear fashion and to do so with some annual volatility based on economic, political, and social conditions, not consistently with a fixed rate over the course of a decade. These data come from the Brazilian Institute for Applied Economic Research and are available here: www .ipeadata.gov.br/

[8] See Roodman (2014) and Arellano and Bond (1988) for more information on this method.

general levels of statistical significance are all similar to those in the primary models. We also use dummy variables for each year to ensure that the assumption holds that there is no correlation across units. We supplement this technique with propensity score matching with a focus on voluntary councils related to poverty (Ho et al. 2007). We match municipalities on all other independent variables in the model and then compare municipalities that are otherwise similar (the nearest neighbor to one another) on all of the independent variables where one municipality has councils that we relate to poverty and the other, very similar municipality, does not. Our estimates of voluntary policy councils' impact on poverty indicators are somewhat lower than in the primary models presented above, but the relationships surrounding policy councils and poverty identified in Tables 4.2 and 4.3 the tables above are robust to the use of propensity score matching. The results in Tables A4.2a–A4.2c of the appendix thus provide supporting evidence for Tables 4.2 and 4.3, and emphasize the strong connection between participation, federal social programs, local public expenditure, and municipal development scores.

An additional, important consideration is that certain municipalities might simply be predisposed to assist the poor more so than other municipalities for some unobserved reason. These municipalities might then promote participatory governance, the expansion of federal programs, and greater spending on public goods as means to a poverty-reducing end, along with many other unobserved programs or policies. Any relationships between participatory governance, federal programs, state spending, and poverty could therefore only reflect municipal predispositions, as opposed to any impact from the specific institutions or programs. We find little evidence to support such a scenario; there are only low correlations between municipalities with voluntary policy councils related to poverty, social program coverage, and public goods spending programs.[9] This may be surprising, but it suggests that municipalities do not tend to excel in all three areas simultaneously and that a commitment to participatory governance, social program coverage, and local social spending does not stem from an unobserved penchant for poverty reduction. Instead, this observation provides some evidence for each area's independent role for improving well-being.

---

[9] Voluntary policy councils related to poverty are *negatively* correlated with Bolsa Família coverage at –0.31. All other correlations between primary independent variables are less than 0.2.

CONCLUSION

Increasing access to income and employment as well as reducing income inequality are crucial for improving well-being. Individuals need money to pay their rent, to purchase food, medicine, and clothes, as well as to invest in schooling or equipment that improve their capabilities and future lives. Increasing income also provides the opportunity for governments to expand their revenue base by increasing economic activity. This, then, creates the opportunity for governments to support programs that reduce income inequality and improve well-being. We begin the empirical evaluation of our democratic pathways with a focus on income and other material elements of poverty because of their basic nature: People need a basic income and basic opportunities to live dignified lives.

Not surprisingly, we find that economic conditions are closely connected to employment, income, consumption, and living standards. Of the four arenas for human development we explore in the book, access to income is the most sensitive to the overall economic conditions within municipalities. Stronger local economies promote greater employment, higher incomes, and lower income inequality. This conforms to much of the existing literature on poverty. However, our results also show that variation in local policies explains poverty outcomes after accounting for local economic conditions. The economy matters, to be sure, but so do local governments' decisions and national programs. The evidence and the argument presented in this chapter demonstrate that Brazil's reductions in poverty are strongly tied to economic expansion, as well as democratic expansion.

The three democratic pathways we identify as theoretically important – rights-based social programs, participation, and inclusionary state capacity – all also work to produce improvements in income poverty. Among our three pathways, the delivery of rights-based social programs provides the most robust explanation for variation in income, employment, and income equality. This makes sense as Brazil's Bolsa Família, a conditional cash transfer program, is a clear example of a rights-based poverty alleviation program that puts money directly into citizens' hands. Poor families now have access to additional money, which allows them to buy food and clothes, and to meet other basic needs. Our work corroborates previous research that demonstrates that the Bolsa Família program reduces poverty (Hall 2006; Ferreira, Leite, and Ravallion 2010; Soares et al. 2010; Bither-Terry 2014) and that conditional cash transfers generally improve household living standards (Fiszbein and Schady 2009;

Araujo et al. 2017). Bolsa Família beneficiaries suffer less hunger, eat better, and buy essential items that improve their lives.

Our two other pathways, inclusive state capacity and participatory institutions, also have significant and positive effects on income, employment, and income equality, although their overall effect is smaller than rights-based social programs. Inclusive state capacity and participatory institutions reduce poverty less directly than the conditional cash transfer approach because they do not directly distribute income to poor citizens. For example, participatory institutions arguably produce better oversight and better management of public goods delivery to better target vulnerable populations. Inclusive state capacity leads to an increase in public goods spending that creates an independent multiplier effect that also improves the lives of the poor.

There are a variety of ways that the three pathways also interact to improve well-being. However, the quantitative analysis does not identify the causal mechanisms driving these improvements or those that stem from independent effects of each pathway. We therefore complement our quantitative analysis in this chapter with causal process tracing that we use in Chapter 8 to provide a closer analysis of the causal mechanisms at work. We show how the expansion of Bolsa Família, a rights-based social program improves citizens' capabilities and agency as it adds critical income, which aids these citizens in their daily lives and also facilitates their demands for rights. There is also considerable overlap with the participatory institutions and an inclusive state apparatus as citizens demand these rights through a variety of local policy councils and engage the local state as it implements national programs. Our case studies show that effective service delivery of anti-poverty programs results when complementary activities are in place. For instance, governments deliver services effectively when local officials engage in rights-based framing, closely monitor Bolsa Família and related programs, engage with policy councils surrounding social assistance on program implementation, and collaborate in intra-departmental exchanges to problem-solve. The municipalities we examine with weaker records on poverty reduction lack these connections and ultimately administer programs poorly, even when they have a strong local economy and municipal governmental revenue is relatively high.

Chapter 5 focuses on health, where we examine the ways our pathways connect to infant mortality. Surviving birth is a prerequisite for a dignified life and all three of our pathways show great benefits for reducing infant mortality. In our study of health as in our study of income poverty, we find that our three democratic pathways all work to save lives. Unlike income poverty and employment, infant mortality is much less dependent on the local economy. It is easier for relatively poor municipalities to achieve strong outcomes through health interventions than for similarly poor municipalities to use public policy to reduce income poverty or to create jobs. This prospect emerges from our analysis: municipalities with robust commitments to our three pathways outpace wealthier municipalities that do not make similar commitments in reducing infant mortality. We thus uncover specific reasons why infant mortality is more responsive to policy interventions than are basic income or employment, which are structured by long-term economic forces to a greater degree.

5

Improving Health: Saving Lives

Health is a right of all and a duty of the state and shall be guaranteed by means of social and economic policies aimed at reducing the risk of illness and other hazards and at the universal and equal access to actions and services for its promotion, protection, and recovery.

Brazil's 1988 Constitution, Article 196

Access to health care is at the core of efforts to improve well-being. At the most fundamental level, infants must survive birth and children need to live beyond their first five years of life in order to benefit from human development programs, such as public schooling. To live a dignified life, people must also be able to maintain their health by avoiding deadly diseases and receiving life-saving treatment. In many countries around the world, childbirth is a risky endeavor for women. Therefore, women must also be able to survive the birth of their children. All to say that individuals need to lead healthy lives if they are to eventually develop capabilities that allow them to more productively engage the market, politics, and civil society (Sen 1999; McGuire 2010; Nussbaum 2011). Over several decades, the international development community has increasingly linked health to issues of human development and economic development. This trend is most clearly evidenced in the United Nations Millennium Goals (United Nations 2000) and Sustainable Development Goals (United Nations 2015), which elevated challenges related to infant mortality, maternal mortality, malaria, and HIV/AIDS to a global human development agenda. While worldwide in scope, the need to advance basic health has been of particular concern for the world's poorest and least developed countries and regions.

For the world's poor, health is about saving lives, pure and simple. For the developing world, that means first addressing the staggeringly high rates of infant mortality. Every day, more than 2,000 children under age five die across low and middle-income countries (United Nations 2018). Over the course of a year, that translates to more than 700,000 people. Why do so many babies die? Health challenges emerge very early in life in the vast number of cases. According to the World Health Organization, three-quarters of all newborn deaths occur in the first week of life. Yet, the WHO estimates that nearly two-thirds of newborn deaths could be prevented (2012). After birth, malnutrition is another serious problem, which is why international health agencies recommend mothers breastfeed their infants. Making it past these precarious early days, weeks, and years of life can be the most significant challenge the poor will face. This is why turning to the topic of health is so urgent. After all, we cannot talk about living one's chosen life without having a life to live.

Countries across the globe have demonstrated different abilities to advance the global health agenda, which emphasizes "health for all," access to primary health care, disease prevention, and community-based participation (World Health Organization 1978; Basilico et al. 2013). Access to health care is increasingly recognized as a "human right" and a responsibility of state action (Chapman 2016). Yet governments have faced different environmental, social, political, and economic challenges to meeting these obligations. Where public health experts may focus on identifying disease vectors and biomedical solutions, social scientists have increasingly sought to identify broader political and structural factors to explain the variation of worldwide health. Factors such as regime type, wealth, ethnic fragmentation, social segregation, income inequality, and type of spending priorities are all thought to matter for key health-related outcomes (see for example, Przeworski et al. 1999; Gauri and Lieberman 2006; McGuire 2010; Pickett and Wilkinson 2015).

Overall cross-national trends suggest that higher levels of economic development and democracy track with improved health outcomes for citizens (Franco et al. 2004; Besley and Kudamatsu 2006). The benefits of democracy for health are well-established. Yet, research also shows that some authoritarian regimes can produce good health outcomes: for example, China, Singapore, and Cuba have made remarkable strides in universal health care. Nevertheless, there is a wide body of literature that suggests democracies have gone farther than authoritarian regimes to promote health-related outcomes (Przeworski et al. 1999; Franco et al. 2004; Besley and Kudamatsu 2006).[1] This chapter focuses on the role of democracy in particular, and investigates the linkages between democratic practice and good health for citizens. We draw on McGuire (2010), who finds that regime type matters, but emphasizes that the structure of spending also contributes to advances in infant mortality. McGuire's comparative research links broader questions about wealth and democracy to important public health debates. Rather than focus on overall spending, he argues, policymakers should focus on policies that are essential for saving lives, namely, prioritizing primary health care and providing basic access for the poor.

This chapter investigates how democratic practices further health outcomes when coupled with provisioning of primary health care. We identify three pathways that improve health and well-being outcomes, thereby allowing us to contribute to public health scholarship. The variation in health outcomes is explained by multiple factors, all operating independently and interactively: the presence of institutional channels for citizens to participate in policy design, implementation, oversight, and evaluation; inclusive social programs that deliver health services to poor families as well as the establishment of a national primary health care system; and local state capacity.

Brazil is an excellent case to test the intersections between democracy and health because the country has extensive variation in local experiences with (a) public participation in democratic institutions, (b) the implementation of national reforms that depend on extensive municipal-level implementation, and (c) the administrative capacity to deliver primary health care. The stakes are particularly high for Brazil, as the country has had remarkably high rates of infant mortality. We focus on infant mortality as a proxy for well-being in this chapter because survival at birth is a necessary precondition to lead one's chosen life (Nussbaum 2011: 33; Gerring et al. 2015).

We advance knowledge surrounding local democratic performance and health outcomes in this chapter as follows: Section two begins with an overview of the political and policy frameworks used to

---

[1] Ross (2006) finds that authoritarian regimes are able to better ensure access to primary care (specifically vaccinations) than democratic regimes due to the ability of middle-class groups in democratic regimes to capture more resources than low-income individuals and communities.

explain variation in health outcomes. Section three then moves to a discussion of why our three pathways provide a more thorough theoretical explanation of health outcomes in general, followed by a discussion of the three pathways and health outcomes in Brazil. Section four describes the data and methods we use to test these hypotheses. Finally, we present the results of analysis and discuss the implications for arguments surrounding governance and health around the world.

To preview our findings, participatory institutions, national social programs, and local state capacity are all associated with lower infant mortality levels, all else equal, both independently and through interactions with each other. The lowest infant mortality levels occur through interactions, where performance is high across all three pathways. It is important to note that we also hold economic conditions and political characteristics constant at their means. These factors are not statistically significant determinants of health outcomes in our data. Thus, health outcomes stem not from how many resources municipalities have or how much money they spend, but from how they deploy these resources and how they spend their money.

THEORIZING HEALTH OUTCOMES

Global health practitioners have long grappled with the question of how countries can achieve improved health outcomes given the costs associated with health care delivery. The World Health Organization's (WHO) international meeting on primary health, held in Alma Ata, Kazakhstan, from September 6–12, 1978, brought together three thousand delegates from 134 countries and 67 international organizations. The meeting and ensuing Alma Alta Declaration represented a watershed moment for the international health community (Cueto 2004: 1867; Basilico et al. 2013). The Alma Ata Declaration (World Health Organization 1978) set an ambitious goal of "health for all by the year 2000." The question of how to achieve "health for all" given large disparities in economic and social development spurred debates within and among international health agencies (such as UNICEF, WHO, and the Pan American Health Organization); these debates shaped domestic actors' adoption of new models for primary care delivery. Here we briefly highlight how health policy and health reforms, in particular, operate through our three democratic pathways to reduce infant mortality.

Participatory Institutions

The Alma Ata Declaration advanced several important principles that highlight the value of community and lay engagement in health care. The Alma Ata attendees promoted preventive health care and broad benefits by deploying larger teams of trained lay health personnel and by focusing on community engagement (Cueto 2004: 1867–1868). The Pan American Health Organization, another major global health player, also advocated for greater community participation in health services. The idea was "to spark change from the bottom-up, giving priority to what the community needed, felt, and could itself contribute" (Cueto 2007: 97). In this way, ideas about primary health care design from the 1960s and 1970s opened the door to community medicine which integrated citizens' voices and experiences into health care delivery.

Reorienting public health from a medical "elite" model (i.e., specialization and attention to curative care) to include community engagement meant that primary health care was redesigned to incorporate trained community health workers, traditional healers, and community participation. A vibrant epistemic community of public health professionals, national health actors, and Pan American Health Organization (PAHO) and WHO representatives drew on primary health models from Costa Rica, China, and elsewhere (Cueto 2004; 2007). Cuba's revolution also led to radical health reform, which loomed large as a potential model for the developing world. However, Cold War politics limited this model's replicability. As Cueto's detailed historical research on the Pan American Health Organization shows, Latin American and Caribbean countries received ideas about bottom-up engagement positively, particularly in the context of deploying hundreds of community health agents throughout the region (2007:111–112).

Health reformers seek to integrate health into broader socioeconomic development by linking public health to community engagement and participation. Poverty, illiteracy, and poor sanitation are socioeconomic conditions that render the poor vulnerable to poor health outcomes, including maternal mortality, infant death, and chronic diseases. Bringing the poor into discussions about health thus serves as an important step for transforming primary health care. The precise institutional mechanisms for participation differ across countries in terms of whether community engagement takes place at local clinics or citywide health councils. But, the key lesson is that "bottom-up" participation can play an important role in advancing community knowledge, promoting the use of health care systems, and monitoring the quality of health services. When done well, these actions can ultimately save lives.

Social Programs

Public health specialists have long recognized that health outcomes such as infant mortality and maternal mortality depend greatly on policy design (World Health Organization 2016; Rasella et al. 2013; McGuire 2010). Spending is less effective for reducing infant and maternal mortality when diverted to high-cost curative care (e.g., specialized doctors and hospital care) at the expense of primary care (McGuire 2010). But, what should primary care look like? Since Alma Ata, there has been a lively debate over which strategies governments and international agencies should pursue. Some actors advocate for more targeted "selective primary health care" focused on growth monitoring, oral rehydration, breastfeeding, and immunization (GOBI) for its cost-effectiveness while others promote universal "primary care for all" (Cueto 2005; Basilico et al. 2013).

The Alma Ata Declaration framed health within a broader development approach, had a significant impact on many countries' health agendas, and reflected the broader framework now found in the Millennium and Sustainable Development Goals. Global public health research has found that the expansion of primary health care has made inroads on maternal and infant mortality and on the prevention of malaria (Basilico et al. 2013; Farmer et al. 2013: 308–309; McGuire 2010). Expanded access to high-quality primary care is crucial if medical practitioners are to reach vulnerable groups (e.g., the poor, disabled, women, elderly, and children). Community-based health care delivery is an important policy instrument to achieve improved health outcomes. In the context of democratic governance, such policy instruments are challenging to create and execute in the context of historic exclusion of marginalized groups. For this reason, it is important that health care access is tied to rights-based access for all citizens. The "health for all" framework established by the Alma Ata Declaration has become an important global health norm (Chapman 2016).

State Capacity

Global health experts have long cautioned against overspecialization in developing country contexts (Cueto 2005). Sophisticated medical machines and equipment, and overreliance on highly trained medical personnel can deplete resources unnecessarily. In areas like primary health care, governments must balance the benefits of "bottom-up" engagement and community health agents with the need for highly specialized care. The role of state capacity in health care is therefore particularly complex. It requires a nuanced understanding of socioeconomic development context, coordination, and an ability to manage appropriate health approaches for diverse populations. Health care needs to reach different groups that face differential complexities of care. For instance, public health systems need to address everything from fundamental sanitation vigilance, to primary health delivery, to advanced specialized care. This requires not only fiscal resources, but the ability to recruit and manage personnel, space, and complex information systems.

Many cross-national studies emphasize the importance of state capacity for health care service delivery and health outcomes (Porter 1999; Fukuyama 2003; Scutchfield et al. 2004; Burkle 2006; Schell et al. 2013; Cao and Ward 2015; Brownson et al. 2017). There is obviously wide variation in how countries deliver these services. Some countries, such as Cuba, provide most services directly. Other countries use parallel public and private systems, such as those in the United States and Brazil; public resources in these countries pay for both public and private provision of health care.

Uneven access to health care remains a significant challenge for uniform, universal health care delivery in large federal systems with internal socioeconomic diversity. Decentralization around the world also showcases the importance of local state capacity to manage and pay for complex health care service delivery. Local governments must have the capacity to raise revenue to supplement any federal transfers and to deliver health services. (See Arretche and Marques 2002.) Health care is a complex policy area and requires sophisticated administrative structures to manage personnel and resources effectively. Municipalities with low administrative capacity thus face particularly serious challenges that undermine service delivery, health outcomes, and well-being.

BRAZIL'S HEALTH CARE NEEDS AND CHALLENGES

Brazil began its return to democracy with notably poor health care outcomes and a great need to address them. For instance, in 1990 its infant mortality rate was an astoundingly high 51.5 deaths per 1,000 live births (Ministry of Health 2016). Life expectancy in the same year was 6.5 years below the Organization for Economic Cooperation and Development (OECD) average. These national figures obscure deeply unequal experiences across the country, where the north and northeast have historically faced far worse health conditions when compared to more affluent regions in the industrialized south and southeast (see Table 5.1).

Federal health care reform undertaken in the 1990s and 2000s greatly improved access to health care services. This resulted in extraordinary gains in life expectancy and reductions in infant mortality. Brazil continued to make important strides in basic indicators related to infant and maternal mortality through 2014. For example, infant mortality dropped to 12 per 1,000 births and life expectancy rose to 75 years.

Overall, Brazil's trajectory in the health sector is one of contradictions. On one hand, the country has made remarkable progress in addressing areas like infant and maternal mortality and HIV/AIDS prevention and treatment (Gauri and Lieberman 2006; Hunter and Sugiyama 2009). On the other hand, Brazil still lags far behind on basic health indicators for its peer group of OECD countries. According to a recent OECD study, Brazil has 50 percent fewer doctors than the OECD average and 80 percent fewer nurses (OECD 2014). While total health spending is on par with the average of all OECD country expenditures (9.3 percent of GDP), only 46 percent of

TABLE 5.1 *Regional health differences across Brazil, 1990–2010*

	1990		2000		2010	
	Infant mortality	Life expectancy	Infant mortality	Life expectancy	Infant mortality	Life expectancy
North	45.9	66.9	32.8	69.5	21.0	72.4
Northeast	75.8	62.8	35.9	67.2	19.1	70.8
Center-West	34.4	68.6	22.3	71.8	15.9	74.5
Southeast	32.6	68.8	20.1	72.0	13.4	74.9
South	28.3	70.4	16.9	72.7	11.6	75.5
National average	47.1	66.9	26.1	70.4	16.0	73.4

Source: Ministry of Health (2017)

Brazil's health spending was funded by public sources, making it one of the lowest of all OECD countries. When compared to other middle-income countries, Brazil still has room for significant improvement (OECD 2014).

Early Challenges and Reforms

Brazil's democratic opening coincided with well-organized pressure from progressive public health reformers, called *sanitaristas* (sanitarians), who advocated for significant reforms in universal health care. Many were inspired by international health debates surrounding "health for all" as part of the Alma Ata Declaration (World Health Organization 1978), principles of community-oriented health participation, as well as Cuba's well-regarded family doctor model, which sent physicians throughout the countryside to remedy the nation's historic urban bias with respect to health care access. The *Sanitarista* movement held sway in the Constituent Assembly, helping to enshrine the right to health in the Brazilian constitution under Article 196 (Weyland 1996; Gibson 2013). Later, these actors would engage within the state apparatus to significantly reform the federal health care model to deliver a unified health system (Falleti 2010; Niedzwiecki 2015). Health reformers sought to address several challenges that contributed to Brazil's relatively low levels of health performance: unequal access to health care by sectors of society, uneven geographic access to high-quality health care, and a historical focus on curative health care at the expense of preventive primary health care.

Reform would require that Brazilian politicians confront the country's exclusionary social welfare system, which provided generous health care benefits to formal sector workers and privileged sectors (e.g., members of the military, judiciary, and government workers) and relegated the vast majority of the population to an underfunded public health system.[2] This social insurance system was a cornerstone of Brazil's corporatist political model (Collier and Collier 2002). Workers in formal sectors of Brazil's economy had access to doctors, clinics, and hospitals. The quality of this system was very high, particularly in the major cities. Organized under a federal office, called the

---

[2] Brazil's social insurance system dates back to the 1930s. Under this Bismarkian model, the cost of social insurance was split between three parties: employers, employees through payroll tax contributions, and the government. The costs associated with the Ministry of Health were paid from general revenue.

National Institute of Medical and Social Services (INAMPS), beneficiaries had wide access to doctors and hospitals. In contrast, informal workers and the poor received only very basic services, such as immunizations, through clinics operated by the government's underfunded Ministry of Health. Outside the state apparatus, civil society would make some efforts to address health care needs. For example, philanthropic organizations administered hospital and clinics, where most citizens accessed health services. The Catholic Church administered a network of hospitals that sought to provide minimal health care. But overall, charitable health services and government clinics geared toward the poor were insufficient to meet the needs of Brazil's large population.

Brazil also had a deeply unequal health infrastructure, which hindered access for vast numbers of the poor. Large capital cities have always benefited from greater investment in hospitals and clinics. Smaller and more remote communities have been historically underserved, both in terms of infrastructure and personnel. These challenges were compounded by regional inequalities. Doctors and nurses are not only concentrated in large capital cities, but regionally as well; more health professionals reside in the more developed south and southeast. As Table 5.1 shows, Brazil has faced serious problems with geographically uneven outcomes. The poor north and northeast have always fared much worse on basic health outcomes when compared to other regions of the country.

Progressive public health advocates would need to confront the powerful institution, INAMPS, the agency responsible for administering social insurance. INAMPS favored higher-cost curative services geared toward eligible beneficiaries. Physicians, hospitals, and medical businesses fared very well under the agency and lobbied to maintain the existing model that privileged their economic interests and clients (Weyland 1996). Federal spending was largely directed to the top tier of the health system, which meant that hospitals serving elite sectors had excellent hospitals, well-trained surgeons, and equipment that focused on curative care. Sanitaristas critiqued this model as regressive; INAMPS left out the needs of the majority, those who worked informally as well as the poor. The Sanitarista movement lobbied effectively in the Constituent Assembly for universal access to health care. Their vision would entail "health for all" with a right to health care. They would also press for a model of health care delivery which prioritized primary health care over curative care.

Reforms: The SUS and the Family Health Program

Brazil's democratic constitution established a social right to health but it would take years to implement this vision. Health reformers would make important advances by instituting a *Sistema Único da Saúde* (Unified Health System, or SUS). The federal government would dissolve INAMPS and centralize all health policy under the Ministry of Health. The SUS would require the federal government to regulate health care and to finance services through fiscal transfers to states and newly empowered municipalities. The municipalization of health services would occur through the 1990s as municipalities built their capacity to contract and manage the provision of medical services.

As the Ministry of Health worked to implement the SUS, reformers at national and local levels sought to advance progressive health reforms that would expand access to the poor and informal workers. Reformers sought to prioritize primary health care, including a focus on preventive medicine over curative models. They also advocated for community-based primary health care. The culmination of this effort would be Brazil's introduction of the *Programa Saúde da Família* (Family Health Program or PSF). This program, supported nationally and administered locally by municipalities, would provide preventive medical services in a residential, team-based manner with the goal of addressing most health care needs for families.

Contemporary Challenges

Despite significant gains, Brazil's health care sector continues to face major challenges. First, the SUS is relatively underfunded and officials must weigh the aspirations for universal free medical care against the costs associated with provision for that care.[3] Another financial challenge relates to the high cost of pharmaceuticals that benefit few patients versus spending that benefits more people. Second, access to high-quality health care remains uneven. Officials have found it challenging to convince doctors to work in remote and poorer parts of the country. For this reason, Brazil has occasionally contracted with Cuba

---

[3] SUS coexists alongside private insurance markets and it is common for insurers to relegate their insured customers to the SUS when it comes to the highest cost curative care (e.g., transplants).

to fill vacancies left by the domestic medical marketplace (Collar et al. 2015). Third, extension of basic health care coverage is also uneven across municipalities. Local control over health care delivery means that municipal officials can weigh and prioritize different facets of medical care. Deepening coverage of preventive health through the Family Health Program may not be a political priority. As such, there is a great deal of diversity in local population coverage under the PSF program.

THREE PATHWAYS TO HEALTH OUTCOMES IN BRAZIL

Participatory Institutions

The health care movement was the strongest social movement that mobilized in Brazil during the 1970s and 1980s (Jacobi 1989; Cardoso and Faletto 1969). At the core of health advocates' demands were the creation of a universal health system, the establishment of health care as a constitutional right, and the creation of policy management councils that would allow citizens to be directly involved in policy-making venues. The *Sanitarista* movement was founded by medical personnel (doctors, nurses) and public health specialists (Escorel 1999). But this movement also connected with community-based organizations, first in São Paulo and then in other urban centers, to build a broad-based movement (Gibson 2017; Mayka 2019).

During the early 1980s, reformist mayors, including those mayors appointed by the military government, established health care councils. In São Paulo, the appointed government of Mayor Montero adopted a health council in 1983, indicating the development of a policy and political reform group that linked a social movement to an emerging group of policy reformers.

Brazil's health-related participatory architecture was built largely during the 1990s. Municipal health councils are required by federal legislations in order for the municipality to receive the transfer of federal revenues. Table 5.2 shows that a large majority of Brazilian municipalities adopted one health-specific council and two health-related councils (children's rights and school nutrition) because of the federal requirement. In addition, there are at least five health-related councils (women's rights, food security, health sanitation, environmental sanitation, and urban policy) that are voluntarily adopted by municipal governments.

TABLE 5.2 *Health-related policy councils across Brazil, 2001–2013*

Council Type	2001	2005/2006	2009	2013
Health	5,426	5,541	5,417	5,389
School nutrition	N/A	5,375	5,466	5,032
Children's rights	4,306	5,201	5,084	4,623
Urban policy	334	731	981	1,280
Women's rights	N/A	438	594	640
Food security	N/A	2,038	786	1,503
Health sanitation	N/A	N/A	306	349
Environmental sanitation	N/A	N/A	1,577	2,036
Total	10,066	19,324	20,211	20,852

Source: Authors' compilation of data published on ibge.gov.br

We expect to see strong health performance in the presence of voluntary councils because their presence suggests a commitment to including citizen voice at multiple stages of the policy cycle. We believe that those municipalities that voluntarily adopt additional councils are likely to generate greater support for health care, from both the state and civil society, than are generated by the induced councils. We would thus expect that municipalities with a higher number of more active voluntary councils will work on refining policies to better serve citizens' needs. We would also expect that a higher number of more active voluntary councils will be associated with better use of public resources and less corruption.

This data draws attention to the gradual spread of a participatory architecture in the fields of health and public health policy. The 1990s and 2000s saw a massive proliferation of councils that allowed tens of thousands of people to engage in health-and policy-related processes. We conservatively estimate (at ten members per council) that at least 200,000 individuals are now directly involved in health-related policy-making venues. If we consider that most council members have an official replacement (*suplente*), there are more than 400,000 individuals involved in formal health-related public policy health councils.

Citizens and community leaders are motivated to engage in participatory institutions for a number of reasons. First, councils represent an opportunity to set spending and policy priorities. Annual budgets and new programs must be approved by the municipal health council, which gives citizens an opportunity to influence policy direction. Second, citizens elected as council members have the ability to monitor the ongoing implementation of services in health care clinics and hospitals. They are able to gain access to information and public facilities based on their elected role. Third, councils are linked to annual or biannual health policy conferences, which allow civil society leaders an opportunity to set a larger policy agenda as well as to influence public officials. Fourth, the formal participation of most health care councils is strongly weighted in favor of representatives from the "user/citizens" group. Typically, 50 percent of the seats are reserved for "user/citizen" representatives, 25 percent are for representatives from health care-related unions (e.g., nurses, doctors), and government officials and service providers split the remaining 25 percent. The formal participatory architecture thus produces new policy networks, allowing citizens, union officials, and government officials to coordinate their actions.

Social Programs

The establishment of the Universal Health System (SUS) represents the cornerstone of Brazil's health reform. The SUS not only created free universal health care but also decentralized resources so that municipalities would manage service provision. Many credit the SUS with improving health care performance and health outcomes (Schramm and Szwarcwald 2000). While there are many components associated with the SUS, one of the most important for public health has been the widespread implementation of the Family Health Program (*Programa Saúde da Família* or PSF), which dramatically expanded preventive health care and promoted universal accessibility (Viana and Poz 1998).

The design of Brazil's Family Health Program (PSF) drew from local administrative experiments that developed in the late 1980s and early 1990s from municipalities such as Londrina (southern state of Parana) and Niterói (from the southeastern state of Rio de Janeiro), which independently established Family Doctor Programs (*Programa Médico da Família*) that were similar to Cuba's Family Doctor model. Others, in the northeast, would modify and expand the existing Community Health Agents Program *(Programa de Agentes Comunitarios de Saúde)* – initially designed to address prevention of diseases like dengue through community education – to provide more integrated primary health. The PSF was formally created in 1994 at a meeting at the Ministry of Health (Viana and Poz 1998). This program combines insights from Brazilian municipalities' experiences by creating a community health program that integrates teams of health professionals (family doctor, nurse, nurse's aides, and community health agents) located in geographically defined service areas. PSF services are typically concentrated in poor and underserved areas to reach vulnerable groups. Through the mid-1990s to the 2000s, the PSF program diffused to municipalities throughout the country (Sugiyama 2012). By the mid-2000s, this approach became so central to Brazil's public health model that the Ministry of Health called it their main strategy for primary health care (Ministry of Health 2016).

In practice, PSF health teams work closely with geographically defined communities to map each family's health needs and social context. Integrated health teams are located in the communities they serve to facilitate meaningful engagement with patients. Their daily practice includes medical checkups, vaccinations, and other complementary education-based programming. Occasionally, doctors and nurses make home visits to check on postpartum mothers, newborn infants, and other homebound patients. Some cities link their PSF programs to complementary activities, such as expansions of the Dental Health (*Saúde Bucal*) program. This model of health service delivery is thus designed to provide preventive and primary health care, with the goal of addressing most health needs.

Today, PSF is widely credited with helping Brazil achieve improvements, such as lower hospitalization rates (Macinko and Harris 2015). Importantly, interventions in maternal and infant health – such as prenatal checkups for expecting mothers, postnatal checkups for mothers and their infants, and programs to encourage breastfeeding – are credited with improving infant and maternal mortality (Macinko et al. 2006). For this reason, we would expect that municipalities with greater coverage of PSF, as a percent of the total population, will have lower rates of infant mortality. As Table 5.3 shows, rates of PSF coverage vary across Brazil.

In recent years, Brazil's social welfare system has fostered linkages and synergies across social service sectors to advance integrated human development goals. Most notably, policymakers in the Ministry of Social Development (MDS) who are responsible for the country's largest poverty-relief program, Bolsa Família, made health compliance a requirement for receipt of monthly cash grants. Bolsa Família beneficiaries must ensure that their children receive scheduled

TABLE 5.3　*PSF coverage rates across Brazilian municipalities, by region*

	PSF Coverage (2000)	PSF Coverage (2006)	PSF Coverage (2013)
North	62%	66%	75%
Northeast	74%	82%	89%
Center-West	69%	84%	87%
Southeast	69%	76%	86%
South	72%	84%	91%
National Average	70%	80%	87%

Source: Authors' compilation based on data obtained at ms.gov.br

vaccinations and meet nutritional targets, as determined by regular height and weight checks. Pregnant women must also receive prenatal health care and later encouraged to breastfeed their infants. PSF health teams track compliance with these requirements and send information back to the MDS. By linking these two programs together, officials hope to spur demand for health services.

Inclusive State Capacity

The delivery of high-quality health care requires multiple layers of complex coordination for national and local administrators. Decentralization of health services and implementation of the Unified Health System represent key features of Brazil's constitutional reforms. In theory, these reforms would bring about virtuous outcomes, including improved responsiveness and effectiveness of health systems (Mills et al. 1990). Beyond administrative efficiencies, local control over primary health care was thought to facilitate community participation and improve collaboration between delivery of primary and specialized hospital care (Kolehmainen-Aitken 2004). The process of decentralization or "municipalization" of health services occurred gradually, beginning in 1994, as local governments took on increasing responsibility for a range of health services (Guanais and Macinko 2009).[4]

---

[4] The Ministry of Health regulated decentralization of health services through a series of internal regulations, known as *Normas Operacionais Básicas* (or NOBs). NOB 1/93 defined enabling conditions for states and municipalities to participate in the SUS. Although passed in 1993, it went into effect in 1994. The NOB 01/96, extended NOB 01/93 by amplifying municipal responsibilities.

The most visible demonstration of municipalization was the local adoption of the Family Health Program. But as Sugiyama (2012) notes, the diffusion of the PSF program across Brazil's municipalities took place slowly and unevenly. This was largely because local governments were unevenly situated to take on health responsibilities that had been previously ascribed to state governments.

The federal government primarily used fiscal transfers, technical support, and detailed Ministry of Health regulations to facilitate decentralization of health services. By federal law, municipalities must spend 25 percent of their total budgets on health care (see *Lei de Responsabilidade Fiscal* 2000). Moreover, municipalities must also demonstrate compliance with the Ministry of Health's operational rules to receive federal transfers. Finally, public health specialists in Brasília provided technical training, hosted conferences and meetings, and worked with local administrators to design and implement services. Despite these efforts, municipal governments have faced uneven capacity to deliver high-quality health care. For instance, most cities are unable to offer full coverage of PSF for their entire population. For this reason, the MDS does not penalize Bolsa beneficiaries if they are unable to access PSF services. Overall, we expect that cities with well-managed Bolsa programs and available PSF services will experience superior infant mortality outcomes than those that do not.

Several factors may account for the significant variation in municipal-level capacity in the local health sector. First, municipal officials nearly uniformly lament that federal transfers are insufficient to meet the full and actual costs associated with health care. (See Chapter 8, the case study chapter, in this book.) Thus, local governments that have revenue raising capacity can better divert resources to supplement federal transfers (see Arretche and Marques 2002). Second, health care delivery is administratively complex to manage. Government officials need to create an administrative structure that allows them to manage the complex duties of building appropriate physical infrastructure, staffing facilities with skilled personnel, and stocking necessary supplies and medicine. Smaller and more remote municipalities are especially challenged in these areas. Finally, municipal authority over capital investments, procurement, and personnel in the health sector have historically been grist for politicians' corrupt practices. While some municipalities hire staff through competitive merit-based civil service exams, many key personnel are still hired through short-term contracts. At best, this structure yields administrative instability and compromises long-term health care engagement with citizens. At worst, the health sector can become a vehicle for politicians' political and personal agendas, rendering health care efforts ineffective.

Interactive Effects

Participatory institutions, social programs, and state capacity interact to support health care delivery and health outcomes. First, we expect health care councils to contribute to decision-making regarding how municipal governments spend resources and implement new programs. The councils provide a specific opportunity for citizens and organized interests (unions, service providers) to publicly debate the allocation of scarce resources. For example, policy councils may advocate for increased allocation of resources to the Family Health Program or they may advocate for the reallocation of resources within the Family Health Program. Participatory institutions interact with national social programs and influence the resources devoted to their administration. Conversely, public administrators responsible for SUS and programs like the Family Health Program are required by law to gain the council's approval for new programs. Thus, public administrators must engage in knowledge-sharing and information-building to gain council members' support.

Second, we would also expect health-related councils to directly influence administrative capacity through the use of oversight mechanisms. Council members are formally responsible for overseeing ongoing implementation as well as for approving quarterly and year-end budgeting reports. Thus, administrative capacity should improve in the context of more robust councils because council members can hold administrators accountable for their actions. This relationship also works in the opposite direction. Administrators provide councils with information that can improve their knowledge base and learning. This means that local administrative capacity influences the quality of council-based deliberation and oversight.

Finally, social programs can also influence state capacity and vice versa. Social programs, such as the Family Health Program, educate citizens about their constitutional rights to health care and thus create incentives for citizens to pressure local public officials to improve health care services in local programs as well. The Family Health Program does not carry performance-based federal resources like the Bolsa Família program. However, federal social programs still carry more oversight from national ministries than most state and local policies. In this case, the Ministry of Health makes an effort to monitor local program administration and work to improve performance. Improving professional management in one health care program likely has spillover effects into other health programs that the local government runs. Local governments' ability and willingness to deliver health care is essential for administering national health programs, like the PSF, as well. Local administrations that have greater health care resources, more professional personnel, and better infrastructure have greater capacity to administer all health programs, including national health programs like the PSF.

VARIABLES AND METHODOLOGY

Dependent Variable: Infant Mortality per 1,000 Live Births

Infant mortality rates serve as an assessment of health care outcomes that can change rapidly in the face of new funding and outreach efforts (Aquino et al. 2009). Any connections between participatory institutions, elections, federal social programs, and service delivery should emerge in data on infant mortality. We use the Brazilian Ministry of Health's estimate for the rate of infant mortality per 1,000 live births in each Brazilian municipality over the previous fifteen years. The mean is 21.14 with a standard deviation of 22.21. The data comes from the Ministry of Health's DataSUS website (www.datasus.gov.br), which reports rates on an annual basis.

Independent Variables:

We describe our primary independent variables in Chapter 3. The material below provides information on variables specific to this chapter and also identifies the independent variables that we use to estimate infant mortality levels that are common across the other chapters.

Adoption of Health-Related Policy Councils

We evaluate connections between policy councils and health through indicators of voluntary councils related to health. These include women's councils, food security councils, health sanitation councils, environmental sanitation councils, and urban policy councils. A greater presence of these councils may improve health by increasing and monitoring public goods spending and programs related to health and, in turn, improving service delivery.

The second variable records whether municipalities use the councils that do carry federal funds with them and may be related to health care. These are health councils, children's rights councils, and school nutrition councils. Sixty-three percent of municipal observations feature all four policy councils and are coded "1." The remainder are coded "0." Finally, we code a dummy variable to indicate municipalities with a high frequency of policy council meetings. Many municipalities adopt policy councils to gain federal funds, but may not promote active councils or sustain them over time. We capture variation in commitment to using these councils by coding municipalities "1" when they feature multiple council meetings each month and "0" if the councils meet monthly, quarterly, annually, or never meet at all. Thirteen percent of municipal policy councils meet frequently (more than one meeting a month), while 87 percent do not.

Bolsa Família Coverage

We assess connections between Bolsa Família program coverage and health in Brazil. Expanding coverage of the Bolsa Família program to eligible families may improve health outcomes as the program's conditionalities require mothers to receive prenatal and postnatal checkups and children to be monitored for nutritional gains and timely vaccinations. Moreover, some families may use the program's grant to cover health-related expenses.

Family Health Plan Coverage

We assess connections between municipal coverage of the Family Health Plan and health. Extending Family Health Plan coverage to a greater percentage of the eligible population may improve health by increasing access to preventive care and increasing knowledge surrounding health.

Bolsa Família Management Quality

We use the *Índice de Gestão Descentralizada* (Index of Decentralized Management, or IGD) to reflect the broader capacity to include citizens in rights-based programs. Inclusive state capacity may improve health by enrolling more residents in these programs and transferring money directly to them.

Percentage of Per Capita Municipal Spending on Public Goods

We use the percentage of per capita municipal spending devoted to health care, sanitation, and education to test connections between commitments to public goods that improve health.

Per Capita Municipal Health Care Spending

We evaluate the extent to which public spending is a component of improvements in health. Greater municipal commitments to public health may improve health outcomes by extending care to a greater percentage of residents and by improving the quality of that care.

Competitive Elections

We evaluate the extent to which local electoral competition alters government priorities and influences health. Higher mayoral vote shares may reflect lower political competition. In turn, fewer electoral incentives to fund health services may thus be associated with higher rates of infant mortality.

Left-Leaning and PT Mayors

We evaluate whether PT mayors are associated with health outcomes. PT mayors have an electoral base among poorer residents, who suffer from many health problems. PT mayors might therefore have more political incentives to adopt and support public health at the local level. In turn, municipalities with PT mayors might have lower infant mortality levels than other municipalities, all else equal.

ESTIMATION STRATEGY

We base our estimation strategy on previous efforts to explain infant mortality and other health care outcomes of interest. Rasella et al. (2013) and Macinko et al. (2006) test hypotheses connecting Brazil's Bolsa Família and Family Health Program (PSF) to public health outcomes at the municipal level. Both studies use conditional negative binomial models with fixed effects to model medical count and rate outcomes of interest. We follow suit in our study; negative binomial regression models for panel data resolve several statistical challenges in estimating the relationships between policy councils, new social programs, and indicators associated with well-being over time and across space. Specifically, negative binomial regressions provide improved estimation in cases where count-outcome data is widely dispersed – as it is in our case, where the unconditional mean of infant mortality is much smaller than its variance (Hilbe 2007).[5] We then use panel data models with fixed effects to account for correlations between unobserved, time-invariant characteristics of the panel and our independent variables.[6]

For our data, the time-invariant characteristics include those of the municipality, such as its historical or sociopolitical experience, that remained fixed over the timeframe of our study. These fixed, unobserved elements could influence municipal adoption of voluntary policy councils as well as local management of federal social programs such as Bolsa Família and the Family Health Plan. For instance, policy councils may have emerged first in areas with lower infant mortality rates that were already committed to reducing infant mortality before we recorded data on their efforts. The estimates of policy councils' impact on infant mortality could thus suffer from selection bias if our models failed to account for fixed, unobserved characteristics that might influence our independent variables. Using fixed, not random, effects adds a term to our models that allows us to control for this potential selection bias (Shahidur et al. 2010).

RESULTS AND DISCUSSION

Participatory Health Councils

The model in Table 5.4 offers several important findings. Our first finding surrounds the role of local policy councils for reducing infant mortality. The presence of voluntary policy councils that are related to

---

[5] The negative binomial regression is similar to the Poisson regression model, but with a component to model the over-dispersed nature of the dependent variable. The result is narrower confidence intervals that provide more targeted estimates of the relationships in the data (Cameron and Trivedi 2009). Our results are very similar for all independent variables when using cross-sectional time-series Poisson regression as well as negative binomial regression.

[6] We choose fixed effects over random effects based on the results of Hausman tests and on the arguments in Wooldridge (2014), Shahidur et al. (2010), and Frees (2004) surrounding fixed effects models and impact evaluations.

TABLE 5.4 *Explaining infant mortality, 2006–2013: Federal social programs, voluntary policy councils, and local state capacity*
This model uses cross-sectional time-series negative binomial estimation with fixed effects.

Variable	Coefficient (SE)
Voluntary council commitment	–0.05**
	(0.01)
Family Health Program coverage	–0.002**
	(0.0002)
Bolsa Família coverage	–0.0003*
	(0.0001)
Bolsa Família management	–0.17**
	(0.04)
Per capita health care spending	–0.00003
	(0.00002)
Competitive elections	–0.05
	(0.03)
Left-leaning mayor	0.04
	(0.03)
Constant	2.20**
	(0.04)
N	17,712
Wald Chi² (6)	199.20
Prob> Chi²	0.000

* Indicates significance at better than 0.05 (two-tailed test).
** Indicates significance at better than 0.01 (two-tailed test).

medical care in general and to the well-being of women and children in particular have a strong, negative, statistically significant connection to infant mortality in Brazil. We estimate that the presence of these councils is associated with a .05 decrease in infant mortality per 1,000 births in Brazil's municipalities. This may seem like a small influence relative to the mean infant mortality rate of 21.15 per 1,000 births in the data, but the effects are important. These coefficients reflect the difference in the logs of the expected counts of the infant mortality indicator. A .05 coefficient translates to a 1.12 reduction in infant mortality per 1,000 births, which represents an 11 percent reduction in infant mortality. On average, we estimate that voluntary councils related to health care save approximately 300 lives per year across Brazil and over 3,000 for the years in our study. Over a decade, the estimate of total lives saved if all municipalities had shown a commitment to voluntary councils related to health care is 30,000. Of course, there are many differences between Brazilian municipalities beyond the presence of local policy councils. Our results suggest these councils are relevant for reducing infant mortality while holding all other observed influences on infant mortality constant at their mean. By extension, our results also highlight the importance of committing to local, demand-side participatory institutions for improving well-being.[7]

Second, we do not identify connections between competitive elections and infant mortality in our data. Neither are the mayor's vote share or margin of victory statistically significant determinants of infant mortality in either first- or second-round elections. Furthermore, the local presidential vote share is not significant, nor is the mayor's party or the mayor's ideological orientation. The only significant relationship we identify between electoral variables and well-being is a negative connection between mayors who run unopposed and infant mortality, which is consistent with arguments connecting a total lack of political competition with clientelism and poor government performance.[8] As discussed above, these results do not impugn previous scholarship on elections, democracy, and well-being in a cross-national context. Instead, our results highlight the importance of more proximate aspects of electoral democracy, namely citizen participation, social policy reform efforts, and municipal administration at the local level.

The model in Table 5.5 assesses whether the frequency of health council meetings affects infant mortality. Many municipalities may happily accept federal funds to create a council, but never ensure it meets regularly. The results in Table 5.5 show how municipalities with health councils that meet every two weeks or more, as opposed to monthly, quarterly, annually, or never, are associated with lower levels of infant mortality than municipalities with less frequent council meetings. These results highlight the role of commitment to participatory institutions for well-being from a different angle. Health councils are nearly ubiquitous across Brazilian municipalities, but their presence

---

[7] We present the results of estimation using the presence of federally induced health councils as the primary independent variable in Table A5.5a in the technical appendix. The results show how the presence of local policy councils that the federal government induces municipalities to create are not statistically connected to infant mortality levels in and of themselves.

[8] These models appear in the technical appendix.

TABLE 5.5 *Explaining infant mortality, 2006–2013: Federal social programs and incentivized policy council meetings*
This model uses cross-sectional time-series negative binomial estimation with fixed effects.

Variable	Coefficient (SE)
Incentivized council meetings	–0.07* (0.03)
Family Health Program coverage	–0.001* (0.0003)
Bolsa Família coverage	–0.005 (0.003)
Bolsa Família management	–0.15** (0.03)
Per capita health care spending	–0.004 (0.003)
Competitive elections	–0.03 (0.02)
Left-leaning mayor	–0.08 (0.10)
Constant	1.64** (0.28)
N	20,369
Wald Chi^2 (6)	295.16
Prob> Chi^2	0.000

* Indicates significance at better than 0.05 (two-tailed test).
** Indicates significance at better than 0.01 (two-tailed test).

does not always correspond with meaningful activity. Many health councils and others that are induced with federal funds meet infrequently, at best, and may not engage in any activity. Capturing data on the frequency of health council meetings provides leverage to address the question of whether these induced institutions, and other, mandated programs, can be meaningful for well-being. The frequency of health council meetings thus serves as an indicator of local commitment to participatory governance. We do not have data on the frequency of meetings for other types of induced councils. However, our results surrounding health councils suggest that federally induced or other top-down institutions can work to improve well-being if they are coupled with a local commitment to take advantage of these institutions.

We estimate that municipalities with active health councils exhibit a 1.20 decrease in infant mortality per 1,000 live births. This figure translates to a 12 percent reduction in infant mortality for the municipalities in our sample. *On average, we estimate that active health councils save approximately 1,800 lives per year across Brazil and over 12,000 for the years in our study.* Over a decade, the estimate for total lives saved if all municipalities had shown a commitment to very active health councils is over 20,000. In this case, the estimate for commitments to very active health councils is higher than for voluntary councils not only due to the larger coefficient on the "incentivized council meetings" variable in Table 5.5 but also because many more municipalities show a commitment to very active health councils than to health care-related voluntary councils.

Federal Social Programs

Our third finding showcases the importance of top-down, federal social programs representing expert-led approaches to service delivery and poverty reduction. Measures of municipal Bolsa Família and Family Health Program coverage as a percentage of eligible families are associated with lower levels of infant mortality. These results replicate prominent findings in the literature on both programs such as Rasella et al. (2013) and Macinko et al. (2006). Importantly, we underscore the importance of local management of the Bolsa Família program. The federal indicator for the quality of local Bolsa Família management, "IGD," is also a statistically significant determinant of infant mortality rates. The coefficient on this variable results in an estimated impact on infant mortality. For instance, moving from the mean municipal management score (0.76) to two standard deviations above the mean (0.99) results in an estimated reduction in infant mortality approximately the same as for the presence of voluntary health-related policy councils. On average, we estimate that very good Bolsa Família management saves approximately 200 lives per year across Brazil and over 2,000 for the years in our study. Over a decade, the estimate for total lives saved if all municipalities had very good Bolsa Família management is over 10,000. This estimate is independent of participatory institutions' influence and speaks to the considerable importance of local state capacity for improving well-being.

Reducing infant mortality is not simply a matter of having a program, such as Bolsa Família or the Family Health Program, but of administering these programs well. It is important to note these results control for per capita municipal spending on health care. This variable is also connected to lower levels of infant mortality in our data, as expected. The point here is that reducing infant mortality is not only a matter of how much municipalities spend on health care, but of how well they spend their *own* money (as monitored by policy councils) and how well they manage the federal Bolsa Família (as evident through management scores). We argue these areas are connected: local monitoring and local program management interact with one another through connections between citizen participation in local politics, the presence of civil society organizations, and the presence of motivated municipal officials to generate strong municipal governance. Thus, Bolsa Família is much more than a simple cash transfer to the poorest households; these programs work well when the local administration is able to properly enroll eligible poor families in the Bolsa Família and allocate the necessary resources to ensure that recipients are being embedded into a larger network of policy support programs.

Finally, our results show that three main components – the active presence of participatory institutions, rights-based social programs, and a more inclusive municipal state – have an independent effect on infant mortality. But it is the ongoing interaction among these areas that we estimate to have the strongest influence on infant mortality. The results in Table 5.6 show how the presence of voluntary policy councils surrounding health care interact with Bolsa Família management to produce estimates of reduced infant mortality levels in our data. Municipalities in the top quintile of Bolsa Família management scores and with a commitment to voluntary policy councils related to health care are associated with 4.34 fewer infant deaths per 1,000 births. This corresponds to a mean estimated reduction in infant mortality of 15 percent nationwide, but as much as 40 percent in some municipalities. The combination of the two areas translates to an estimated 2,000 lives saved per year among the municipalities in our dataset, 14,000 over the entire timeframe we cover in our study, and approximately 140,000 lives saved over a decade if all of Brazil's municipalities had featured strong commitments to participatory institutions and strong Bolsa Família management.

Interactions across our three pathways also influence infant mortality rates. All combinations of commitment to participatory institutions, Bolsa

TABLE 5.6 *Explaining infant mortality: Voluntary policy councils, federal social programs, and local state capacity, 2006–2013* These models use negative binomial estimation.

Variable	Councils, top 20% mgmt. scores Coeff (SE)	No councils, top 20% mgmt. scores Coeff (SE)	Councils, bottom 80% mgmt. scores Coeff (SE)	No councils, bottom 80% mgmt. scores Coeff (SE)
Councils*BF management	-0.21** (0.05)			
Per capita health care spending	-0.0002 (0.0002)	-0.0003 (0.0004)	-0.0004* (0.0002)	-0.001** (0.00002)
Bolsa Família coverage	-0.003 (0.002)	-0.06* (0.03)	0.003 (0.003)	-0.005 (0.006)
Family Health Plan coverage	-0.00001* (0.000004)	-0.0003** (0.0001)	Dropped	-0.0006* (0.0003)
Voluntary councils	0.004 (0.009)	Dropped	-0.02 (0.05)	Dropped
Bolsa Família management	-0.0007 (0.005)	-0.04 (0.04)	Dropped	Dropped
Competitive elections	-0.03 (0.04)	-0.04* (0.02)	-0.05 (0.03)	-0.05* (0.02)
Left-leaning mayor	-0.01 (0.02)	-0.02 (0.05)	-0.03 (0.02)	-0.04* (0.02)

(continued)

TABLE 5.6 *(continued)*

Variable	Councils, top 20% mgmt. scores	No councils, top 20% mgmt. scores	Councils, bottom 80% mgmt. scores	No councils, bottom 80% mgmt. scores
	Coeff (SE)	Coeff (SE)	Coeff (SE)	Coeff (SE)
Constant	1.29	1.33*	1.55*	1.20
	(0.69)	(0.58)	(0.71)	(0.74)
N	5,840	5,210	6,135	4,570
Wald Chi²	305.46	318.79	299.58	328.66
Prob> Chi²	0.00	0.00	0.00	0.00

* Indicates significance at better than 0.05 (two-tailed test).
** Indicates significance at better than 0.01 (two-tailed test).

TABLE 5.7 *Explaining infant mortality through interactions among policy councils, Bolsa Família coverage, and local state capacity*

	Infant mortality
Councils and Bolsa Família	Reduce mortality
Councils and state capacity	Reduce mortality
Bolsa Família and state capacity	Reduce mortality

Família coverage, and inclusive state capacity are associated with low levels of infant mortality.

ROBUSTNESS CHECKS

We perform a variety of tests to assess the robustness of our results. First, our results in supplemental negative binomial and Poisson regressions with lagged dependent variables are similar to those in Tables 5.4, 5.5, and 5.6. This check addresses the prospect of serial autocorrelation driving the results in our models; in this case, the lagged dependent variables are statistically significant determinants of infant mortality, but the central variables of interest all retain their approximate magnitudes, directions, and levels of statistical significance.[9] Next, we use several different specifications in our models. First, we present the results of models excluding the Bolsa Família management variable, which limits our data coverage to the period 2006–2013 in our primary models. Dropping this variable extends our coverage back to 2000 and increases the number of observations in each model. The results for our primary remaining variables, the policy council indicators and federal social program coverage indicators, are broadly similar to those in our primary models. We also evaluate different model specifications surrounding control variables that might also influence infant mortality rates. For example, models that use per capita municipal spending instead of per capita municipal health care spending produce results that are broadly similar to those in Tables 5.4, 5.5, and 5.6. Replacing the "left-leaning mayor" variable with a dummy variable for a PT mayor also produces similar results. Geographic dummy variables are sometimes significant determinants of infant mortality, especially the north and the northeast compared to the south. However, the central explanatory variables

---

[9] The models we describe in this section all appear in the technical appendix.

retain their significance, magnitude, and direction in models with geographic dummies, too.[10]

We also account for endogeneity in our models in several different ways. Specifically, it is possible that previous levels of infant mortality influence municipalities' future choices surrounding health care spending and service provision. For example, a municipality struggling with infant mortality might have adopted health care-related councils and increased health care spending to address this problem. Macinko et al. (2006) address a similar endogeneity issue surrounding infant mortality and federal social programs through instrumental variable regression using the mayor's party as an instrument for Bolsa Família and PSF coverage. However, previous scholarship connects the mayor's party directly to infant mortality rates in Brazil (Touchton and Wampler 2014), which suggests that this variable violates the exclusion restriction for instrumental variables and would therefore be inappropriate to include as an instrument in our models (Wooldridge 2014). Instead, we use Arellano-Bond dynamic panel models to account for this potential concern for our estimates.[11] The Arellano-Bond models use the "system" generalized method of moments (GMM) with one lag of the dependent variable. The instruments used are the policy council variables, Bolsa Família and PSF coverage, Bolsa Família management, and per capita health care spending, beginning with the second lag and going back as far in time as the data exists for each variable. The direction of the coefficients and the general levels of statistical significance are all similar to those in the primary models. We also use dummy variables for each year to ensure that the assumption holds that there is no correlation across units. Finally, we use propensity score matching with treatment effects, as in other chapters, to address concerns for endogeneity in our models. The results in Tables A5.4b–d of the appendix are robust to these techniques and thus provide supporting evidence emphasizing the strong connection between participation, federal social programs, local administrative capacity, and infant mortality.

---

[10] We replicate findings in Rasella et al. (2013) by dividing Bolsa Família and Family Health Plan coverage into terciles and using low, medium, and high coverage as independent variables. This results in similar estimates, only with our voluntary, health-related councils and Bolsa Família management variables also present in the models. These results are available in the online appendix.

[11] See Roodman (2014) and Arellano and Bond (1988) for more information on this method.

An additional, important consideration is that certain municipalities might simply be more predisposed to assist the poor than other municipalities for some unobserved reason. These municipalities might then promote participatory governance and strong management of federal programs as means to a poverty-reducing end, along with many other unobserved programs or policies. Any relationships between participatory governance, state capacity, and infant mortality could therefore only reflect municipal predispositions, as opposed to any impact from the specific institutions or programs. We find little evidence to support such a scenario; there are only low or negative correlations between municipalities with voluntary policy councils related to health care, social program coverage, and management of these social programs.[12] This suggests that municipalities do not tend to excel in all three areas simultaneously and that a commitment to participatory governance, social program coverage, and social program management do not stem from an unobserved penchant for poverty reduction. Instead, this evidence provides some support for each area's independent role for improving well-being.

CONCLUSION

Robust democratic practices that extend principles of participation, citizenship, and an inclusionary state save lives by expanding the breadth and quality of primary health services. Our findings surrounding the positive influence of democratic governance aligns with established international health norms. Much like the prescriptions found in the Alma Ata Declaration (1978) of the World Health Organization, we find that governmental investments in community-based health care as well citizen engagement in the design and oversight of health services, are very important. Our pathways approach provides strong evidence that robust governmental support for community engagement and implementation of universal, rights-based health programs improves health outcomes. Furthermore, we see no tradeoff between expert-based health care provision and democratic, community-based engagement. Rather, our approach demonstrates how municipal-level investment in three democratic pathways offers great opportunities to improve basic health care.

---

[12] Voluntary policy councils related to health care are *negatively* correlated with Bolsa Família coverage at −0.45. All other correlations between primary independent variables are under 0.2.

Health care provision is distinct from the other three policy arenas covered in this book (poverty reduction, women's empowerment, education) because it depends on a unique combination of highly skilled technical experts (e.g., doctors, nurses, hospital administrators), lay health workers (e.g., community health agents), and community activists working to improve basic services. We find that the lowest levels of infant mortality occur in municipalities that invest in a combination of participatory institutions, rights-based social programs, and inclusive state capacity. Thus, the slow, complex process of building and then sustaining new democratic institutions and rights-based social policies is of paramount importance to improving health outcomes.

In comparison to Chapter 4, which focused on poverty reduction, we find that all three of our democratic pathways are of crucial importance for health. In Chapter 4, we showed how the presence of a conditional cash transfer program was the most important pathway to ensure greater access to income; this finding makes a lot of sense because the Bolsa Família program is designed to do just that – get cash into the hands of extremely poor families. This finding is interesting as it illustrates the interconnections between poverty and health. The positive influence of Bolsa Família on health outcomes shows its reach in other key areas related to human development. We then found that the other two pathways – inclusive state capacity and participation – have important complementary effects. But in health, we do not see any one pathway as being more important than the others. Rather, our quantitative results demonstrate that the robust presence of any one pathway can have a positive effect. Nevertheless, municipalities generate the strongest results when all three pathways are present at high levels.

Our quantitative results demonstrate strong associations between each pathway and reductions in infant mortality. Yet, they cannot show how key causal connections operate in practice. In Chapter 8 we therefore move beyond the quantitative analysis to trace the processes connecting specific policies, programs, and institutions to health outcomes. Specifically, we show how teams from the Family Health Program work closely with both community members and public health experts to deliver targeted services to poor, underserved communities. We also demonstrate how community activists use multiple policy councils (e.g., health, nutrition, sanitation, children's rights) to draw attention to their community's needs. Finally, we explain how the municipal governments employ professional experts to allocate health resources and encourage participation in health and health-related councils.

In Chapter 6, which focuses on women's empowerment, we examine how our pathways contribute to reductions in maternal mortality. Saving mothers' lives involves similar, but distinct public health strategies, suggesting that municipalities can support multiple types of improvements in health when they invest in health care. We also look at other key arenas for women to achieve greater autonomy, including the need for women's economic and political agency. Unlike the health arena, women's empowerment is harder to measure. It is also harder to advance. Poverty and health outcomes are difficult to alter in the short term, to be sure, but are much easier to change than long-term structural, social, and political challenges surrounding women's empowerment or educational attainment. We explore why that is in Chapter 6. As we move to even more complex areas of human development, we uncover the opportunities and constraints for these democratic pathways to produce more immediate successes.

6

Empowering Women: Saving Mothers and Enhancing Opportunities

"Men and women have equal rights and duties under the terms of this Constitution."

Brazil's 1988 Constitution Article 5, Section I

Over the last three decades, governments and international development agencies have recognized the importance of women's status and gendered exclusion for the overall population's well-being. Women are more likely to face poverty and greater social, economic, cultural, and political barriers to address their vulnerabilities than men. A focus on women and girls is normatively justified given that they constitute more than half of the world's population. Yet beyond their numerical size, there is growing consensus that women's status affects development outcomes for everyone (Sen 1999; Nussbaum 2011). Historical and existing barriers for women and girls to fully develop as individuals – due to patriarchy, paternalism, and other forms of gender discrimination – violate international human rights norms and hinder instrumental goals to further broader human development. For instance, research reveals that gender discrimination that creates barriers to girls' education has negative spillover effects in a number of domains related to development. For this reason, education is widely promoted as a mechanism for development as it contributes to cognitive ability, health, and well-being for women themselves and for their children (Kabeer 2005: 16–17). Economic agency is also important for women and members of their family, as a study on the effects of microenterprises demonstrates. For example, mothers who received Grameen Bank loans invested more in their household and in children's health and education, thus improving their life prospects

(Pitt and Khandker 1998). Sen's capabilities approach focuses on fostering human capabilities as a way to promote productivity and also includes a large role for gender equity (Evans and Heller 2015). In other words, countries must expand agency for women and girls if they want their population to enjoy greater well-being (Sen 1999).

The stakes are high for women in low- and middle-income countries. Women in the developing world face systemic discrimination that renders them less likely than their male counterparts to obtain the skills they need to reach their full capabilities. For instance, women and girls face higher rates of illiteracy: of the roughly 800 million illiterate people worldwide, more than two-thirds are women (UNESCO 2017). Poverty also has a gendered component, as women constitute a disproportionately large share of the poor. This is due, in part, to gendered norms that render women subject to the economic activity of their husbands and fathers. But women also face systemic barriers to paid employment; the International Labor Organization estimates that only 49 percent of the world's women participate in remunerated economic activity, often with a stark gender pay gap (2018). Uneven access to reproductive health means that maternal mortality rates are exceedingly high, particularly for the world's poorest nations (World Health Organization 2012). Surviving childbirth therefore becomes a significant life event with implications for generations. Finally, women are less likely to serve in elected office in their countries, making it harder to advocate for political solutions to their social, economic, and political isolation. For all these reasons, international development agencies have placed the status of women and girls front and center on the international development agenda and elevated their focus on girls and women's empowerment.

The United Nations' development goals serve as the clearest illustration of the international development community's recognition that gender empowerment should be mainstreamed into development commitments. The Millennium Development Goals (MDGs) include three aims with explicitly gendered components: achieving universal primary education (Goal 2), promoting gender equality and empowering women (Goal 3), and improving maternal health and improving maternal mortality (Goal 5) (United Nations 2000). The new and broader Sustainable Development Goals reinforce areas identified in the MDGs and also call on governments around the world to "achieve gender equality and empower all women and girls" (Goal 5) (United Nations 2015).

The international development community clearly aims to empower girls and women, but we must ask: What is gender empowerment? We begin by distinguishing between the concept of "sex" and "gender;" the former refers to biological differences between males and females, while the latter refers to the socially constructed norms surrounding differences between males and females. Gender thus captures not only socially embedded norms about what constitutes "feminine" and "masculine" roles but also captures the power hierarchies between men and women. The concept of "gender empowerment" is itself complex, murky, and fluid (Mason 1987; Batliwala 1998; Rowlands 1997). Nevertheless, development practitioners generally agree that gender empowerment entails structural changes to gendered power relations between men and women. Gender empowerment necessitates that political and social systems that limit women's decision-making power be reconfigured. To achieve these aims, international agencies such as the United Nations have advocated for gender equality and women's empowerment in all governmental activities, including poverty reduction, democratic governance, access to political institutions from the judiciary to the civil service, as well as in the private sector (UN Women, 2016).

The agenda to empower girls and women has both normative and functional aims. First, gender empowerment fits within international human rights norms:

Whereas the peoples of the United Nations have in the Charter reaffirmed their faith in fundamental human rights, in the dignity and worth of the human person and in the equal rights of men and women and have determined to promote social progress and better standards of life in larger freedom . . . (Preamble, UN Declaration of Rights).

Other UN treaties, such as the Convention on the Elimination against All Forms of Discrimination against Women (CEDAW), go further to specify equality of rights between men and women.[1]

The concept of gender empowerment is tied to both political and instrumental aims. As Batliwala (2007) highlights, demands for gender empowerment are born out of international feminist movements and date back to the 1970s and 1980s, where activists critiqued the largely apolitical economic framework international development agencies advocated at the time.[2] Feminists pressed for conceptualizations of empowerment that would upend power hierarchies between men and women. However,

---

[1] Adopted by the United Nations General Assembly in 1979. There are ninety-nine signatories and 188 state parties to CEDAW.
[2] Those frameworks included the "women in development," "GAD," and "WID" development models. (See Batliwala 2007: 558.)

critics contend the agenda has lost its politically transformative goals and now serves the development agencies' more instrumental policy aims as the push for gender equity has become mainstream within the international development field (Cornwall et al. 2007). For this reason, the concept of "gender empowerment" can now include such diverse dimensions as women's psychosocial well-being, feminist consciousness, economic independence, physical autonomy, and autonomous decision-making, just to name a few (Batliwala 1994; Sen 1999; Kabeer 2005). We acknowledge the importance of social transformation that gender empowerment should bring, including transformations of patriarchal structures that limit opportunities for girls and women to realize their full potential. A full exploration of progress toward gender empowerment would necessarily entail evaluations of such factors as changes in feminist consciousness and realization of more balanced family household relations, e.g., household time-use studies. While essential, these more nuanced understandings are difficult to implement in large-N, comparative, municipal-level analysis. Instead, we take a narrower approach that allows us to compare advances in women's status across place and time and for which data is more readily available.

THEORIZING GENDER EMPOWERMENT

How does democracy empower women? Political theorists argue that improved "descriptive representation" will alter governance so that policy better reflects women's and girls' interests, resulting in "substantive representation" as women gain suffrage and the right to run for office worldwide (Philips 1995; Mansbridge 1999). On balance, there is some indication that countries with greater representation of women in electoral office, such as Nordic countries, have made greater strides in women's socioeconomic and political inclusion. Yet suffrage alone has been insufficient to overcome women's barriers to full social, economic, and political participation. Here we highlight the ways that democratic pathways can empower women.

Participatory Institutions

Local participatory institutions represent one potential arena through which women can organize, participate, and influence decision-makers because the barriers to entry in these venues are much lower than those for running for elected office or becoming a high-level government administrator (Cornwall 2003; Lüchmann et al. 2016). This is because meetings for participatory institutions are often held at times and places that are more convenient for women and mothers of young children, discussions often call on individuals to propose solutions drawn from their local knowledge, and participants can engage in actions that are community-based or specific to a single policy arena.

Given their lower entry barriers, participatory institutions may empower women in several distinct ways. Participatory institutions often focus on building knowledge and information-sharing, both of which empower participants. Some governments and international organizations adopt citizen's budgets and gendered budgets, which teach citizens about how budgets and policies directly affect specific communities (Budlender 2000). Participatory institutions are also for-ward-looking, allowing participants to channel their plans into con-crete steps that governments and civil society organizations can take to tackle key problems. From an ideal-type perspective, participatory institutions are "schools of democracy" whereby participants learn about their rights and learn to engage in spirited public deliberation (Baiocchi 2005).

Participatory institutions can also facilitate women's community engagement because they often focus on community-based issues that are central to women's "practical" interests in their "maternalist" roles as caretakers and mothers (Molyneux 1985; Alvarez 1990). Women in poor communities are particularly vulnerable to low levels of access to soup kitchens, schools, health clinics, and daycare services, and thus, many women focus their demands on those immediate needs. We are not sug-gesting the existence of a core set of "women's issues" that women across the world are likely to agree upon. (See for example, Baldez 2002.) Rather, we note that poverty and limited access to public services often have a strongly gendered component as women are more likely to be poor and responsible for others' primary care. Some participatory venues create women-only forums, which are designed to create a physical space that increases women's opportunities for active deliberation (Polletta 2015). Other venues have experimented with a combination of women-only forums and secret ballots, which are intended to allow the most socially vulnerable participants to better express their preferences (Olken 2010).

Social Policies

Social policies represent a second democratic pathway to empowerment, as social provisioning can advance human agency and freedom, both as ends in themselves and as means for further freedom (Drèze and Sen 2002: 8). Studies of advanced democracies reveal that social policies can have long-term consequences (Pierson 2000). Research from advanced industrialized countries also illustrates how the structure of social policies matters. For instance, governments can create new groups of "deserving" beneficiaries by ascribing a special status to those who gain privileged membership (e.g., United States Civil War widows and WWII veterans were granted special access to federal benefits) (Skocpol 1992; Mettler 2007). Any state provisioning that elevates women's status through inclusionary frameworks can be valuable because women have historically faced exclusionary systems politically, socially, and economically.

The design and scope of social welfare policy can have profound effects on markets and families. As Esping-Andersen's (1990) typology of welfare capitalism shows, western European democracies have developed varied social welfare regimes – including liberal, conservative, and social democratic models – that imbed different assumptions about the role of the state in shaping families and markets. We know that women face greater pressures related to their double and triple burden: paid work in the labor market, unpaid household and care labor, and unpaid community service. Policies that affect wages, family benefits, and the structure of the labor market thus have important gendered effects for men and women. Policies related to maternity and paternity leave also matter, influencing such varied decisions as family size, part-time or full-time employment status for women, and the proportion of women in service sectors of the economy (Esping-Andersen 2002; Thévenon 2011). The size and scope of the welfare state both reflects gendered norms and reinforces gendered outcomes for men and women through policy feedback effects (Pierson 2000).

Access to social provisioning presents both a barrier and an opportunity for women's advancement in low- and middle-income countries. Not only do women in these countries experience poverty in greater numbers overall, but discriminatory legal, economic, political, and cultural practices make escaping poverty especially difficult for women and girls. However, policymakers increasingly realize that poverty-reduction programs need to explicitly embrace gendered perspectives that acknowledge socially constructed differences between men and women, boys and girls. Cash transfer programs, either conditional or unconditional, have become popular strategies to alleviate poverty worldwide (Fiszbein and Schady 2009; Sugiyama 2011; Garay 2017). Importantly, most cash transfer programs prioritize women as beneficiaries for their households.

Programs that include conditionality requirements, usually behavioral changes related to school attendance and health care, sometimes also include special incentives to address gaps in girls' educational attainment. This approach has become a standard development model to both alleviate poverty and promote human development among international financial institutions (Fiszbein and Schady 2009). International organizations such as the United Nations also consider social transfers, like conditional cash transfer programs, to be a significant strategy to empower women worldwide (UN Women 2015, 137–138).

State Capacity

Finally, we examine the role of state capacity as a third democratic pathway for women's empowerment. The mainstreaming of "gender empowerment" as a core feature of government activity is part of a relatively recent agenda that emerged worldwide in the 1970s. Since then, international agencies have played an important role in highlighting the need for governments to alter their administrative practices and develop the personnel and tools to address women's unequal status. For instance, delegates at the UN's International Women's Year Conference (1975) called on all governments to establish agencies to advance women's equality and improve their status. Later, in 1995, the UN Platform for Action reinforced the need to address discrimination against girls and women and prescribed recommendations for changing states' administrative and electoral apparatuses to further gender equality. The UN Platform for Action (United Nations 1995b) strengthened the importance of "women's machineries" even further, highlighting the crucial role of administrative reforms in how governments address gender inequality. Remarkably, by 1995 more than 100 such women's "agencies" or "machineries" had spread throughout the world (True and Mintrom 2001: 30). Women's agencies are most visible at the national level, as governments have increasingly created them to respond to international human rights conventions and reports on women's human development progress. In principle, women's machineries can employ a gendered framework to analyze girls' and women's needs. These agencies may administer their own portfolio of programs or help coordinate across ministries to maximize impacts and promote a "mainstreaming" agenda across the bureaucracy.

In practice, women's ministries have varied levels of success in advancing women's rights agendas. Some countries have established influential agencies, such as Chile's SERNAM, while many other women's ministries are relatively powerless and do not influence other government agencies (Goetz 2007). Moreover, such state capacity reforms are typically concentrated at the national level (True and Mintrom 2001); the adoption of women's bureaucracies as tools for advancing women's rights in other jurisdictions varies widely across subnational governments, such as those in provinces and cities. As a result, decentralized systems, which are supposed to render government closer and more accountable to citizens, still have dramatic variation in local administrative structures and trained personnel to address gender inequality.

Beyond specialized women's machineries, overall state capacity can have gendered impacts that influence the extent to which public policies empower women and girls. It is especially important that bureaucracies properly administer programs that affect women and girls because they face differential obstacles for inclusion. For example, conditional cash transfer programs, where women are the preferred and direct beneficiaries, need to be well-funded and well-operated. Similarly, in the health sector, high state capacity theoretically produces well-run maternal and primary health care services, contributing to lower maternal mortality. Ultimately, state capacity is important because development scholars have noted that low levels of administrative independence and poor staffing can undermine effective service delivery, even when public policies are designed to empower women.

BRAZILIAN WOMEN'S STATUS: NEEDS AND CHALLENGES

Brazilian women's social status reflects contradictions and puzzles, with areas of progress amid entrenched gender discrimination (Htun 2003). In some respects, Brazilian women have fared well compared to women in other middle-income and developing countries; Brazil is home to a vibrant women's movement, women's workforce participation is relatively high, and girls and women have improved their access to education. Yet women's opportunities vary considerably across socioeconomic classes and serious challenges persist for all women in areas related to economic independence, gender-based violence, gendered health outcomes, and women's access to political power. Brazilian law has sought to address challenges in some of these areas over the last several decades with mixed results. We discuss these issues in turn.

Brazil has a history of vibrant organizing by women who have pressed for legal changes to improve women's status. The women's movement dates as far back as the nineteenth century, as advocates pressed for female literacy, the abolition of slavery, and the establishment of the Republic. (See Beltrão and Alves 2009.) In the twentieth century, the women's movement pressed for suffrage (gained in 1932) and was among the most important groups to lobby for democracy during the transition from military rule (1964–1985). Women's rights advocates were active in supporting democracy during the liberalization period in the 1980s (*abertura* period) and pursued the creation of the constituent assembly to enshrine important political and civic rights for women in the democratic constitution. Among the most important of those rights was the establishment of full citizenship for women in the constitution of 1988 (Piovesan 2009: 117),[3] which included the establishment of "equality in the family, condemnation of domestic violence, equality among sons and daughters, [and the] recognition of reproductive rights," among others (Barsted and Hermann 2001: 35). Through the 1990s and 2000s, the women's movement successfully advocated for changes in Brazilian law to strengthen protections for women in the workplace, including areas such as employment discrimination, regulation of domestic labor, and family planning. (See Piovesan 2011.) One of the most important legal gains in this area was the 2006 passage of the Maria da Penha Law (Law 11.340), which framed domestic violence as a human rights violation instead of a minor criminal infraction as previously described in the civil code. (See Piovesan 2009: 122.)[4] Brazil has benefited greatly from an active and autonomous women's movement that has pressed for legal equality between men and women. Nevertheless, there are still many remaining areas where contemporary women's rights advocacy is needed to achieve further advances.

Access to education represents another significant advance for Brazilian girls and women in the twentieth century (Alves 2003, as cited in Beltrão and Alves 2009). Contemporary access to education for girls is largely on par with that of their male counterparts. Beltrão and Alves's (2009) cohort analysis of the gender gap in educational attainment reveals successive and growing waves of girls' completion of elementary education for cohorts born between 1960 and 2000; girls started enrolling in

---

[3] As Barsted (2001) notes, prior to constitutional changes in 1988, married women were still considered their husband's "collaborators," with the husband responsible for directing the marriage (as cited in Piovesan 2009: 126).

[4] The Maria da Penha Law represents decades of women's movement advocacy on issues of domestic violence. Prior to 2006, Brazil had no specific legislation to address violence against women. For more on the significance of the Maria da Penha legislation, see Piovesan 2009: 121–125.

high school in significant numbers by the 1960s and then made gains in higher education in the 1970s. Today, much like in other OECD countries, Brazilian girls are more likely than boys to complete their secondary (high school) education (OECD 2014). The gender gap is also reversed at the tertiary (university) level, where women's educational attainment rates surpass men's by 29 percent (OECD 2011:15). Many interpret these data to reflect improvements in girls' empowerment and likely future improvements in women's empowerment. However, it is important to recognize that the national data mask important gender biases within educational fields, with men overrepresented in mathematics and some science disciplines and women overrepresented in the humanities (OECD 2011: 15). Recent efforts to address racial exclusion of Afro-Brazilians at the tertiary level through affirmative action policies have only started to make inroads for some Afro-Brazilian women. These programs have not yet addressed barriers for Afro-Brazilian girls at the primary and secondary level.[5]

Challenges: Maternal Well-Being, Economic Independence, and Political Power

Maternal health is a crucial area for women's empowerment. Pregnancy and childbirth are not inherently dangerous when accompanied by adequate health care, which includes having access to prenatal health checkups and a skilled attendant at birth. As public health specialists note, many complications that contribute to maternal mortality can be prevented with early and adequate care (Campbell and Graham 2006).[6] Yet for generations of poor women, maternal mortality has been exceedingly high. For example, a study by the World Health Organization and the UN estimated a national ratio of sixty-five maternal deaths per 100,000 live births in 2010 (WHO 2016). These rates are dropping across Brazil, with the most recent national estimates falling to forty-four maternal deaths per 100,000 live births in 2015. Socioeconomic improvements related to women's education, access to conditional cash transfers, and expanded access to health care through the unified health system (SUS) are thought to be main contributors to advances over the last thirty years (Victora

---

[5] See Marteleto (2012) on Afro-Brazilian educational gaps at the primary and secondary levels.

[6] Worldwide, 80 percent of deaths are estimated to occur as a result of severe bleeding, high blood pressure during pregnancy, and unsafe abortion (WHO 2012).

et al. 2011). The government needs to prioritize these services to continue these improvements. Improving conditions surrounding other contributors to maternal mortality, including high rates of illicit abortions, would require legislative changes to make safe and legal abortions available to all women.[7] For this reason, women's ability to make autonomous decisions about their bodies and reproductive life goes beyond abstract discourse about rights to the realities of life and death.

A second area of concern relates to women's economic autonomy and ability to meet basic needs. Unfortunately, advances in female education have not easily translated into women's economic gains. Like much of the world, Brazil has a significant gender gap in workforce participation. As Beltrão and Alves 2009 explain: "Female conquests in the educational field have not been accompanied to the same degree by conquests in the labor market. Women have reversed the gender gap in education, but they have not reversed the occupation and salary gaps" (29). The paid labor force participation rate for females fifteen years and older was 51.9 percent in 2016. This represented a decrease from a high of 57.9 percent in 2009, prior to the economic downturn (World Bank 2018). Brazilian women are also more likely to work in the informal economy (e.g., microenterprise) where salaries are lower and few workers receive social protections that come with formal employment (e.g., disability compensation, paid holidays, paid sick days, and other benefits). Additionally, precarious working conditions for women in the informal sector are unevenly distributed by race. For instance, Afro-Brazilian women are far more likely to face poverty than other women and those who are college-educated earn just 40.6 percent of what college-educated white men make (IPEA 2014, as cited in Wylie, in press: chapter 7). In sum, there are multifaceted dimensions to economic discrimination that restrict women from realizing their full economic potential. All women face barriers to economic empowerment, with many also facing intersectional challenges related to racial exclusion.

Women's limited access to political decision-making remains one of the most significant challenges for advancing gender equity in politics. Women gained the right to vote in 1932, but their representation in

---

[7] Abortion is illegal in Brazil except in cases of rape and incest. Nevertheless, research suggests that abortion is a common and persistent occurrence. Diniz et al. (2017) find that in 2016, one in five women have had at least one abortion by the age of forty. Further, they find that despite heterogeneity among women who have had an abortion, they are more frequent among black, brown, and indigenous women, as well as those who live in the poorer north, northeast, and center–west.

national elective office remains one of the lowest in the region. (See Interparliamentary Union 2016.) Brazil's first quota law (#9.100), enacted in 1995 for municipal elections, required that women comprise 20 percent of the candidates included by political parties on their lists for legislative office. Two years later, a new electoral law (#9.540) extended minimum and maximum quotas for candidates of each sex for elections for national, state, and local legislators.[8] While the legislation requires a minimum of one-third and a maximum of 70 percent be reserved for candidates of each sex, in practice this has not meant that political parties "reserved seats" for women. Brazil's quota has been largely ineffective in raising the number of women elected under proportional representation rules because parties can name candidates for up to 150 percent of all vacant seats, thereby undermining the effectiveness of the quota. For example, parties fulfill the quota requirement by placing women in the lowest positions on the ballot, ensuring they will not be seated unless the party performs surprisingly well at the polls. Furthermore, Brazil's open-list, proportional representation, weak party system and weakly worded legislation makes it relatively easy for parties to evade the law (Htun 2003; Marx, Borner and Caminotti 2009: 52). As Table 6.1 shows, women remain vastly underrepresented in the Senate and Chamber of Deputies.[9] Racial disparities also persist for Afro-Brazilian women in Congress. As Ollie A. Johnson has noted, only three black women were elected to Congress between 1983 and 1995 (1998: 108), confirming the reality that not only is women's electoral representation low, it remains overwhelmingly white. Dixon and Johnson (2018) draw on historic data (using largely hetero-classification) and newly available data on self-declared racial identification from the 2014 election to show that only 11.7 percent of Afro-Brazilian federal deputies were women (Wylie, in press: chapter 7). Stated differently, only 10 percent of deputies in the 2014 Congress were women, and fewer than 20 percent of those female deputies were Afro-Brazilian. This disparity is even starker at the local level, where fewer than 2 percent of mayors elected in 2016 identified as black and none as black women. Afro-Brazilian women comprised less than 1 percent of municipal legislators elected in 2016 (Superior Electoral Tribunal 2017).

---

[8] Brazil's quota law does not apply to the Senate.
[9] Brazil ranks 153rd worldwide in the percentage of women in legislatures. In May 2016, women made up 9.9 percent of the lower house and 16 percent of the Senate. The regional average for Latin America was 27 percent (Interparliamentary Union 2016).

TABLE 6.1 *Political and economic status of Brazilian women*
Percentages are rounded to the nearest whole number.

	Women in Electoral Politics			Women's Economic Participation	
	Women in Senate[1]	Women in lower house office (%)[2]	Women mayors (%)	Gender wage gap (median female wages as % of male wages)[3]	Gendered poverty (% of men/women living in poverty)
1990s	1990 2 senators (2%) 1994[4] 6 senators (7%) 1998 6 senators (7%)	1990 30 deputies (6%) 1994 32 deputies (6%) 1998 29 deputies (6%)	1993–1996 172 (3%) 1997–2000 304 (5%)	1997 Women's median incomes are 62% of men's.	1997 Men: 32% Women: 58%
2000s	2002 10 senators (12%) 2006 4 senators (15%)	2002 44 deputies (9%) 2006 45 deputies (9%)	2000–2004 317 mayors (6%) 2005–2008 407 mayors (7%) 2009–2012 504 mayors (9%)	2008 Women's median incomes are 65% of men's.	2008 Men: 45% Women: 55%

2010s	2010	2010	2009–2012	2013	2013
	8 Senators (15%)	44 Deputies (9%)	504 mayors (9%)	Women's median incomes are 68% of men's.	Men: 37% Women: 63%

1 Senators serve eight-year terms, with one-third and two-thirds renewed alternatively every four years. Source: Interparliamentary Union, PARLINE database.

2 Deputies in the lower house serve four-year terms. Source: Interparliamentary Union, PARLINE database.

3 These data record the gap between men's and women's median income, not the gap between men's and women's salaries for the same work.

4 Two Afro-Brazilian women (Mariana Silva and Benedita da Silva) were elected to the Senate in 1994.

Source: Brazilian Institute of Geography and Statistics (2017)

When it comes to executive office, women are also underrepresented. Only a handful of women have been elected governors since the mid-1980s (Htun and Piscopo 2014: 5). For instance, in 2015 there was only one woman elected governor out of twenty-six gubernatorial offices. At the local level, women held only 12 percent of mayoral positions in 2015 (Superior Electoral Tribunal 2017). While the election of Brazil's first woman president, Dilma Rousseff (2011–2016) was a significant historic milestone, her election did not signal the end of a *machista* political culture for women in politics. All to say, women's access to the corridors of political power has been and continues to be highly restricted.

THREE PATHWAYS FOR BRAZILIAN WOMEN'S EMPOWERMENT

Participatory Institutions

Since Brazil's political opening (*abertura*), the women's movement has called for the creation of participatory democratic institutions so women can better engage with the state (Alvarez 1990). The women's movement that emerged with democratization was one of the largest and most vibrant in Latin America (Baldez 2003: 254). Importantly, this movement has broadly engaged diverse groups and taken up varied areas for action. Rather than display a single or shared interest, scholars identify the movement as engaging both "practical" interests – derived from women's gendered roles as mothers, daughters, and "caretakers" – and other "strategic" interests, which challenge gender hierarchies (Molyneux 1985; Alvarez 1990). Alvarez (1990) coined these distinctions in terms of the women's movement's prioritization of "feminine" interests versus "feminist" political interests. The feminist wing of the movement advocated a more radical line, advocating for legal rights that would establish women as equal to men under the law and expand women's rights in general, especially in the areas of reproductive health and domestic violence. This portion of the women's movement was initially located among Brazil's middle classes and in the more affluent regions of the country. In parallel fashion, a feminine wing of the women's movement emerged and did not explicitly advocate for formal equality between women and men. Instead, the feminine wing pursued the expansion of public services that they perceived as being of greater interest to women than to men. These included "bread and butter" issues directly linked to women's access to income as well as "care" issues related to health, education, and childcare services. Beyond the intersectionality of class and gender, Caldwell (2007) notes that racial cleavages have spurred the development of an autonomous Afro-Brazilian feminist movement. This phenomenon is evidenced by the creation of new organizations by black women, who work to highlight the differential impact of issues related to reproductive and sexual health, violence, and racial justice (Caldwell 2007).

Brazil's diverse women's movement has been instrumental in advocating for participatory spaces so that women can better engage in policymaking processes (Alvarez 1990; Hochstetler 2000; Friedman and Hochstetler 2002). The clearest linkage between the women's movement and participatory institutions is the voluntary adoption of more than 600 women's councils at the municipal level. There have also been national conferences on women's rights policy held throughout the 2000s. Additionally, many municipalities adopted participatory institutions in the 1990s and 2000s and many different types of participatory governance mechanisms now operate at the municipal level. The central venues for engagement include participatory budgeting, policy councils, and policy conferences, all of which provide these diverse social movements with a direct mechanism to engage the state.

The broad participatory architecture available at the local level allows for more diverse entry points for women citizens and activists. For instance, those concerned with more "feminine" interests related to maternal roles can engage with voluntary thematic councils, such as those focused on children and adolescents, on social assistance, or on "bread and butter" venues such as participatory budgeting. "Feminists" may prioritize engagement in women's councils or human rights councils, which are more likely to address topics such as domestic violence or the expansion of rights and protections for the LBGT community. Afro-Brazilian advocates, who want to highlight problems of racial and gendered discrimination, may want to engage both "feminine" and "feminist" venues.

The expansion of women's councils has not been as extensive as in other arenas, even in those without federal funding, such as environmental and urban policy councils. Although the National Secretariat for Women's Policy promoted the use of participatory spaces to discuss women's status and gender discrimination, the formal establishment of municipal-level councils depended on the actions of mayors and legislators. Women's councils have been adopted less frequently than other policy communities such as housing or environmental policy. Nevertheless, Brazil has witnessed a steady increase in interest in women's councils. In 2013, 640 municipalities (out of 5,570, or about 11 percent) had adopted women's councils, up from 594 in 2009 and 438 in 2005. Policy councils in other key areas such as health, education, social assistance, and human rights have created complementary spaces to advocate for women's access to state resources. For these reasons, we hypothesize that policy councils will be associated with outcomes that empower girls and women and improve their well-being.

As women's councils have lower entry barriers to participation when compared to formal electoral politics, we should see women's increased presence in these venues. Lüchmann, Almeida, and Gimenes (2016) argue that "if the field of electoral politics favors men, the same does not occur in other spaces of political action, as is the case of the policy councils" (790). Lüchmann et al. conducted a gender-focused study that included an analysis of 105 municipal councils across three areas: health, social assistance, and the environment. Differential access is most evident in the health sector, where they found that 82 percent of the health department heads (secretaries) were men, but that 51 percent of the council presidents were women (795). In the social assistance arena, most council presidents and department heads were female, whereas in the environmental fields most participants and department heads were male (796). Overall, this suggests that the councils can play an important role in expanding women's access to public policy venues, but that we also need to be a bit cautious about universal claims to access surrounding the councils; some policy arenas (environment, in this case) are not necessarily as open to women's participation as others.

We would also expect to see the expansion of policy venues that concentrate on issues that are of central importance to women's and feminist's movements, including themes such as domestic violence, childcare, reproductive rights, health care, and education. The council system allows for women's movements to focus more narrowly on policy issues as well as to engage in oversight. In addition, the council system is intimately linked to the national conference system, which allows for the expansion of legal protections for women. Pogrebinschi and Samuels (2014) argue that the presence of women's conferences galvanized support for the national legislature to pass a domestic violence law (324).

Finally, councils can provide an opportunity for women to develop coalitions and networks that might expand their presence in other policy and political realms. A study by Almeida, Lüchmann, and Ribeiro (2012) finds a clear link between women's electoral representation and their previous volunteer experience serving on participatory policy councils. "In the 2003–2007 legislative session, 48 percent of female legislators had participated in a council, in the 2007–2011, 40 percent, and in the 2011–2015, 34 percent. These data allow us to assert that the councils are important steps in the political careers of women who manage to pass through the gender barriers of the Brazilian electoral system" (2012: 800).

Inclusive Social Policies

Brazilian federal policy for women's empowerment has lacked a singular focus, unlike other policy arenas examined in this book where the federal government has advanced a single, large, social-sector reform or instituted a large-scale public policy to address a key area of human development. Gender empowerment was not necessarily part of the overall policy goal, even though some of the policy efforts identified in this chapter have helped elevate women's status. Three large-scale federal programs serve as the best examples of public policies that are thought to contribute to improvements in women's well-being in the short term, with potential for gender empowerment in the longer term.

The Bolsa Família (Family Grant) is the country's largest poverty-alleviation program. Importantly, it has an explicit gendered component in its design as women are the preferred designated beneficiaries of the program for their households. This means the grants are associated with their names and they are responsible for ensuring their households comply with the conditionality requirements. Nearly all, or 93 percent, of Bolsa recipients are women (Camargo et al. 2013: 175). With bankcards in their names, female beneficiaries are instructed to create and maintain private PIN numbers to withdraw funds. The prioritization of women as beneficiaries is important because fewer than half (42.2 percent) of total household beneficiaries were female-headed (Camargo et al. 2013: 164).[10] While "gender neutral" in its design, in that men are also eligible to apply for the grant and serve as cardholders if there is no eligible female in the household, Bolsa Família has gendered impacts by providing women with control over resources.

A new line of impact evaluations on the program explores whether the grant improves women's status or empowers them. For example, Leão Rêgo and Pinzani (2013) provide one of the most comprehensive studies

---

[10] As the *Cadastro Único* database changes monthly, the authors report descriptive statistics for March 2013.

on the effects of Bolsa Família on poor women. Their research, which spans 2006 to 2011, includes interviews and focus groups with the poorest and most vulnerable women from regions of the country that have been long abandoned by the state. They found that their subjects all experienced significant improvements in material well-being, thought it was beneficial to have benefits in their names, and changed their pessimistic outlook and resignation over poverty (2013). Greater personal reproductive autonomy is another outcome for Bolsa Família recipients who, as women, are more likely to make key decisions about their reproductive lives (de Brauw et al. 2014). Further into the political realm, scholars show that the grant provides a pathway to citizenship, as beneficiaries begin to interact with the state, participate in local councils, or gain essential identity documentation (Leão Rêgo and Pinzani 2013; Hunter and Sugiyama 2014; Hunter and Sugiyama 2017). All to say, this poverty program has important spillover effects that can enhance women's prospects.

The health sector is a second policy arena with gendered impacts for women. The establishment of the Family Health Program (PSF) – part of the Unified Health System, SUS – broadly extended primary health care to vulnerable families and did so in an integrated fashion. A team of health professionals tracks families and contextualizes their health through an integrated, community-based lens. The expansion of the PSF has also vastly improved access to primary health care across Brazil. Importantly, women now have better access to basic preventive care that includes access to prenatal checkups, postpartum care, and support for breastfeeding. Not surprisingly, there is also evidence that the Family Health Program has contributed to a decrease in maternal mortality (Victora et al. 2011; Filippi et al. 2016).

More recently, the federal government extended financial support for local governments to make *crèches* (early childhood education centers) available under President Dilma Rousseff's *Brasil sem Miséria* (Brazil without Extreme Poverty) campaign. By law, municipal governments are responsible for providing daycare centers as part of their educational responsibilities. Public daycare centers are free – either government-run or contracted – centers that provide daily care for children from birth to five years of age. Bolsa families receive priority for coveted spots under the expansion of daycare centers through Brasil sem Miséria (Farah et al. 2015). These daycare centers are framed as an education initiative, but also have the potential to alter socioeconomic relations in ways that empower women. Women are typically their children's primary caretakers and childcare thus frees them to pursue employment during regular working hours. Previous cross-national research shows that access to daycare is associated with higher income and greater formal employment (Esping-Andersen 2002; Sorj and Gama 2013). We have every reason to believe that Brazil's daycare centers would bring similar economic benefits for Brazilian mothers.

Inclusive State Capacity

Building inclusive state capacity represents a third pathway where local governments can advance a gender-equitable policy agenda. Some local governments have sought to specifically address their capacity to deal with public policy issues related to women by creating municipal-level women's machineries, such as secretariats for women. These entities work broadly on issues related to women and/or gender empowerment. Their agendas vary, with some taking on more "materialist" agendas and others taking on "feminist" ones. They also vary organizationally, operating as independent bodies (or *coordenadorias* in Portuguese), as subdivisions within other agencies, or as offices within the mayor's office (Secretaria Nacional de Políticas para Mulheres 2014). In theory, these municipal women's administrative units bring expertise on issues related to women and gender to advocate for administrative and policy changes in existing practices. These bodies can be particularly important for enhancing local state capacity to address ways to improve women's status as centers of expertise on girls, women, and gender. For instance, it can be difficult for municipal administrators to mainstream this expertise across an entire bureaucracy and these bodies can help by lending expertise across sectors.

Municipalities are not required to establish local women's agencies and there are no federal incentives for them to do so. For this reason, local governments that make this investment are particularly dedicated to enhancing their administrative structure to address women's status. The national Women's Secretariat (SPM) has tracked the growth of these entities from 2004 to 2017. The first year for which data is available reveals that only thirteen municipalities had such women's agencies; by April 2017, 800 municipalities had adopted them (personal communication, December 11, 2017). We would expect that cities that have municipal women's machineries would have higher capacity to address women's status. However, a lack of data makes it difficult to test this feature of state capacity.

A more gender-neutral democratic pathway to examine gender empowerment involves the municipal government's general approach to providing services. As the discussion above suggests, social services related to health, education, and poverty relief have gendered impacts for girls and women. For example, women, as primary beneficiaries of the program, have a large stake in whether the local government properly administers Bolsa Família. Similarly, women benefit when the Family Health Program is well-run and accessible to poor families. Local governments provide these crucial services but they have experienced serious difficulties doing so cleanly without patronage and corruption (see Ames 1987; Graham 1990; Leal 1997). Furthermore, even well-designed social programs can fall prey to local political manipulation as politicians use them for personal advantage. For example, politicians may use job training workshops to target their allies or alter staffing for health facilities based on a community's political support rather than on identifiable policy need. Some of the national social policies we highlight here, particularly Bolsa Família, have sought to avoid the perils of local manipulation (Lindert et al. 2007). For these reasons, we expect that municipalities that administer federal social programs in ways that deliver rights-based access as a public good will see better results for poor women.

VARIABLES AND METHODOLOGY

Dependent Variables

Maternal Mortality
We collect data on outcomes associated with gender empowerment across health, economics, and political issue areas. We begin with maternal mortality rates per 1,000 live births across Brazil. This area reflects gendered survival and health care performance outcomes and therefore serves as a proxy for women's empowerment in health care. The data for this measure comes from Brazil's Ministry of Health (2017).

Women's Income
Next, we include data on women's economic empowerment through women's wages at the municipal level. Specifically, we use Brazilian women's median income in the lowest income quintiles. Higher income among low-income earners expands women's access to shelter, water, and food as well as women's ability to live independently of male relatives or

spouses who might be abusive. Higher income thus empowers women from a variety of perspectives and improves women's quality of life. The measure we use is in constant 2010 reais (logged) and comes from the Brazilian Institute for Geography and Statistics (IBGE).

Women Running for Political Office

Third, we use data on women's political empowerment. Political empowerment reflects women's ability to pursue their chosen life through representation in local policy-making bodies, and, theoretically, incorporating women's preferences into local policies. We include several variables from the Superior Electoral Tribunal as proxies for women's political empowerment. The first two reflect the representation of women candidates in terms of the percentage of mayoral candidates who are women and the percentage of candidates for the municipal legislature (similar to a city council in the United States) who are women. Our third variable in this area reflects the extent to which political parties honor gender quota requirements that a minimum of 30 percent of municipal legislature candidates be women. We divide the actual percentage of women candidates by 30 percent to generate a ratio of gender quota compliance, and thus, we argue, openness to women's political empowerment at the local level.

It is important to be clear about what our political empowerment variables represent. We do not have access to data on individuals that would allow us to determine whether women who participated in women's rights councils participated in other political activities, later sought political office, or gained political power in terms of holding office. Similarly, we do not have data on the passage of local legislation or policy implementation that might ultimately connect to policies designed to achieve gender equity. We do, however, have access to data on a potential early step on the path to accessing political power and pursuing gender equity. Whether women are putting themselves in the political arena to seek elected office and whether the parties support them by filling or surpassing their quota on party lists serves as an early bellwether for political empowerment. Running for office also represents a lower hurdle than actually winning an election, which could result from any number of factors that we currently cannot evaluate, such as local party dynamics or structure. In contrast, running for office and insisting on the enforcement of existing legislation, such as gender quotas for party lists, is an early area that could lead to access to power – and one that we can evaluate with our data. Moreover, these measures also have the potential to change during the relatively short timeframe of our study. Thus, we are likely to see connections between participatory institutions, social programs, and political empowerment in this area, should they exist in the data.

Independent Variables

We provide very brief descriptions of the independent variables we use in each thematic chapter. Full descriptions of each variable appear in Chapter 3.

Policy Councils
Our indicator for participatory governance is the municipal adoption of women's rights councils.

Bolsa Família Coverage
Our indicator for Bolsa Família coverage is the percentage of the eligible municipal population that receives program benefits each year.

Family Health Plan Coverage
Our indicator for the Family Health Plan is the percentage of the eligible municipal population receiving benefits in a given year.

Daycare Center Coverage
We assess connections between municipal coverage of daycare centers that provide childcare for young children in Brazil. Our indicator is the percentage of the eligible population with access to public daycare.

Bolsa Família Management Quality
We use municipal scores on the *Índice de Gestão Descentralizada* (Index of Decentralized Management, or IGD) to reflect inclusive state capacity.

Per Capita Municipal GDP
This is an annual measure of per capita municipal Gross Domestic Product in constant reais.

Women's Median Education Levels
We include an annual, municipal measure of women's median education in models of women's empowerment.

Competitive Elections
We measure electoral competition as the winning mayoral candidate's vote share in the previous municipal election.

TABLE 6.2 *Explaining variation in maternal mortality, 2006–2013.*
The model uses negative binomial regression with fixed effects.

Variable	Maternal mortality coefficient (SE)
Women's rights council	−0.44**
	(0.10)
PSF coverage	−0.003**
	(0.0001)
Bolsa Família coverage	−0.005
	(0.005)
Bolsa Família management	−0.04**
	(0.01)
PT mayor	−0.09
	(0.07)
Per capita health spending (logged)	−0.10**
	(0.02)
Women's median education	−0.06*
	(0.03)
Municipal per capita GDP (logged)	0.12**
	(0.01)
Constant	6.04**
	(1.59)
N	16,361
F	245.70
Prob> F	0.000

* Indicates significance at better than 0.05 (two-tailed test).
** Indicates significance at better than 0.01 (two-tailed test).

Left-Leaning and PT Mayors
This indicator is a dummy variable coded "1" for Mayors from the PT and "0" for all other mayors. We recode this variable to distinguish between parties on the political left as "1" and others as ("0") as a robustness check.

Results and Discussion
We use negative binomial regressions for our primary models of maternal mortality. We use Arellano-Bond dynamic panel estimation for models of economic and political empowerment.

Tables 6.2–6.5 present the results of estimation for women's health, economic, and political empowerment across Brazil from 2006 to 2013 when we have full coverage of all indicators. We begin with maternal mortality in Table 6.2.

The first stage of our analysis provides support for hypotheses surrounding women's health. Participatory institutions are associated with women's empowerment in health care. Having municipal women's rights councils or women's offices are associated with low levels of maternal mortality. We estimate that municipalities with a women's rights council enjoy 8 percent lower maternal mortality, on average, relative to those that do not.[11] *This translates to 300 lives saved each year among Brazilian municipalities and roughly 2,400 over the course of our study.* Next, both high levels of education for women and greater access to care through municipal Family Health Program (PSF) coverage are associated with low levels of maternal mortality. Bolsa Família coverage is not statistically significant for maternal mortality. However, the quality of municipal management of the program, our proxy for local administrative capacity, is connected to maternal mortality. Municipalities with higher management scores feature lower maternal mortality levels, on average. Furthermore, higher per capita health spending is also associated with lower maternal mortality.

Neither mayors from the PT nor mayors from left-leaning parties are systematically associated with maternal mortality. This suggests that other aspects of governance beyond the mayor's ideological or partisan orientation have tighter connections with women's empowerment. Finally, larger cities are associated with lower maternal mortality. These results suggest that incorporating women in policy making through targeted, issue-oriented venues for participation pays dividends in terms of access to maternity care and maternal mortality. Municipalities' ability to fund and deliver maternal care, as evidenced by health care spending and administrative quality, also pays off. In contrast, partisan politics does not have a statistical connection to women's health empowerment. Maternal mortality is no different in municipalities with mayors from the PT or left-leaning parties than in municipalities with mayors from other parties, on average.

Next, we present the results for women's economic empowerment in Table 6.3.

Table 6.3 demonstrates connections between innovative, targeted social programs and women's economic empowerment. Higher levels of Bolsa Família program coverage are associated with higher levels of

---

[11] We calculate this figure using 2013 mean maternal mortality rates per 100,000 live births.

TABLE 6.3 *Explaining variation in earnings for low-income women,*
2006–2013
This model uses Arellano-Bond dynamic panel estimation.

Variable	Earnings for low-income women (logged) coefficient (SE)
Instrumental variable (L1)	0.79** (0.18)
Women's rights council	0.13 (0.08)
Bolsa Família coverage	0.05* (0.02)
Family Health Plan coverage	0.03 (0.02)
Bolsa Família management	0.27** (0.06)
PT mayor	−0.04 (0.04)
Local GDP (per capita, logged)	0.19** (0.04)
Per capita enrollment in daycare centers	0.05** (0.01)
Women's median education levels	0.13** (0.03)
Constant	1.33* (0.46)
N	15,237
Wald Chi² (7)	183.65
Prob> Chi²	0.000

* Indicates significance at better than 0.05 (two-tailed test).

income for women at the municipal level. This relationship is particularly strong among the lowest quintile of earners, which suggests that Bolsa Família is having the desired effect of raising low-income women's earnings and empowering them from an economic perspective.[12] Per capita gross local product is also connected to women's income, with high levels of municipal productivity associated with higher income levels. Finally,

---

[12] Yet the quality of Bolsa Família management is not statistically connected to women's incomes. This suggests that delivering money to low-income women raises their income even if the program is administered poorly.

TABLE 6.4 *Explaining variation in women's political participation,*
2006–2013
These models use Arellano-Bond dynamic panel estimation.

Variable	% of mayoral candidates coefficient (SE)	% of legislative candidates coefficient (SE)	Candidate-to-quota ratio coefficient (SE)
Instrumental variable (L1)	0.69** (0.14)	0.75** (0.20)	0.63** (0.27)
Women's rights council	0.15** (0.03)	0.14** (0.05)	0.24* (0.11)
Bolsa Família coverage	0.07 (0.05)	0.04 (0.03)	0.04 (0.03)
Family Health Plan coverage	0.05 (0.05)	−0.06 (0.04)	0.10 (0.08)
Bolsa Família management	0.06 (0.05)	0.12 (0.08)	0.05 (0.05)
PT mayor	0.03 (0.02)	0.02 (0.02)	0.05 (0.03)
Per capita gross local product (logged)	0.11 (0.06)	0.06* (0.03)	0.08* (0.03)
Constant	0.29** (0.03)	0.36* (0.12)	0.94 (0.61)
N	14,059	13,926	14,383
Wald Chi² (6)	220.86	235.66	215.40
Prob> Chi²	0.000	0.000	0.00

* Indicates significance at better than 0.05 (two-tailed test).
** Indicates significance at better than 0.01 (two-tailed test).

the percentage of eligible children enrolled in public daycare centers in the municipality is also associated with women's income. This result suggests that access to childcare frees many women to work outside of the home and/or to enter the formal marketplace for employment. Neither participatory institutions nor political variables are connected to women's income. These last results are to be expected: only a very long, indirect logical chain would connect participatory institutions to city-wide income. Similarly, for the mayor's party to impact women's income across the city would require a longer timeframe than our study and extraordinary policy success in very specific areas.

TABLE 6.5 *Explaining women's empowerment through interactions among policy councils, Bolsa Família coverage, and local state capacity*

	Maternal mortality	Women's income	Women running for office
Councils and Bolsa Família	Reduce mortality	No impact	Increase candidates
Councils and state capacity	Reduce mortality	No impact	Increase candidates
Bolsa Família and state capacity	Reduce mortality	Increase income	No impact

Finally, we present the results of analysis surrounding women's political empowerment in Table 6.4.

Participatory institutions are associated with women's political empowerment. Municipalities with a women's rights council are associated with greater percentages of women mayoral candidates, municipal legislature candidates, and higher ratios of women candidates relative to the 30 percent quota for women on party lists. Municipalities with women's rights councils feature 18 percent more women in mayoral races, 25 percent more women in municipal legislative races, and a 25 percent greater women candidate-to-quota ratio relative to municipalities without women's rights councils, on average. These results show how political empowerment can stem from opening spaces intended to incorporate women's voices and supporting policies targeting women. Many proponents hope that women who attend council meetings will gain knowledge of the political process, engage with policymakers, and potentially run for office as a member of a party list. Our results offer some support for that interpretation, though they could also reflect a municipal predisposition to empower women, a prospect we address in the robustness checks section below.

Next, municipalities with higher average levels of education among women residents are associated with greater women's political empowerment for each political measure. Bolsa Família coverage, Bolsa Família management, and Family Health Program coverage are not associated with women's political empowerment in our data. The results for political independent variables and women's political empowerment is mixed. Municipalities with PT mayors have statistically greater percentages of women candidates for city council, but no greater percentages of women running for mayor and no greater candidate-to-quota ratio than other municipalities. Similarly, municipalities with higher per capita gross local product are associated with a greater percentage of women candidates for the municipal legislature and higher candidate-to-quota ratios than other municipalities, but not with women candidates for mayor.

Finally, we report the results for interactions across our three pathways and their influence on women's empowerment. There is more variation in these effects on women's empowerment than in the effects on areas of human development examined in other chapters; this is because of the nature of the dependent variables, which are more distant from direct program outcomes and are potentially slow to change over time. Interactions across all three pathways reduce maternal mortality and empower women from a health perspective. From the standpoint of economic empowerment, an interaction between Bolsa Família coverage and local state capacity improves outcomes, but policy councils are not statistically relevant. In contrast, policy councils interact with Bolsa Família coverage and state capacity to empower women politically, but the Bolsa Família program and state capacity do not interact with each other to influence women's decisions to run for office. Table 6.5 presents the interactive effects we identify in our data.

ROBUSTNESS CHECKS

We perform a variety of tests to assess the robustness of our results as in earlier chapters. First, we supplement our primary models with new models, but with lagged dependent variables, where appropriate. Next, we use several different specifications in our models. We have many fewer observations surrounding participatory budgeting programs relative to women's rights councils. However, we do find support for this program's efficacy in terms of women's health. Having a participatory budgeting program is also associated with lower levels of maternal mortality and with greater odds of maternity care. Geographic dummy variables are sometimes significant determinants of women's empowerment indicators, especially for the north and the northeast compared to the south. However, the central explanatory variables retain their significance, magnitude, and direction in models with geographic dummies, too.

We also account for endogeneity in our models in several different ways. Specifically, it is possible that previous levels of women's empowerment or lack thereof in the context of health, economic independence, and access to political representation influence municipalities' future choices surrounding gendered institutional adoption, public goods spending, and service provision. For example, a municipality struggling with maternal mortality due, in part, to a lack of funding or support for maternity clinics or prenatal checkups, might have committed to women's rights councils, to extending Family Health Program coverage, or to increasing health care spending to address this problem. Similarly, some municipalities may simply be predisposed (for unobserved reasons) to assist women residents by promoting women's participation in policy making and public services designed to improve women's well-being. Relationships between women's rights councils and women's empowerment would be epiphenomenal under such circumstances and policy recommendations that might result from the analysis would be misplaced.

We use Arellano-Bond dynamic panel models to account for this potential concern surrounding our estimates for some models, as described in this chapter and in previous chapters.[13] Additionally, we use propensity score matching with a focus on women's rights councils to address concerns for endogeneity (Ho et al. 2007). Like with poverty indicators, our estimates of women's rights councils' impact on empowerment indicators are somewhat lower than in the primary models presented above, but the relationships surrounding policy councils and women's empowerment are robust to the use of propensity score matching. We estimate that having a women's rights council reduces maternal mortality by 5 percent. Women's rights councils are also associated with 9 percent more women running as candidates for the municipal legislature and with a 12 percent increase in candidate-to-quota ratios.[14]

CONCLUSION

Global commitments to expand women's and girls' rights have elevated gender empowerment on the human development agenda. We know that structural barriers to girls and women's development hinders their ability to achieve agency, an integral component for advancing capabilities (Sen 1999; Nussbaum 2011). More recently, international development research shows that gender bias also hinders overall development as the exclusion of women and girls from markets, schools and universities, and

---

[13] See Roodman (2014) and Arellano and Bond (1988) for more information on this method.

[14] These models appear in the appendix.

political venues all limit countries' ability to advance their societies. Yet generations of economic, political, and social exclusion make progress on these fronts difficult to achieve. Our focus on women in Brazilian municipalities shows how key features of democratic practice can empower women. While democracy advances women's status, this chapter underscores the opportunities and constraints women and girls still face.

Our empirical tests show the importance of several democratic pathways for empowering women. Like the findings in the health chapter, which emphasize infant mortality, we find that local governments' robust participatory spaces, rights-based social programs, and investments in a capable state save mothers' lives. This result demonstrates that maternal mortality is a domain where immediate investments can produce important gains. Other barriers to women's agency – economic dependence and low levels of political engagement – are "stickier" and harder to dislodge.

Gender empowerment is different from the three other policy arenas we cover in this book (poverty reduction, health, and education) because of the conceptual and empirical complexity associated with the root causes of gender discrimination. The state and society would need to "mainstream" gender empowerment into all activities to fully advance girls' and women's agency. Unlike the other policy domains addressed in this book, gender empowerment has been largely absent from Brazil's national focus. The Women's Ministry lacks the political clout and budget associated with other federal ministries, such as the Ministry of Social Development, Ministry of Health, and Ministry of Education. Thus, the mechanisms we identify as important components of our pathways – participatory institutions, rights-based social programs, and an inclusive state – are the least developed to specifically empower girls and women. Despite these limitations, we uncover important lessons for how democratic practices can improve women's lives.

We find uneven results for our causal pathways on the economic and political dimensions. For instance, the Bolsa Família program produces immediate, positive effects for women's economic status but has no direct, identifiable effect on the number of women running for local office. This result makes sense in that Bolsa Família was specifically designed to increase women's income, but the process of encouraging women to run for office is not part of the program. But we do find that women's rights councils have a positive effect on the number of women running for office, suggesting that municipalities' voluntary adoption of participatory spaces creates the conditions to encourage more women to run for office. However, having a women's rights council is not associated with elevating women's economic status. Thus, the uneven results for our causal pathways reveal that each pathway is likely to generate different outcomes for women; in this case, social programs increase women's income and participatory venues foster women's involvement in formal electoral politics.

The analysis in this chapter identifies the statistical determinants of three features of women's empowerment: maternal mortality, women running for office, and women's access to income. This bird's-eye view covers all of Brazil, but cannot address the causal processes that drive these relationships in practice. Looking ahead to Chapter 8, our case studies provide a narrative of how women's engagement in councils contributes to important oversight of services and program design. The case studies also illuminate how women's activism and engagement with councils and civil service reformers make advances that are important to women, including access to maternity wards and domestic violence services. In particular, we highlight how variation in engagement with women's rights council's helps to explain variation in women's well-being for our three cities.

In Chapter 7 we turn to the issue of education, a more clear-cut policy arena for human development. Evaluating girls' and women's empowerment is analytically and empirically hard to pin down, but educational outcomes are clearer and easier to evaluate and measure. For instance, international comparisons of country performance on such indicators as school enrollment, attendance, and learning are well-known. Yet, education is perhaps one of the hardest areas in which to observe the long-term benefits of shorter-term investments. For instance, education outcomes include intergenerational effects, stemming from parents' levels of educational attainment. Poverty is another important mitigating factor that hinders students' learning. Moreover, major educational reforms – funding, teacher training, employment contracting, school construction, and curricular changes – are politically difficult to undertake (Kaufman and Nelson 2004). For these reasons, we turn next to the challenge of enhancing human development through education.

7

Educating Society: Promoting Public Education and Learning

Education, which is the right of all and duty of the state and of the family, shall be promoted and fostered with the cooperation of society, the full development of the individual preparation for the exercise of citizenship, and seeking qualification for work.

Brazil's 1988 Constitution, Article 205

At the broadest level, education is essential for generating well-being (Cremin and Nakabugo 2012). It provides the means to build basic stocks of human capital and to create individual capabilities (Nussbaum 2011). Individuals armed with information, knowledge, and new skills can better engage markets, civil society, and politics (Sen 1999). For these reasons, access to primary education is now recognized as a key component of social and human development. The United Nations Millennium Goals (United Nations 2000) and the United Nations Sustainable Development Goals (United Nations 2015) both identified education as integral to their efforts to improve basic social development among the world's poorest and least developed countries. Investments in primary education are thus widely viewed a significant strategy for enhancing capabilities and furthering individuals' ability to engage the wider world.

There is a broad body of literature that demonstrates empirically that the extension of primary education is strongly associated with sustaining economic growth in the developing world (Brown and Hunter 2004; Ravallion 1997; Kohli 2004; Glewwe and Kremer 2006; Hanushek 2013). Amartya Sen notes that the investment in primary and secondary education was a crucial component of East Asian countries' (Japan, South Korea, Taiwan) industrialization (Sen 1999: 41; see also Kohli 2004).

More narrowly, access to education is associated with improvements in health outcomes, such as infant mortality (Touchton et al. 2017). It is also associated with creating a more productive workforce that enables companies to profit by hiring better-prepared workers (Duflo 2001; Glewwe and Kremer 2006; World Bank 2013). Advances in educational attainment are also associated with enhanced democratic activity as individuals learn to become citizens (Dewey 1937, 2004; Nussbaum 2011).

We know education is critical for social and economic development, but what explains education performance around the world? Some educational systems benefit from ample funds, resources, and infrastructure to deliver educational services. Others lack these benefits and struggle to serve students – especially in the developing world. Access to economic resources is one key area that influences the presence and quality of educational infrastructure, the quality of instruction and materials, class sizes, and many other areas that relate to educational outcomes. Countries with large economic resources and high tax-collection capacity provide opportunities to improve education performance at all levels. Moreover, greater wealth (surplus or slack resources) generates the conditions for citizens to demand greater access to education as well as to pique government interest in providing education (Fritscher et al. 2010). Increases in wealth generate shifts in citizens' attitudes and behaviors: as citizens gain greater financial security, they tend to invest more resources into their children's education. This then creates a virtuous cycle as higher levels of education are associated with greater wealth production, which then leads to greater demands for education (Putnam et al. 1994; Sen 1999).

Yet there is wide variation in educational outcomes across environments with similar economic conditions. Some common explanations for this variation include: policy goals of improving labor productivity in support of industrialization; preferences for low taxes; preferences for private or religious education; choices in relative spending levels across primary, secondary, and tertiary education; and cultural norms surrounding education (Huntington and Harrison 2000; Kohli 2004). We readily acknowledge the role of these distinct political, social, and economic factors in educational performance. We argue that these factors are often constant at the subnational level or very difficult to measure in the local context. They may have diffuse effects and be difficult to alter directly in the short term. In contrast, governments can deliberately focus policy efforts on educational performance to directly improve citizens' capabilities, human capital, and, in the long run, economic growth.

Global interconnectedness and technological advances have fundamentally reshaped economies and social relations in the twenty-first century. Yet it is also evident that billions of individuals are ill-prepared to engage this interconnected world and advocate for themselves. Low levels of educational attainment in developing countries remain a significant barrier to achieving agency. For instance, more than 700 million people are functionally illiterate in low- and middle-income countries (UNESCO 2017). Literacy is important because it provides individuals with crucial information for decision-making in a wide variety of important areas, whether it be safe sex practices, family planning, or politics. Beyond this, completing primary school is another important marker. There are still roughly 750 million people who have not completed their primary education (World Bank 2018) and 1.5 billion who failed to complete lower secondary education. This means large populations are woefully underprepared to enter the workforce. It is essential that people have the necessary educational preparation to obtain employment as a growing number of countries such as Argentina, Brazil, India, Indonesia, Mexico, Peru, Philippines, South Africa, and Turkey shift from labor-intensive industries (e.g., agriculture and manufacturing) to service sector work (World Bank, 2018). Work in itself is not a guarantee for escaping poverty, but without it people are much less likely to obtain employment and the corresponding wages that will allow them to meet basic needs. Education is therefore essential for upward mobility out of poverty.

We test hypotheses connecting our three theoretical pathways to well-being in this chapter, which is laid out as follows: The chapter begins with an overview of the political and policy frameworks used to produce educational outcomes, followed by a theoretical discussion of connections between our three pathways and educational performance. Then we apply these theoretical insights to build hypotheses for how our three pathways influence educational performance in Brazil. The chapter then describes the data and methods we use to test these hypotheses. Next, we present the results of analysis and discuss the implications for arguments surrounding governance and education around the world.

PATHWAYS TO EDUCATION FOR ALL

The "right to education" was included in the United Nations' Declaration of Human Rights (1948: Article 26). "Education for All" was the guiding theme of a United Nations and World Bank-sponsored conference held in Jomtien, Thailand, in 1990. The Jomtien conference issued a "joint framework for action" that recognized the millions of children who lack access to basic primary education and the hundreds of millions of adults who were functionally illiterate and were thus denied their basic human rights. The joint framework for action then called on governments and international organizations to increase access to education by investing greater resources in education and improving state capacity to deliver education; the framework also called for increased access to primary, secondary, and adult education. Subsequently, the Dakar Declaration (2000) expanded the original framework to include greater participation of civil society organizations in the "formulation, implementation and monitoring of strategies for educational development" (World Education Forum 2000: 8).[1] The Dakar Declaration also placed greater emphasis on primary education and gender parity as the means through which to improve human development and well-being.

The United Nations' Millennium Declaration of 2000, Millennium Development Goals (2000), and Sustainable Development Goals (2015) all emphasized access to primary education (especially for girls) as a fundamental right and participation as key to improving well-being. The Millennium Development Goals and Sustainable Development Goals also advanced policy recommendations and set specific targets to achieve universal primary education.

Rights-Based Social Policies

One particularly difficult challenge in low- and middle-income countries is in encouraging children from poor and extremely poor families to attend school on a regular basis. School attendance is a necessary condition for achieving a useful education and developing human capabilities. However, school attendance is very low and irregular in many low- and middle-income contexts. Children may not attend school because they need to work to earn money, they may not have the necessary uniforms and school supplies, or the cost of transportation is too high.

Conditional cash transfer programs (CCTs) have emerged as an important strategy to overcome these barriers. By design, they seek to enhance educational outcomes by requiring that parents send their children to school on a regular basis. These programs have both immediate and long-term aims. In the short term, the cash grants raise families' standards of living. In the longer term, they also seek to increase the children's

---

[1] http://unesdoc.unesco.org/images/0012/001211/121147e.pdf

capabilities and to disrupt the intergenerational transmission of poverty. School enrollment and regular attendance will theoretically improve student learning outcomes, provide life and job skills for the future, and, potentially, prevent poverty. Inclusive social policies extend beyond CCTs, and can also include nutrition, transportation, and social programs, all of which increase the likelihood that students will perform better.

There is a strong basis for transforming capabilities into agency when inclusive social programs are framed around rights. Then, citizens will be more likely to exercise agency to engage their communities, their government, and the market after they achieve the minimum threshold of a dignified life based on the concept of access to public resources as a basic human right. Brazil's social programs are based on these rights because they are directly tied to constitutional guarantees and participation (Garay 2017).

Participatory Institutions

Establishing education-related participatory institutions allows parents, teachers, and school administrators to work together in public formats to resolve pressing problems. The Dakar Declaration (World Education Forum 2000) advocated for greater involvement of civil society organizations in setting education policies and monitoring implementation. However, the declaration did not include language surrounding specific types of participatory institutions related to education. In many countries, education-focused participatory institutions provide a formal means to encourage a public discussion regarding broader educational policy as well as more specific issues related to spending, teacher performance, and administrative support. In addition, youth-related participatory institutions expand the terrain of the educational debate beyond schools to focus on a broader range of social issues (e.g., homelessness, sexual abuse, underage employment, etc.). These participatory institutions also provide parents, social workers, and teachers with an opportunity to monitor the implementation of publicly funded programs. These oversight processes increase the likelihood that public resources will be used as they are intended.

Beyond formal institutions, the type of civil society mobilization may also explain education outcomes, especially in the context of institutional venues designed to harness this mobilization to improve governance. For example, societal pressures for greater inclusion can encourage activists and community leaders to lead the way in education reform. Religious organizations may teach adults to read (Warren 2005; Kosack 2012). Feminist movements may advocate for preschool spending as well as support for primary and secondary education, especially for girls (Nussbaum 2011). Educators may lead efforts to conceptualize new ways of educating citizens, which may spur support for K-12 education. These actors may pursue their interests in promoting education through participatory venues, where available. The venues, as discussed above, provide opportunities for CSO advocacy as well as for CSOs to connect citizens' preferences to government resources.

Inclusive State Capacity

Building inclusive state capacity is a crucial component for expanding and improving public education. States need to invest in basic infrastructure, teacher training, school materials, and transportation to create the conditions that allow students to succeed, especially those from poor and extremely poor backgrounds. Governments alter these basic conditions when they improve state capacity. Children gain short-term benefits in educational performance and long-term benefits in building capabilities when they have more opportunities to thrive in the classroom. "Inclusive" state capacity broadens state capacity further to provide better education services to otherwise underserved children. Improving local state capacity is especially important in the context of decentralization, where local governments deliver services and often have discretion to dedicate greater or fewer resources to education, depending on political support (Chaudhary et al. 2012). There is then a greater likelihood that students develop the necessary capabilities to engage markets, governments, and civil society when local states deliver education to students from poor and extremely backgrounds.

Expanding access to education produces tangible benefits for citizens and their broader communities. Improvements in education also improve workforces' human capital and their comparative advantage in national and international markets. Kohli argues that Japanese and Korean governments' expansion of primary education was a key component of their successful entry into global markets (2004). These countries transitioned away from agriculture and light industry into more sophisticated manufacturing and research and development, which all required a more educated workforce. Enhancing education was thus a process through which individuals' basic capabilities improved, thus allowing for better engagement with changing market forces.

In addition, better education creates citizens with a broader knowledge base and skills beyond the market. Under this logic, education builds residents' basic capabilities so that they can develop into "democratic citizens" who engage their communities and governing offices. In turn, creating better informed citizens generates greater opportunities for these citizens to claim rights formally established under democratic rule. Inclusive state capacity is thus mobilized to help transform children into "rights-bearing" members of the polity, who then exercise agency in the public domain.

EDUCATION IN CONTEMPORARY BRAZIL

The return to democracy opened the door for potential transformation in Brazilian education. The 1988 Constitution cemented the right to an education and made school enrollment and attendance compulsory for children. Voters would be able to use the ballot box to place demands on their elected representatives. Parents would use more local participatory mechanisms to make their interests heard locally. Finally, decentralization would, in theory, create opportunities for local governments to respond to local needs and interests, allowing for laboratories of democracy to flourish throughout the country. In practice, education reformers would face four major challenges: decades of underinvestment; uneven quality; disproportionate spending on tertiary education; and poor learning outcomes despite high spending. All to say, reformers faced historical and structural challenges that make the "promise of democratic governance" for educational outcomes one of the toughest tests of the three pathways analyzed in this book.

Brazil experienced decades of insufficient and inefficient investment in education, creating lasting legacies for the quality of education (Birdsall et al. 1996: 30). In 1960, the country's coverage of primary education was about the same as others with similar per capita incomes. Yet, by 1990, Brazil had fallen significantly behind its peers, particularly its high-performing East Asian counterparts. As Birdsall et al. note, Brazil played its hand badly when it came to education.[2] Demographics, slow economic growth, along with a hostile macroeconomic fiscal context, would highly

---

[2] Political and economic conditions influenced Brazil's educational system, including: the country's inward-looking development strategy; the structure of federal, state, and local

constrain government investment in education. The cuts would affect generations of Brazilians. The country's relative global standing in education has not yet recovered.

Progressive reformers have encountered challenges associated with Brazil's regressive education spending system, one that has favored highly specialized university training over broader access to quality primary and secondary education (Hunter and Sugiyama 2009). Well-organized sectors, such as university students and professors, effectively protected prestigious national public universities from privatization and high student fees. Free tuition at universities has benefited privileged groups. Upper-class Brazilians tend to opt out of the public primary and secondary school system, which are generally of poor quality, only to enter the public system at the university level under "meritocratic" competitive university entrance exams. Poorer families have little choice but to stick with the public primary schools, despite poor educational performance, which makes it extremely difficult for these students to prepare for university-level entrance exams. The poor have fared badly under this system, with lower high school graduation rates (Bruns et al. 2012). They are also underrepresented among students at elite public universities.

Uneven economic development has rendered poorer areas at a structural disadvantage in the provisioning of education. States in the poor north and northeast have had fewer resources to leverage for educational investments, instead relying heavily on federal transfers. Students in the rural north and northeast also face the hurdles of access that are brought on by remoteness. The more industrially developed regions in the south and southeast have, by contrast, benefited from a robust local tax base that allows them to complement federal funding. Brazil's decentralized federal model for delivering education has also produced uneven outcomes, with state systems outperforming municipal ones.[3] One of the most important educational reforms efforts under the Cardoso administration tackled this problem. The *Fundo de Desenvolvimento do Ensino Fundamental* (FUNDEF) sought to reduce the stark disparities among municipalities by: (1) establishing a national minimum level of spending per student in primary education, which would follow the student; (2) creating a redistributive funding system managed by the federal government; and (3) establishing a requirement

power; and slow economic growth combined with a rapidly growing school-age population (Birdsall et al. 1996).

[3] See Appendix, Table A7.3.c for educational delivery by level of government.

TABLE 7.1 *Education across Brazil*

	Literacy rate (%)			Functional literacy Rate (%)			School attendance, ages 7–14 (% attending)		
	1992	2001	2011	1992	2001	2009	1992	1999	2009
Brazil	83	88	91	63	73	80	59.7	86.6	95.7
North	88	89	90	67	74	77	72.4	88.9	95.5
Northeast	67	76	83	45	57	69	56.3	79.7	94.1
Center-West	85	90	94	66	74	81	61.6	89.2	96.0
Southeast	89	92	95	71	80	85	63.2	90.9	96.7
South	90	93	95	71	79	84	52.4	88.4	96.5

Source: Ministry of Education 2018.

that 60 percent of the total student allocation go toward teacher salaries and the remaining 40 percent go toward operating costs (Bruns et al. 2012: 4–5). Importantly, FUNDEF created a competitive incentive for schools to enroll students.

Brazil must overcome learning gaps if the country is to make gains relative to international peers. Despite significant expenditures in education, Brazil is a relatively poor performer for a middle-income country. In 2013, public expenditure in primary through tertiary levels represented 16.1 percent of total government spending, far above the OECD average of 11.2 percent (OECD 2016: 3). Importantly, primary, secondary, and post-secondary nontertiary levels saw the greatest increases, as a share of GDP, from 2005 to 2013 (OECD 2016: 3). Yet Brazil's investments in education have not resulted in substantial gains in learning. Grade repetition is a problem, with one in three (36 percent) of 15-year-old students having repeated a grade at least once in primary or secondary school (Knobel 2014). The most recent comparative PISA assessment of student learning, in 2015, found that the average score (401 points) of young Brazilian students in science was substantially lower than the average score of students from OECD member countries' studies (493 points) (Instituto Nacional de Estudos e Pesquisas Educacionais Anísio Teixeira 2016: 11). A similar tendency occurs with reading, with the average score of 15-year-old Brazilian students at 407 points, compared with the OECD average of 493 points (Instituto Nacional de Estudos e Pesquisas Educacionais

Anísio Teixeira 2016: 22). To put this in perspective, Brazil is among the lowest-performing countries in the region, fairing only slightly better than the Dominican Republic and Peru. Differences in learning outcomes across regions and schools are also a pronounced feature of uneven educational outcomes, as shown in Table 7.1.

THREE PATHWAYS TO EDUCATION PERFORMANCE IN BRAZIL

Participatory Institutions

The mobilization of civil society around the demands for universal access to education and the corresponding institutionalization of participatory councils were central features of Brazilian education reforms during the 1980s and 1990s. Although the education social movement was not as robust as the health movement, there was strong growth in participatory architecture in the areas of education and youth during the 1990s and 2000s.

The roots of education-oriented civil society activity come from at least four complementary fields. First, Brazilian educator Paulo Freire became world-renowned for his teaching philosophy that emphasized imparting critical thinking skills as teenagers and adults learned to read and write. *Pedagogy of the Oppressed*, first published in 1970, remains a widely cited work that served as the backbone of a national movement to improve education for the large majority of poor and socially excluded Brazilians. Second, the Christian Base Communities, supported by the socially progressive faction of the Catholic Church, emphasized literacy and learning as a key component to individuals' liberation (Mainwaring 1986; Burdick and Hewitt 2000). Third, social movements and community organizations mobilized in urban areas in order to demand universal education for poor children. Finally, public employee unions, often composed of teachers, were also key political actors fighting to expand educational opportunities.

The institutionalization of municipal-level and school-level education councils and youth-related councils in the 1990s and 2000s fostered the direct inclusion of citizens, community-based organizations, and union officials in education policy. We include youth-related councils in our discussion of participatory institutions surrounding education because they are charged with the responsibility of providing support to particularly vulnerable youth who lack familial and community support. We hypothesize that participatory policy management councils will be associated with strong educational outcomes.

A significant rationale for the creation of policy councils is that a public debate surrounding education issues will produce better policy proposals than if policy had been designed without deliberation and community knowledge. Thus, the ongoing interaction among parents, community leaders, teachers, union representatives, and government officials should improve educational outcomes by bringing together invested stakeholders and broadening the deliberative public sphere around education. The principal interest groups in the education field – unions, governments, and parents – all have specific representation in the councils, which generates the opportunity to produce broader, more comprehensive policy (Avritzer 2009). The council system is particularly important for parents as they are among the hardest group to organize and face collective action problems (Corrales 1999). Union leaders – who represent teachers, administrators, and staff – actively participate in education-related council venues to promote their policy interests and, in the process, they defend their proposals to the public. Finally, municipal-level policymakers need buy-in for their education plans as well.

These venues also provide participants with an opportunity to monitor the activities of community leaders, union representatives, and government officials and to engage in oversight over schools, staffing, and curricular issues. There are now an increasing number of municipalities that permit schools to establish school-level councils, which allow local parents, teachers, and administrators to meet on a regular basis. With larger numbers of people monitoring how public resources are spent, there is the potential for less corruption and misuse of public resources. We would expect that municipalities using a broader array of education-related councils would have a greater number of individuals involved in the policy-making process, which contributes to the density of engagement but, even more importantly, indicates that a wide range of citizens are interested in trying to work on relevant policy issues.

Brazil's participatory architecture was built during the 1990s and 2000s. The education and youth councils are strongly induced by federal legislative requirement. Table 7.2 shows that there are four education-specific councils (education, FUNDEF, school nutrition, school-level) and two youth-related councils (children's rights and children's protection) that a large majority of Brazilian municipalities adopt because of the

TABLE 7.2 *Number of councils related to education and youth*

Council type	2001	2005/2006	2009	2013
Education	4,072	5,037	4,403	4,258
FUNDEF/FUNDEB	–	5,372	5,267	5,119
School nutrition	–	5,375	5,466	5,032
School-level	–	3,867	4,290	4,007
Children's rights	4,306	5,201	5,084	4,623
Children's protective services	3,798	4,857	5,472	5,423
School transportation		2,165	2,201	2,238
Food security		2,038	786	1,503
Total	12,176	33,912	32,969	32,203

Source: Authors' compilation of data published on ibge.gov.br

federal incentives. In addition, there are two councils (school transportation and food security) that are voluntarily adopted by municipal governments to address issues of great importance to children. These two councils serve as a proxy for general municipal-level support for participation in education.

We expect to see strong education performance in the presence of voluntary councils because of the deliberate commitment to better policy design and use of public resources. We make what we think is a reasonable assumption: those municipalities that adopt additional councils are likely to generate greater support for education, from both the state and civil society, than those that only adopt the induced councils. We would thus expect that municipalities with more active voluntary councils will work on refining policies to better serve students' needs. We would also expect that a greater number of more active voluntary councils will be associated with better use of public resources and less corruption.

This data draws attention to the gradual spread of a participatory architecture in the fields of education and youth services, from virtually no policy-specific venues in the 1970s and 1980s to the massive proliferation of councils that allowed tens of thousands of people to engage in processes related to education and policies. There were roughly 30,000 councils established that pertained to education and youth-related services. A conservative estimate (ten council members per council) suggests that at least 300,000 individuals are now directly involved in education or youth-related policy-making venues.

Inclusive Social Programs

We also expect that public investment in education will improve basic human development if the resources are targeted to primary education. Brazil has long spent a relatively high level of resources on public education, but a considerable portion of it funds higher education. However, Bolsa Família has the potential to help close this gap because the program spurs demand for primary and secondary education by requiring regular school attendance among children of beneficiaries. Brazil's Bolsa Família includes a requirement that beneficiaries' children attend at least 80 percent of school days. This provides a direct, instrumental interest that creates a strong incentive to send children to school. It also sends a powerful signal that the national government vigorously supports including poor children in the educational system; this was thought to habituate families to providing greater support for education in general and to taking a more active role in their children's educational experience.

In addition, the Brazilian government has invested in nutrition programs, school transportation, and basic infrastructure to overcome deep educational deficits. For example, the expansion of nutrition programs provides a mechanism to ensure that poor children have access to at least one decent meal a day. Similarly, the expansion of free transportation programs is vital in rural areas where children previously had to walk long distances to attend school. The national school construction program is part of an effort to expand local schools to meet basic educational demands; Brazilian schools often host two or three "shifts" of students across the school day. The use of multiple shifts means that many children are only in school for four hours a day, an unacceptably short time.

Inclusive education policies have sought to treat a wide range of issues that might account for poor school attendance and weak educational results. The Bolsa Família program provides an incentive to get children to school; the expansion of free transportation increases the likelihood that children arrive at school; school nutrition programs improve basic health and provide another incentive for children to go to school; and, finally, building more schools creates more opportunities for children to attend school.

State Capacity

State capacity to deliver educational services has been a historical challenge for municipal governments. Creating and administering basic educational infrastructure should make it easier for students to study and stay enrolled in school. We believe that more administratively capable municipalities are more likely to use their limited resources to build and maintain the necessary infrastructure to allow students to study. By basic infrastructure, we mean items such as access to clean drinking water, indoor plumbing for bathrooms, regular trash collection, desks, textbooks, etc. Providing this basic infrastructure increases the likelihood that students will have the minimum conditions to succeed in school.

Despite these challenges, local administrative capacity has improved following Brazil's return to democracy. Several new programs and pieces of legislation have contributed to these improvements. First, Brazil's 2000 Fiscal Responsibility Law increases fiscal transparency and regulates municipal government spending. Municipal governments must now devote half of their annual budget to health care and education and file end-of-year fiscal reports with the federal government. Next, Brazil established the Federal Accounting Tribunal and the Federal Comptroller's Office to foster regular evaluation and formal auditing of policy implementation, including at the municipal level (Speck 2011). These offices publicize audit results and theoretically make municipal administrative practices more transparent.

Federal ministries involved with education have also improved their coordination and management practices to strengthen educational outcomes. The Ministry of Social Development has provided financial incentives for strong municipal performance surrounding Bolsa Família by evaluating municipal record keeping and reporting on an annual basis, publishing the results, and delivering extra funds to municipalities that perform well (Lindert et al. 2007). These incentives and federal oversight insulate Bolsa Família from local clientelistic practices and also promote local capacity building (Lindert et al. 2007; Sugiyama and Hunter 2013). New public management (Grindle 2007), new federal offices to oversee municipal governance, and incentives to improve governance all influence local state capacity to deliver critical education services.

In sum, our three pathways – participatory institutions, inclusive social programs, and local state capacity – are directly connected to education performance. These features involve parents and education activists in policy making to improve educational quality: the state providing narrow and broad incentives to the poorest children's parents; and state officials working to supply the basic infrastructure that creates the conditions for student success. In the next section, we evaluate connections between the extensive participatory architecture that emerged in the 1990s and expanded in the 2000s, social programs designed to incentivize school attendance, and local administrative capacity on educational outcomes. The dependent variables include educational outcomes and performance that are specific to this sector. Other independent and control variables are very similar or identical to those we use to evaluate outcomes associated with health care, poverty, and women's empowerment in other chapters.

VARIABLES AND METHODOLOGY

Dependent Variables

School Attendance
We collect outcomes associated with education including attendance, and test-results. School attendance is the first dependent variable we explore because it is a necessary condition for a complete education. Attending school is an obvious factor that helps to account for students' ability to access public education. It is virtually impossible for students to learn the appropriate material if they do not attend classes. School attendance is thus the most fundamental first step toward a quality education, but attendance is far from guaranteed. The literature identifies numerous reasons why Brazilian students do not attend school, such as the need to work, lack of transportation, overcrowding, and poor quality of teachers (Birdsall et al. 1996; Bruns et al. 2012). We therefore begin our analysis with school enrollment in five different areas: daycare (*crèche*), preschool, elementary, middle school, and high school. The data for all five of these measures comes from Brazil's Ministry of Education.

Graduation Rates and Standardized Test Scores

School attendance is the first step toward an education, but attendance alone is clearly insufficient for achieving an education that builds capabilities and empowers Brazilian students. The quality of education that students experience while in attendance is the next step toward well-being through education. We therefore seek to explain variation in educational quality across Brazil's municipalities. Assessing educational quality is difficult, but we attempt it by using three different measures: high school graduation rates; the percentage of students passing a national, standardized test at the high school level (ENEM); and specific test scores on the same standardized test at the high school level.

It is important to be clear about what our education variables represent. We do not have access to individual-level data on students that would allow us to assess how their involvement in different social programs might affect their performance. Similarly, we do not have neighborhood-level data on enrollment in programs that might boost performance at the school level. Instead, we aggregate individual- and school-level results upward to the municipality, where we have consistent data on participatory institutions, such as public policy councils; social programs, such as Bolsa Família; and measures of municipal administrative capacity. We therefore use dependent variables reflecting municipal education to test hypotheses connecting our primary independent variables to educational outcomes across municipalities.[4] We do not expect participatory institutions, new social programs, and local administrative capacity to influence education equally across all issue areas. Yet we do hypothesize that our primary independent variables will generally have a positive influence on education outcomes.

Independent Variables

We provide very brief descriptions of the independent variables we use in each thematic chapter. Full descriptions of each variable appear in Chapter 3.

Policy Councils

Our indicator for participatory governance is the municipal adoption of policy councils that are related to education, including education councils, school councils, school nutrition councils, children's rights councils, juvenile rights councils, tutelary councils, and school transportation councils.

---

[4] We aggregate to the municipal level while recognizing the extensive submunicipal variation in Brazil. However, considerable variation across municipalities remains to be explained. For example, 72 percent of schools had internet access across Brazil in 2013. However, the mean percentage at the municipal level is only 54 percent with a standard deviation of 38. The bulk of Brazil's 5,570 municipalities are small. Many of these small municipalities have very few schools and those schools frequently lack internet access. This is especially true in rural Brazil. Thus, aggregating upward to the municipal level obscures some variation, but considerable variation remains to be explained.

Bolsa Família Coverage

Our indicator for Bolsa Família coverage is the percentage of the eligible municipal population that receives program benefits each year.

Family Health Plan Coverage

Our indicator for the Family Health Plan is the percentage of the eligible municipal population receiving benefits in a given year.

Basic Educational Infrastructure

We compile data on six different facets of the quality of educational facilities to capture school infrastructure: the presence of indoor plumbing for drinking water, indoor plumbing for bathrooms, waste disposal, computers per pupil, internet access, and broadband internet access. We aggregate these data at the municipal level and use the mean percentage of schools with basic infrastructure (indoor water systems, bathrooms, and waste disposal) as well as advanced infrastructure (internet and broadband access).

As in other chapters, we also use the *Índice de Gestão Descentralizada* (Index of Decentralized Management, or IGD) to reflect the broader capacity to include citizens in rights-based programs.

Per Capita Municipal GDP

This is an annual measure of per capita municipal Gross Domestic Product in constant reais.

Competitive Elections

We measure electoral competition as the winning mayoral candidate's vote share in the previous municipal election.

Left-leaning and PT Mayors

This indicator is a dummy variable coded "1" for Mayors from the PT and "0" for all other mayors. We recode this variable to distinguish between parties on the political left "1" and others ("0") as a robustness check.

ESTIMATION TECHNIQUES

We use time-series, cross-sectional regressions with municipal and year-fixed effects for our primary models of school attendance, facilities, and test scores. We use logit for variables with binary outcomes and supplement these analyses with Arellano-Bond dynamic panel estimation to address questions surrounding a short time-series relative to the broad number of cross-sectional observations and the possibility for endogeneity in the data.

The results of our analysis provide support for many, though not all, of our hypotheses. At the broadest level, there is strong evidence that path-dependent, long-term economic and political development are most closely associated with education outcomes. Thus, state, economic, and social development are closely intertwined. We also find that short-term policy interventions such as Bolsa Família and voluntarily adopted councils are associated with higher levels of school attendance. This suggests that short-term policy and democratic interventions might be part of a broader package of reforms that heightens citizens' access to public education, but it is vital to recall that educational performance is quite stubborn and can take a very long time for change to appear in the data.

Our analysis demonstrates that several factors consistently explain variation in school attendance, most particularly among younger children and students. Municipal-level wealth, federally led policy interventions (Bolsa Família and PSF), local state capacity, and local participatory institutions (policy councils) are associated with high attendance for children enrolled in daycare, preschool, and elementary education. Quite simply, our results here suggest that active states and democratic interventions can have meaningful effects on producing change where it is most likely and possible.

The presence of greater municipal wealth is associated with higher school attendance among younger children as well because of a better school infrastructure, a higher property tax base that can support less prioritized programs (such as preschool and daycare), and a greater demand for employment that leads parents, especially mothers, to place their children in early childhood education programs.

For younger students, we also see that Bolsa Família coverage has a positive impact on attendance. This impact is stronger at the elementary and preschool levels, we believe, because parents have greater influence regarding their younger children's school attendance than they do among older children. *Moving from mean Bolsa Família coverage to one standard deviation above the mean translates to roughly 200,000 additional students in elementary school each year and 1.6 million over the course of our study.* The federal government is offering a clear incentive for very poor women to send their children to school. During the 2000s, Bolsa Família strongly encouraged recipients to view their access to the cash transfer program as well as the education and health services as a combination of rights and responsibilities (Sugiyama and Hunter 2013). Thus, school attendance is a right for children but it is also the family's responsibility to ensure attendance. Relatedly, the quality of Bolsa Família management was also positively related to school attendance. We can infer that better management in this area is similar to other areas of state capacity. Municipalities with higher management scores "supplied" better educational facilities and services to parents.

Our index of basic educational infrastructure is consistently associated with attendance across the different cohorts. These results also suggest that better infrastructure is a proxy for the quality of education, which drives students to attend at greater rates than they might have otherwise. Our results surrounding state capacity confirm much of the existing academic literature that demonstrates a fairly strong connection between state capacity and educational outcomes (Kohli 2004; Afonso and Aubyn 2006; Glewwe and Kremer 2006). Using the quality of Bolsa Família management instead of the educational infrastructure measure is also associated with attendance rates for every cohort.

Finally, the presence of participatory institutions in education is also associated with higher attendance rates among younger children. The explanation is twofold. First, the presence of a denser civil society is associated with parental demands for greater public investment in education. Parents aligned with teachers and educational activists to ensure greater access to higher-quality educational programs. Second, the council system includes a public deliberation aspect, which involves discussion of new programs and votes on the annual budget. This also includes an oversight mechanism, through which council members have access to budgetary information and end-of-year financial reports. The presence of these councils increases the number of political actors involved in the proposal and oversight stage of the policy process, which makes it more difficult for government officials to be involved in corruption.

Importantly, the short-term policy interventions (Bolsa Família) and new participatory institutions have no effect on junior high or high school attendance. This result may stem from parents having less control over their older children, despite their desires for them to stay in school. This finding may also reflect that more time is needed before early elementary school cohorts that benefited from Bolsa Família make their way through high school graduation. Municipal wealth is the only variable that is statistically significant as a determinant of attendance in these models, which is likely due to a combination of supply and demand issues. There is weaker supply of infrastructure, of quality teachers, and of a good educational experience in poorer municipalities. There is also weaker demand in poorer municipalities because older students may need to work, may have fallen significantly behind in the age-appropriate grade level (Bruns et al. 2012), and may also live greater distances from schools. Older students therefore drop out of the school system at greater rates in poorer municipalities and drag down attendance numbers. It is also possible that the older students had poor attendance records when they were young (no strong incentive to attend school), which led to weaker performance, which then led them to drop out because they were performing poorly. In addition, it is possible that these older students were never habituated to think of education as a right and responsibility, thus leading them to drop out.

Overall, we find that short-term policy interventions have positive effects on school attendance, thus indicating that the programs are producing some desired results among preschool and primary school students. The recent introduction of new democratic institutions (education-related councils) and policy innovations (Bolsa Família) contribute to behavioral changes among the groups most susceptible to change, i.e., increased school attendance of young children from communities with high levels of Bolsa Família coverage.

We also find that long-term structural factors, such as municipal-level economic conditions, account for higher attendance at the K-6 level and were the only statistically significant factors that explained attendance at junior high and high school levels. It is possible that younger children will be habituated to attend school and local government officials will continue to invest in high-quality public education, but the results indicate that two decades of reform are not sufficient to overcome the long-term educational deficits across municipalities for all cohorts.

EDUCATION QUALITY

Improving the quality of public education was a key goal when President Cardoso initiated public education reform in the mid-1990s. As noted above, one of the Cardoso administration's primary strategies was the use of national testing for high school students. The purpose was to establish a baseline that would allow for a comparative evaluation of school performance. In this section, we use three different measures to assess school performance: high school graduation rates, the percentage of high school students passing a college-entry exam (ENEM), and specific test scores on the ENEM test.

Municipal wealth and educational infrastructure are the only factors that are statistically significant for graduation rates. This is similar to our results for high school attendance rates in Table 7.3. Wealthier municipalities have more resources to devote to education and likely benefit from residents with more education as well. In addition, wealthier municipalities are also more likely to have a labor market that induces students to graduate from high school. Municipalities with basic infrastructure are also associated with stronger graduation rates, potentially because more high school students may be induced to stay in school and eventually graduate when the quality of educational resources are better. Similarly, replacing the basic infrastructure variable with an advanced infrastructure indicator also generates a statistically significant impact on graduation rates and test scores. Using Bolsa Família management instead of the educational infrastructure as an indicator suggests that the quality of Bolsa Família management is also associated with attendance rates for every cohort.[5]

Two factors are consistently associated with higher test scores in our models – municipal wealth and state capacity. As with the infrastructure findings, this suggests that long-term structural conditions are the most significant factors that account for variation in test scores. The short-term interventions of social policies and the recent introductions of participatory processes have limited statistically significant connections with test scores.[6]

There are several factors that are associated with *lower* test scores. As the number of students and families covered by Bolsa Família increases, there is a decrease in the percentage of students who pass the college entrance exam (ENEM). We argue that there are several reasonable explanations for these results. First, the poorest municipalities have the highest percentage of families eligible for Bolsa Família and there is a strong general association between low test scores and low family income (Carnoy 2015). Second, a greater number of students in poor municipalities now take the

---

[5] These models appear in the appendix.

[6] Interestingly, we find that the presence of a nutritional council is also positively associated with test scores. This could signal the presence of a denser civil society – although none of the other councils are statistically significant – but it could also signify support for governments committed to producing "healthier students." Municipal governments with nutrition councils are better able to deliver services (such as breakfast or lunch) that help students perform at higher levels.

TABLE 7.3 *Explaining variation in school attendance, 2003–2013*
These models use time-series, cross-sectional regression with municipal and year-fixed effects.

Variable	Daycare attendance Coefficient (SE))	Preschool attendance Coefficient (SE)	Elementary school attendance Coefficient (SE)	Junior high and high school attendance Coefficient (SE)
Education-related councils	0.22** (0.02)	0.25** (0.03)	0.17** (0.06)	0.15 (0.12)
PSF coverage	0.04 (0.06)	0.08 (0.10)	0.11 (0.14)	0.06 (0.09)
Bolsa Família coverage	0.07* (0.02)	0.12* (0.05)	0.23** (0.03)	0.13 (0.12)
Basic infrastructure index	0.02** (0.003)	0.04** (0.001)	0.05** (0.002)	0.03* (0.008)
PT mayor	0.17 (0.15)	0.06 (0.08)	0.12 (0.12)	−0.07 (0.09)
Mayoral vote share	0.05 (0.06)	0.04 (0.03)	−0.04 (0.03)	0.05 (0.05)
Per capita GDP (logged)	0.36** (0.01)	0.37** (0.01)	0.25** (0.03)	0.26** (0.07)
Constant	0.46** (0.15)	0.51* (0.20)	0.84** (0.15)	0.70* (0.34)
N	46,245	48,119	47,280	49,067
F	199.46	212.38	163.26	205.60
Prob> F	0.000	0.000	0.000	0.00

* Indicates significance at better than 0.05 (two-tailed test).
** Indicates significance at better than 0.01 (two-tailed test).

standardized tests. Brazil's changing social situation may have inspired these students to stay in school as well as to take the test that would help them to attend college. Unfortunately, students from municipalities with high Bolsa Família coverage rates performed poorly, thus suggesting that these students are not prepared academically for the test.[7] Disappointingly,

---

[7] We also find that test scores are low in rural areas; these scores are strongly correlated with wealth and access to the broader social infrastructure that facilitates student learning. Finally, we also find that municipalities with a higher percentage of students who self-identify as members of ethnic or racial minorities (e.g., indigenous, black, Afro-Brazilian) are also

TABLE 7.4 *Explaining college entrance exam scores (ENEM), 2006–2013*
These models use cross-sectional time-series regression with municipal
and year-fixed effects.

Variable	High school graduation rates	Total ENEM score (logged)	% of students with passing scores
	Coefficient (SE))	Coefficient (SE)	Coefficient (SE)
Education-related councils	0.16 (0.22)	0.61 (0.56)	0.15 (0.14)
PSF coverage	0.13 (0.09)	0.30 (0.24)	0.45 (0.10)
Bolsa Família coverage	−0.08 (0.10)	−0.71** (0.22)	−0.13* (0.05)
Basic infrastructure index	0.02* (0.01)	0.19** (0.03)	0.03** (0.005)
PT mayor	−0.15 (0.20)	−0.39 (0.35)	−0.11 (0.14)
Mayoral vote share	0.17 (0.13)	0.32 (0.46)	0.07 (0.08)
Per capita GDP (logged)	0.27** (0.07)	0.82** (0.18)	0.25** (0.04)
Constant	0.54* (0.21)	2.27** (0.96)	0.58** (0.10)
N	56,486	53,691	54,278
F	152.93	162.35	138.79
Prob> F	0.000	0.000	0.000

* Indicates significance at better than 0.05 (two-tailed test).
** Indicates significance at better than 0.01 (two-tailed test).

our data analysis did not identify any significant relationships between participatory institutions, social programs, and test scores during the latter years of our data, when early changes in performance due to Bolsa Família or participatory governance might emerge.[8]

Overall, the wealth of a municipality and local state capacity are the strongest factors that account for high school performance. Thus,

---

negatively associated with passing scores on the standardized test. This finding is similar to a substantial body of research that demonstrates that poor students, many of whom are black, receive very poor education. These models are included in the online appendix.

[8] These models appear in the extended, online appendix.

long-term economic trends and the associated improvements in basic state capacity best account for education performance. The construction of a participatory architecture as well as investments in social programs aimed at low-income students are not yet sufficient to overcome the long-term structural differences in education across municipalities. Quite simply, students living in wealthier municipalities receive a better education than students living in poorer municipalities.

Interactive Results

Tables 7.5 and 7.6 present the results of interactive models of school attendance and test scores. The interactions we present are between different configurations of policy councils related to education and municipal scores on the Index of Decentralized Management, which we use to proxy for local state capacity.

The results of estimation show interactive effects in favor of a commitment to participatory institutions and high levels of state capacity. School attendance and test scores are highest in the presence of both participatory institutions and strong performance on the Index of Decentralized Management. Moving from mean municipal levels of both variables to one standard deviation above the mean is associated with 24 percent higher attendance rates and 18 percent higher standardized test scores. As with other issue areas, education outcomes benefit greatly from multiple, complementary pathways whose total impact is greater than the sum of the individual parts when they operate at high levels.

ROBUSTNESS CHECKS

We perform a variety of tests to assess the robustness of our results for education outcomes, as in other chapters. First, we use several different specifications in our models. For example, models that include per capita municipal education spending instead of per capita gross municipal product produce results that are broadly similar to those in Tables 7.3–7.6. Replacing the "left-leaning mayor" variable with a dummy variable for a PT mayor also produces similar results. Geographic dummy variables are sometimes significant determinants of education performance, especially in the north and the northeast compared to the south. However, the central explanatory variables retain their significance, magnitude, and direction in models with geographic dummies too.

TABLE 7.5 *Explaining elementary school attendance, 2006–2013: Interactions among policy councils, Bolsa Família coverage, and local state capacity*

These models use cross-sectional time-series regression with municipal and year-fixed effects.

Variable	Councils, top 20% management Coefficient (SE)	No councils, top 20% management Coefficient (SE)	Councils, lesser management Coefficient (SE)	No councils, lesser management Coefficient (SE)
Councils* BF management	0.18** (0.03)			
BF management	0.0004 (0.0003)	0.0004 (0.0004)	0.0005* (0.0002)	0.002** (0.0002)
Bolsa Família coverage	0.06* (0.02)	0.12* (0.06)	0.20** (0.05)	0.16 (0.12)
Family Health Plan coverage	0.06 (0.08)	0.11 (0.10)	0.09 (0.10)	0.08 (0.06)
Voluntary councils	0.006 (0.005)	Dropped	−0.05 (0.05)	Dropped
Bolsa Família management	−0.009 (0.007)	−0.05 (0.04)	Dropped	Dropped
Competitive elections	0.06 (0.05)	0.06 (0.04)	−0.05 (0.03)	−0.05 (0.04)
Left-leaning mayor	0.11 (0.14)	0.09 (0.10)	0.10 (0.07)	−0.05 (0.07)
Per capita local GDP (logged)	0.31** (0.05)	0.33** (0.09)	0.27** (0.08)	0.29** (0.04)
Constant	0.51** (0.19)	0.47* (0.22)	0.86** (0.27)	0.64* (0.30)
N	5,840	5,210	6,135	4,570
Wald Chi^2	296.39	307.40	290.13	337.28
Prob> Chi^2	0.00	0.00	0.00	0.00

* Indicates significance at better than 0.05 (two-tailed test).
** Indicates significance at better than 0.01 (two-tailed test).

We also account for endogeneity in our models in several different ways because previous levels of education performance may influence municipalities' future choices surrounding institutional adoption, public goods spending,

TABLE 7.6 *Explaining high school test (ENEM) performance, 2006–2013: Interactions among policy councils, Bolsa Família coverage, and local state capacity*
These models use cross-sectional time-series regression with municipal and year-fixed effects.

Variable	Councils, top 20% management Coefficient (SE)	No councils, top 20% management Coefficient (SE)	Councils, lesser management Coefficient (SE)	No councils, lesser management Coefficient (SE)
Councils* BF management	0.14** (0.02)			
Bolsa Famila management	0.004 (0.006)	0.009* (0.004)	0.005 (0.004)	0.002* (0.001)
Bolsa Família coverage	0.04 (0.05)	0.03 (0.02)	0.06 (0.04)	0.04 (0.03)
Family Health Plan coverage	0.02 (0.02)	0.06 (0.11)	0.07 (0.10)	0.06 (0.06)
Voluntary councils	0.03 (0.02)	Dropped	0.02 (0.02)	Dropped
Bolsa Família management	0.004 (0.006)	0.06 (0.04)	Dropped	Dropped
Competitive elections	−0.09 (0.13)	−0.06 (0.06)	−0.07 (0.05)	0.04 (0.03)
Left-leaning mayor	−0.07 (0.09)	−0.06* (0.03)	−0.15 (0.12)	−0.04 (0.04)
Per capita local GDP (logged)	0.24** (0.08)	0.21** (0.06)	0.23** (0.09)	0.30** (0.10)
Constant	0.22** (0.09)	0.28* (0.12)	0.19** (0.10)	0.16** (0.05)
N	5,618	5,072	5,966	4,323
Wald Chi²	316.93	324.37	315.75	338.42
Prob> Chi²	0.00	0.00	0.00	0.00

* Indicates significance at better than 0.05 (two-tailed test).
** Indicates significance at better than 0.01 (two-tailed test).

and service provision. We use Arellano-Bond dynamic panel models to account for this potential concern surrounding our estimates.[9] The Arellano-

[9] See Roodman (2014) and Arellano and Bond (1988) for more information on this method.

TABLE 7.7 *Explaining educational outcomes through interactions among policy councils, Bolsa Família coverage, and local state capacity*

	Elementary school attendance	High school graduation rates	ENEM test scores
Councils and Bolsa Família	Increase attendance	No impact	No impact
Councils and state capacity	Increase attendance	Increase graduation rates	Increase test scores
Bolsa Família and state capacity	Increase attendance	Increase graduation rates	No impact

Bond models use the "system" generalized method of moments (GMM) with one lag of the dependent variable. The instruments used are the policy council variables, Bolsa Família coverage, Bolsa Família management, and the percentage of per capita municipal spending devoted to public goods, beginning with the second lag and going back as far in time as the data exists for each variable. The direction of the coefficients and the general levels of statistical significance are all similar to those in the primary models. We also use dummy variables for each year to ensure that the assumption of no correlation holds across units. Finally, we present the results of propensity score matching with treatment effects as another way to isolate the role of our variables of interest and address the prospects for endogeneity in our primary models. The results in Tables A7.3 a-b and A7.4 a-b of the appendix thus provide supporting evidence for Tables 7.3–7.6, and emphasize the strong connection between participation, federal social programs, local public expenditure, and municipal education outcomes.

An additional important consideration is that certain municipalities might simply be predisposed to educate the poor more than other municipalities for some unobserved reason. These municipalities might then promote participatory governance, the expansion of federal programs, and greater education spending as means to improve education. Any relationships between participatory governance, federal programs, state spending, and education performance could therefore only reflect municipal predispositions, as opposed to any impact from the specific institutions or programs. We find little evidence to support such a scenario; there are only low correlations between municipalities with voluntary policy councils related to education, social program coverage, and public goods spending programs.[10] This provides further evidence that municipalities do not tend to excel in all three areas simultaneously and that a commitment to participatory governance, social program coverage, and local social spending does not stem from an unobserved, underlying commitment to education.

CONCLUSION

Access to education is essential for human development, especially in aiding individuals and families to escape intergenerational poverty. The "right to education" was included in the United Nations' Declaration of Human Rights (1948: Article 26), setting the tone for seventy years of efforts across the world to expand access to primary education. More recently, access to education was included in the United Nations' Millennium Goals (2000) and Sustainable Development Goals (2015); both of which identified universal primary education as key components of their efforts to improve social development among the world's poorest countries. Our pathways approach, and the accompanying policy programs, provide strong evidence that robust government support for investing in education-related infrastructure, incentivizing poor families to send their children to school, and supporting community engagement in education policy making can improve education.

Different from the other three policy arenas covered in this book (poverty reduction, health, women's empowerment), advances in education are more influenced by historical patterns of infrastructure investment. We find that variation in education outcomes stems foremost from longer-term investments in educational infrastructure that was built – and sometimes neglected – over decades. This finding suggests that investments in education are part of a long-term, path-dependent developmental approach, which is generally associated with greater wealth and more general investment in schools, books, new technologies, and teacher training. Thus the broader, long-term improvements in wealth and local state capacity are the strongest factors that explain improvements in basic education indicators. The field of education also differs from the other arenas we examine in that it may take decades to assess whether current policy changes have a broader impact. For example, having more young children attend school is thought to have positive, lifelong effects, but researchers will not be able to assess how current primary school attendance may affect university enrollment, job prospects, or income for

---

[10] Voluntary policy councils related to poverty are *negatively* correlated with Bolsa Família coverage at -0.31. All other correlations between primary independent variables are under 0.2.

more than twenty years. Thus, unlike with infant or maternal mortality, we are less likely to see results for longer-term educational performance, such as standardized test scores or high school graduation rates, because the results of policy interventions take a very long time to appear in the data. What we can do is identify short-term changes in education indicators that can have important consequences for the future.

Our pathways approach accounts for several important short-term gains in education, which may be associated with more significant long-term changes later on. We find that Bolsa Família coverage is positively associated with school attendance, especially among younger children. Similarly, participatory institutions have a moderate, positive association with elementary school attendance. But neither Bolsa Família nor participatory institutions are associated with school-age attendance among middle school and high school students. This demonstrates that rights-based social programs and participatory institutions have a more immediate effect among young children, which is similar to the findings surrounding infant mortality. Reducing infant mortality and increasing school attendance are both areas in which active state provisioning and active civil society participation are more likely to produce these positive outcomes. The implications of these findings are that our pathways start the process of creating virtuous circles of change, but that deeper structural changes are more difficult to achieve and that we should not necessarily expect to see such fundamental changes for years, if not decades.

As researchers have noted elsewhere, expanding access to education is a necessary first step toward improving human development. However, broader improvements in educational performance and the development of human capabilities may require intergenerational efforts. Universal primary schooling for millions of poor Brazilian students may help many later access opportunities available through secondary and tertiary education, which was largely previously out of reach. Although we find no positive impact for our pathways on high school standardized test scores, we do see the possibility that early school attendance will eventually generate positive benefits later in students' lives.

Like the previous chapters on income poverty, health, and gender empowerment, this chapter has systematically identified quantitative associations between our pathways and key indicators of well-being. These relationships for education are generally strong. But the analysis for education also demonstrates the pathways' limitations as long-term patterns of state development and economic growth produce headwinds that hinder the potential of democratic pathways to accelerate human development performance (e.g., access to income; high school atten-dance). In Chapter 8, we narrow our analytical focus to three cities to trace these causal processes to better explain how these pathways work in practice to further educational outcomes. For instance, we explain how advocates in a high-performing municipality – Camaragibe – use partici-patory institutions to demand inclusive access to education. In contrast, other municipalities display weaker civil society engagement with educa-tion councils and civil servants have less meaningful interactions to pursue educational reforms.

We turn next to our case studies of three northeastern municipalities to show how a commitment to these democratic pathways improve human development across a variety of issue areas. At the same time, we also demonstrate how the absence of such efforts leave municipalities and their residents behind.

8

Pathways at Work: Lessons from
Brazil's Poor Northeast

Brazil is known for its vast internal diversity. Whether we consider its historical patterns of colonization, industrial development, internal migration, or ecological diversity, Brazil offers amazing contrasts. During the 1990s and 2000s some Brazilian municipalities were the sites of an amazing array of reforms: universal health programs, participatory budgeting programs, public policy councils, and conditional cash transfer programs flourished across Brazil. Multiple Brazilian municipalities were internationally recognized for creating innovative policy and institutional solutions to address a wide range of social and political problems, such as extreme poverty, low rates of vaccination, and a disengaged citizenry (United Nations 1996). However, patronage, clientelism, administrative malfeasance, corruption, and poor provision of public goods continue to plague many citizens and municipalities and limit efforts to improve well-being. In this chapter, we narrow the analytical lens to three municipalities to examine how participatory institutions, inclusive social policy, and local state capacity work on the ground to advance well-being.

The municipalities of Camaragibe, Jaboatão dos Guararapes, and Garanhuns, all located in the northeastern state of Pernambuco, contain within them a great diversity of social and political life. Within these cases, mirroring the points made above, we find examples of government officials and citizens working together within participatory councils to improve policy outcomes, expand access to rights, and deepen the quality of democracy. We find examples of government officials working hard to overcome legacies of policy neglect, clientelism, and misuse of public resources. But we also find examples of policy neglect, in which elected officials make few policy initiatives to improve the lives of the poorest groups. Importantly, these cities' economic conditions are not destiny for their citizens' well-being. High levels of economic wealth do not necessarily produce better outcomes for residents, nor do low levels necessarily undermine human development performance. Instead, the degree to which each municipality fosters citizenship, participation, and an inclusionary state influences their human development outcomes and their residents' well-being.

A former government official from Jaboatão noted that the process of implementing reform must contend with a long history of government officials using public resources to subvert rights and democratic practices. She commented, "The history of social assistance policy in Brazil is a history of clientelism, handouts, paternalism, all the 'isms' in life used to promote local officials (Socorro Araújo, Jaboatão)."[1] Efforts to build democratic pathways across Brazil require that government officials and civil servants devise new programs and practices to overcome these legacies. These include building councils to help improve policy formulation and implementation. "The Social Assistance Council follows [issues related to poverty] because it is responsible for oversight; this is why it accompanies the families that receive Bolsa Família benefits, those who have the *Benefício de Proteção Continuada* (Social Protection Benefit), or BPC, those who have some type of benefits" (Givaldo José da Silva Nascimento, Camaragibe). It also includes investment by the federal government to provide the programmatic and financial support to increase the likelihood that municipal government could support the expansion of social rights. In this chapter, we trace out the independent and interactive processes that citizens, community leaders, civil servants, and government officials use to build pathways.

This book's analysis thus far has taken a "birds-eye" view of human development, with a specific focus on municipalities; the quantitative analysis presented in Chapters 4–7 examines how a range of factors affected health, education, poverty, and gender inequality outcomes. In this chapter, we shift from our preceding analysis of 5,570 municipalities to an analysis of three municipalities in order to tease out the causal processes connecting our three pathways to outcomes surrounding well-being. We show how high performance in participation, inclusive social programs, and local administrative capacity contribute to "virtuous

---

[1] Throughout this chapter we will refer to interviews conducted with council members, elected officials, and civil servants in the three municipalities. A complete list of the type of communication, names, dates, and locations appears in the front of this book.

circles" of high human development performance. Of course, this confluence of high performance is difficult to achieve and many municipalities
have middling or low performance results related to participation, social
policy implementation, and state capacity; these municipalities are prone
to "vicious circles" of underperformance on human development. This
chapter's analysis contextualizes how participatory councils, local social
service delivery of federal programs, and the local administrative apparatus impact critical stages of the policy cycle, from agenda setting, policy
formulation, and approval to implementation and oversight (Howlett and
Ramesh 2003; Jann and Wegrich 2007; Dye 2016).

Exploring three municipalities in Brazil's northeast informs the
work of researchers and development practitioners who have long
questioned how to get "good government in the tropics" (Tendler
1997; Grindle 2004). The combination of democracy and underdevelopment is thought to create political and economic conditions that are
not necessarily conducive to delivering essential services needed for
human development. A society's wealth has long been used as a proxy
to capture the social, cultural, and institutional impediments that hinder individual-level improvements in well-being. (See Chapter 1.)
Underdevelopment is also thought to create conditions that entrench
power among elites and undermine prospects for vibrant democratic
governance (Weyland 1996; O'Donnell 1998; Ross 2006; Cleary 2007;
Gibson 2013). For example, citizens' poverty may render them subject
to the whims of oligarchs with strong political machines. Low levels of
economic development make it difficult for individuals to escape intergenerational poverty. But our work shows that economic wealth is not
destiny. Both Garanhuns and Jaboatão are relatively well resourced,
yet underperform expectations based on wealth. Camaragibe, with
limited industry and lower GDP per capita, beats expectations based
on wealth alone. Our three pathways best explain this variation in
human development outcomes while wealth alone does not (Sen
1999; Nussbaum 2011).

This chapter is organized as follows: The next section provides
a broad overview of the three municipal cases, Camaragibe,
Jaboatão dos Guararapes, and Garanhuns. The third section provides
a detailed account of the causal mechanisms that connect councils,
social policy, and local state capacity to well-being. The fourth section
examines the mutually reinforcing effects across these factors. We
show how these pathways interact to produce even greater human
development outcomes when they all function at a high level, but

also how these "fragile links" can be derailed and undermine democracy's influence on well-being. Finally, we draw conclusions from our cases to fill in gaps in our understanding of democratic processes and human development.

SETTING THE STAGE: A TALE OF THREE CITIES

Each of the three municipal case studies offers a fascinating portrait of the political, social, and economic challenges that medium- and large-sized municipalities face in Brazil's northeast. Table 8.1 summarizes these municipalities' main socioeconomic characteristics. The underlying economic and political conditions vary significantly across the three municipalities. But explanations for improvements in well-being do not readily conform to prominent theoretical explanations. Most notably, municipal-level wealth is unable to account for the variation in well-being, reminding us that the level of economic development does not fully explain improvements in well-being. Among the three cases, the poorest, Camaragibe, outperforms the other two municipalities. Simply, economic development

TABLE 8.1 *Case study municipalities: Socioeconomic summary statistics*

	Camaragibe	Jaboatão dos Guararapes	Garanhuns
Population	144,466	691,125	137,810
Geographic size (sq. km)	51.2 sq. km	258.7 sq. km	458.9 sq. km
Poverty rate (1991)	53%	41%	53%
Poverty rate (2000)	36%	32%	42%
Poverty rate (2010)	17%	18%	27%
Gini index (1991)	0.53	0.61	0.60
Gini index (2000)	0.58	0.63	0.60
Gini index (2010)	0.51	0.58	0.59
GDP per capita (2000)	R$ 1,874	R$ 3,727	R$ 2,795
GDP per capita (2010)	R$ 5,653	R$ 11,767	R$ 9,283
HDI (1991)	0.47	0.52	0.47
HDI (2000)	0.58	0.63	0.53
HDI (2010)	0.69	0.72	0.66

Source: IBGE Cidades (2010); Brazilian Institute of Geography and Statistics (2003); IBGE MUNIC (2013); Ministry of Social Development (2013).

is not destiny as local governments can build democratic pathways that enable them to improve well-being.

Similarly, elections are a necessary but insufficient mechanism to explain variation in outcomes for these municipalities. We acknowledge the role that elections and mayoral leadership – of various ideological strains – can have on the lives of citizens because mayors are a dominant political actor in most municipalities. In our cases, Camaragibe has an established electoral history of left-leaning politics. Jaboatão has experienced electoral turnover, with episodes with nonprogrammatic mayors and a reformist centrist mayor. Finally, the Garanhuns electorate has voted for mayors from major parties, including the right, center-right, and center-left, with the variation on vote choice reflecting a general tendency around personalism in vote choice. Having competitive elections in these cities is important because it sets the stage for other pathways to be established and consolidated. Elected leaderships is needed for policies and programs that promote citizens' access to their citizenship rights. Yet the human development outcomes for Camaragibe, Jaboatão, and Garanhuns are not easily explained by electoral politics. Instead, it is the process of building institutions, implementing rights-based programs, and building an inclusive state that matters. Accomplishing these democratic processes requires the steady work of broad numbers of civil servants, government officials, and community leaders.

The three municipalities included in this chapter illustrate how the building (or lack thereof) of the three democratic pathways better explains the variation in social well-being improvements. Table 8.2 summarizes different aspects that illuminate the extent to which each municipality was able to build the democratic pathways. This chapter begins with a brief overview of the broader socioeconomic context of each municipality and then explains how our variables of interest – participation, social policy, and inclusive state capacity – contribute to divergent outcomes in human development. The reader should recall that these municipalities were selected based the "nested case" logic (Lieberman 2005), which uses mixed-method research strategies pairing large-N quantitative analysis with intensive case studies. In this chapter, we use process tracing to analyze specific characteristics of three Brazilian municipalities. Process tracing is a method that "provides information about mechanism and context" by meticulously tracing the steps in causal processes that connect inputs to outcomes (Collier et al. 2004: 253).

TABLE 8.2 *Case study municipalities: Social summary statistics*

	Camaragibe	Jaboatão dos Guararapes	Garanhuns
Infant mortality (1991)	43.1	41.6	52.2
Infant mortality (2000)	34.8	27.5	47.7
Infant mortality (2010)	14.2	16.0	19.5
School attendance ages 6–17 (1991)	65%	67%	71%
School attendance ages 6–17 (2000)	70%	71%	68%
School attendance ages 6–17 (2010)	84%	81%	77%
ENEM exam (percent passing in 2001)	70%	73%	66%
ENEM exam (percent passing in 2006)	82%	79%	74%
ENEM exam (percent passing in 2013)	91%	83%	80%
Women running for office (2004)[1]	0	6%	0%
Women running for office (2008)[1]	12%	6%	5%
Women running for office (2012)[1]	12%	8%	7%

Sources: Ministry of Social Development (2013); Ministry of Health (2013); Ministry of Education (2013); Superior Electoral Tribunal (2013).
[1] Includes female candidates running for municipal legislator and mayor.

FIGURE 8.1: Brazil and the state of Pernambuco

TABLE 8.3 *Case study municipalities: Democratic pathway summary statistics*

	Camaragibe	Jaboatão dos Guararapes	Garanhuns
Voluntary Policy Councils (2006)	8	1	0
Voluntary Policy Councils (2013)	15	5	2
Bolsa Família coverage (percent of eligible population receiving benefits in 2006)[1]	95%	58%	90%
Bolsa Família coverage (percent of eligible population receiving benefits in 2013)	74%	74%	64%
PSF coverage (percent of eligible population receiving benefits in 2006)	98%	22%	74%
PSF coverage (percent of eligible population receiving benefits in 2013)	90%	50%	79%
Administrative capacity score (2006) (IGD)	0.84	0.48	0.84
Administrative capacity score (2013) (IGD)	0.80	0.76	0.78

Source: IBGE Cidades (2010); IBGE MUNIC (2013); Ministry of Social Development (2013); Ministry of Health (2013); Ministry of Education (2013).
[1] The way Brazil's Ministry of Social Development calculated eligibility and coverage rates changed over time; these cities did not necessarily get worse at tracking and enrolling PBF recipients during this timeframe. Most cities in our dataset had coverage that exceeded 90 percent of the eligible population in the mid-2000s, with many exceeding 100 percent.

CAMARAGIBE, PE: STRONG PERFORMANCE

Among development scholars, Camaragibe is undoubtedly the most widely known of the three case study sites (Farah and Barboza 2000; Baiocchi et al. 2011; Hunter and Sugiyama 2017). The municipality is located in the greater metropolitan region of Recife and enjoys a reputation as a "good governance development city" for its administrative and policy reforms. Beginning in the 1990s, local leaders have won numerous awards for their innovations in public health, participatory public management, and services for women (Reis 2004; Baiocchi et al. 2011). The municipality's vibrant civil society and engagement with policy councils and conferences have been well documented (Santos 2002; Araújo 2003; Negreiros and da Fonte 2003; Oliveira 2003; Reis 2004; Moura 2009; Baiocchi et al. 2011). Importantly, the municipality's human development outcomes now rival those of far more affluent neighbors. For this reason, Camaragibe stands as an example of a "high-performing" municipality that has accomplished a great deal, despite serious structural challenges.

Camaragibe is a relatively new municipality, achieving its independence in 1982 when it broke away from a municipality that was economically geared toward the interior of the state (Farah and Barboza 2000). Camaragibe was much more focused on its eastern neighbor, the state capital of Recife. When Brazil returned to democratic rule in the mid-1980s, Camaragibe's citizens and democratically elected officials confronted a number of socioeconomic challenges including high poverty rates, housing vulnerability, and food insecurity. Economic vulnerability in Camaragibe is largely tied to low levels of economic development, both within the municipality's borders as well as in the greater metropolitan region. Notably, one study put 82 percent of Camaragibe's economic activity in the informal sector (Santos 2002). In this way, the municipality resembles smaller towns in the interior of Brazil's northeast because there are no major industries, government-based employment is limited, and there are few job opportunities. Camaragibe neighbors the state capital of Recife but it does not enjoy prime coastal real estate that can draw in tourism.

During the 1990s, Camaragibe began to build strong pathways to well-being. The emphasis on participatory institutions and citizenship rights was advanced by a political coalition of new social movements, community organizations, and the rural workers' labor union (*Sindicato dos Trabalhadores Rurais*) (Baiocchi et al. 2011).

Civil society strengthened during the democratization period, with community-based social movements in Camaragibe connecting with movements in *Casa Amarela*, a nearby neighborhood located in Recife. In the 1980s, this area [Camaragibe and *Casa Amarela*], experienced an expansive social mobilization around issues related to health and the urbanization of favelas (Oliveira 2003: 52).

The mobilization of civil society coincided with the election of a series of left-of-center mayors who strongly supported the inclusion of citizens into the formal, institutionalized governing systems (Baiocchi et al. 2011). Camaragibe was an early adopter of councils; they established the Municipal Health Council as early as 1991 (Law No. 104/91).

Camaragibe was a pioneering municipality, in Pernambuco, of citizen participation in public administration. Demands for citizen participation began with the political struggle, which occurred between 1989 and 1991, to establish municipal councils for health, and children and adolescents (Oliveira 2003: 52).

Camaragibe's elected governments were also pioneers in the area of rights-based social policies and in building an inclusive state apparatus. Camaragibe was also an early adopter of the Family Health Program (PSF), which allowed community-based health agents to work directly with families as early as 1994 (Rodrigues 1996). The government also invested in maternal health programs to address the dreadfully high rates of infant and maternal mortality. Beyond health, the government also adopted pioneering public policies for women, geared at reducing domestic violence and addressing social and economic exclusion (Farah and Barboza 2000). In addition, the government emphasized merit-based, professional hiring to ensure that quality services were provided. The government reoriented civil servants to develop and implement programs that would better enable citizens to access social rights formally guaranteed by the 1988 Constitution (Rodrigues 1996; Farah and Barboza 2000).

In sum, Camaragibe is a very poor municipality, lacking industry, tourism, and a property tax base and deriving much of its income from its location on the outskirts of a major city. It was the emergence of a new political coalition that sought to build new institutions that would lead to important advances in well-being. Despite numerous disadvantages, the municipal government greatly improved basic well-being among its citizens during the 2000–2013 period under review. Camaragibe is an excellent example that "wealth is not destiny," as it significantly over-performed to produce measurable improvements in well-being for their residents.

JABOATÃO DOS GUARARAPES: MIDDLING RESULTS

Jaboatão dos Guararapes offers important contrasts when compared to our other case study sites. Situated on the beautiful coast of Pernambuco and just south of the capital, Recife, Jaboatão has more municipal resources than most municipalities in Pernambuco and Brazil's northeast, but faces greater income inequality. The municipality is home to urban, industrial, and rural areas that create starkly different socioeconomic conditions for its population. Jaboatão's middle and upper classes reside in lovely coastal areas and generally work in Recife. Also noteworthy, Jaboatão has two distinct city centers. One is along the coast with high-rise apartment buildings that line the beach. A second center is a 30-to-45-minute drive from the vibrant beach region; the old city center feels like a distant small town of the interior. Poorer neighborhoods dominate the interior and rural regions of the geographically large municipality; many residents must travel an hour or two by bus to reach either of the two economic centers. Despite its relative wealth, Jaboatão's human development outcomes are "middling" and thus somewhat consistent with similar municipalities in Pernambuco and in the northeast.

During the 1990s, citizens and governments officials faced a complex set of challenges. Jaboatão has the second largest economy in the metropolitan region of Recife, with a combination of industry, services, tourism, and agriculture (IBGE MUNIC 2013). As a result of its relatively large local economy, the municipality is twice as wealthy as Camaragibe, when measured by GDP per capita. Despite greater overall resources, high rates of income inequality have meant that a large minority (32 percent) of residents in the early 2000s were poor (IBGE Cidades 2010). The poor in Jaboatão face many of the same physical infrastructure challenges common in Brazil's northeast, including low rates of sanitation, substandard housing, and high unemployment rates (IBGE MUNIC 2013). The poor in Jaboatão have encountered unreliable services, both in terms of access and in quality of essential municipal services, which hinder their prospects for improved quality of life.

During the 1980s and 1990s, Jaboatão did little to build the pathways that help to improve well-being. Civil society was weak, with few municipal-wide organizations, an absence of national-based NGOs, and a limited number of community-based organizations. This limited number of community organizations did not form the necessary alliances to pressure state and government officials to build programs and policies to address gaps in social needs (Fatima Lacerda, Jaboatão). There was no organized pressure to induce elected governments to create policies or programs that might produce an inclusive local state.

In addition, the municipality of Jaboatão has had a tumultuous political trajectory that has included numerous state interventions due to administrative mismanagement and local malfeasance (Lima 2011). Personalism, rather than programmatic party politics and an engaged civil society, and clientelism have been the main drivers in municipal electoral politics. Personal exchanges with voters for electoral support, such as offers of everything from free food baskets to coffins, helped solidify electoral victories for mayors elected in 1997 and 2001. During the 2000–2008 period, mayors in Jaboatão did not fully support existing councils or the national social programs it was responsible for managing and there was little to no administrative reform (Fatima Lacerda, Jaboatão).

Until 2009, Jaboatão's elected governments did not support public participation or national social programs, nor did they devote sufficient resources to bolster administrative performance and improve service delivery (Fatima Lacerda, Jaboatão). This dynamic appeared to reverse in 2009 with the entry of reformist mayor, Elias Gomes da Silva (2009–2012; 2013–2016). His election led to a political project of renewal that was based on the expansion and strengthening of councils, the restructuring of the administrative state, and expansions of social policies to eligible beneficiaries. Our research showed that the Gomes administration began the necessary steps of building pathways but was hampered by decades of weak administrative structures and a weak, disorganized civil society. Unfortunately, Jaboatão's results are not unusual and are similar to many Brazilian municipalities' weak improvements in well-being.

In sum, it is helpful to conceptualize Jaboatão as a relatively wealthy municipality that lies on the outskirts of a major city (Recife, the state capital). In Jaboatão, basic social indicators improved over the course of this study (2000–2013) but did not catch up to other, more highly performing municipalities in the region despite its economic advantages. As we explain in greater detail below, one mayoral administration (Gomes 2009–2012; 2013–2016) pursued opportunities to advance well-being through our pathways, but this administration faced significant challenges. Decades of poor administrative practices, corruption, and clientelism limited the Gomes mayoral administration's ability to implement reforms because it had to contend with decades of mismanagement. Thus, in many ways, Jaboatão reflects many Brazilian municipalities' general experience with participatory institutions, social programs, and state capacity.

GARANHUNS: LOW PERFORMANCE

Garanhuns, located 239 kilometers from Recife, is situated in the high plains in the interior of the state. This small municipality is best known for cooler temperatures, its Winter Festival, and the nearby birthplace of former President Luiz Inácio Lula da Silva (2003–2006;

2007–2010).[2] The local economy consists largely of tourism and major industries, including general services, agriculture, and the production of folk art (Gomes and Barboza 2003). Garanhuns markets itself as the "Pernambucan Switzerland" to attract tourists to the interior of the state. As the regional hub for thirty-two neighboring municipalities, the city is home to many essential services utilized by area residents, including hospital care and tertiary education. Compared to Camaragibe, annual per capita income in Garanhuns is higher USD 3714 but its poverty rate is also ten percentage points higher, at 27 percent (IBGE MUNIC 2013). Despite some economic advantages, Garanhuns has the lowest rates of human development of all our case study municipalities.

The municipality of Garanhuns, similar to Jaboatão, has high rates of income inequality because it is a relatively wealthy city with a large class of poor and extremely poor citizens. For some groups, the struggle for equality dates back centuries to conflicts between Portuguese settlers and African slaves. Afro-Brazilians have faced continuous persecution and the legacy of racial discrimination is still reflected in area settlement patterns. For example, the Castainho community (population 728) is a remaining *quilombo* (former runaway slave community) located within the municipality of Garanhuns (Machado 2009). Racial inequality remains a feature of current social context in Garanhuns; 62 percent of the population who earn up to one monthly minimum wage identify as either *pardo* (mixed-race) or *preto* (black).[3] Social investments in areas that particularly benefit the poor, such as primary health, education, and sanitation, have lagged behind investments in other areas that are thought to produce economic growth. The

---

[2] President Luiz Inácio Lula da Silva was born in Caetés, Pernambuco, part of the Garanhuns microregion. When President Lula was born, Caetés was formally part of the municipality of Garanhuns, but Caetés would later break off to become its own municipality.

[3] Brazilian census data on race relies on self-identification. A considerable body of research suggests Brazilians display "racial fluidity," where racial self-identity can vary across situations and contexts, or over time. Both social status and skin color are thought to matter for racial classification. Telles and Paschel argue that contemporary Brazil displays features of "polarization" for some "pardos" (mixed-race individuals) where higher status whitens them into a "branco" (white) category, whereas for others higher levels of education darken them as they become more likely to affirm their identity as "preto" (black) (2014: 887). Afro-Brazilian political mobilization, along with new federal affirmative action policies, are thought to contribute to growing and positive self-identification among Afro-Brazilian. Racial demographics in Garanhuns likely reflect these broader trends as well as the lack of civil society mobilization to raise black consciousness. Brazil Census 2010.

government has not pursued pro-poor policies and civil society has not effectively pressed local governments to address housing, sanitation, health, or gender equality.

During the 1980s and 1990s, Garanhuns made little progress on building pathways that might improve well-being. As is often the case in medium-sized, rural municipalities, civil society organizing in Garanhuns is weak; civil society has therefore not generated consistent pressure on the government to create a robust participatory system or to support rights-based social programs. In addition, candidates for elective office tend to run on personal appeals rather than on national party platforms (Marta, Garanhuns).[4] Since democratization, the municipality has elected mayors affiliated with major parties, including the rightist PFL/ DEM, the center-right PMDB, and the center-left PDT. Recent mayors have advanced general economic development goals, but pro-poor policy priorities have been largely absent from their political agendas (Silvia, Garanhuns). Worse, political leadership in Garanhuns has actively undermined public participation in policy-making processes and provides little support to national social programs. Garanhuns's mayors have also diverted resources away from service delivery in areas that impact well-being, such as health care and education.

In sum, it is helpful to conceptualize Garanhuns as a relatively well-off municipality in the poorer interior of the state. It is characterized by decades of poor administrative practices, corruption, and clientelism, and by a weak civil society. There are few organized groups advocating for policy or political reform. For all these reasons, Garanhuns has the potential to do better on human development but falls short on building its citizens' capabilities.

This brief overview of socioeconomic and political dynamics in Camaragibe, Jaboatão dos Guararapes, and Garanhuns offers a snapshot of three municipalities. Table 8.1 summarizes these municipalities' main socioeconomic characteristics. It is important to note that their challenges are not unique to Brazil's northeast or other developing settings. Camaragibe has gone far to overcome serious obstacles to advance well-being. In Jaboatão, extensive efforts, during the 2009–2016 period, to induce change confronted a history of policy neglect that required policy reformers to build from a very low point, complicating efforts to catch up. Finally, Garanhuns has yet to initiate broad efforts to improve

---

[4] We use pseudonyms to refer to interview respondents who wished to remain anonymous. We refer to these sources only by first names that were assigned to them.

its citizens' well-being – a failure reflected in its poor outcomes surrounding well-being.

Importantly, these municipalities' economic conditions are not destiny for their citizens' well-being. High levels of economic wealth do not necessarily produce better outcomes for residents, nor do low levels necessarily undermine human development performance. As McGuire (2010) notes for the health sector, the overall level of resources can be less important than decisions on how to invest resources. Decisions about how to spend public resources often come down to political and administrative priorities. Camaragibe is noteworthy because it made the most significant strides toward building pathways that contributed to citizens' well-being. A reformist government in Jaboatão, led by Mayor Gomes, sought to build these pathways but they had to contend with decades of administrative malfeasance and limited state capacity; Gomes also had very limited partners in civil society. Thus, even where reformist leadership is in place, it may not be enough to overcome decades of policy neglect.

In the next sections, we draw on case studies of these three municipalities to examine how democratic practices worked to further well-being. Tables 8.2 and 8.3 provides a brief snapshot of summary statistics on the quantitative pathway mechanisms for these municipalities. The qualitative analysis focuses on our three theoretically motivated factors: participatory institutions, federal social policy, and local state capacity. These three pathways impact all stages of the policy cycle to improve well-being. Councils influence agenda setting, formulation, approval, implementation, and oversight. Social policy influences policy implementation and oversight, but municipalities that perform well can innovate to create new programs and influence the next policy cycle at all stages. Finally, state capacity is central to policy implementation, but well-trained, funded personnel may also innovate to create programs and engage the policy cycle anew.

EXPLAINING OUTCOMES: HOW COUNCILS AFFECT WELL-BEING

Public policy councils are democratic policy-making venues designed to link citizens, union representatives, civil servants, and municipal public officials in an effort to improve the quality of public goods provisions. A growing body of evidence, as demonstrated in previous chapters and elsewhere, shows that councils are associated with improvements in well-being. In this section, we seek to illuminate how the variation in councils' presence and performance contributes to differences in well-being. We draw on interviews with civil society leaders, municipal civil servants, and local political appointees to show how policy councils can alter policy-making processes, thus changing the provision of public goods. It is important to keep in mind that the mere presence of councils will not necessarily produce positive impacts; rather, public policy management councils offer the opportunity to generate and influence new governance processes.

Field research in Camaragibe, Jaboatão, and Garanhuns reveals important variation regarding how councils are incorporated into policy-making processes. Put simply, not all municipalities have vibrant councils and it can be difficult to sustain them over time. In Camaragibe, we find that government officials and their civil society allies created a robust council system that contributed to improvements in well-being. In Jaboatão, we find that a newly elected reformist mayor invested heavily in the expansion of a council system but these new councils were hampered by a legacy of underperforming councils and a poorly functioning administrative state. Finally, Garanhuns has a very poorly performing council system, thereby limiting the development of cogovernance processes and oversight mechanisms that might improve public goods provision.

We identify several mechanisms that theoretically contribute to building better functioning councils, which in turn promote better public policies, and ultimately improve well-being. The following features are basic components of vibrant councils. First, councils are able to incorporate a cross section of community members, which expands the number of voices and interests represented in meetings. Second, councils connect public officials to citizens, which creates an information exchange that builds a shared knowledge base. This knowledge generates better awareness of citizens' needs and of how governments might be able to meet those needs. Third, councils institutionalize participation throughout the policy-making cycle. These participatory institutions allow citizens to engage in agenda setting, deliberation, program evaluation, and oversight. When government officials formally institutionalize these procedures for citizen engagement, they advance the democratic and policy spirit behind them.

We posit that improving policy provision is crucial to improving well-being because it enables the state to deliver a broader range of better-quality services in underserved communities. We begin this section with an explanation of a context where the council system works well, contributing to improvements in public goods provision and well-being.

GOVERNING WITH COUNCILS

Brazil's policy councils reflect one part of a broad effort to establish participatory institutions and incorporate citizens in policy-making processes. Some Brazilian municipalities created vibrant council systems that directly influence policy debates, provide policy oversight, and enable meaningful public engagement in policy making (Avritzer 2009; Lüchmann and Almeida 2010; Abers and Keck 2013; Gurza Lavalle et al. 2015).

Commitments to Councils Advance Well-Being

Among our three cases, Camaragibe emerges as the clearest example of the benefits of state-society engagement through policy councils and conferences. The municipality was an early adopter of councils – they established the Municipal Health Council as early as 1991 (Law No. 104/91). In addition, they created a large number of councils. By 2017, there were twenty operational councils (five mandated by federal legislation and fifteen voluntarily adopted) in the municipality. Numerous governments and a broad cross section of neighborhood associations, community groups, and social movements invested heavily in the council system, which then positively affected public deliberation, public goods provisions, and, ultimately, well-being. We briefly turn to basic features of how these councils function in Camaragibe.

Camaragibe incorporates a wide range of citizens, which expands the number and breadth of interests represented in the policy councils. These venues are not "captured" by a small segment of the population but successfully incorporate neighborhood associations, social movements, labor unions, service delivery providers, and government officials (Eduardo Santos, Camaragibe; Vera Leão, Camaragibe; Júlio Antão, Camaragibe; Denivaldo Freire, Camaragibe; Baiocchi et al. 2011). We find that civil society representatives view themselves as intermediaries between government officials and community members. Most also emphasize their role in promoting knowledge and awareness to the wider community. As one member of the health council explained: "The challenge we must overcome is related to participation and awareness. When it comes to 'social control,' it's the people who vote. . . The people need to be aware of their power to monitor representatives" (Eduardo Santos, Camaragibe). Governments thus provide information, which allows citizens to monitor a wide swath of actors – council representatives, civil servants, political appointees, and elected officials – which increases the likelihood of producing better policies.

Successive municipal administrations have supported a diverse set of policy councils. Several of our interviewees in Camaragibe reported that once new councils are created there are very few differences between voluntary and mandated councils, suggesting that the government invested in them equally (Cynthia Barbosa, Camaragibe; Fernando Antonio, Camaragibe; Laudicea Ramos de Oliveira, Camaragibe; Eduardo Santos, Camaragibe). Administrative, logistical, and political support helps to institutionalize these entities, which means that they are no longer isolated from key policy issues but are integrated into how the government selects and then implements policy projects. (See Wampler 2015.)

Many of our interviewees worked with multiple councils, often beginning with the education or health council and then moving to other, more specialized councils (Júlio Antão, Camaragibe; Eduardo Gaspar, Camaragibe). Some civil society representatives engage with more than one council at the same time. Civil servants also tend to meet with two or more councils on a regular basis. When this level of engagement happens, participants report that they are more aware of debates in other councils and platforms from municipal policy conferences, and that they can therefore reinforce policy agendas across venues (Laudicea Ramos de Oliveira, Camaragibe). As one administrator explained, "The health council meets twice a week and the councils related to health meet at least once a month. This ensures that no one forgets what we're working towards and that we can take small steps to achieve it" (Lúcia Teixeira, Camaragibe). Another official in the social assistance sector used a metaphor to convey a similar sentiment: "The councils all work together and do it through the Social Assistance Center, with the Social Assistance Council as the hub and the councils as spokes on a wheel. The wheel connects the councils to each other too" (Eduardo Gaspar, Camaragibe). From this we infer that the government recognizes that most policy problems cannot be tackled within a single council, but that it is necessary to support multiple councils across related issue areas. The presence of multiple voluntary councils therefore creates a "ratcheting-up effect" that produces mutually reinforcing effects on the policy-making process.

Councils affect well-being by creating a space for meaningful exchange of information between civil society and municipal officials. For instance, councils inform government policy by providing municipal administrators with better information on citizens' needs and demands. Camaragibe's Secretary of Social Assistance reported: "Every day I spend the afternoon out of the office speaking at council meetings and conferences to hear what the people need and help them enroll in social assistance programs" (Edvaldo Ferreira, Camaragibe). Civil society representatives also share information with municipal authorities. "We are working to identify needs in each region, bring that to the council, and then the council takes it to city hall" (Givaldo José da Silva Nascimento, Camaragibe). Thus, an ongoing exchange of information involves both government officials and civil society representatives. Camaragibe recruits a broad cross section of the population to participate in policy-making processes, which enables the government to receive inputs from a variety of areas. In addition, government officials share information with council members. This expands representatives' policy knowledge, but also has spillover effects as council members take this information back to their communities. The councils thus connect government officials to hard-to-reach citizens.

Policy councils also serve an important role by assisting citizens and CSOs to engage the policy-making process. Numerous interviewees asserted that policy councils play an important role in preparing the biannual, thematic municipal policy conferences as well as incorporating policy recommendations from these conferences. In contrast with councils, conferences engage a greater number of citizens and are intended to establish an agenda for key sectors, such as health, education, and social assistance (Pogrebinschi and Samuels 2014). These conferences provide important opportunities to stipulate policy priorities, advance new agenda items, and highlight areas that have not yet advanced. Policy proposals developed at conferences are submitted to councils and the mayor's office. Between the biannual conferences, councils are useful venues to allow for participation that shapes the ongoing, current policy-making process. Interviewees provided specific issues whereby participants were demanding improvements in policy design or delivery. For example, officials in the education council expressed concern over access to education for disabled students (Fernando Antonio, Camaragibe; Cynthia Barbosa Camaragibe). The council's intervention in the area of student disability led the city council to reallocate funds to make schools more wheelchair accessible (Edvaldo Ferreira, Camaragibe; Denwaldo

Freire, Camaragibe). More narrowly, in Jaboatão, Moisés explained that his health council convinced civil servants to purchase a safer kind of disposable needle that was produced locally (Moisés Gomes dos Santos, Jaboatão).

Beyond agenda setting and policy design, policy councils have the clear function of providing ongoing monitoring and oversight of existing municipal service delivery. For example, in Jaboatão, one council member asserted: "The role of the [social assistance] council is to oversee and monitor, principally the institutions that operate here: Bolsa Família, the Social Assistance Reference Centers, the Specialized Social Assistance Reference Centers – this is the role of the council" (Agenilda Ramos Nascimento, Jaboatão). Citizens working in councils use oversight mechanisms much as legislators do in national and state legislatures – to monitor the actions of elected officials, civil servants, and private, third-party service providers. In some instances, council members' oversight responsibility can lead them to seek advice or remedies from a wide range of state actors. Council members' routes into and across the state vary depending on the sector in which they serve. For instance, some council members directly engage the federal-level Ministry of Health because of the ministry's role in directing the PSF. Others engage state-level ministries as well as government officials in other municipalities.

Part of the health council's oversight role over the PSF program is to monitor officials and service delivery. For example, in Camaragibe, council members recognized that many of the *Agentes Comunitario de Saúde* (Community Health Agents) were themselves sick and could not work due to cancer diagnoses, depression, and other illnesses. Council members noted that the population has grown, there are greater needs, and the municipality has not resolved the problems facing community health agents. Rather than rely on responses from municipal authorities, they scheduled a meeting with an auditor from the federal Ministry of Health who explained federal hiring regulations and why it would be difficult to simply reassign these dedicated health workers (Eduardo Santos, Camaragibe). The council demonstrated a willingness to seek external guidance to fulfill its oversight role, which suggests that the councils are now part of an increasingly intricate governing process.

Fiscal oversight represents yet another way that councils monitor policy implementation. Councils are responsible for overseeing public accounts related to their policy area. In sectors where local administrators receive federal transfers for the provision of services – such as education and health – this fiscal responsibility is particularly important for transparency. In theory, fiscal oversight should also hinder the diversion of funds for other areas (public or otherwise). "There are a lot of resources that get to the city and we have to be certain that those resources are being used for those objectives" (Elaine Alves de Britto, Camaragibe). Again in the health sector, a council member asserted: "The council is the monitor of public policies and the fiscal watchdog of public resources that come into the municipalities from all three levels of the federal state. . . . Thus, social control is the society's control. It is this [type of] participation that we defend from having been part of the process" (Eduardo Santos, Camaragibe).

Finally, we learned that council members engage in day-to-day service delivery practices that help individuals and even save lives. They directly intervene to provide support to specific individuals in need. For example, a Camaragibe council member affiliated with both the health and women's councils reported: "The tutelary council has been very helpful for girls and mothers because it helps us find help for people who are abused and can't get away" (Laudiceas Ramos de Oliveira, journalist and member of the health and women's councils, Camaragibe). The immediate assistance for individuals in crisis was also a theme brought up by Elaine Alves de Britto, who worked on the Children's and Youth Council in Camaragibe. As she explained,

We've had to do some difficult things, such as be with a child, and arrive at an institution and demand that this institution, at that instant, guarantee the child's safety. For example, we've had various instances where adolescents will have to spend the night at a police station; I've taken children into my home; I've taken a child to a health center, so that they can be housed overnight, for example. We know very well that these were inadequate responses given what is needed. But we've done this to guarantee the rights of the child and adolescent, who needed the help of the Tutelary Council.

While these kinds of activities go above and beyond the scope of responsibility for policy councils, it is clear that members who are passionate and dedicated to the advancement of social rights take steps to engage directly with the population they serve.

In sum, municipal governments that adopt and support public policy management councils produce several policy and democratic advances that improve well-being. We highlight three important mechanisms for advancing well-being. First, councils allow for the inclusion of a cross section of diverse perspectives, which expands the number of voices and interests represented in meetings. Second, councils promote information-sharing between government officials and citizens. This type of exchange is mutually beneficial and allows administrators to improve services based on ongoing feedback. Third, these venues help institutionalize participation throughout the policy-making cycle; citizens can engage in agenda setting, ongoing monitoring, and oversight functions. Altogether, these features assist in improving services and reaching the neediest populations.

An Attempt to Build Councils Falls Short

Our field research reveals that not all municipalities have vibrant councils; some governments will have to take steps to build effective participation. As noted above, governments must be actively involved in building and sustaining councils. Similarly, civil society must readily engage these participatory spaces. The municipality of Jaboatão illustrates the challenges a reformist government faces when attempting to build a meaningful council system.

Jaboatão spent the 1990s and most of the 2000s with a weak council system because a series of governments was disinterested and because civil society was not strong enough to force governments to provide additional support (Fatima Lacerda, Jaboatão; Karina Antunes, Jaboatão). The federally mandated councils, Health and Education, operated during that time, but did so minimally. The year 2009 marked a shift in support for participatory institutions as a reformist mayor sought to inject life into the moribund council system. Importantly, Elias Gomes's mayoral administration invested heavily in three areas of reform – building participatory councils, overhauling the administrative state, and improving delivery of social programs. When the Gomes administration entered office, they were unable to verify the names of the officially elected members of existing councils because the outgoing administrators did not keep clear records and the elections had not been properly recorded in the municipality's Official Record (Fatima Lacerda, Jaboatão). The previous mayoral administrations provided limited administrative support for the councils as well. All interviewees indicated that in 2008 the council system was very weak, which made it difficult for the government to collect policy input from citizens and limited activists' ability to monitor government officials and policy implementation. Quite simply, the council system was not an institutionalized part of the policy-making process between 2000 and 2008.

The Gomes mayoral administrations (2009–2012, 2013–2016) sought to actively expand the council system. During Gomes's first two years in office, the municipality created seven new councils, including those in such new policy areas such as human rights and LBGT affairs. The government also invested in existing councils by providing logistical support that included proper staffing and by providing physical space for council members to meet. More importantly, the government expended considerable effort to link the different policy areas. Administrators sought to expand connections across government departments because social and economic problems could not be solved by working within specific departments (e.g., health or education) (Fatima Lacerda, Jaboatão). Finally, the government hired skilled policy professionals from across the metropolitan area – people with extensive experience working in formal policy fields as well as with citizen-engagement councils.

The results of these efforts are decidedly mixed. Interviewees clearly identify how the government invested extensive time and effort to expand the role of councils. High-level political appointees attended meetings. Government officials served on multiple councils with the intention of building a base of knowledge about citizens' needs and policy options. Government officials built new ties with civil society and established policies that addressed problems in a more comprehensive fashion. However, government officials also struggled to incorporate a broad cross section of the population into the policy process due to civil society's underdevelopment. Citizen participants were unable to make the councils into vibrant, independent democratic venues because their numbers were low and they lacked a history of engaging in either contentious or deliberative politics. One administrator's comments on Jaboatão aptly capture the sentiments of all of our interviews: "Civil society is very disorganized" (Jantene Torres, Jaboatão).

Jaboatão's council system expanded during two mayoral administrations. Jaboatão now has more councils than Garanhuns, but far fewer than Camaragibe. Government support for councils was greater in Jaboatão than in Garanhuns, but far less than in Camaragibe. Government officials recruited some new participants and incorporated their demands into some policies. We have extensive anecdotal evidence that suggests that the council system contributed to specific, immediate policy changes (e.g., building a women's shelter; working more closely with parents of school-aged children) but we were unable to marshal any compelling evidence that systematically connects this expansion to improved policy outcomes. The Gomes administration's efforts to build a more robust council system failed to move Jaboatão above the middle of the pack in terms of local democratic performance and citizens' well-being.

An Absence of Councils Hinders Well-Being

Some Brazilian municipalities have not built well-functioning councils or council systems. It is first necessary to recall that policy management councils are relatively new institutions. By the mid-2000s, the federal government required municipalities to adopt councils in five areas – education, health, social services, human rights, and children's rights. Municipal governments had to work internally as well as reach out to interested citizens to create councils. The case of Garanhuns demonstrates how government's unwillingness to strengthen these venues and the inability of civil society actors to successfully pressure government officials has the effect of undermining these new institutions.

Our interview subjects in Garanhuns and Jaboatão identified several culprits that explain why councils do not perform well. First, municipal officials can undermine the effectiveness of councils by only doing the minimum necessary. Under this scenario, the council may exist on paper but government officials are not involved in the heavy lifting of bringing these councils to life. For example, councils may not hold elections regularly to elect new council members as was the case in Jaboatão. Additionally, meetings may be held too infrequently to create a policy debate. Garanhuns's experience reflects this concern in the sense that it has councils in the required areas, but many of them meet very infrequently. For instance, we heard that the health council only meets once a year (Marta, Garanhuns; Dorvalina Maria Maciel de Vasconcelos, Garanhuns). Garanhuns has only voluntarily adopted a small number of councils, all of which are related to education. Thus, some participatory institutions exist on paper in Garanhuns, and those that do exist tend not have the government support necessary to improve performance in their issue areas.

Government officials in Garanhuns were also reluctant to foster the growth of an independent council system. Councils are thus not independent from the government officials and may serve only to rubber-stamp government decisions. For instance, the education council lay largely dormant for a four-year period (Dorvalina Maria Maciel de Vasconcelos, Garanhuns). As one member explained, municipal officials never attended education council meetings, which depressed interest on the part of citizens. Without citizen engagement, you have a self-fulfilling prophecy that makes the councils less effective than they could be (Washington Silva Vieira, Garanhuns). Some of the council members associated with social assistance reported the municipality made the necessary fiscal contributions to councils by providing office space, a computer, car, and driver for the education council (Yacy Novaes, Garanhuns; Diana Maria da Conceição, Garanhuns). However, this support does not extend across all councils that exist on paper in the municipality.

The absence of an independent and robust civil society can also undermine the potential effectiveness of policy councils. The initial push for councils is associated with the health care movement in São Paulo in the early 1980s. The idea for the councils centered on a larger role for citizens than for government officials. When municipalities lack a vibrant civil society and citizens willing to participate, it becomes more much more difficult for nongovernment actors to influence these bodies. In the case of Garanhuns, civil society is too weakly organized to make use of councils (Marta, Garanhuns). In the absence of organized interests, personal and kin-based loyalties tend to motivate participation. When such personal loyalties exist, we are less likely to find the kind of autonomous oversight and engagement intended with councils. Most of our respondents in Garanhuns reported that the municipality lacks a commitment to vibrant civic engagement through policy councils. When this happens, the benefits of a shared participatory policy venue for citizens and officials to monitor policy fall by the wayside. The result is a missed opportunity to educate citizens, engage with civil society, and meaningfully pursue policy that promotes well-being.

As a result, municipalities with weak councils lose the benefit of information exchange because governments are not necessarily interested in gathering information and demands from citizens in these formal venues. In turn, citizens and CSOs are not encouraged to work within these venues because they function poorly (Washington Silva Vieira, Garanhuns). Participating in council meetings is often a frustrating experience for those citizens who are present because their efforts do not influence policy. The lack of results then discourages the growth of a stronger civil society. This can compound the disenchantment with the participatory process that occurs when municipalities are unable to respond to the feedback that councils provide. For instance, council members in Garanhuns cited low levels of fiscal capacity as a serious challenge (Yacy Novaes, Garanhuns; Diana Maria da Conceição, Garanhuns). José Juca, also from Garanhuns, provided a clear example where the municipality has not yet been able to address uneven access to Social Assistance Reference Centers (CRAS). All of these centers are in the urban part of the municipality; this makes access much more difficult for rural residents who have to travel far for social assistance services. Limited federal and local resources have prevented the government from adequately addressing this issue (José Juca de Melo Filho, Garanhuns).

Councils present opportunities to share information, enrich the public debate, directly intervene to solve immediate problems, and monitor past and current policy implementation when governments, civil society organizations, and citizens work together within the council system. These processes contribute to improvements in well-being, most notably in Camaragibe. Camaragibe's policies improved well-being, despite relatively high poverty rates and low economic productivity. However, incorporating the councils into a policy-making process is not easy. Officials in Garanhuns made little effort to create vibrant councils. Officials in Jaboatão successfully expanded the number of councils and incorporated a greater number of actors, but did not support the councils at the same level as Camaragibe.

EXPLAINING OUTCOMES: HOW SOCIAL POLICY AFFECTS WELL-BEING

In principle, well-designed and operated social programs advance well-being by addressing basic needs. We expect peoples' lives to improve if health, education, and social assistance programs work properly; children will learn more, misery will decline, and people will live longer, healthier lives. Yet development practitioners note that even well-designed social policies can fail to achieve promised results. The diversity of local experiences can sabotage well-planned national programs, especially in large federal countries like Brazil. For instance, fiscal corruption can divert funds from the needy into the pockets of the powerful and local politicians may divert state or federal funds for personal gain (Ames 2001; Hagopian 1996). Similarly, disinterested local leaders may hinder proper implementation of programs through neglect or outright political manipulation, such as vote buying (Desposato 2007). All to say, well-designed social policies should advance well-being but there are reasons why they may not do so.

Field research in Camaragibe, Jaboatão, and Garanhuns revealed important variation in the ways social policies contribute to human development outcomes. We find that Garanhuns has the lowest performance in operating federal social programs. Its administration of health and social assistance centers displays low levels of administrative autonomy coupled with local political interference and indifference. The municipality also lacks locally designed and implemented equity-enhancing, pro-poor initiatives. Jaboatão represents a middling case. Interviewees reported that the municipality largely neglected the implementation of social policies prior to 2009. Administrative reforms under Mayor Elias Gomes sought to better organize social service delivery in areas like health, social assistance, education, and poverty relief. Local authorities also developed new initiatives in the area of human rights. Yet historic neglect has meant advances in this area have been slow to produce improvements in well-being. Finally, we found evidence of robust implementation of federal programs in Camaragibe. A technocratic approach to service delivery across multiple sectors has served their citizens well. Successive governments created inclusive social programs that were equity-enhancing and focused on improving well-being.

Several factors account for the variation regarding how the delivery of social policy at the municipal level affects well-being. Social programs work best when administrators frame their work in terms of the state's responsibilities and social rights. Each of the programmatic areas we explore here is protected under Brazil's 1988 Constitution. However, not all local governments view social policy in rights-based terms. A rights-based framework is particularly important because it signals that program benefits are not personal handouts and that all citizens have equal access. Social policies also work best when there are low levels of political interference in everyday operations. Mayors and municipal legislators' political interference on behalf of friends, political supporters, and potential voters greatly compromises the integrity of these programs. Finally, administrators must have the latitude to operate programs through technocratic decision-making based on their communities' unique needs. This enables local innovation, unique program development, and synergies across sectors. As Socorro Araújo explained, "The history of social assistance policy in Brazil is a history of clientelism, handouts, paternalism, all the 'isms' in life, used to promote local officials... Today, the federal government has played a very important role [in reversing this]" (Socorro Araújo, Jaboatão). That means that in practice the municipal government has sought to identify the neediest population and to focus its energies for greater effectiveness.

Program framing, administrative autonomy, and a technocratic approach are important because they play a role in the administration of essential services. The social policies we explore in this book have varying program designs with nuanced operational rules. The Bolsa Família is designed to insulate it from local political interference (Lindert et al. 2007;

Sugiyama and Hunter 2013; Fried 2012). Other programs, such as the Family Health Program, Social Assistance Reference Centers (CRAS), and Specialized Social Assistance Reference Centers (CREAS), have fewer protections against local manipulation as municipalities enjoy greater autonomy in local administrative decision-making. Federal transfers and regulations make these programs available locally, but they are more prone to political machinations as local officials handle areas such as hiring, procurement, and the geographic distribution of services. Other sectors such as women's rights, human rights, anti-racism, and LGBT policy lack large-scale federal programs altogether. Policies in these issue areas occur more autonomously and vary locally, although they may receive moral and ideological support from national social movements, NGOs, and federal agencies. To preview our argument in this section, Camaragibe has all three administrative mechanisms in place – a social rights framework, low levels of political interference, and a technocratic approach to decision-making – and thus drives human development by performing better across all policy arenas. Jaboatão made efforts to address these areas beginning in 2009, but faced extensive administrative deficits and thus produced some middling results. Finally, Garanhuns has trouble across all three areas and displays the lowest levels of human development outcomes.

Strong, Rights-Based Social Programs Advance Well-Being

Camaragibe's administrators were early adopters of a rights-based framework for service delivery. Throughout our interviews, administrators and council members representing civil society consistently framed social policies as fitting within a rights-based framework. Our interviewees made reference to general "social rights" as well as to specific rights, such as the "rights of the child." They often cited federal statutes and constitutional principles for why their programmatic areas were important and to define their obligations to fulfill those rights through public policy. For instance, government officials view spending associated with the Family Health Program, Bolsa Família, and primary education as part of the state's duty to fulfill citizens' rights. Eduardo Antonio, an education council member, commented that the promotion of rights was part of their aims and responsibilities on councils. Similarly, municipal administrator Fernando Antonio in Camaragibe emphasized that his department works hard to incorporate everyone into the educational system: "The government administration believes that education has the power to change people's lives. For this reason, they have regular campaigns to ensure people are aware of their right to education, no matter their special needs." This inclusionary discourse was important because it informed their professional outlook as well as how they communicated with beneficiaries. One sees the potential to enhance citizenship when beneficiaries come to see social programs in rights-based terms, rather than handouts.[5]

Low levels of political interference and administrative autonomy are a second important feature of Camaragibe's success in managing social policies. Remarkably, our respondents reported that they operate federal social programs without local political interference from mayors or city council members. According to Cynthia Barbosa from Camaragibe:

There have been major gains in women's and children's education and health because of national programs that the local politicians can't mess up; Bolsa, Minha Casa, Minha Vida [My House, My Life], and SUS [Universal Health System] programs have all been very helpful. . . The politicians can't mess with the national programs very much because we have so much support from the public and organized civil society.

In this case, local managers of federal social programs have been effective in managing programs and collaborating with civil society to protect them from local political interference. These federal programs are administered largely as technocrats in Brasília designed them to be run. As we note below, this is not the case everywhere. In other municipalities, issues such as the geographic distribution of public services can be distorted due to local politicians' interventions.

Administrative autonomy matters because it contributes to an administrative culture of technocratic decision-making. We found evidence that Camaragibe's administrators were using technocratic tools to reach vulnerable groups in the areas of social assistance and health. The Bolsa Família program staff explained the value of information from the Unified Registry to understand their municipality's needy population. The registry, with hundreds of questions, provides municipal officials with details on the social, economic, and living conditions of the poor in their city. For instance, they can learn about family composition, housing conditions, and access to clean water. As part of the conditionalities associated with the program, public officials also determine which families are in need of additional social support. Interviews

---

[5] Previous research by Hunter and Sugiyama (2014) uncovered the linkages between policy rights-based framing and beneficiaries' sense of agency in Camaragibe.

with local coordinators reinforced the importance of the Unified Registry for their work with vulnerable populations. For instance, the Bolsa Família coordinator and the Social Assistance department work closely together and use the Unified Registry to identify families at risk and deliver services at the individual, neighborhood, and microregional levels (Edvaldo Ferreira, Camaragibe). Specifically, they use the Unified Registry to connect beneficiaries to other programs, such as the Social Assistance Protection for Families program, as well as to identify those who have special needs and are eligible for additional services (Eduardo Gaspar, Camaragibe).

The health sector is more administratively complex, yet the municipality has managed to sustain preventive care programs and outcomes. Camaragibe has the longest-running experience in Brazil with preventive medicine through the PSF program. As such, it is possible to see the benefits of sustained and inclusive efforts to provide primary health care. According to one municipal health worker, the health secretariat's general focus on preventive medicine and education in the poor areas has led to health care advances (Lúcia Teixera, Camaragibe). Overall, Camaragibe has fared much better than other municipalities and managed to achieve nearly full coverage of PSF for the entire city.

In the end, these federal programs work as they were intended to. The civil servants we interviewed emphasized the important role of these programs to address basic needs. As one municipal administrator explained: "Bolsa Família works directly to give people money and I think a big part of Camaragibe's good performance comes from these programs. They are designed to help people and that's exactly what they do" (Eduardo Gaspar, Camaragibe). Edvaldo reinforced this notion: "Social assistance programs [such as Bolsa Família] put money in the people's pockets and gives them services they need. Camaragibe has done well in signing up more eligible Bolsa recipients than elsewhere" (Edvaldo Ferreira, Camaragibe). As a former coordinator of the Bolsa Família program explained, the municipality has had some success stories where children stayed in school where they would not have otherwise, and now they attend university (Gabriela Nascimento Dos Santos; Camaragibe).

In sum, Camaragibe stands out among our three municipalities as having successfully implemented federally funded social programs. The social programs, by and large, worked on the ground as they were designed to work.

Incomplete Social Policy Produces Modest Gains

Jaboatão's mixed political trajectory allows us to examine how the effectiveness of federal social policy can change over time. Our interviews reveal that, prior to 2009, the municipality faced many challenges related to social service delivery. Administrative reform in 2009 attempted to deal with existing challenges and had modest success.

As the new mayor, Elias Gomes's first challenge was to reverse a traditional political culture where social policies were viewed as grist for machine politics. Previous mayors were known for vote-buying practices where they distributed everything from food baskets to coffins near elections. As a result, progressive reformers had to change the way the municipality framed social provisioning. The administrators we spoke with from the Elias administrations (2009–2012; 2013–2016) all held the opinion that social policies fit within a rights-based framework. We heard this rights-based discourse from civil servants and CSO members across various sectors, including health, education, and social assistance. Some new areas of work such as human rights and LBGT rights also clearly incorporated rights-based discourse. Public officials' framing of social policy in rights-based terms is particularly important because it represents an attempt to reverse historical practices where political brokers captured public resources for personal and political gain.

Administrative autonomy from local political interference reflected a second challenge for the government officials to overcome. Through much of the early 2000s, Jaboatão was known for ineffective social policy, at best, and, at worst, for the political distribution of public resources. As one source explained, Jaboatão had made few administrative investments prior to 2009. "The neighboring city, Recife, underwent administrative reforms in the mid-1980s and 1990s to modernize civic engagement and management, but these reform efforts never went as far in Jaboatão; I'm afraid Jaboatão was known as a lost cause, unfortunately" (Fatima Lacerda, Jaboatão). Thus, Jaboatão was twenty years behind the state capital in terms of the administrative reforms necessary to support decent social policy provision. However, reformist Mayor Gomes began operating autonomously to promote more equitable service delivery when he established his administrative team in 2009. The new leadership team created seven districts to distribute personnel and resources, decentralized service delivery, and established new venues to directly engage citizens. Jaboatão finally initiated reforms in 2009 that most large Brazilian municipalities had initiated during the 1990s.

Once the municipality's leadership signaled interest in an autonomous and technical administrative state, Jaboatão's municipal workers demonstrated willingness to use analytic tools to build new programs to meet local needs. One important example relates to the human rights work led by Jaboatão's administrators. Social workers recognized that the poor had few of the documents necessary to apply for Bolsa Família benefits. The city has high rates of flooding and precarious housing, which leads many families to lose essential documents, such as birth certificates and state identification cards. To address this problem, the municipality created a program called *Balcão da Cidadania* (Citizen Kiosk). Administered by the Department of Human Rights under Mayor Gomes, this outreach program facilitated the acquisition of documents for itinerant residents. These documents are not only necessary to apply for Bolsa Família and other social benefits but help residents become voters and consumers and make workers eligible for legal protections (Hunter and Sugiyama 2017).

When Social Policy Is Less Effective

What does a municipality with lower levels of success in operating social programs look like? Garanhuns offers important lessons in this regard and highlights the importance of three factors we identified above: rights-based framing, administrative autonomy, and technocratic decision-making.

Garanhuns administrators rarely discussed their work in rights-based terms during our interviews. Of course, many displayed strong personal commitments to the policy areas in which they worked. We spoke to dedicated teachers, health professionals, and social workers who care deeply about helping people. But civil servants from Garanhuns were the least likely of all our interviewees to spontaneously adopt rights-based language to justify and defend their areas of work. Instead, their analysis focused more on "needs" rather than "rights." When they did refer to rights, it was most often in a comment acknowledging that the population did not recognize they have rights (Humberto Granja Neto, Garanhuns). This nuanced distinction is important because administrators who use rights-based frameworks are more likely to replicate that language with beneficiaries they serve. When social programs are framed in terms of a right to education or a right to housing, it is clear that the state has an obligation to provide them and citizens have a right to demand them.

Garanhuns also displayed signs of being vulnerable to local political interference. The nature of political interference, whether the result of clientelism, patronage, or partisan horse trading, can be difficult to ascertain because interview subjects were often reluctant to discuss it directly. Nevertheless, both direct and indirect evidence suggests that administrators in Garanhuns face challenges in this area. Officials in Garanhuns were the most likely of all interviewees to request anonymity for fear of reprisals or diminished career prospects. Despite some apprehension from our interviewees, we nonetheless heard about administrative program implementation that suffered from political interventions. For instance, one individual reported that he faced constant challenges in managing the health budget because "city hall" would often want to divert funds from health to infrastructure projects (Marta, Garanhuns). Another reported that a former secretary of education had to buy school supplies personally because the mayor and city council members would not allocate funds for the purpose, despite the obligation of the municipal government to cover such expenses (David, Garanhuns). Politicians seemed especially keen on interfering with decisions related to the allocation of resources:

City hall tells us what we can and cannot do with the money [we request]. It's usually not what we want to do with it or what we would do it with it. They almost never give us resources to spend in poor communities (Silvia, Garanhuns).

Another individual admitted that PSF clinics had been located in middle-class neighborhoods instead of poorer neighborhoods. As a result, they remained underutilized by the middle class, who are more likely to use private health insurance, while the poor were underserved (Marta, Garanhuns). However, when public health clinics are located in middle-class neighborhoods, local middle-class residents will use the free services for preventive health care, such as vaccinations (Eduardo Bezarra, Jaboatão). Similarly, Garanhuns chose to invest resources for advanced hospital-based care in lieu of investments for preventive health (Gilberta, Garanhuns), which have the greatest impact for improving basic outcomes like infant mortality (McGuire 2010). We heard that the social assistance sector faced similar problems. Garanhuns located all the CRAS (Social Assistance Reference Centers) and CREAS (Specialized Social Assistance Reference Centers) in the urban part of the municipality, leaving the predominately poor rural sectors underserved (José Juca de Melo Filho, Garanhuns). The tendency in Garanhuns to divert health and social assistance resources to middle-class neighborhoods and the services they use, parallels Michael Ross's research in which he found that representative democracy allows middle-class groups to capture public goods (2006).

Given the limited administrative autonomy, it is not surprising we would find little evidence of technocratic decision-making. None of our subjects referred to any insights they gained by accessing data from the Unified Registry. Nor did we hear specific examples of local policy innovation. Areas of work that are unsupported by federal grants were especially hindered by low levels of resources and political commitment. As the department head for women explained, their office depends entirely on cooperative interagency agreements to run programs and respond to new legislation (Eliane Simões, Garanhuns). In short, Garanhuns has failed to leverage resources and support made available through federal programs. Nor have they moved on their own to develop unique social policy solutions to address their citizens' needs.

Garanhuns serves as a cautionary example of why municipalities need technocratic and federal support to advance federal and local social policy. If basic program operations are not functioning well, even well-designed programs will achieve little. Basic program operations need to be in place if municipalities are to take additional steps of attempting to coordinate work across sectors or creating new programs that can respond to local needs. All to say, a minimum floor of local administrative competency is necessary for federal programs to work as intended. The next section explains how state capacity works to advance well-being.

In sum, rights-based administrative frameworks, low levels of political interference, and technocratic approaches to decision-making all improve service delivery for national social programs. In turn, improved services promote human development performance. Camaragibe showcases these connections at a high level. Jaboatão's efforts are better than nothing, but only produce middling results. Finally, Garanhuns operates at low levels across all three areas and subsequently displays the lowest levels of human development outcomes.

EXPLAINING OUTCOMES: HOW INCLUSIVE STATE CAPACITY AFFECTS WELL-BEING

Inclusive state capacity is essential for governments to properly deliver basic services that contribute to human development. We ground our analysis in those features of democratic administrative practices that are essential for universal service delivery. In this context, municipal governments are responsible for administering inclusive services that align with areas of municipal responsibility, including education, health, and social assistance. State capacity and social programs thus overlap in our analysis, as they overlap in local practice. Brazil's movement toward greater fiscal transparency represents one example of this confluence, as federal regulations require local administrators comply with open records laws, follow rules for personnel and procurement, and deliver services equitably. Whistleblowers and the public can pursue legal channels to denounce administrative malfeasance, most commonly through complaints to the Public Ministry. Similarly, the Federal Comptroller (*Controladoria Geral da União*, or CGU), established in 2003 under the arm of the executive office of the presidency also administers random audits of municipal governments to monitor fiscal practices. These measures theoretically increase performance and improve service delivery for marginalized populations.

In practice, we know that Brazil's diverse local governments still display varied levels of inclusivity in state capacity. Clientelism and patronage practices continue under democracy and municipalities struggle to meet their basic administrative obligations – especially for vulnerable groups. Other municipalities have better intentions from a public administration standpoint, but simply lack resources to hire and train competent staff, construct buildings for offices, or purchase appropriate equipment. The result here is also low capacity to administer government programs, even with well-meaning officials who may pursue social inclusion. Many municipalities simply have not yet achieved a "new public administration" approach that centers public management around democratic citizenship.

Our case study municipalities present a picture of varied levels of inclusive state capacity, which result in differential outcomes for well-being. Camaragibe is relatively small and economically challenged, but represents our high-performing municipality with respect to state capacity for social inclusion. Jaboatão's experience is varied and demonstrates middling outcomes. Through much of the 2000s, Jaboatão had numerous public management problems that led to investigations of corruption and state interventions into municipal operations (Silva 2012). Reform efforts in 2009 specifically targeted the administrative state and we see some evidence of improvement as a result. Finally, Garanhuns displays the lowest levels of inclusive state capacity among our three municipalities. We found little evidence that local leaders prioritized administrative reform for delivering services and programs that work toward social inclusion, which undermined human development performance.

What explains this variation in local experiences? We identified three main areas where state capacity promotes social inclusion and well-being:

appropriate staffing, administrative continuity, and resources. Proper administrative staffing is one of the most important indicators of a capable, inclusive state. Stated simply, local governments need to hire individuals with appropriate professional training for the positions they will occupy. A professional civil service means that those who work in the health sector should have a medical background or familiarity with public health, those who work in education should have training in education, and so on. When staff have proper training, they are able to carry out day-to-day operations with greater programmatic success. Properly trained staff are also able to contextualize the work they do, situate their work within federal regulations, and explain their roles within a broader administrative structure. Importantly, professional training matters not only for street-level bureaucrats and mid-level administrators but also for senior political appointees who need to justify overall policy and spending strategies to mayors.

Administrative continuity emerged as another important indicator of inclusive state capacity that also contributes to human development performance. Continuity in staffing at the street- and middle-management levels is essential to long-term programmatic development related to education, health, and social assistance. In many municipalities, each four-year electoral cycle can result in major reshuffling of personnel. When this happens local governments have to hire new personnel to staff reconfigured teams to deliver federal programs, reestablish operations of locally run social programs, develop new ties with policy councils and their members, and establish new contracts with service providers. Municipalities that can sustain some degree of administrative continuity across mayoral administrations are less likely to lose time rebuilding. In practice, this means that the poor can expect more programmatic continuity and maintain longer-lasting relationships with day-to-day service providers. Advocates for the poor also benefit by having more sustained interactions with councils and mid-level public officials.

Finally, field research revealed the importance of adequate resources to administer social programs. This is a particularly difficult condition for local governments to meet; all of the officials we interviewed reported that their municipality was underfunded, had limited ability to raise revenue, and operated with serious fiscal constraints. Federal transfers for education, health, and other services were also cited as equally insufficient across municipalities. Thus, the question is not necessarily what level of funding administrators need to operate effectively, but how municipalities maximize services with the resources they have. Are municipal officials effective at prioritizing resources for programs that advance basic needs? Are municipal managers savvy at identifying fiscal opportunities? We found that our municipalities performed very differently on this dimension.

How Inclusive State Capacity Advances Well-Being

Camaragibe's administration stands out for having well-qualified municipal administrators. Importantly, the city has been able to hire capable, dedicated workers with a firm commitment to areas in which they work and a deep-seated personal commitment to improving people's lives. Interestingly, Camaragibe does not always hire permanent staff through competitive exams. Yet they have been able to attract talented public servants from around the metropolitan region. Some of these public servants passed competitive exams in neighboring municipalities and work "on loan" to Camaragibe.

Camaragibe also stands out as the most stable example of mid-level civil service continuity. While senior political appointees naturally change from one mayoral administration to the next, Camaragibe has the greatest permanency in staffing of street-level and mid-level municipal employees. We found no evidence of wholesale departures of entire staffs, as was common elsewhere. In practice, this means that municipal administrators have more long-term experience with their municipality and longer-serving ties with councils, coworkers, and the greater community. Many of our interview subjects could reflect on policy changes over several administrations and could talk about their experiences working in several councils over the course of their careers (Gabriela Nascimento Dos Santos, Camaragibe; Eduardo Santos, Camaragibe; Júlio Antão, Camaragibe). Program administrators also had more continuity in their day-to-day practices with beneficiaries.

Municipalities are also better situated to use existing resources when they have a technocratic approach to inclusive governance. Interview respondents identified IGD, the small federal transfers associated with good administration of the Bolsa Família program, as an important source of revenue. Social Assistance teams reported using those funds to strengthen their sector and the Bolsa Família program in particular. For instance, the social assistance office used those funds to buy computers and equipment and to fund outreach (Gabriela Nascimento Dos Santos, Camaragibe). In this sense, the IGD became part of a virtuous circle.

We use the IGD resources to cover infrastructure and personnel costs. That lets them hire more people and use better tools to reach the population. These resources are very important and we try to get more of them (Eduardo Gaspar, Camaragibe).

Camaragibe's higher level of performance on the IGD meant they received more funds than other municipalities, which did more to enhance their operations. Unfortunately, this is the only federal transfer that depends on administrative performance. Other areas such as health, education, and women's empowerment lack a similar mechanism to encourage building local capacity for inclusion and rewarding strong practice.

Middling Levels of Inclusive State Capacity Hinder Well-Being

Jaboatão has experienced significant internal variation in state capacity for inclusion over time. At the start of our study, the municipality showed signs of very low levels of capacity. The entry of a reformist mayor in 2009 led a reform of the municipality's administrative infrastructure by first addressing shortcomings in the area of personnel. Municipal administrators also sought to redistribute resources according to more technocratic criteria. Nevertheless, legacies of poor administrative management made it difficult to achieve a "quick fix" that improved administrative capacity and subsequent human development performance.

   Jaboatão was known for its poor administrative management and lack of capacity for inclusion from 2000 to 2008. Critics charged that the municipal government had little interest in administrative reforms that would produce the kind of advances in human development undertaken elsewhere in the metropolitan region (Fatima Lacerdo, Jaboatão). Beyond charges of outright corruption (Silva 2012), the municipality was also described as generally poorly administered, which was due, in part, to poorly selected personnel. We met with one longstanding municipal employee who exemplified a disconnect between her professional background and the work she had undertaken. This individual, who was originally hired to work in the municipal police and had training in education, ended up working in the municipality's social assistance office. She had no formal training related to social assistance and yet became the coordinator of the municipality's social assistance council. She was unable to frame her work in terms of federal aims, regulations, or social rights. Moreover, she criticized Bolsa Família for perpetuating dependency and suggested it might be wise to eliminate it (Alberta, Jaboatão). This kind of discourse runs entirely counter to the Ministry of Development's framing of the program in terms of social rights and the state's obligations. A long-time administrator asserted that governments, prior to 2009, "didn't know how to work with the [poor, needy] population" (Maria do Carmo Mendes de Oliveira, Jaboatão). The implication is that municipal public officials were disconnected from the poor majority who were in desperate need of even the most basic public services.

We encountered administrative problems in other social sectors as well. In the educational arena, the municipal education system enrolled students in one of four daily schedules (7 a.m. to 11 a.m., 11 a.m. to 3 p.m., 3 p.m. to 7 p.m., and 7 p.m. to 10 p.m.). With time needed to rotate students in and out of buildings, the majority of students were only getting three-and-a-half hours of daily instruction. This is far less than the federally mandated number of hours of instruction (Ministry of Education 2017). Given the exceedingly low number of instructional hours, it is not surprising that students in the municipal public system would fare badly on national exams. One long-time teacher and administrator asserted, "We were unable to improve quality because we didn't have capacity" (Renata Cristina Lopes, Jaboatão). Quite simply, the administrative state in Jaboatão had never been modernized, which made it very difficult to address grave social problems in anything but the most superficial and immediate ways.

From 2009 to 2016, Jaboatão rebuilt its administrative capacity by hiring many experienced civil servants from neighboring municipalities, including Cabo de Santo Agostino and Recife. As one senior administrator from Jaboatão recounted:

We arrived in Jaboatão on January 5, 2009. The first shock I encountered was that the department didn't have a staff. We brought a very small team in with us and made a presentation. We then asked the professionals who had been there to stay and continue working for the city. The workers, everyone left, only three or four professionals stayed. (Socorro Araújo, Jaboatão)

The social assistance teams were put to the test very quickly. Their biggest challenge was a massive backlog of paper applications for Bolsa Família benefits. The municipality had collected over 21,000 paper registrations for the Unified Registry and stored them in boxes throughout municipal offices. Yet the municipality had not entered any of these forms into the national database, the Unified Registry, so that families could be assessed for program eligibility. The new team quickly identified several additional problems, including low levels of capacity in the previous administration, poor internet access, and poor geographic organization and outreach. The social assistance team therefore worked to completely restructure outreach and services and to obtain the computing equipment they needed to properly register families (Socorro Araújo, Jaboatão). These kinds of administrative issues were not abstract problems: They severely hurt poor families in Jaboatão who waited months, perhaps years, to receive cash transfers from the Bolsa Família program.

Low levels of administrative continuity were clearly a feature of public administration in Jaboatão. The near-wholesale evacuation of mid-level and senior-level administrators as each new mayor enters office means that many of the previous administration's policies are less likely to endure. In cases where progressive reformers enter office, such departures from the previous administration may facilitate renewal efforts. In cases where traditional politicians replace progressive reformers, such departures may signal the fleeting nature of any reform efforts. With the entry of a more socially conservative mayor, we expect much of the rights-based discourse for progressive LBGT and race-related initiatives will decline. Whether the rights-based framework will continue for areas such as education, health, and social assistance is largely unknown.

Finally, we acknowledge the role that resources came to bear on the municipality of Jaboatão. The municipality had greater resources, on a per capita basis, than most municipalities in the state and region but they were hampered by high inequality and two distinct city centers. Although geography was not destiny, having two distinct city centers placed a greater burden on public resources.

How Low State Capacity for Inclusion Undermines Well-Being

Garanhuns best exemplifies the case of a municipality that has not undertaken any major administrative reforms and suffers from a lack of inclusive state capacity. Low inclusive capacity creates challenges related to personnel, high turnover, and poorly managed resources that ultimately harm prospects for human development.

Hiring qualified administrative personnel is difficult in Garanhuns for several reasons. Garanhuns is located in the interior of Pernambuco, more than a four-hour drive from Recife, the political and economic capital of the state. Convincing well-trained administrators to move to Garanhuns is challenging, as is paying them. Those qualified administrators and personnel who do elect to stay in Garanhuns (education officials, teachers, and council members) typically do so because of personal ties to the area. Others would work for city hall, but may not qualify for positions elsewhere due to their low levels of experience or lack of university training. These problems persist at all levels of public employment. As several informants explained: Garanhuns has difficulty attracting qualified doctors associated with the Family Health Program. Nearly all are there to complete their residency training. They "do their time" until they can get their medical credentials and move on. As a result, they don't build connections with the community, which affects overall care (Leandra Magalhaes dos Santos, Garanhuns). As another person explained: "We can tell in practice that these doctors are not interested in the social aspect of the work; many prefer to work in hospitals, engage in specialized care, so we don't have a cadre of professionals who want to engage in public health and work as generalist physicians" (Ana Claudia, Garanhuns). At city hall, we saw the disconnect between the administrators and their lack of commitment to public services. Very low levels of professionalism among the administrative ranks was evident when all municipal offices were empty by 2:00 p.m. and many closed (unofficially) hours earlier.

Administrative turnover represents another area where Garanhuns performs poorly. There is considerable turnover of appointed secretaries even within administrations. For example, the secretary of health recently resigned under pressure from the mayor after less than one year in the position; several respondents suggested that this was due to the secretary's insistence on using budgeted money for health services. The education secretary who paid for school supplies for municipal schools out of his own pocket threatened to resign when the mayor would not comply with the municipal obligation to provide schools with resources. Department heads do not necessarily last long either, even if they are tied to federal, rather than local, programs. For example, the administrator in charge of Garanhuns's Bolsa Família program cautiously agreed to an interview and then cancelled, reportedly for fear of criticizing the mayor on the record. We were informed of this turn of events by the deputy administrator who agreed to the interview in his stead. The deputy administrator was willing to do the interview because of his own "lack of political ambition."

Finally, Garanhuns is wealthier than Camaragibe and has greater access to funding for social programs. Garanhuns generates these resources by virtue of its position as a regional agricultural center and the hub of economic activity for hours of travel time in any direction. Nevertheless, Garanhuns is still a relatively poor municipality in the interior of Brazil's northeast, one of the country's poorest regions.

Garanhuns uses the resources it does have poorly. Public employees connected to the education ministry spoke of diversion of school funds toward the mayor's pet projects and respondents with knowledge of health funding spoke of similar machinations in that area (Catalina, Garanhuns). The result is a missed opportunity to hire better-trained personnel, improve services, and enhance well-being, just like in Jaboatão.

In sum, our fieldwork shows how state capacity is essential for government service delivery and human development performance. Our case study municipalities vary in terms of administrative personnel, turnover, and resources, which result in differential outcomes for well-being. Our analysis also shows, however, that resources alone do not make or break efforts to improve well-being. Places with relatively few resources, such as Camaragibe, can perform at high levels if they devote their attention to hiring strong personnel, maintaining administrative continuity, and ensuring that budgeted funds actually reach their official destination. Similarly, municipalities with greater resources, like Jaboatão and Garanhuns, will miss out on human development gains by administering their resources poorly.

INTERACTIVE EFFECTS

Our three pathways – participatory councils, inclusive social programs, and inclusive state capacity – have independent and interactive effects on well-being. In the final part of this chapter, we demonstrate how our three pathways complement one another and become mutually reinforcing. Camaragibe, as the reader has already surmised, is noteworthy for the additive effects on well-being that each independent pathway generates. The additive effects are important but interactions among these pathways multiply their impact and help to build out the virtuous circle that we identified earlier. In Camaragibe, for example, council members work to improve social policies and monitor the local state; social policy administrators promote councils and strengthen local state capacity. Well-trained administrators use resources efficiently to support the councils and run social programs better than in other municipalities.

Figure 8.2 (identical to Figure 1.2) identifies the interactive effects across participatory institutions, social programs, and local inclusive capacity.

It is important to acknowledge that the interactive effects among these mechanisms can both undermine and enhance performance for each area of democratic governance. For instance, a lack of inclusive state capacity

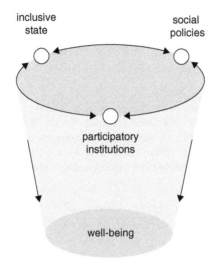

FIGURE 8.2: Interaction of pathways

can sabotage effective social programs and council operations. Similarly, low levels of council operations can limit potential contributions to social policy operations and enhancements to state capacity for inclusion. Finally, low-quality rights-based social policy delivery can dampen council engagement and can thwart the momentum for state reform efforts. As the negative interactive relationships are easier to understand, we focus here on ways in which our mechanisms produce positive ratcheting-up effects. This final section focuses primarily on Camaragibe, where the positively reinforcing connections are most evident. We also include insights from Jaboatão because government officials attempted to build these connections there as well.

COUNCILS AND SOCIAL POLICY PROGRAMS

Councils interact with social policy programs in several different ways. At the broadest level, council members exchange information with government officials about citizens' needs and resource availability. More narrowly, council members work with civil servants to help individual citizens navigate the bureaucracy to secure their social rights, as guaranteed under the 1988 Constitution. These interactions are reciprocal in the sense that both sides initiate contact and sustain interactive connections.

Policy councils and related conferences allow for the presentation of ideas and demands from citizens and CSOs in ways that contribute to governmental improvements in policy design and implementation. As Moisés Gomes dos Santos, a citizen representative on the health council, explained:

The department engages with the councils a lot. We work with them and sometimes with the PSF. It's more common for the department to ask to do something to support PSF or for us to ask support of PSF or the hospitals, clinics, etc. through the department. The civil society connection is very important, but PSF or the department don't connect directly with them – they go through the councils and the conferences.

For example, in Camaragibe, health council members formally rejected the proposed annual health budget on several occasions, thus requiring the municipal government to address their demands (Eduardo Santos, Camaragibe; Lúcia Teixera, Camaragibe). Municipal and state health conferences have led to new health legislation as well as adoption of useful policies devised elsewhere in the region (Edvaldo Ferreira, Camaragibe; Eduardo Santos Camaragibe).

Council members also play an important role at the individual level by assisting citizens and hard-to-reach communities to access social programs such as Bolsa Família and the Family Health Program. This often involves connecting the individual with the appropriate civil servant or administrative agency responsible for the implementation of the program. Civil servants acknowledge the benefit of reaching out to council members who are key intermediaries between the local state and hard-to-reach populations (Lubania Barbosa dos Santos, Jaboatão). For one example, less visible groups might consist of families living in isolated pockets along rivers or highways. Community members will then inform council members or civil servants about the needs of these communities.

The information exchange that takes place between council members and municipal officials can play an important part in regular and effective program operations. For instance, Camaragibe's social assistance secretary and staff attend social assistance council meetings to present information about their programs. The lead administrator of Camaragibe's Bolsa Família program also attends council meetings so she can learn directly of community needs and takes steps to ensure individuals and families she learns about receive the services they need.

Overall, information exchange is at the heart of the interaction between the council system and implementation of social programs. This interaction represents an ongoing learning process that enriches short- and long-term understandings of policy and policy outcomes. This process enhances well-being because it improves citizens' access to public goods and government officials' ability to deliver services.

COUNCILS AND INCLUSIVE STATE CAPACITY

Councils interact with the administrative state primarily through monitoring and oversight of budgets, policy proposals, and end-of-year reports. Municipalities with greater capacity provide the necessary information and logistical support that permits members to engage in this monitoring; this allows dedicated civil servants to carry out their job duties without having to worry about politicians and others who might be interested in capturing or misappropriating these resources.

Policy councils serve as venues that have direct oversight over the implementation of social programs. In Camaragibe, our interviewees explained how the federal technocrats worked directly with municipal-level public officials. In turn, these municipal officials then worked with council members. This moves monitoring from a post hoc oversight to an "ongoing, continual" oversight process. We saw this in practice in Camaragibe when the council for the disabled informed the local education department of their lack of compliance with national access requirements for disabled students in new and existing schools. Then, they worked with education administrators to incorporate access ramps into plans for new schools, which is more efficient than having to find new funding to add ramps to existing schools (Fernando Antonio, Camaragibe; Cynthia Barbosa, Camaragibe).

Beyond implementation, council members also engage in post hoc oversight, which involves approving end-of-year accounts. This feature serves as a general review of what the government accomplished during the year but it also helps council members make plans for the future. In Camaragibe, the health council, in at least two different years, rejected the year-end report because it lacked enough detail for the council members to understand how resources had been spent. The health department was thus required to submit a new end-of-year report (Eduardo Santos, Camaragibe).

Thus well-functioning councils provide a great opportunity for citizens and council members to directly engage in oversight, which has the effect of moderating behaviors of government officials. Council members are relatively well-informed about what government officials and service providers should be doing. In addition, direct engagement with councils allows government officials to move beyond the isolation associated with modern bureaucracies. Ongoing participation creates a mutually reinforcing system where public officials change their behavior as they know they are being monitored and participation becomes more relevant as it changes officials' behavior.

INCLUSIVE STATE CAPACITY AND SOCIAL POLICY PROGRAMS

A capable, inclusive state supports social policy programs through internal bureaucratic processes that are necessary to deliver public services. Brazil's local governments rely heavily on federal transfers for their budgets. However, well-being improves when a competent local administrative apparatus manages those resources well and takes advantage of the opportunities that federal social programs create. There are several different ways that the local, state, and national social programs interact to improve well-being.

Although federally designed and funded, local administrations carry the brunt of service delivery associated with the implementation of Bolsa Família, the Family Health Program, and the School Nutrition Program. Municipal governments make decisions regarding the quality and quantity of personnel dedicated to the programs, how to create efficiencies (e.g., decentralizing intake or digitizing enrollment), and the degree of autonomy their employees have to run programs. In Jaboatão, Gomes's reformist government invested in reorganizing its citizen outreach and digitizing enrollment into the Unified Registry because of the requirement for people to re-enroll every two years. These efforts required a significant one-time start-up cost, but eased the burdens on recipients in future years.

The federal government incentivizes good municipal performance through regulations that accompany federal funds for health, education, and social assistance. Notably, the Bolsa Família program created several opportunities to enhance local administrative practices. The federal government's Unified Registry allows municipal authorities access to information about poor families in their municipality. Our interviews in Camaragibe and Jaboatão also demonstrate that social workers use this information as they seek to address key needs in their communities.

In Camaragibe, the municipality used the data to work across sectoral divides and to conduct outreach to poor families with greater effect. In Jaboatão, municipal officials used the data to design new local programs. Thus, administrators in the local social assistance office use the registry from a national social program to advance local programs that fall beyond the federal purview. The "Decentralized Management Index" spurred improvements in local governance by awarding monthly fund transfers on the basis of solid administrative performance; both Camaragibe and Jaboatão made good use of those funds to enhance their state capacity.

In sum, this section illustrates the interactive process of building virtuous, democratic, policy circles that are then associated with improvements in well-being. This qualitative case study analysis complements our large-N analysis that demonstrates how each pathway can have an independent effect on well-being; it shows that the improvements in well-being grow even stronger when participatory councils, social policies, and local administrative capacity join forces.

CONCLUSION

Our fieldwork identifies important, causal connections among participatory institutions, rights-based social programs, inclusive state capacity, and well-being. Case studies of three municipalities contextualize the ways that public policy councils (*conselhos*), rights-based social programs (nationally-funded, but administered locally), and the local state create "virtuous circles" of high performance that improve well-being. Our methodological approach in this chapter utilizes process tracing to better illuminate the varied pathways that government officials and civil society actors can take to improve well-being. Our qualitative process tracing, combined with our decades of research experience in Brazil, suggests that it is difficult to build high levels of performance; it is far more challenging to construct and maintain these virtuous circles of democratic change than to derail them. In this chapter, we have shown how the absence of government and civil society support for participatory institutions, half-hearted commitments to rights-based social programs, and low levels of state capacity result in lower levels of human development. Drawing from quantitative findings, as presented in Chapters 4–7, we find that many municipalities remain mired in "vicious circles" of disengagement that produce lower levels of human development. Others are at risk of backsliding into poor performance after achieving gains in governance and human development.

The municipality of Camaragibe is far and away the poorest among our three cases, but it generated robust results for well-being because government officials and their civil society allies invested in improving the quality of participatory institutions, rights-based social programs, and inclusive state capacity. Most key social indicators for Camaragibe, such as infant mortality and education test scores, are more positive than those in either Jaboatão or Garanhuns despite Camaragibe having considerably fewer financial resources. In Camaragibe, our three pathways also interact to produce mutually reinforcing effects that improve citizens' well-being. Camaragibe most clearly lays bare the deficiencies of wealth-focused arguments surrounding human development because government officials and their allies were still able to build social and policy processes that improved public goods provisions, which in turn led to improvements in well-being. Economic health and access to resources clearly matters, but a key lesson from Camaragibe is that building new democratic institutions and making advances in inclusive state capacity can improve well-being, even under relatively poor economic conditions.

The cases of Jaboatão and Garanhuns show how moderate levels of wealth are not enough to improve well-being on their own. Garanhuns is a regional economic pole in Pernambuco's interior. It had relatively high levels of overall wealth and relatively strong economic conditions during the timeframe of our study, but also had high levels of poverty and income inequality. Government officials there did not invest in social and political processes to expand democratic venues or improve social policy provisions. Moreover, Garanhuns only weakly implemented political and policy reforms; the local government did not actively initiate or strengthen policy reforms to improve citizens' well-being.

The case of Jaboatão is a mixed case, not just due to its middling results but also because we identify two distinct moments in its political and policy history. In the first moment, which covered redemocratization in the mid-1980s through 2008, government officials in the municipality were infamous for their clientelistic practices and extensive corruption. Social programs were poorly administered, funds did not get where they were supposed to go, and there was little citizen-based oversight. The election of a reformist mayor in 2008 ushered in an era of policy change and active efforts to improve governance. Interestingly, the mayor's reform efforts coincided with our three pathways – expanding democratic participation, improving social program delivery, and building local administrative capacity. However, these reforms were partial and not well-supported, either during or after this administration. The result has been middling outcomes surrounding well-being that exceed those in Garanhuns, but lag far behind Camaragibe, despite Jaboatão's much stronger economic foundation.

Our analysis in this chapter demonstrates more clearly the causal mechanisms that produce changes in well-being by developing a richer understanding of how our three pathways operate in practice to improve well-being on the ground. Other municipalities can potentially emulate the successes we identify here. But we acknowledge why it is difficult for many municipalities to escape the vicious circle of poverty. Local governments that invest in democratic and policy reform are more likely to improve their citizens' well-being. Although democratic practices are sometimes cumbersome and untidy, there is a clear advantage to investing in participatory processes, rights-based social programs, and inclusive state capacity. Local governments that support policy reform through these three pathways achieve much greater human development success than those that do not.

Conclusion

How Democracy Improves Well-Being

The complexity, richness, and messiness of democratic politics generates opportunities for governments to expand citizens' basic capabilities, agency, and rights. In turn, these advances contribute to individual and collective well-being. This book demonstrates how multiple pathways within democratic regimes connect participatory institutions, rights-based social policies, and inclusive state capacity to human development. Of course there is no simple formula that permits citizens and governments to advance human development. We find that the slow, often cumbersome work of building democracy through participation, citizenship, and inclusive state capacity are crucial to initiate and sustain efforts to improve well-being. Each of these pathways can have a positive independent influence, but we find the strongest outcomes when two or all three pathways are activated simultaneously.

At the broadest level, our theoretical framework and mixed-methods approach demonstrate how a more comprehensive, fuller examination of democratic practice permits us to explain how governments, civil servants, and citizens work together to produce social and political change. Democratic regimes have multifaceted policy-making processes that alter basic governance patterns and generate new state-society relationships. Although free and fair elections are an important part of representative democracy, they do not constitute the entirety of democratic politics that contributes to human development. Our democratic framework better accounts for the myriad ways that citizens and governments use different pathways to promote well-being.

DEMOCRACY: CORE DIMENSIONS AND KEY PATHWAYS

Democracies share the same broad characteristics, including three core principles: participation, citizenship, and an inclusive state (Marshall 1950; Dahl 1971; Linz and Stepan 1996). We show how variation in the robustness of these democratic components explain variation in well-being. Yet, not all democracies fully develop these dimensions, which helps to explain why they struggle to deliver services, social programs, and participatory opportunities that might improve well-being.

Each democratic dimension – participation, citizenship, and a usable state – represents a point of departure for distinct pathways that contributes to well-being. No pathway, by itself, is necessary for improving well-being and each pathway is sufficient for affecting change. However, we see the strongest results for well-being when all three pathways are present. Based on these findings, governments seeking to improve well-being could invest their scarce resources in any one of the three areas: enhancing participation, promoting rights-based social policies, and developing a more inclusive state can all produce important changes in peoples' lives. Importantly, it is the configuration of each pathway that best explains the extent to which governments and citizens are able to use democratic processes to improve change.

We link these dimensions with specific mechanisms to develop a "pathway" for social well-being. In the Brazilian context, we highlight the importance of policy councils as a vehicle for participatory citizen engagement to advance better governance. Within the citizenship domain, we find that inclusive social policies related to the Family Health Program (PSF) and Bolsa Família have provided the poor with essential support that allows them to build capabilities and enhance their well-being. Finally, we identify the importance of an inclusive state for directing state action to deliver public goods and services in ways that are consistent with democratic values; this entails professionalizing the civil service, operating transparently, and allocating resources to reward effective management practices. These pathways have independent impacts on well-being, but they also reinforce one another and can initiate virtuous circles of change.

Importantly, our explanation allows us to capture the full range of democratic experiences, from "thicker" to "thinner" local democratic practices. Understanding what happens when municipalities develop democratic institutions, commit to citizenship development, and enhance state capacity is crucial for both theorists and policy practitioners.

Municipalities that make extensive commitments to these areas do so by building more robust participatory institutions, implementing rights-based social policies consistently, and harnessing local state capacity for inclusion and social change. We then see significant improvements in basic human development indicators when governments and their civil society allies invest in these democratic practices, especially when compared to those places that do not invest. As our case studies reveal, some municipalities do not build the necessary institutions and policy-making processes that can improve well-being because local officials and their civil society allies display limited interest in doing so. Our theoretical framework allows us to explain wide variation in democratic practice as well as human development outcomes in Brazil. Though our study occurs in Brazil, the resulting lessons are applicable to new democracies in the developing world, where hundreds of millions of people work to build basic capabilities and exercise their rights. As we explain in this chapter, our framework makes important contributions to scholarship on democracy and human development. Researchers can utilize this approach to uncover pathways for social change for other developing and middle-income democracies.

ADVANCING THE DEBATE

We advance theoretical and empirical debates in three ways. We first link theoretical debates on democracy and human development, showing how core dimensions of democracy are inextricably intertwined with efforts to build capabilities and thus promote human development. We then provide a more comprehensive, fuller definition of democracy, which allows us to move beyond elections to better identify how core dimensions of democracy, along with their corresponding mechanisms, contribute to efforts to improve well-being. Finally, we draw upon new sources of data, which allow us to test these theoretical propositions in ways that no one has previously been able to do.

Democracy and Human Development

Our analysis explicitly links democracy and human development as inter-related processes. We unpack the democratic process to show how a broader democratic ecosystem works to enhance human capabilities. Unlike authoritarian regimes, democracies are grounded in principles of citizenship that enable individuals to exercise rights and develop capabilities. The capabilities approach has always been about the goal of helping individuals achieve agency. For agency to be meaningful, people must be incorporated into a democratic citizenship-based system of government that fosters free decision-making. Democracy is well suited to advance human capabilities because its core components and processes, particularly the concepts of citizenship and creation and protection of social rights, are mutually reinforcing. As such, scholarship on human development that examines simpler relationships between regime type and basic human development indicators, misses, the mark. Simply put, enhanced "human development" metrics under authoritarianism do not constitute enhanced capabilities if people are not free to make fundamental life choices.

Recognizing the linkages between democracy and freedom, Amaryta Sen (1999) highlights the vital role that democracies can play in supporting the expansion of capabilities and agency. However, Sen does not specify which democratic dimensions and mechanisms might be of greater fundamental importance to promoting capabilities and well-being (1999: 146–159). In this way, we advance Sen's "development as freedom" approach by identifying how specific features of democracy produce capabilities and, subsequently, improve well-being. The adoption of democracy is a positive first step, but we argue that analysts need to dig deeper to identify the conditions under which governments and civil society actors are more likely to develop the institutional participatory mechanisms, social programs, and inclusionary state reforms that improve capabilities.

We advance debates on human development because our three pathways capture the complexity of democratic processes in ways that previous studies have not. Much of the previous scholarship on regime type and human development has not explicitly connected democratic practices to human development in the way we do here. This is because previous analyses largely occurred at the national level, which obscures subnational politics where people are more likely to access and exercise social and political rights. Moreover, cross-national research, because of its complexity, tends to use simpler, elections-based proxies to measure the effect of democracy. (See for example, Brown and Hunter 2004; Przeworski et al. 1999; Bellinger 2018.) Such choices are certainly understandable; it is currently impossible to find cross-national comparative data that would allow for meaningful comparison of our democratic pathways. These limitations drove us to subnational analysis, which provides a richer, more thorough picture of democratic practice.

Our approach also broadens the context in which we explain variation in well-being. Much of the extant research on the expansion of social programs focuses narrowly on specific types of programs (conditional cash transfer programs, universal health care) or participatory institutions (health councils, participatory budgeting) (Rasella et al. 2013; Touchton and Wampler 2014). These studies make important contributions to show how either social programs or participation improve well-being, but we argue that they do not sufficiently account for additional factors that also influence well-being. For instance, isolated approaches cannot adequately consider the interactive processes at work between local participation and social policy. Our emphasis on democratic pathways positions us to draw upon the groundbreaking work of Sen and Ostrom who assert that citizen engagement and participation are vital for producing better social outcomes (Ostrom 1990; Sen 1999; Evans, Huber, Stephens 2017: 407). But, we advance this understanding by identifying how specific features of democratic regimes account for human development across thousands of cases. We leverage the Brazilian case for theory building and testing; we can uncover the messy process of democratic politics because we have this information for Brazil.

Deepening Democracy

We provide a more comprehensive analysis of democracy's multifaceted components to show how variation across its core dimensions helps explain improvements in well-being. Importantly, we look beyond procedural minimums and elections to better understand how the democratic architecture surrounding rights, social programs, and an inclusive state can improve human development. This approach departs from a focus on procedural minimums, which has long been a mainstay of comparative politics. Scholars in the 1980s and 1990s rightly sought to clarify transition moments and identify criteria to distinguish between democratic and authoritarian regimes (Schmitter and Karl 1991; O'Donnell 1994). This starting point was important as analysts needed to identify cutoff points for regime change and democratic consolidation. Yet the emphasis on procedural minimums has had lasting effects on the operationalization of research that investigates the role of regime type on various outcomes. The widespread use of national elections and national-level indicators runs the risk of omitting important components to assess the quality of democracy. Moreover, it obscures examination of how democratic regimes' internal characteristics are associated with variation in outcomes.

Working in parallel, another set of research inspired by the "third wave" of democracy embraced a different approach by taking an in-depth look at democratic practice to investigate whether regime change, as countries moved out of authoritarianism to democracy, would pro-duce tangible improvements in their citizens' lives. Researchers in this area asked whether democracy contributed to improved performance, however conceived; most studies were designed as country case studies or medium-N studies. Answers to these questions were elusive. Confounding variables, such as historical legacies, the character of the preceding regime, levels of development, and the nature of economic reform, complicated prospects for a generalizable causal narrative. This scholarship made important contributions by opening up the "black box" of democratic practice and linked actions by citizens, politicians, and bureaucrats to different performance outcomes and good govern-ance (Putnam et al. 1994; Fox 1996; Tendler 1997; Grindle 2004; Haggard and Kaufman 1997; McGuire 2010). However, differences in data availability, analytic techniques, research questions, and theoretical frameworks across these and other studies made it difficult to draw broader conclusions. From our perspective, this body of research helped identify the importance of complicating democratic practice beyond elections. As found in Chapter 2, we build on these insights by develop-ing a pathways framework that can be applied to other developing third wave countries.

The three analytically distinct concepts we highlight as part of democ-racy – participation, citizenship rights, and a usable state – show how institution-building and policy implementation between elections are cru-cial ways that governments can improve well-being. Here we highlight how our three main dimensions and their corresponding mechanisms work in practice to build virtuous circles for human development.

Participation in formal policy-making venues is crucial because it engages community leaders and government officials in ongoing policy deliberations and discussions. Participatory democratic institutions con-vey information in both top-down and bottom-up fashions. Community leaders thus "practice" democracy on a regular basis because they are in constant dialogue and negotiations with the communities they represent as well as with government officials in positions of power. Democratic policy making is thus not the result of elections contested every four years, but is actively determined on a daily basis.

Improving democratic governance through participatory institutions is, therefore, one important mechanism for enhancing well-being. The expansion of democratic institutions, in our case through policy councils, enables citizens and civil society organizations (CSOs) to actively exercise individual and collective agency as they exercise their rights. Democratic processes are then no longer distant ideals, but become part of citizens' everyday experiences, allowing them to work within deliberative policy-making institutions to pursue public policies that address their concerns.

Citizenship guarantees membership in the polity. For most democratizing countries, citizenship also necessitates the incorporation of previously excluded groups – ethnic minorities, indigenous, the poor, women – just to name a few. Building rights-based social programs expands rights by enabling socially vulnerable groups to secure dignified lives. At the most basic level, this involves caring for infants and mothers so that they survive the birth process, but it also extends to building capabilities that permit citizens to better engage markets, governments, and communities. We show that inclusive social programs that deliver public goods based on rights, rather than clientelistic exchanges, expand rights in other areas. This includes basic civil and political protections, thus ensuring that neither the state nor private entities systematically violate the rights of vulnerable groups. Citizens' lives will be transformed when inclusive social programs, such as universal health programs, are directed to reshape society. These transformations are material – surviving birth – but also political and cultural as recipients begin to learn how to exercise their rights in the public sphere.

Designing, funding, and implementing inclusive, rights-based social programs that provide basic public goods to poor citizens is an important mechanism for citizenship in democracy. It is obviously no surprise that a conditional cash transfer (CCT) program will provide additional income to targeted populations. Bolsa Família is a rights-based program, with explicit controls designed to prevent clientelistic implementation at the local level (Lindert et al. 2007). Hunter and Sugiyama (2017) also argue that its broad-scale, means-tested design, and strong rights-based framing matter for citizenship development. CCTs and other inclusive social programs may provide the poor with income in authoritarian environments, but our line of analysis demonstrates that implementing these programs within a democratic ecosystem is necessary to build capabilities and agency that are integral to the realization of social rights. Thus, the virtuous circle of change needs both democratic renewal and inclusive social programs in order to sustain improvements in well-being.

Finally, we bring the state back into central focus (Evans et al. 1985; Centeno et al. 2017). Most democratic theory implicitly addresses the role of the state in fostering citizenship and participation by highlighting rule of law. Where we differ is in drawing analytic emphasis on the "inclusive state" for advancing well-being. Redirecting the state to provide inclusive services that are grounded in democratic principles is essential. As is common in new, "third wave" democracies, elected governments interested in investing in democratic practices may inherit states with deep authoritarian roots and practices. Governments must then reform the state to support and expand social and political rights. When private interests capture public resources through patronage and clientelism, the potential is high for well-designed social programs to fall short of their transformative potential.

Our focus on the usable state allows us to redress a problem that has long befuddled the deliberative democracy debates, which is that the state seemingly disappears. We highlight those mechanisms that are part of local state capacity building that are important for governments to implement potentially transformative social policy. Administrative capacity is a key component supporting a virtuous circle because public resources and state authority are central to the efforts to build capabilities and support the institutionalization of both democratic institutions and inclusive social programs. Sufficient resources, rights-based access to services, well-trained technocratic personnel with the freedom to deliver services without favoritism, and local administrations that operate without patronage are all directly relevant to high-quality provision of public goods and resulting impacts on well-being.

Methodological Advances

Our third major contribution is in the realm of methodology. Advances in data availability, statistical modeling, and research design allow us to make new methodological contributions. We draw from extensive material covering outcomes surrounding well-being and potential explanatory factors for over 5,500 municipal governments. This comprehensive data lets us accurately incorporate key dimensions of daily democratic life over time and across space, while also accounting for traditional explanations for well-being. This type of analysis has not been possible to this point because such rich municipal data has never been available. We employ a nested-case logic that draws on mixed-methods as our main empirical strategy (Lieberman 2005).

We first use quantitative analysis to show how our democratic pathways affect four policy arenas. Quantitative models explain ten distinct outcomes (e.g., infant mortality, women's political candidacies, school attendance), thus providing a robust and meaningful explanation for distinct levels of well-being across Brazil. Despite some important nuances across issue area, we find a consistent story: the democratic pathways and their corresponding mechanisms contribute to well-being. We then use case studies and process-tracing to identify causal mechanisms that connect democratic pathways to well-being. The cases – all located in the poor northeast – are reflective of challenges found in the poorest regions of the world. They are also of keen interest to Brazilianists and development practitioners because this region has experienced some pockets of excellence amid an otherwise very challenged social, economic, and political context. Taken together, our research shows how the specific activities of citizens, community leaders, CSOs, and elected governments reflect variation in commitment to each of our democratic pathways. In turn, that commitment leads to a fuller explanation of well-being across Brazilian municipalities than we could achieve with quantitative or qualitative methods alone.

KEY FINDINGS: DIFFERENT PATHWAYS FOR DIVERSE POLICY ARENAS

Our quantitative findings demonstrate that the adoption of one or more of our three democratic pathways saves lives (infant and maternal), increases early school attendance, expands access to basic income, and begins to empower women. However, we also find that different configurations of the pathways within distinct policy arenas help account for variation in how they affect well-being. For example, we find that some pathways matter more in the health arena whereas others are more important in education. This is to be expected because distinct processes drive changes in areas such as access to income, infant and maternal mortality, school attendance, high school test scores, and women's political engagement. Thus, the pathways converge in terms of promoting well-being, but diverge across policy arenas and their direct impact on specific issues.

In the health sector, all three democratic pathways save lives by reducing infant and maternal mortality. Fortunately, infant and maternal mortality are public health problems that can be solved fairly rapidly through greater involvement of community health agents, public health specialists, medical professionals, and community leaders. Our findings support a growing body of research that demonstrates that community participation in health governance is a vital component of change (Lasker and Weiss 2003; Zakocs and Edwards 2006; Oakes and Kaufman 2017). The broader implication of this finding is that universal health programs would greatly benefit from participatory governance processes that engage communities, build their rights, and expand their capabilities, especially when working with poor populations in the Global South and extremely poor populations in the Global North.

In terms of poverty reduction, extending rights-based conditional cash transfers (Bolsa Família) expands access to income and reduces poverty. This finding confirms considerable academic and policy work on conditional cash transfer programs (Lindert et al. 2007; Macinko et al., 2006; Fiszbein and Schady 2009; Rasella et al., 2013; Bither-Terry 2014). Importantly, the features of participation and state capacity also influence poverty reduction. Poverty falls when local governments operate efficiently and effectively implement policies as well as when citizens work within participatory institutions to design policy and monitor government behavior. The broader implication of these findings is that conditional cash transfer programs are likely to have a larger impact on poverty and act as a democratic multiplier, if they are part of a broader set of institutional, democratic reforms.

Empowering women requires multifaceted advances in political, economic, and social domains. As our analysis shows, our democratic pathways work somewhat differently across these areas. For instance, the presence of women's councils that had been voluntarily adopted by municipal governments is positively associated with political empowerment as measured by the number of female candidates running for local office. This is likely because councils can serve as training grounds for women to develop political skills and cultivate the necessary support to run for office. Similarly, the Bolsa Família program lowers women's economic vulnerabilities. These nuances reflect the complexity of gender discrimination and the multiple interventions that are necessary for women to make gains toward equality. Taken together, participation, social policy, and an inclusive state can help women enhance their capabilities. But much of the advances reflect the secondary effects that come with participatory institutions and universal social policies in the absence of a large and sustained national social policy effort for gender equality.

In the education sector, school attendance, like poverty levels, is driven by the presence of a rights-based conditional cash transfer program and, to a lesser extent, by other supporting democratic pathways. Conditional cash transfer programs work better when embedded in a democratic ecosystem, which then allows parents and teachers to engage in public processes to promote better schooling. An important caveat is that municipalities' economic conditions have a strong impact on test scores and graduation rates, whereas none of the three pathways are statistically relevant. Bolsa Família can help to get children to school, but school attendance is not enough to overcome decades of economic stagnation and educational neglect. The lack of connections between our pathways and longer-term educational performance may stem from the recent expansion of local democracy; it may take a generation or two of investment in inclusive, rights-based democratic institutions to alter outcomes. This suggests that democratic pathways help to improve well-being, but they are also embedded within macro-structural conditions that are hard to overcome.

There is no single, linear narrative that connects our three democratic pathways to well-being. Rights-based social policies are more likely to generate change in some policy arenas because they deliver specific benefits. In other areas, participatory institutions are more important because they alter state-society relations. Our approach thus shows that governments should not necessarily focus solely on a single path to improve peoples' lives. There is no single "magic bullet" for development practitioners who want to enhance well-being. Investment in one pathway is certainty better than none. Similarly, investment in all three democratic pathways provides the greatest chance for social transformation. But practitioners will need to determine which pathway or pathways make most sense to tackle first given the unique country context in which they work. Extending rights, promoting participation, and redirecting the state to support rights-based programs are all important components of promoting well-being.

ENCOURAGING VIRTUOUS CIRCLES

In the broadest sense, this book demonstrates that local governments can initiate virtuous circles of change when they are able to take advantage of new participatory venues, nationally designed inclusive social programs, and improved administrative capacity. The three pathways we identify in this book support one another and form a virtuous circle for well-being when they all operate at high levels. For example, formally institutionalizing democratic practices within policy-making processes enables citizens to express *voice* and *vote*, which is more likely to lead to meaningful impacts if a capable state is also present to carry out citizens' demands. The positive interactions run the opposite way as well; states are more likely to make better use of resources when they receive inputs via democratic institutions as well as when citizens exercise oversight. In this sense, the ideal whole is much greater than the sum of its parts, both in terms of statistical results surrounding well-being and in local evidence of different areas working simultaneously to improve citizens' lives. Governments that invest in core dimensions of democracy are more likely to produce the types of changes in human development that citizens desire and have come to expect from their governments.

Our analysis shows that the confluence of all three factors is difficult to achieve, but that change is more widespread than among just a few award-winning municipalities: hundreds of municipalities perform at high levels on all three pathways and hundreds more on at least two of the pathways. We are therefore cautiously optimistic about the prospects for generating high-quality democratic governance and improving well-being, even in poor cities in the developing world. Achieving good local governance through democracy is hard work, but it is encouraging that it does occur in some municipalities. It is also encouraging that we find no trade-off between strengthening state capacity and deepening the quality of democracy. Rather, they are complementary and reinforcing.

However, the links in the virtuous chain we describe above are fragile and can be broken when governments abandon their support of any one area. Our results show that the three pathways' virtuous interaction can also become vicious: the lack of participatory institutions and an incapable state drag down social program performance, and vice versa. Our work thus shows that the pathways to well-being are full of pitfalls and the price of sustaining good governance and fragile gains is vigilance across as many areas as possible. Moreover, our analysis covers a period where national democracy and the economy were functioning relatively well. As our "lessons" explain, democratic practice cannot be taken for granted; it is fragile and human development is also sensitive to economic conditions. What happens when a national government faces a political and economic crisis? For example, what happens when a country faces its worst economic recession since the Great Depression, when champions of social inclusion are ousted from office, and when the federal government faces fiscal austerity measures that threaten to roll back more inclusionary social protections provided by their welfare state? We do not have the data to evaluate these areas directly, but our discussion below addresses our findings in the context of Brazil's post-2014 political and economic crisis.

SUSTAINABLE RESULTS? IMPLICATIONS OF BRAZIL'S
POLITICAL AND ECONOMIC CRISIS

Brazil entered a profound economic downturn and a political crisis just as we finished our data collection. Our data coverage is through 2013, which we collected in 2015 and 2016. The Brazilian federal government often publishes data several years after it collects it, which means that researchers face a lag in the timing of data collection and its availability for analysis. The political crisis illuminates the fragility of new democratic institutions and inclusive social programs. The economic downturn highlights the importance of economic growth to support improvements in well-being.

With regard to the political crisis, 2013 is commonly cited as the year that marked a sharp turn in Brazil's political trajectory. (See Kingstone and Power 2017.) A wave of protests against a small increase in public bus fares morphed into a widespread political mobilization in which multiple social and economic sectors called for reform. The 2014 presidential election, which the opposition expected to win because of a slowing economy and the mobilization of conservative sectors, nonetheless led to the narrow reelection of incumbent President Dilma Rousseff. Following her inauguration, the decade-long commodity boom (early 2000s to early-mid 2010s) ended, weakening economic growth. Brazil then entered its worst economic recession since the 1930s.

Compounding the national political and economic crisis was a corruption investigation that ensnarled multiple senior members of the Workers' Party, many of whom were close to President Lula (2002–2006; 2007–2010) and President Dilma Rousseff (2011–2014; 2015–2016). The corruption scandal deepened Brazil's economic and political problems by convincing the Workers' Party's opponents that the party was deeply corrupt, which led to a decrease in support for its social and political agenda. An investigation into widespread corruption and kickbacks involving Brazil's largest company, Petrobras, also implicated broad swaths of the economic and political elite, including politicians from all major parties. The elites' feelings of increasing vulnerability added to the volatile national mood. It was in this context that President Dilma Rousseff was impeached and removed from office. The official reason for her impeachment was budgetary malfeasance; she was accused of obscuring the country's fiscal crisis ahead of the 2014 elections. Observers note, however, that Rousseff followed a common executive practice of moving money from one part of the budget to the other. While

Congress adhered to procedural rules in impeaching Rousseff, she and many of her supporters considered her impeachment a political "coup." Brazilians were deeply divided over her impeachment.

In 2018, as we were finishing the book, Jair Bolsonaro was elected Brazil's president with 55 percent of the vote in the country's second round of elections. The campaign season reflected a highly charged political climate that revealed deep divisions within society. Political opportunity, partisan realignment, and dissatisfaction with the status quo opened the door for Bolsonaro's electoral victory. Bolsonaro's win worried those concerned about social inclusion. Throughout his decades-long political career, he has been on the extreme far-right of the ideological spectrum. Although Bolsonaro was elected through a democratic process, he has lauded Brazil's authoritarian past and reveres former military leaders who tortured political opponents during the military era (1964–1985). He has also voiced opinions that run counter to Brazil's more inclusionary trends since democratization. For instance, he has openly espoused racist, misogynist, and anti-LBGTQ views. He has also suggested the country embrace harsh policing tactics in response to the country's high homicide rates. This approach would render the poor and predominantly Afro-Brazilian population vulnerable to human rights violations. For now, Bolsonaro's public declarations suggest that his presidential administration will be unlikely to support investments in the core democratic pathways that improve well-being.

We would expect the deep economic recession, a national-level political crisis and Bolsonaro's election to have negative effects on efforts to improve well-being. Indeed, recently published data reveals infant mortality rose in 2016 for the first time in a quarter-century (Collucci 2018). In our analysis, we found that economic growth was significantly associated with improvements in well-being. We thus expect that a decrease in economic growth will, at best, lead to a decrease in the rate of improvements in well-being and, at worst, unravel the improvements from the 2000s. A deep economic crisis restricts government revenues and resources, which then limits governments' ability to support rights-based social programs and improve state capacity. Individuals also have lower personal income during an economic crisis because of job losses and pay cuts. As a result, they are more likely to rely on public services, which are often more difficult to obtain due to higher demand amid government cutbacks. Yet, it is not a lack of revenue or jobs alone that will likely impact efforts to provide services to the poor and improve their lives. Our pathway-based analysis points to several additional ways to conceive of the relationships between the current economic and political crisis and well-being.

The federal government's fiscal resources, administrative support, and leadership role are also crucial components to improving well-being. Three of Brazil's key inclusive social programs – Bolsa Família, Family Health Program (PSF), and the noncontributory pension (BPC) – relied on support from the two political parties that controlled the presidency from 1994 to 2016. These two decades of support for inclusive, rights-based social policies profoundly changed millions of Brazilians' lives. The inclusive social programs were influential because of their design (rights-based, technocratic), their oversight mechanisms, federal coordination to implement the programs, and an active, federal role in the programs' ongoing administration during the 2000s. A withdrawal of resources and technical support in the post-2016 period could therefore limit these programs' capacity to improve well-being. In particular, the Family Health Programs and Bolsa Família had a wide and extensive impact, improving health outcomes and delivering more resources into the hands of the very poor. Thus, local governments will be hard-pressed to sustain the programs contributing to improvements in well-being if the federal government reduces financial transfers and technical support.

Brazil's municipal participatory infrastructure is arguably the most insulated from the national economic and political crisis. There is little doubt that the federal government under President Michel Temer (who took over when President Rousseff was impeached) has substantially downplayed the importance of policy conferences and national-level policy councils (Avritzer 2017). However, the withdrawal of federal support did not explicitly undermine the existing participatory infrastructure at the municipal level. This mechanism may well withstand national headwinds if local officials and civil society leaders continue to defend the need for participation.

We theorize that the political and economic crisis could produce two starkly different effects on the municipal policy council system. It is possible that the increased attention to public spending and corruption could lead more individuals to participate in local democratic venues, which would improve public dialogue, increase oversight, and enhance service delivery. In this scenario, a municipality with a robust participatory system may fare better under the dual crises than those municipalities without these citizen engagement processes. However, we can also envision scenarios where the economic and political crises drive people away from public participation venues. For example, poor citizens may have less time to devote to community and political activities because they need to spend more time generating income. Politically mobilized individuals may change their political focus away from local issues and choose to dedicate their scarce time and energy to national-level issues. Additionally, participation through free exchange of ideas would be hindered if Brazil's relatively open political sphere begins to stifle dialogue. All of these factors could make participatory institutions less effective and lead some individuals to grow disenchanted with public participation.

Finally, local state capacity increased in the first decade of the 2000s (this book's timeframe), because the federal government invested in improving public management of policies and programs. We expect that many municipalities will lack the internal dynamics to improve state capacity and well-being, should the federal government withdraw technical support or limit oversight. For example, we would expect local government officials interested in maintaining the status quo to avoid reform in municipalities similar to Garanhuns and Jaboatão. (See Chapter 8.) In contrast, we anticipate continued internal pressures to improve state capacity in municipalities similar to Camaragibe. Given the national spotlight on corruption, it is possible to envision newfound interest in addressing transparency at the local level. But it is also possible to envision efforts to strengthen local state capacity giving way to personalistic politics if the traditional political forces that supported Bolsonaro's election have their way. In this scenario, Brazil's legal institutions will likely be put to the test.

Brazil's recent national political and economic trajectory has been sobering and disconcerting for organizations and individuals advocating the expansion of rights, democratic participation, and social well-being. However, we note that the institutional foundations for Brazil's continued social transformations remain in place. We know what works for improving human development. The democratic principles and social rights that improve well-being are enshrined in the constitution. We also know how their related mechanisms work to improve peoples' lives. It will ultimately be up to engaged citizens, civil servants, and politicians to defend democratic principles and promote an inclusive state.

MOVING BEYOND BRAZIL: BUILDING PATHWAYS TO IMPROVING WELL-BEING AROUND THE WORLD

This book focuses on Brazil but we believe that our theoretical explanation and findings are relevant for countries across the Global South and, increasingly, among the older, more consolidated democracies. These countries face similar problems that Brazilian citizens and government officials must contend with: high inequality, expansive citizen needs, misallocation of public resources, fragmented states, and poorly performing democratic institutions. Governments, NGOs, CSOs, and citizens are seeking to address these problems through the creation of social and political institutions. Similarly, multilateral organizations such as the World Bank are also investing in both "supply-side" (state capacity, state leadership) and "demand-side" strategies (community-driven development, participatory budgeting) to improve well-being. International donors, such as the Ford Foundation and the Open Society Foundation, have invested their resources and energy to support civil society. Our argument and supporting evidence suggests that there are no simple answers or magic formulas to improving well-being.

We are now well into the twenty-first century. Democratic governments around the world can draw on considerable evidence to adopt policies that improve well-being. The stakes for these efforts are high: globally, the poor have made great gains since 2000 but billions of people remain stuck in grinding, multigenerational poverty. Billions more are in a precarious position of meeting their basic needs, but still facing serious, daily challenges. Concurrently, democracy is now the most acceptable form of government, at least rhetorically, and many highly restrictive, authoritarian regimes now hold regular elections. Democratic governments using free and fair elections respond to their citizens and seek to improve well-being, but these governments face political challenges as well. Democratic rollbacks, restrictions on rights, and growing inequality all combine to undermine democracies' efforts to empower their citizens and improve their lives. Free and fair elections thus represent one important way that citizens pursue well-being, but elections are not the only path forward and, perhaps, not the most important one either. Building institutions and targeting public policy toward poor, marginalized populations are also key to human development performance around the world. Our evidence and analysis demonstrate that building democratic institutions into a broader state architecture is an important element of improving state capacity. Hierarchical, authoritarian models of state development continue to be in vogue in places like Singapore and China and were previously used in South Africa, South Korea, and Taiwan. Yet, our evidence suggests that combining coherent, capable states and participatory institutions is an important step forward for enhancing citizens' capabilities and autonomy.

There are multiple, independent, parallel democratic pathways that improve marginalized citizens' well-being. None of the three pathways is absolutely necessary to improve well-being and all are sufficient to produce change. The presence of one pathway is better than none, and two pathways are better than one. Moreover, deficits in one area can be offset by gains in others – for example, local governments do not necessarily require inclusive federal programs to begin reform processes that lead to well-being. Similarly, municipalities need not invest in all three areas at once; even poor governments can initiate processes that improve peoples' lives by developing any one of the pathways to well-being. Democratically elected governments and their civil society allies have the power to invest in programs, policies, and institutions that foster participation, citizenship, and inclusive state capacity. Ultimately, these investments can make democracy work to support human development and advance citizens' well-being.

APPENDIX

Democracy at Work Pathways to Well-Being in Brazil

Brian Wampler, Natasha Borges Sugiyama, Michael Touchton

4: REDUCING POVERTY: BROADENING ACCESS TO INCOME

TABLE A4.2.A *Explaining poverty outcomes, 2006–2013: Federal social programs, voluntary policy councils, and local public goods spending*
Model 1 uses Arellano-Bond Dynamic Panel Estimation and Model 2 uses Fixed Effects. These models use a continuous measure of policy councils related to poverty, which is coded 0 to 6.

	Model 1	Model 2
Variable	Coefficient (SE)	Coefficient (SE)
Instrumental variable (L1)	0.70** (0.13)	
Voluntary councils	0.01** (0.003)	0.02* (0.01)
Bolsa Família coverage	0.003* (0.0005)	0.006** (0.002)
Bolsa Família management	−0.04 (0.03)	−0.06 (0.04)
Per capita municipal public goods spending (% of total spending)	0.17** (0.03)	0.11* (0.05)
Median earnings for low-income residents	0.18** (0.03)	0.20** (0.04)
Competitive elections	−0.08 (0.06)	−0.04 (0.04)
Left-leaning mayor	0.03 (0.03)	−0.10 (0.08)
Constant	0.40 (0.32)	0.57 (0.46)
N	20,312	20,312
Wald Chi² (6), F	124.78	39.43
Prob> Chi², Prob> F	0.000	0.000

* Indicates significance at better than 0.05 (two-tailed test).
** Indicates significance at better than 0.01 (two-tailed test).

TABLE A4.2.B *Explaining poverty outcomes, 2006–2013: Federal social programs, voluntary policy councils, and local public goods spending* The dependent variables in these models are the percentage of each municipality's population in the lowest quintile of national income distribution, the percentage that lives below the national poverty line, and the percentage below the extreme poverty line. Model 1 uses Arellano-Bond Dynamic Panel Estimation and Model 2 uses Fixed Effects.

Variable	Model 1 Coefficient (SE)	Model 2 Coefficient (SE)	Model 3 Coefficient (SE)
Instrumental variable (L1)	0.66** (0.18)	0.60** (0.04)	0.71** (0.13)
Voluntary council commitment	−0.07* (0.03)	−0.09* (0.04)	−0.13** (0.03)
Bolsa Família coverage	−0.02* (0.01)	−0.03* (0.01)	−0.02* (0.01)
Bolsa Família management	−0.04* (0.02)	−0.05** (0.01)	−0.04** (0.01)
Per capita municipal public goods spending (% of total spending)	−0.06** (0.02)	−0.08** (0.01)	−0.14** (0.01)
Median earnings for low-income residents	−0.03** (0.01)	−0.02* (0.01)	−0.04** (0.01)
Competitive elections	−0.16 (0.09)	− 0.14 (0.09)	− 0.16 (0.12)
Left-leaning mayor	0.14 (0.10)	−0.11 (0.08)	−0.15 (0.12)
Constant	0.47** (0.07)	0.23** (0.05)	0.14* (0.07)
N	17,490	17,490	17,490
Wald Chi² (6), F	59.32	106.27	133.84
Prob> Chi², Prob> F	0.000	0.000	0.000

* Indicates significance at better than 0.05 (two-tailed test).
** Indicates significance at better than 0.01 (two-tailed test).

TABLE A4.2.C *Explaining poverty outcomes: Voluntary policy councils, 2006–2013*

This model uses Nearest-Neighbor Propensity Score Matching with Treatment Effects.

Variable	Coefficient (SE)
Voluntary council commitment	0.12**
	(0.04)
N	20,325

* Indicates significance at better than 0.05 (two-tailed test).
** Indicates significance at better than 0.01 (two-tailed test).

5: IMPROVING HEALTH: SAVING LIVES

TABLE A5.4.A *Explaining infant mortality, 2006–2013: Federal social programs, voluntary policy councils, and local state capacity*
This model uses continuous counts of the voluntary policy councils and health council meetings instead of dummy variables and uses Negative Binomial Estimation with Fixed Effects.

Variable	Coefficient (SE)	Coefficient (SE)
Voluntary council count Health council meetings	-0.04** (0.004)	0.00004 (0.007)
Family Health Program coverage	-0.002** (0.0002)	-0.002** (0.0007)
Bolsa Família coverage	-0.0004 (0.0002)	0.001 (0.001)
Bolsa Família management	-0.22** (0.03)	-0.12 (0.10)
Competitive mayoral race	0.02 (0.01)	0.11 (0.11)
PT mayor	-0.01 (0.02)	0.05 (0.11)
Presidential vote	0.002 (0.001)	-0.001 (0.003)
Per capita health care spending	0.000004 (0.00002)	0.00001 (0.00003)
Median low income wage	0.0007** (0.0002)	0.001** (0.0004)
Constant	2.31** (0.07)	1.90** (0.22)
N	20,268	6,490
Wald Chi²	265.44	23.42
Prob> Chi²	0.000	0.00

* Indicates significance at better than 0.05 (two-tailed test).
** Indicates significance at better than 0.01 (two-tailed test).

TABLE A5.4.B *Explaining infant mortality, 2006–2013: Federal social programs, voluntary policy councils, and local state capacity*
These models use Arellano-Bond Dynamic Panel Estimation for different terciles of infant mortality.

Variable	Coefficient (SE) (lowest tercile)	Coefficient (SE) (middle tercile)	Coefficient (SE) (highest tercile)
Infant mortality (L1)	0.51** (0.05)	–0.09** (0.04)	–0.70** (0.08)
Infant mortality (L2)	0.31** (0.05)	–0.02 (0.02)	–0.35** (0.05)
Voluntary council commitment	–8.41** (1.06)	–9.07** (3.18)	–3.11 (5.28)
Family Health Program coverage	–0.06** (0.02)	–0.01 (0.01)	0.04* (0.02)
Bolsa Família coverage	–0.08** (0.01)	–0.02** (0.01)	0.18** (0.02)
Bolsa Família management	–22.06** (1.93)	–5.09 (1.12)	21.30** (2.31)
Competitive elections	1.17 (0.62)	–0.85 (0.49)	–2.44* (1.15)
PT mayor	–3.06** (0.97)	0.44 (0.78)	–1.52 (1.39)
Presidential vote	1.34** (0.24)	1.12** (0.18)	–1.03* (0.40)
Per capita health care spending	–0.01* (0.002)	–0.01* (0.001)	0.02** (0.004)
Median low income wage	–0.16** (0.05)	–0.12* (0.05)	0.51** (0.13)
Constant	Omitted	Omitted	Omitted
N	5,350	4,338	2,708
Wald Chi² (6)	1254.26	3923.64	1571.45
Prob> Chi²	0.000	0.00	0.00

* Indicates significance at better than 0.05 (two-tailed test).
** Indicates significance at better than 0.01 (two-tailed test).

TABLE A5.4.C *Explaining infant mortality, 2006–2013: Federal social programs, voluntary policy councils, and local state capacity*

The first model uses Arellano-Bond Dynamic Panel Estimation. The second uses the same estimation, but with year dummies. 2007–2010 are significant and positive. The third model uses Difference-in-Difference Estimation.

Variable	Coefficient (SE)	Coefficient (SE)	Coefficient (SE)
Infant mortality (L1)	−0.10**	0.03	
	(0.03)	(0.03)	
Infant mortality (L2)	−0.02	0.05**	
	(0.02)	(0.02)	
Voluntary Council commitment	−8.41**	−6.01**	−7.23**
	(0.84)	(0.85)	(0.92)
Family Health Program coverage	−0.03**	0.01	−0.005
	(0.007)	(0.01)	(0.006)
Bolsa Família coverage	−0.03**	−0.01	0.01
	(0.01)	(0.01)	(0.007)
Bolsa Família management	−10.41**	−1.82	−1.54
	(0.95)	(1.18)	(1.16)
Competitive elections	−0.05	−0.59	−0.13
	(0.38)	(0.41)	(0.43)
PT mayor	−1.33**	−0.76	−0.59
	(0.53)	(0.57)	(0.55)
Presidential vote	0.65**	0.32**	Omitted
	(0.12)	(0.11)	
Per capita health care spending	−0.003**	0.0004	−0.001
	(0.001)	(0.0005)	(0.001)
Median low income wages	0.06*	0.05	0.23**
	(0.03)	(0.03)	(0.04)
Constant	Omitted	Omitted	−0.32**
			(0.09)
N	12,396	12,392	14,033
Wald Chi² (15)	5072.72	11659.35	105.76
Prob> Chi²	0.000	0.000	0.000

* Indicates significance at better than 0.05 (two-tailed test).
** Indicates significance at better than 0.01 (two-tailed test).

TABLE A5.4.D *Explaining infant mortality, 2006–2013: Federal social programs, voluntary policy councils, and local state capacity*
This model uses Nearest-Neighbor Propensity Score Matching with Treatment Effects.

Variable	Coefficient (SE)
Voluntary council commitment	−0.79** (0.22)
N	20,515

* Indicates significance at better than 0.05 (two-tailed test).
** Indicates significance at better than 0.01 (two-tailed test).

TABLE A5.5.A *Explaining infant mortality, 2006–2013: Federal social programs and incentivized (rather than voluntary) health councils*
This model uses cross-sectional time series Negative Binomial Estimation with Fixed Effects.

Variable	Coefficient (SE)
Incentivized council commitment	0.05 (0.24)
Family Health Program coverage	−0.002** (0.0002)
Bolsa Família coverage	−0.004* (0.0002)
Bolsa Família management	−0.23** (0.03)
Competitive mayor	0.02 (0.01)
PT mayor	−0.01 (0.02)
Presidential vote	0.002 (0.001)
Per capita health care spending	−0.000006 (0.00002)
Low-income wages	0.0006** (0.0002)
Constant	1.99** (0.25)
N	20,268
Wald Chi^2 (6)	199.57
Prob> Chi^2	0.000

* Indicates significance at better than 0.05 (two-tailed test).
** Indicates significance at better than 0.01 (two-tailed test).

6: EMPOWERING WOMEN: SAVING MOTHERS AND ENHANCING OPPORTUNITIES

TABLE A6.3.A *Explaining maternal mortality, 2006–2013: Federal social programs, voluntary policy councils, and local state capacity*
The first model uses Arellano-Bond Dynamic Panel Estimation. The second uses the same estimation, but with year dummies; 2007–2010 are significant and positive.

Variable	Coefficient (SE)	Coefficient (SE)
Maternal mortality (L1)	−0.08** (0.02)	−0.03 (0.04)
Maternal mortality (L2)	−0.03* (0.01)	0.04* (0.02)
Voluntary council commitment	−6.33** (0.74)	−6.57** (0.91)
Family Health Program coverage	−0.05** (0.004)	−0.03** (0.01)
Bolsa Família coverage	−0.02* (0.01)	−0.02* (0.01)
Bolsa Família management	−11.65** (0.52)	−10.54** (1.27)
Competitive elections	−0.15 (0.20)	−0.44 (0.36)
PT mayor	−1.05 (0.62)	−0.84 (0.75)
Presidential vote	0.61* (0.29)	0.46* (0.26)
Per capita health care spending	−0.003* (0.001)	−0.0004* (0.0002)
Median low income wages	−0.06 (0.04)	−0.05 (0.03)
Constant	Omitted	Omitted
N	11,893	11,670
Wald Chi² (15)	3169.21	9530.72
Prob> Chi²	0.000	0.000

* Indicates significance at better than 0.05 (two-tailed test).
** Indicates significance at better than 0.01 (two-tailed test).

This model uses Nearest-Neighbor Propensity Score Matching with Treatment Effects. These estimates are for maternal mortality.

Variable	Maternal mortality Coefficient (SE)
Voluntary council commitment	−0.37**
	(0.05)
N	20,248

* Indicates significance at better than 0.05 (two-tailed test).
** Indicates significance at better than 0.01 (two-tailed test).

TABLE A6.4.A *Explaining variation in women's income, 2006–2013: Federal social programs and voluntary policy councils*
The first model uses Arellano-Bond Dynamic Panel Estimation, but with year dummies; 2007–2010 are significant and positive. The second model uses difference-in-difference estimation

Variable	Coefficient (SE)	Coefficient (SE)
Earnings for low-income women (L1)	0.17** (0.05)	
Earnings for low-income women (L2)	0.10* (0.04)	
Voluntary council commitment	0.15 (0.10)	0.10 (0.08)
Family Health Program coverage	0.05 (0.03)	0.06 (0.04)
Bolsa Família coverage	0.04* (0.02)	0.06* (0.03)
Bolsa Família management	0.23** (0.04)	0.20** (0.01)
PT mayor	−0.07 (0.06)	−0.05 (0.05)
Per capita GDP	0.22** (0.03)	0.24** (0.01)
Median low income wages	0.17** (0.05)	0.19** (0.04)
Constant	Omitted	1.21* (0.54)
N	15,196	14,540
Wald Chi² (15)	188.24	170.93
Prob> Chi²	0.000	0.000

* Indicates significance at better than 0.05 (two-tailed test).
** Indicates significance at better than 0.01 (two-tailed test).

TABLE A6.4.B *Explaining variation in women's income,*
2006–2013: Federal social programs and voluntary policy councils
This model uses Nearest-Neighbor Propensity Score Matching with
Treatment Effects. These estimates are for the economic
empowerment variables.

Variable	Earnings for low-income women Coefficient (SE)
Voluntary council commitment	0.16 (0.12)
N	17,464

* Indicates significance at better than 0.05 (two-tailed test).
** Indicates significance at better than 0.01 (two-tailed test).

TABLE A6.5.A *Explaining variation in women's political participation,*
2006–2013
These models use Arellano-Bond estimation and include year dummies.
2011–13 are positive and significant.

Variable	% of mayoral candidates	% of legislative candidates	Candidate-to-quota ratio
	Coefficient (SE)	Coefficient (SE)	Coefficient (SE)
Instrumental variable (L1)	0.72**	0.73**	0.65**
	(0.13)	(0.20)	(0.29)
Women's rights council	0.14**	0.11*	0.21*
	(0.03)	(0.05)	(0.10)
Bolsa Família coverage	0.06	0.04	0.04
	(0.05)	(0.04)	(0.04)
Family Health Plan coverage	0.07	−0.07	0.10
	(0.05)	(0.04)	(0.06)
Bolsa Família management	0.06	0.12	0.05
	(0.06)	(0.10)	(0.03)
PT mayor	0.04	0.03	0.03
	(0.03)	(0.03)	(0.02)
Per capita gross local product (logged)	0.11*	0.06**	0.09**
	(0.05)	(0.02)	(0.03)
Constant	0.27**	0.33*	0.90
	(0.04)	(0.10)	(0.66)
N	14,057	13,921	14,374
Wald Chi^2 (6)	226.52	237.19	210.39
Prob> Chi^2	0.000	0.000	0.00

* Indicates significance at better than 0.05 (two-tailed test).
** Indicates significance at better than 0.01 (two-tailed test).

TABLE A6.5.B *Explaining women's political empowerment, 2006–2013: Federal Social Programs, voluntary policy councils, and inclusive state capacity*

These models use Nearest-Neighbor Propensity Score Matching with Treatment Effects to generate estimates for political empowerment variables.

Variable	% of mayoral candidates Coefficient (SE)	% of legislative candidates Coefficient (SE)	Candidate-to-quota ratio Coefficient (SE)
Voluntary council commitment	0.11** (0.02)	0.10** (0.03)	0.21* (0.09)
N	16,278	15,961	15,955

* Indicates significance at better than 0.05 (two-tailed test).
** Indicates significance at better than 0.01 (two-tailed test).

7: EDUCATING SOCIETY: PROMOTING PUBLIC EDUCATION AND LEARNING

TABLE A7.3.A *Explaining school attendance, 2006–2013*
These models use Arellano-Bond Dynamic Panel Estimation.

Variable	Crèche attendance Coefficient (SE)	Preschool attendance Coefficient (SE)	Elementary school attendance Coefficient (SE)	High school attendance Coefficient (SE)
Instrumental variables (L1)	0.53**	0.45**	0.62**	0.66**
	(0.14)	(0.12)	(0.09)	(0.20)
Instrumental variables (L2)	0.21	0.15	0.24	0.28
	(0.17)	(0.15)	(0.18)	(0.21)
Education-related councils	0.20**	0.23**	0.19*	0.13
	(0.05)	(0.03)	(0.10)	(0.08)
PSF coverage	0.02	0.05	0.03	0.06
	(0.02)	(0.03)	(0.02)	(0.04)
Bolsa Família coverage	0.05**	0.05*	0.10*	0.12**
	(0.01)	(0.02)	(0.04)	(0.03)
Bolsa Família management	0.13*	0.10*	0.16*	0.15*
	(0.05)	(0.04)	(0.07)	(0.06)
PT mayor	−0.05	0.09	−0.12	−0.08
	(0.04)	(0.06)	(0.10)	(0.08)
Mayor's vote share	0.03	−0.02	0.05	−0.03
	(0.03)	(0.03)	(0.05)	(0.02)
Per capita GDP (logged)	0.34**	0.36**	0.29**	0.29**
	(0.01)	(0.03)	(0.05)	(0.08)
Constant	0.25**	0.40**	0.27**	0.59*
	(0.04)	(0.12)	(0.08)	(0.26)
N	34,870	35,414	35,295	35,584
Wald Chi² (7)	153.91	159.01	164.53	163.27
Prob> Chi²	0.000	0.000	0.000	0.00

* Indicates significance at better than 0.05 (two-tailed test).
** Indicates significance at better than 0.01 (two-tailed test).

TABLE A7.3.B *Explaining school attendance, 2006–2013: Federal social programs and voluntary policy councils*
These models use Nearest-Neighbor Propensity Score Matching with Treatment Effects to generate estimates for political empowerment variables.

Variable	Daycare attendance Coefficient (SE)	Preschool attendance Coefficient (SE)	Elementary school attendance Coefficient (SE)	Junior high and high school attendance Coefficient (SE)
Voluntary council commitment	0.21** (0.02)	0.22** (0.05)	0.14** (0.04)	0.17 (0.12)
N	16,244	15,769	15,873	16,533

* Indicates significance at better than 0.05 (two-tailed test).
** Indicates significance at better than 0.01 (two-tailed test).

TABLE A7.4.A *Explaining ENEM test scores, 2006–2013*
These models use Arellano-Bond Dynamic Panel Estimation and Bolsa
Familia management scores instead of our education infrastructure index.

Variable	High school graduation rates Coefficient (SE)	ENEM score Coefficient (SE)	% of students with passing scores Coefficient (SE)
Instrumental variables (L1)	0.42** (0.05)	0.25** (0.01)	0.33** (0.06)
Instrumental variables (L2)	0.18 (0.10)	0.20* (0.08)	0.11 (0.09)
Education councils	0.18 (0.15)	0.37 (0.30)	0.19 (0.17)
PSF coverage	0.16 (0.12)	0.26 (0.22)	0.23 (0.18)
Bolsa Família coverage	−0.13* (0.06)	−0.53* (0.24)	−0.18* (0.07)
Bolsa Família management	0.06* (0.03)	0.14* (0.05)	0.06** (0.02)
PT mayor	−0.17 (0.17)	−0.36 (0.25)	−0.18 (0.15)
Mayoral vote share	0.14 (0.13)	0.29 (0.26)	0.13 (0.09)
Per capita GDP (logged)	0.34** (0.03)	0.77** (0.12)	0.31** (0.02)
Constant	0.55* (0.21)	1.90* (0.87)	0.58** (0.15)
N	56,349	53,371	54,236
Wald Chi² (7)	147.63	179.27	144.16
Prob> Chi²	0.000	0.000	0.000

* Indicates significance at better than 0.05 (two-tailed test).
** Indicates significance at better than 0.01 (two-tailed test).

TABLE A7.4.B *Explaining high school graduation rates, test scores, and test passage rates, 2006–2013: Federal social programs and voluntary policy councils*

These models use Nearest-Neighbor Propensity Score Matching with Treatment Effects to generate estimates for political empowerment variables.

Variable	High school graduation rates Coefficient (SE)	Total ENEM score (logged) Coefficient (SE)	% of students with passing scores Coefficient (SE)
Voluntary council commitment	0.06 (0.05)	0.09 (0.06)	0.05 (0.05)
N	15,597	14,645	14,639

* Indicates significance at better than 0.05 (two-tailed test).
** Indicates significance at better than 0.01 (two-tailed test).

8: PATHWAYS AT WORK: LESSONS FROM BRAZIL'S POOR
NORTHEAST

Case Studies: Questionnaire for Democracy at Work*

---

1. What are the two or three biggest challenges you face as an administrator?

2. How much autonomy do you have to administer the program as you see fit? Do you find that elected officials want to 'participate'/interfere?

3. How has Bolsa Família/PSF/Ed Program contributed to advances in well-being in your community, if at all?

4. To what extent does the municipal government invest time and resources for participation?

5. To what extent does the municipal government invest time and resources for social programs?

6. To what extent do administrators in health, education, or social assistance secretariats use IGD resources to promote engagement and participation?

7. To what extent do administrators use local capacity to refine social programs, extending into new areas or using the data from the cadastro to address new social needs?

8. To what extent do IGD funds alter how municipal administrators offer services or expand them in new ways? To what extent are IGD resources used to strengthen BF program (as intended by the federal government)?

9. Have civic leaders sought to engage in participatory spaces to specifically address the operations of these programs (BF/PSF/Educ./Gender)?

10. As the manager of BF/PSF/Gender Program, how have you engaged with the participatory councils in your city? Please provide some specific examples, where possible.

11. There are five different councils that address issues related to X dependent variable (Ed/poverty/health/women). To what extent do you work with these different councils?

12. Over the past year, has this council deliberated on policy issues pertaining to X issue? Can you please provide examples of the most meaningful interventions where this council influenced specific policy changes?

13. What were the most significant challenges that limited the council's ability to influence policy change?

14. What types of materials, if any, are provided to council members on the annual budget or year-end reports? If possible, could you please provide examples?

(continued)

(continued)

---

15. Was the council involved in monitoring the ongoing implementation of policy projects? Please provide examples.
16. Please tell me about your current position (Title, Role).
17. Please describe your professional background, training, or previous work experience.

---

* We used three versions of this questionnaire for our fieldwork in Pernambuco, Brazil. Each version is very similar to the one presented here, which is for government officials. However, we made slight modifications to the other versions for interviews with leaders in civil society and members of policy councils. Those additional versions are available on request.

References

Abers, R. (2000). *Inventing Local Democracy: Grassroots Politics in Brazil.* Boulder, CO: Lynne Rienner Publishers.

Abers, R. & Keck, M. E. (2013). *Practical Authority: Agency and Institutional Change in Brazilian Water Politics.* Oxford, UK: Oxford University Press.

Acemoglu, D., Johnson, S. & Robinson, J. (2000). *The Colonial Origins of Comparative Development: An Empirical Investigation* (NBER Working Paper No. 7771). Cambridge, MA: National Bureau of Economic Research.

Acemoglu, D. & Robinson, J. A. (2013). *Why Nations Fail: The Origins of Power, Prosperity, and Poverty.* New York, NY: Crown Business.

Adams, G. (1981). *The Iron Triangle.* New York, NY: Transaction Publishers.

Afonso, A. & Aubyn, M. S. (2006). Cross-Country Efficiency of Secondary Education Provision: A Semi-Parametric Analysis with Non-Discretionary Inputs. *Economic Modelling,* 23(3), 476–491.

Almeida, C., Cayres, D. C. & Tatagiba, L. (2015). Balanço dos Estudos Sobre os Conselhos de Políticas Públicas na Última Década, *Lua Nova,* 94, 255–294.

Almeida, C., Lüchmann, L. & Ribeiro, E. (2012). Associativismo e Representação Política Feminina no Brasil. *Revista Brasileira de Ciência Política,* 8, 237–263.

Alvarez, S. (1990). *Engendering Democracy in Brazil: Women's Movements in Transition Politics.* Princeton, NJ: Princeton University Press.

Alvarez, S. (1999). Advocating Feminism: The Latin American Feminist NGO "Boom." *International Feminist Journal of Politics,* 1(2), 181–209.

Alvarez, S., Rubin, J., Thayer, M., Baiocchi, G. & Lao-Montes, A. (2017). *Beyond Civil Society: Activism, Participation, and Protest in Latin America.* Durham and London: Duke University Press.

Ames, B. (1987). *Political Survival.* Berkeley, CA: University of California Press.

Ames, B. (2001). *The Deadlock of Democracy in Brazil.* Ann Arbor, MI: University of Michigan Press.

Amsden, A. (1992). A Theory of Government Intervention in Late Industrialization. In L. Putterman & D. Rueschmeyer, eds., *State and Market in Development: Synergy or Rivalry.* Boulder, CO: Lynne Rienner Pub, 53–84.

Ansell, C. & Gash, A. (2008). Collaborative Governance in Theory and Practice. *Journal of Public Administration Research and Theory*, 18(4), 543–571.

APSA Task Force (2012). *Democratic Imperatives: Innovations in Rights, Participation, and Economic Citizenship.* Washington, DC: American Political Science Association.

Aquino, R, Oliviera, N. F. & Bareto, M. (2009). Impact of the Family Health Program on Infant Mortality in Brazilian Municipalities. *American Journal of Public Health*, 99(1): 87–93.

Aranha, A. L. M. (2017). Accountability, Corruption, and Local Government: Mapping the Control Steps. *Brazilian Political Science Review*, 11(2): 1–31.

Araújo, A. V. (2003). *Política Educacional e Participação Popular: Um Estudo Sobre Esta Relação no Município de Camaragibe-PE* (Unpublished master's thesis). Recife, PE: Universidade Federal de Pernambuco.

Araujo, M. C., Bosch, M. & Schady, N. (2017). Can Cash Transfers Help Households Escape an Inter-Generational Poverty Trap? in C. B. Barrett, M. R. Carter & J. Chavas, eds., *The Economics of Poverty Traps.* Chicago, IL: University of Chicago Press,

Arellano, M. & Bond, S. (1988). *Dynamic Panel Data Estimation Using PPD: A Guide for Users.* London, UK: Institute for Fiscal Studies.

Arendt, H. (1958). *The Human Condition.* Chicago, IL: University of Chicago Press.

Arias, E. D. (2009). *Drugs and Democracy in Rio de Janeiro: Trafficking, Social Networks, and Public Security.* Chapel Hill, NC: University of North Carolina Press.

Arretche, M. (2015). *Trajetórias das Desigualdades: Como o Brasil Mudou nos Últimos Cinquenta Anos, São Paulo.* SP: Editora Unesp.

Arretche, M. (ed.) (2018). *Paths of Inequality in Brazil: A Half-Century of Changes.* New York, NY: Springer Press.

Arretche, M. & Marques, E. (2002). Municipalização da Saúde no Brasil: Diferenças Regionais, Poder do Voto e Estratégias de Governo. *Ciência & Saúde Coletiva*, 7(3), 455–479.

Attanasio, O., Fitzsimons, E., Gomez, A., et al. (2010). Children's Schooling and Work in the Presence of a Conditional Cash Transfer Program in Rural Colombia. *Economic Development and Cultural Change*, 58(2), 181–210.

Auyero, J. (2007). *Routine Politics and Violence in Argentina: The Gray Zone of State Power.* New York: Cambridge University Press.

Avelino, G., Brown, D. S. & Hunter, W. (2005). The Effects of Capital Mobility, Trade Openness, and Democracy on Social Spending in Latin America, 1980–1999. *American Journal of Political Science*, 49(3), 625–641.

Avis, E., Ferraz, C., & Finan, F. (2016). *Do Government Audits Reduce Corruption? Estimating the Impacts of Exposing Corrupt Politicians* (No. w22443). National Bureau of Economic Research.

Avritzer, L. (2001). Democracia Deliberativa: La Recuperación del Concepto de Deliberación Pública en la Teoría Democrática Contemporánea. *Metapolítica*, 5(18), 50–65.

Avritzer, L. (2002). *Democracy and the Public Space in Latin America.* Princeton, NJ: Princeton University Press.

Avritzer, L. (2009). *Participatory Institutions in Democratic Brazil*. Washington, DC: Woodrow Wilson Center Press.

Avritzer, L. (2017). *The Two Faces of Institutional Innovation: Promises and Limits of Democratic Participation in Latin America*. Northampton, MA: Edward Elgar Publishing.

Azzoni, C. R. (2001). Economic Growth and Regional Income inequality in Brazil. *The Annals of Regional Science*, 35(1), 133–152.

Baer, W. (2001). *The Brazilian Economy: Growth and Development*, 5th ed. Westport, CT: Praeger.

Baiocchi, G. (2005). *Militants and Citizens: The Politics of Participatory Democracy in Porto Alegre*. Stanford University Press.

Baiocchi, G., & Ganuza, E. (2017). *Popular Democracy: The Paradox of Participation*, Palo Alto, CA: Stanford University Press.

Baiocchi, G., Heller, P., & Silva, S., (2011). *Bootstrapping Democracy: Transforming Local Governance and Civil Society in Brazil*. Palo Alto, CA: Stanford University Press.

Baldez, L. (2002). *Why Women Protest*. New York, NY: Cambridge University Press.

Baldez, L. (2003). Women's Movements and Democratic Transition in Chile, Brazil, East Germany, and Poland. *Comparative Politics*, 35(3), 253–272.

Barber, B. (1984). *Strong Democracy: Participatory Politics for a New Age*. Berkeley, CA: University of California Press.

Bardhan, P. (2002). Decentralization of Governance and Development. *The Journal of Economic Perspectives*, 16(4), 185–205.

Barro, R. J. (1973). The Control of Politicians: An Economic Model. *Public Choice*, 14(1), 19–42.

Barsted, L. L., & Hermann, J. (2001). Black and Indigenous Women: Law vs. Reality in L. L. Barsted, J. Hermann, and M. E. V. de Mello, eds. *Brazil: Women and Legislation against Racism*. Rio de Janeiro: Cepia, 39–84.

Barzelay, M. (2001). *The New Public Management: Improving Research and Policy Dialogue* (V3). Berkeley, CA: University of California Press.

Basilico, M., Weigel, J., Motgi, A., Bor, J., & Keshavjee, S. (2013). Health for All? Competing Theories and Geopolitics in P. Farmer, J. Y. Kim, A. Kleinman, M. Basilico, eds., *Reimagining Global Health: An Introduction*. Berkeley, CA: University of California Press, 74–110.

Bastagli, F., Hagen-Zanker, J., Harman, L., et al. (2016). *Cash Transfers: What Does the Evidence Say? A Rigorous Review of Impacts and the Role of Design and Implementation Features*. London, UK: Overseas Development Institute.

Batista de Oliveira, L. F. & Soares, S. S. (2013). *The Impact of the Programa Bolsa Família on Grade Repetition: Results from the Single Registry, Attendance Project and School Census* (IPC Working Paper No. 119). Brasilia, DF: International Policy Centre for Inclusive Growth.

Batliwala, S. (1994). The Meaning of Women's Empowerment: New Concepts from Action in G. Sen, A. Germain & L. C. Chen, eds., *Population Policies Reconsidered: Health, Empowerment, and Rights*. Boston, MA, Harvard University, Harvard Center for Population and Development Studies, 127–138.

Batliwala, S. (1998). *Status of Rural Women in Karnataka*. Bangalore: National Institute of Advanced Studies.

Batliwala, S. (2007). Taking the Power Out of Empowerment: An Experiential Account. *Development in Practice*, 17(4–5), 557–565.

Baud, I. S., Scott, D., Pfeffer, K., Sydenstricker-Neto, J. & Denis, E. (2015). Reprint of: Digital and Spatial Knowledge Management in Urban Governance: Emerging Issues in India, Brazil, South Africa, And Peru. *Habitat International*, 46, 225–233.

Baum, M. & Lake, D. (2003). The Political Economy of Growth: Democracy and Human Capital. *American Journal of Political Science*, 47(2), 333–347.

Beck, T., Clarke, G., Groff, A., Keefer, P. & Walsh, P. (2016). New Tools in Comparative Political Economy: The Database of Political Institutions. *The World Bank Economic Review*, 15(1), 165–176.

Behrman, J. R., Gallardo-Garcia, J., Parker, S. W., Todd, P. E., & Vélez-Grajales, V. (2012). Are Conditional Cash Transfers Effective in Urban Areas? Evidence from Mexico. *Education Economics*, 20(3), 233–259.

Bellinger, N. M., & Son, B. (2018). Political Parties and Foreign Direct Investment Inflows among Developing Countries. *Political Studies*, 1–20.

Beltrão, K. I. & Alves, J. E. D. (2009). Reversal of the Gender Gap in Brazilian Education in the 20th Century. *Cadernos de Pesquisa*, 39(136), 125–156. doi: https://dx.doi.org/10.1590/S0100-15742009000100007.

Bennett, A. (2010). Process Tracing and Causal Inference in H. Brady & D. Collier, eds., *Rethinking Social Inquiry*. New York, NY: Rowman and Littlefield, 207–220.

Besley, T., & Kudamatsu, M. (2006). Health and Democracy. *The American Economic Review*, 96(2), 313–318.

Bhagwati, J., & Panagariya, A. (2013). *Why Growth Matters: How Economic Growth in India Reduced Poverty and the Lessons for Other Developing Countries*. London, UK: Hachette UK.

Birdsall, N., Bruns, B., Sabot, R. S. (1996). Education in Brazil: Playing a Bad Hand Badly in N. Birdsall & R. H. Sabot, eds., *Opportunity Foregone: Education in Brazil*. Baltimore, MD: Johns Hopkins University Press, 7–48.

Bither-Terry, R. (2014). Reducing Poverty Intensity: What Alternative Poverty Measures Reveal about the Impact of Brazil's Bolsa Família. *Latin American Politics and Society*, 56(4), 143–158.

Blais, A., & Lago, I. (2009). A General Measure of District Competitiveness. *Electoral Studies*, 28(1), 94–100.

Bockstael, V. (2017). Rôle des Agences Régionales de Santé (ARS) dans l'organisation des Parcours de Soins. *Médecine des Maladies Métaboliques*, 11 (1), 52–54.

Booth, A. (1999). Initial Conditions and Miraculous Growth: Why Is South East Asia Different from Taiwan and South Korea? *World Development*, 27(2), 301–321.

Boulding, C. & Brown, D. S. (2013). Political Competition and Local Social Spending: Evidence from Brazil. *Studies in Comparative International Development*, 49(2), 197–216.

Brazil (1988). *Constituição da República Federativa do Brasil*. Brasília, DF: Senado Federal.

Brazil (1991). *Decreto No. 104 de 11 de Junho de 1991*. Brasilia, DF: Governo do Brazil.

Brazilian Institute of Geography and Statistics (1995). *Pesquisa Nacional por Amostra de Domicilios 1995*. Rio de Janeiro, RJ: Instituto Brasileiro de Geografia e Estatistica.

Brazilian Institute of Geography and Statistics (2000). *Poverty in Brazil*. Rio de Janeiro, RJ: Instituto Brasileiro de Geografia e Estatistica.

Brazilian Institute of Geography and Statistics (2003). Mapa de Pobreza e Desigualdade: Municípios Brasileiros 2003. Retrieved from: https://biblioteca .ibge.gov.br/index.php/biblioteca-catalogo?id=2100513&view=detalhes.

Brazilian Institute of Geography and Statistics (2010). 2010 Population Census. Retrieved from: www.ibge.gov.br/english/estatistica/populacao/censo2010/def ault.shtm.

Brazilian Institute of Geography and Statistics (2016). Pesquisa de Informacoes Basicas Municipais – Perfil dos Municipios Brasileiros 2015. Retrieved from: https://biblioteca.ibge.gov.br/visualizacao/livros/liv95942.pdf.

Brazilian Institute of Geography and Statistics (2017). *Survey of Employment and Salary*. Brasilia, D.F.: Brazilian Institute of Geography and Statistics.

Bresser Pereira, L. C. (1998). *Reforma do Estado para a Cidadania: A Reforma Gerencial Brasileira na Perspectiva Internacional*. Sao Paulo, SP: Editora 34.

Brown, D. & Hunter, W. (2004). Democracy and Human Capital Formation Education Spending in Latin America, 1980 to 1997. *Comparative Political Studies*, 37(7), 842–864.

Brown, D. & Mobarak, M. (2009). The Transforming Power of Democracy: Regime Type and the Distribution of Electricity. *American Political Science Review*, 103(02), 193–213.

Brown, D., Touchton, M. & Whitford, A. (2011). Political Polarization as a Constraint on Government: Evidence from Corruption. *World Development*, 39(9), 1516–1529.

Brownson, R. C., Colditz, G. A., Proctor, E. K. (eds.) (2017). *Dissemination and Implementation Research in Health: Translating Science to Practice*. New York, NY: Oxford University Press.

Bruns, B., Evans, D. & Luque, J. (2012). *Achieving World-Class Education in Brazil: The Next Agenda*. Washington, DC: World Bank.

Budlender, D. (2000). The Political Economy of Women's Budgets in the South. *World Development*, 28(7), 1365–1378.

Burdick, J. (1993). *Looking for God in Brazil: The Progressive Catholic Church in Urban Brazil's Religious Arena*. Berkeley, CA: University of California Press.

Burdick, J., & Hewitt, W. E. (eds.) (2000). *The Church at the Grassroots in Latin America: Perspectives on Thirty Years of Activism*. Westport, CT: Greenwood Publishing Group.

Burkle F. M., Jr. (2006). Globalization and Disasters: Issues of Public Health, State Capacity and Political Action. *Journal of International Affairs*, 241–265.

Caldwell, K. (2007). *Negras in Brazil: Re-Envisioning Black Women, Citizenship, and the Politics of Identity*. New Brunswick, NJ: Rutgers University Press.

Camargo, C. F., Curralero, C. R. B., Licio, E. C. & Mostafa, J. (2013). Perfil Socioeconómico dos Beneficiários do Programa Bolsa Família in T. Campello

& M. C. Neri, eds., *Programa Bolsa Família: Uma Década de Inclusão e Cidadania.* Brasília, DF: Instituto de Pesquisa Econômica Aplicada, 157–178.

Cameron, A. & Trivedi, P. (2009). *Microeconometrics Using Stata.* College Station, TX: Stata Press.

Campbell, T. (2003). *The Quiet Revolution: Decentralization and the Rise of Political Participation in Latin American Cities.* Pittsburgh, PA: University of Pittsburgh Press.

Campbell, O. M., Graham, W. J. (2006). Strategies for Reducing Maternal Mortality: Getting on with What Works. *The Lancet,* 368(9543), 1284–1299.

Cao, X., & Ward, H. (2015). Winning Coalition Size, State Capacity, and Time Horizons: An Application of Modified Selectorate Theory to Environmental Public Goods Provision. *International Studies Quarterly,* 59(2), 264–279.

Cardoso, F. H., & Faletto, E. (1969). *Dependencia Y Desarrollo En América Latina: Ensayo De Interpretación Sociológica.* Mexico: Siglo XXI Editores.

Carnoy, M. (2015). *International Test Score Comparisons and Educational Policy: A Review of the Critiques.* Boulder, CO: National Education Policy Center.

Centeno, M. A., Kohli, A., & Yashar, D. J. (2017). Unpacking States in the Developing World: Capacity, Performance, and Politics in M. A. Centeno, A. Kohli, D. J. Yashar, eds., *States in the Developing World.* New York, NY: Cambridge University Press, 1–34.

Chapman, A. R. (2016). Health and Human Rights in the Neoliberal Era in A. Chapman, *Global Health, Human Rights and the Challenge of Neoliberal Politics.* New York, NY: Cambridge University Press, 72–114.

Chaudhary, L., Musacchio, A., Nafziger, S. & Yan, S. (2012). Big BRICs, Weak Foundations: The Beginning of Public Elementary Education in Brazil, Russia, India, and China. *Explorations in Economic History,* 49(2), 221–240.

Cheibub, J. A. & Przeworski, A. (1999). Democracy, Elections, and Accountability for Economic Outcomes. *Democracy, Accountability, and Representation,* 222–250.

Cleary, M. R. (2007). Electoral Competition, Participation, and Government Responsiveness in Mexico. *American Journal of Political Science,* 51(2), 283–299.

Cleary, M. R. (2010). *The Sources of Democratic Responsiveness in Mexico.* Notre Dame, IN: University of Notre Dame Press.

Collar, J. M., Almeida Neto, J. B. D., & Ferla, A. A. (2015). Formulação e Impacto do Programa Mais Médicos na Atenção e Cuidado em Saúde: Contribuições Iniciais e Análise Comparativa. *Saúde em Redes,* 1(2), 43–56.

Collier, D., Brady, H. E. & Seawright, J. (2004). Sources of Leverage in Causal Inference: towards an Alternative View of Methodology in H. Brady & D. Collier, eds., *Rethinking Social Inquiry.* New York, NY: Rowman and Littlefield, 161–200.

Collier, D., & Levitsky, S. (1997). Democracy with Adjectives: Conceptual Innovation in Comparative Research. *World Politics,* 49(3), 430–451.

Collier, P. (2008). *The Bottom Billion. Why the Poorest Countries Are Failing and What Can Be Done about It.* New York: Oxford University Press.

Collier, R. B., & Collier, D. (2002). *Shaping the Political Arena: Critical Junctures, the Labor Movement, and Regime Dynamics in Latin America.* Notre Dame, IN: University of Notre Dame Press.

Collucci, C. (2018) Brazil's Child and Maternal Mortality Have Increased against Background of Public Spending Cuts. *BMJ* 362: 3585.

Coppedge, M., Gerring, J., Lindberg, S., et al. (2015). V-Dem [Country-Year /Country-Date] Dataset V4. Varieties of Democracy (V-Dem) Project.

Coppedge, M., Gerring, J., Lindberg, S., et al. (2016). "V-Dem [Country-Year /Country-Date] Dataset V6." Varieties of Democracy (V-Dem) Project.

Cornwall, A. (2003). Whose Voices? Whose choices? Reflections on Gender And Participatory Development. *World Development*, 31(8), 1325–1342.

Cornwall, A. & Coelho, V. S. (eds.) (2007). *Spaces for Change? The Politics of Citizen Participation in New Democratic Arenas* (V 4). London, UK: Zed Books.

Cornwall, A., Harrison, E., & Whitehead, A. (2007). Gender Myths and Feminist Fables: The Struggle for Interpretive Power in Gender and Development. *Development and Change*, 38(1): 1–20.

Corrales, J. (1999). *The Politics of Education Reform.* Washington, DC: World Bank.

Couto, C. G. (1995). *O Desafio de ser Governo: O PT na Prefeitura de São Paulo, 1989–1992*, Rio de Janeiro, RJ: Paz e Terra Editora.

Cox, G. W., & McCubbins, M. D. (1986). Electoral Politics as a Redistributive Game. *The Journal of Politics*, 48(2), 370–389.

Cremin, P. & Nakabugo, M. G. (2012). Education, Development and Poverty Reduction: A Literature Critique. *International Journal of Educational Development*, 32(4), 499–506.

Crocker, D. A. (2008). *Ethics of Global Development: Agency, Capability, and Deliberative Democracy.* New York, NY: Cambridge University Press.

Cruz, M., Foster, J., Quillin, B. & Schellekens, P. (2015). *Ending Extreme Poverty and Sharing Prosperity: Progress and Policies* (Policy Research Note PRN/15/ 03). Washington, DC: World Bank.

Cruz, M. d. C. M. T., Farah, M.F.S. & Sugiyama, N.B. (2014). Normatizações Federais e a Oferta de Matrículas em Creches no Brasil. *Estudos em Avaliação Educacional*, 25(59): 202–241.

Cueto, M. (2004). The Origins of Primary Health Care and Selective Primary Health Care. *American Journal of Public Health*, 94(11), 1864–1874.

Cueto, M. (2005). The Promise of Primary Health Care. *Bulletin of the World Health Organization*, 10(2) 1–27.

Cueto, M. (2007). *The Value of Health: A History of the Pan American Health Organization.* Washington, DC: Pan American Health Organization.

Dagnino, E. (1994). Os Movimentos Aociais e a Emergência de Uma Nova Noção de Cidadania in E. Dagnino, ed., *Anos 90: Política e Sociedade no Brasil.* Tatuape, SP: Editora Brasiliense, 103–115.

Dagnino, E. (1998). Culture, Citizenship, and Democracy: Changing Discourses And Practices of the Latin American Left in S. E. Alvarez, E. Dagnino & A. Escobar, eds., *Cultures of Politics/Politics of Cultures: Revisioning Latin American Social Movements.* Boulder, CO: Westview Press.

Dahl, R. A. (1971). *Polyarchy: Participation and Opposition.* New Haven, CT: Yale University Press.

Dahl, R. A. (1989). *Democracy and Its Critics.* New Haven, CT: Yale University Press.

De Brauw, A., Gilligan, D. O., Hoddinott, J. & Roy, S. (2014). The Impact of Bolsa Família on Women's Decision-Making Power. *World Development,* 59, 487–504.

De la O, A. L. (2015). *Crafting Policies to End Poverty in Latin America.* Cambridge, UK: Cambridge University Press.

De Soto, H. (2000). *The Mystery of Capital: Why Capitalism Triumphs in the West and Fails Everywhere Else.* New York, NY: Basic Civitas Books.

de Souza, P. H. (2012). *Poverty, Inequality and Social Policies in Brazil, 1995–2009* (Working Paper No. 87). Brasilia, DF: International Policy Centre for Inclusive Growth.

Desposato, S. (2007). How Does Vote Buying Shape the Legislative Arena? in F. C. Schaffer, ed., *Elections for Sale.* Boulder, CO: Lynn Rienner.

Dewey, J. (1937). Education and Social Change. *Bulletin of the American Association of University Professors,* 23(6), 472–474.

Dewey, J. (2004). *Democracy and Education,* North Chelmsford, MA: Courier Corporation.

Diamond, L. (1999). *Developing Democracy: Toward Consolidation.* Baltimore, MD: Johns Hopkins University Press.

Diaz-Cayeros, A., Estévez, F. & Magaloni. B. (2016). *The Political Logic of Poverty Relief: Electoral Strategies and Social Policy in Mexico.* New York: Cambridge University Press.

Diniz, D., Medeiros, M. & Madeiro, A. (2017). National Abortion Survey 2016. *Ciência & Saúde Coletiva,* 22(2), 653–60.

Dixon, K., & Johnson, O. A. (eds.) (2018). *Comparative Racial Politics in Latin America.* Abingdon, UK: Routledge.

Dollar, D., Kleineberg, T. & Kraay, A. (2016). Growth Still Is Good for the Poor. *European Economic Review,* 81, 68–85.

Dollar, D. & Kraay, A. (2001). *Trade, Growth, and Poverty* (Working Paper No. WPS 2615). Washington, DC: World Bank.

Dollar, D. & Kraay, A. (2002). Growth Is Good for the Poor. *Journal of Economic Growth,* 7(3), 195–225.

Downs, A. (1957). An Economic Theory of Political Action in a Democracy. *The Journal of Political Economy,* 65(2), 135–150.

Drèze, J., & Sen, A. (eds.). (1995). *Indian Development: Selected Regional Perspective.* New York, NY: Oxford University Press.

Drèze, J. & Sen, A. (2002). *India: Development and Participation.* 2nd ed. Oxford, UK: Oxford University Press.

Drèze, J., & Sen, A. (2013). *An Uncertain Glory: India and Its Contradictions.* Princeton, NJ: Princeton University Press.

Dryzek, J. (2000). *Deliberative Democracy and Beyond: Liberals, Critics, Contestations.* Oxford, UK: Oxford University Press.

Duflo, E. (2001). Schooling and Labor Market Consequences of School Construction in Indonesia: Evidence from an Unusual Policy Experiment. *American Economic Review,* 91(4), 795–814.

Dye, T. R. (2016). *Understanding Public Policy*, 15th ed. New York, NY: Pearson.

Eakin, M. (1997). *Brazil: The Once and Future Country*. New York, NY: St. Martin's Press.

Easterly, W. (2006). Reliving the 1950s: The Big Push, Poverty Traps, and Takeoffs in Economic Development. *Journal of Economic Growth*, 11(4), 289–318.

Eaton, K. & Dickovick, T. (2004). The Politics of Re-centralization in Argentina and Brazil. *Latin American Research Review*, 39(1), 90–122.

Esping-Andersen, G. (1990). *The Three Worlds of Welfare Capitalism*. Cambridge, UK: Polity Press.

Esping-Andersen, G. (2002). A new gender contract in G. Esping-Andersen, D Gallie, A. Hemerijc & John Myles, eds., *Why We Need a New Welfare State*. Oxford, UK: Oxford University Press.

Esping-Andersen, G. (2017). *Politics against Markets: The Social Democratic Road to Power*, Princeton, NJ: Princeton University Press.

Evans, P. & Heller, P. (2015). Human Development, State Transformation and the Politics of the Developmental State in S. Leibfried, E. Huber, M. Lange, J. D. Levy & F. Nullmeier, eds., *The Oxford Handbook of Transformations of the State*. Oxford, UK: Oxford University Press, 691–713.

Evans, P., Huber, E. & Stephens, J. (2017). The Political Foundations of State Effectiveness in M. A. Centeno, A. Kohli, & D. J. Yashar, eds., *States in the Developing World*. New York, NY: Cambridge University Press, 380–408.

Evans, P., Rueschemeyer, D., & Skocpol, T. (eds.) (1985). *Bringing the State Back in*, Cambridge, UK: Cambridge University Press.

Faguet, J. P. (2008). Decentralisation's Effects on Public Investment: Evidence and Policy Lessons from Bolivia and Colombia. *The Journal of Development Studies*, 44(8), 1100–1121.

Falleti, T. G. (2010). *Decentralization and Subnational Politics in Latin America*. Cambridge, UK: Cambridge University Press.

Falleti, T. G., & Cunial, S. L. (2018). *Participation in Social Policy: Public Health in Comparative Perspective*. New York: Cambridge University Press.

Falleti, T. G., & Lynch, J. F. (2009). Context and Causal Mechanisms in Political Analysis. *Comparative Political Studies*, 42(9), 1143–1166.

Falleti, T. G., & Parrado, E. A. (eds.) (2017). *Latin America since the Left Turn*, Philadelphia, PA: University of Pennsylvania Press.

Fan, S., Zhang, L. & Zhang, X. (2002). *Growth, Inequality, and Poverty in Rural China: The Role of Public Investments* (Research Repot No.125). Washington, DC: International Food Policy Research Institute.

Farah, M. F. S. (1997). Gestão Pública e Cidadania: Iniciativas Inovadoras na Administração Subnacional no Brasil. *Revista de Administração Pública*, 31(4), 126–156.

Farah, M. S. F., & Barboza, H. B. (eds.) (2000). *Vinte Experiências de Gestão Pública e Cidadania*, São Paulo, SP: Programa Gestão Pública e Cidadania.

Farah, M. F. S., & Spink, P. (2009). Subnational Government Innovation in a Comparative Perspective: Brazil in S. F. Borins, ed., *Innovations in*

Government: Research, Recognition, and Replication. Washignton, DC: Brookings Institution Press, 71–92.

Farmer, P., Basilico, M., Kerry, V., et al. (2013). Global Health Priorities for the Early Twenty-First Century in P. Farmer, J. Y. Kim, A. Kleinman, M. Basilico, eds., *Reimagining Global Health: An Introduction.* Berkeley, CA: University of California Press, 302–339.

Feld, L. P., Fischer, J. A. & Kirchgässner, G. (2010). The Effect of Direct Democracy on Income Redistribution: Evidence for Switzerland. *Economic Inquiry*, 48(4), 817–840.

Fenwick, T. B. (2009). Avoiding Governors: The Success of Bolsa Família. *Latin American Research Review*, 44(1), 102–131.

Fenwick, T. B. (2015). *Avoiding Governors: Federalism, Democracy, and Poverty Alleviation in Brazil and Argentina.* Notre Dame, IN: University of Notre Dame Press.

Ferraz, C., & Finan, F. (2008). Exposing Corrupt Politicians: The Effects of Brazil's Publicly Released Audits on Electoral Outcomes. *The Quarterly Journal of Economics*, 123(2), 703–745.

Ferraz, C. & Finan, F. (2011). Electoral Accountability and Corruption: Evidence from the Audits of Local Governments. *American Economic Review*, 101(4), 1274–1311.

Ferreira, F. (2010). *Distributions in Motion: Economic Growth, Inequality, and Poverty Dynamics* (ECINEQ Working Paper 2010 – 183). Verona, IT: Society for the Study of Economic Inequality.

Ferreira, F., Leite, P. G. & Ravallion, M. (2010). Poverty Reduction without Economic Growth? Explaining Brazil's Poverty Dynamics, 1985–2004. *Journal of Development Economics*, 93(1), 20–36.

Fields, G. S. (1977). Who Benefits from Economic Development? A Reexamination of Brazilian Growth in the 1960's. *The American Economic Review*, 67(4), 570–582.

Filippi, V., Chou, D., Ronsmans, C., Graham, W., & Say, L. (2016). Levels and Causes of Maternal Mortality and Morbidity in R. E. Black, R. Laxminarayan, M. Temmerman, & N. Walker, eds., *Reproductive, Maternal, Newborn, and Child Health: Disease Control Priorities* (V 2), 3rd ed. Washington, D.C.: World Bank Group.

FIRJAN (2015). Índice FIRJAN de Desenvolvimento Municipal (IFDM). Retrieved from: www.firjan.com.br/ifdm/

Fishkin, J. S. (1991). *Democracy and Deliberation: New Directions for Democratic Reform.* New Haven, CT: Yale University Press.

Fiszbein, A. & Schady. N. (2009). *Conditional Cash Transfers: A World Bank Policy Research Report.* Washington, DC: World Bank.

Fleischer, D. (2002). As Eleições Municipais no Brasil: Uma Análise Comparativa (1982–2000). *Opinião Pública*, 8(1), 80–105.

Font, J. (2005). Participación Ciudadana y Decisiones Públicas: Conceptos, Experiencias y Metodologías in A. Ziccardi, ed., *Participación Ciudadana Y Políticas Sociales En El Ámbito Local.* Mexico: Instituto de Investigaciones Sociales de la Universidad Nacional Autónoma de México, 23–41.

Font, J., Smith, G., Galais, C. & Alarcón, P. (2017). Cherry-Picking Participation: Explaining the Fate of Proposals from Participatory Processes. *European Journal of Political Research*. 57(3), 614–636.

Font, M. A. (2003). *Transforming Brazil: A Reform Era in Perspective*. Lanham, MD: Rowman and Littlefield Publishers.

Food and Agriculture Organization of the United Nations (2018). *The State of Food Security and Nutrition in the World: Building Climate Resilience for Food Security and Nutrition*. Rome, Italy: FAO.

Fox, J. (2015). Social Accountability: What Does the Evidence Really Say? *World Development*, 72, 346–371.

Franco, A., Álvarez-Dardet, C., & Ruiz, M. T. (2004). Effect of Democracy on Health: Ecological study. *BMJ*, 329(7480), 1421–1423.

Freeland, N. (2007). Superfluous, Pernicious, Atrocious and Abominable? The Case against Conditional Cash Transfers. *IDS Bulletin*, 38(3), 75–78.

Frees, E. (2004). *Longitudinal and Panel Data: Analysis and Applications in the Social Sciences*. Cambridge, UK: Cambridge University Press.

Frey, B. S. (1994). Direct Democracy: Politico-Economic Lessons from Swiss Experience. *The American Economic Review*, 84(2), 338–342.

Fried, B. (2012). Distributive Politics and Conditional Cash Transfers: The Case of Brazil's Bolsa Família. *World Development*, 40 (5), 1042–1053.

Friedman, E.J. & Hochstetler, K. (2002). Assessing the Third Transition in Latin American Democratization: Representational Regimes and Civil Society in Argentina and Brazil. *Comparative Politics*, 35(1), 21–42.

Fritscher, A. M., Musacchio, A. & Viarengo, M. (2010). *The Great Leap Forward: The Political Economy of Education in Brazil, 1889–1930* (Working Paper No. 2010–18). Mexico City, ME: Banco de México.

Fukuyama, F. (2003). *Our Posthuman Future: Consequences of the Biotechnology Revolution*, New York, NY: Farrar, Straus and Giroux.

Fung, A. (2006). Varieties of Participation in Complex Governance. *Public Administration Review*, 66, 66–75.

Fung, A. & Wright, E. O. (2001). Deepening Democracy: Innovations in Empowered Participatory Governance. *Politics and Society*, 29(1), 5–42.

Fung, A. & Wright, E. O. (eds.) (2003). *Deepening Democracy: Institutional Innovations in Empowered Participatory Governance*. London, UK: Verso.

Garay, C. (2017). *Social Policy Expansion in Latin America*. New York, NY: Cambridge University Press.

García, S., & Saavedra, J. E. (2017). Educational Impacts and Cost-Effectiveness of Conditional Cash Transfer Programs in Developing Countries: A Meta-Analysis. *Review of Educational Research*, 87 (5), 921-965.

Gauri, V. & Lieberman, E. S. (2006). Boundary Institutions and HIV/AIDS Policy in Brazil and South Africa. *Studies in Comparative International Development*, 41(3), 47–73.

Gaventa, J. & McGee, R. (2013). The Impact of Transparency and Accountability Initiatives. *Development Policy Review*, 31(S1), 3–28.

Gay, R. (1990). Community Organization and Clientelist Politics in Contemporary Brazil: A Case Study from Suburban Rio de Janeiro. *International Journal of Urban and Regional Research*, 14(4), 648–666.

Gay, R. (2010). *Popular Organization and Democracy in Rio de Janeiro: A Tale of Two Favelas*. Philadelphia, PA: Temple University Press.

Geddes, B. (1994). *Politician's Dilemma: Building State Capacity in Latin America* (V25). Berkeley, CA: University of California Press.

Gerring, J., Knutsen, C., Skaaning, S., et al. (2015). *Electoral Democracy and Human Development* (V-Dem Institute Working Paper 2015:9). Retrieved from: http://dx.doi.org/10.2139/ssrn.2652180.

Gerring, J., Thacker, S. & Alfaro, R. (2012). Democracy and Human Development. *The Journal of Politics*, 74(1), 1–17.

Gibson, C. L. (2017). *The Consequences of Urban Brazil's Sanitarist Movement for Primary Public Health Care Expansion and Declining Infant Mortality*, paper prepared for Stanford University GSB Seminar in Organizational Studies, Stanford, California.

Gibson, E. (2013). *Boundary Control: Subnational Authoritarianism in Federal Democracies*. Cambridge, UK: Cambridge University Press.

Gilligan, D. & Fruttero, A. (2011, October). Presentation: The Impact of Bolsa Família on Education and Health Outcomes in Brazil. Report on Select Findings of IFPRI evaluation done by A. de Brauw, D. Gilligan, J. Hoddinott, & S. Roy, presented at Second Generation of CCTs Evaluations Conference, Washington, DC.

Giraudy, A. (2013). Varieties of Subnational Undemocratic Regimes: Evidence from Argentina and Mexico. *Studies in Comparative International Development*, 48(1), 51–80.

Glewwe, P. & Kremer, M. (2006). Schools, Teachers, and Education Outcomes in Developing Countries. *Handbook of the Economics of Education*, 2, 945–1017.

Goetz, A. M. (2007). National Women's Machinery: State Based Institutions to Advocate for Gender Equality in S. Rai, ed., *Mainstreaming Gender, Democratizing the State? Institutional mechanisms for the Advancement of Women*. Abingdon, UK: Routledge.

Goldfrank, B. (2011). *Deepening Local Democracy in Latin America: Participation, Decentralization and the Left*. University Park, PA: Pennsylvania State University Press.

Gomes, E. T. & Barboza, M. S. (2003). A Organização Espacial Através das Redes em Uma Cidade Média do Nordeste do Brasil: Garanhuns-PE. *Scripta Nova*, 7 (146).

Gomez, P., Friedman, J., & Shapiro, I. (2005). Opening Budgets to Public Understanding and Debate. *OECD Journal on Budgeting*, 5(1), 7–36.

Gomide, A. D. A., & Pires, R. (2014). *Capacidades Estatais E Democracia: A Abordagem dos Arranjos Institucionais para Análise de Políticas Públicas*. Brasilia, DF: Ipea.

Gonçalves, S. (2014). The Effects of Participatory Budgeting on Municipal Expenditures and Infant Mortality in Brazil. *World Development*, 53, 94–110.

Gradin, C. (2007). Why Is Poverty So High Among Afro-Brazilians? A Decomposition Analysis of the Racial Poverty Gap. *The Journal of Development Studies*, 45(9), 1426–1452.

Graham, C. (1994). *Safety Nets, Politics, and the Poor: Transitions to Market Economies in Latin America*. Baltimore, MD: Johns Hopkins University Press.

Graham, R. (1990). *Patronage and Politics in Nineteenth-Century Brazil*. Palo Alto, CA: Stanford University Press.

Grindle, M. S. (2004). Good Enough Governance: Poverty Reduction and Reform in Developing Countries. *Governance*, 17(4), 525–548.

Grindle, M. S. (2007). *Going Local: Decentralization, Democratization, and the Promise of Good Governance*. Princeton, NJ: Princeton University Press.

Guanais, F., & Macinko, J. (2009). Primary Care and Avoidable Hospitalizations: Evidence from Brazil. *The Journal of Ambulatory Care Management*, 32(2), 115–122.

Gurza Lavalle, A., Voigt, J. & Serafim. L. (2015). Afinal o que Fazem os Conselhos e Quando o Fazem: Padrões Decisórios e o Debate dos Efeitos das Instituições Participativas. *Dados*, 59(3), 609–650.

Haggard, S. (1990). *Pathways from the Periphery: The Politics of Growth in the Newly Industrializing Countries*. Ithaca, NY: Cornell University Press.

Haggard, S. & Kaufman, R. R. (1997). The Political Economy of Democratic Transitions. *Comparative Politics*, 29(3), 263–283.

Hagopian, F. (1996). *Traditional Politics and Regime Change in Brazil*. New York, NY: Cambridge University Press.

Hagopian, F. (2016). Brazil's Accountability Paradox. *Journal of Democracy*, 27(3), 119–128.

Hall, A. (2006). From Fome Zero to Bolsa Família: Social Policies and Poverty Alleviation under Lula. *Journal of Latin American Studies*, 38(4), 689–709.

Hanushek, E. A. (2013). Economic Growth in Developing Countries: The Role of Human Capital. *Economics of Education Review*, 37, 204–212.

Harding, R., & Stasavage, D. (2014). What Democracy Does (and Doesn't) Do for Basic Services: School Fees, School Quality, and African Elections. *Journal of Politics*, 76(1), 229–245

Hartz-Karp, J. (2012). Laying the Groundwork for Participatory Budgeting – Developing a Deliberative Community and Collaborative Governance: Greater Geraldton, Western Australia. *Journal of Public Deliberation*, 8(2), 1–18.

Heller, P. (2017). Development in the City: Growth and Inclusion in India, Brazil and South Africa in M. A. Centeno, A. Kohli, D. J. Yashar, eds., *States in the Developing World*. New York, NY: Cambridge University Press, 309–338.

Hellmann, A. G. (2015). *How Does Bolsa Familia Work? Best Practices in the Implementation of Conditional Cash Transfer Programs in Latin America and the Caribbean*. IDB Technical Note, 856.

Hilbe, J. (2007). *Negative Binomial Regression*, 2nd ed. Cambridge, UK: Cambridge University Press.

Ho, D. E., Imai, K., King, G., & Stuart, E. A. (2007). Matching as Nonparametric Preprocessing for Reducing Model Dependence in Parametric Causal Inference. *Political Analysis*, 15(3), 199–236.

Hochstetler, K. (2000). Democratizing Pressures from Below? Social Movements in the New Brazilian Democracy in P. Kingstone & T. J. Power, eds., *Democratic Brazil: Actors, Institutions, and Processes*. Pittsburgh, PA: University of Pittsburgh Press, 167–184.

Hodgson, G. M. (2017). Institutions, Democracy and Economic Development: On Not Throwing Out the Liberal Baby with the Neoliberal Bathwater in G. C. Bitros, N. C. Kyriazis, eds., *Democracy and an Open-Economy World Order*. Cham, Switzerland: Springer, 51–63.

Holston, J. (2008). *Insurgent Citizenship: Disjunctions of Democracy and Modernity in Brazil*. Princeton, NJ: Princeton University Press.

Howlett, M., & Ramesh M. (2003). *Studying Public Policy: Policy Cycles and Policy Subsystems*. Oxford, UK: Oxford University Press.

Htun, M. (2003). *Dimensions of Political Inclusion and Exclusion in Brazil: Gender and Race*. Washington, DC: Inter-American Development Bank, Department of Sustainable Development.

Htun, M., & Piscopo, J. (2014). *Women in Politics and Policy in Latin America and the Caribbean* (Conflict Prevention and Peace Forum CPPF Working Papers on Women in Politics, V 2). Brooklyn, NY: Social Science Research Council.

Huber, E. (1996). Options for Social Policy in Latin America in G. Esping-Andersen, ed., *Welfare States in Transition*. London, UK: Sage Publications, 141–191.

Huber, E. & Stephens, J. D. (2001). *Development and Crisis of the Welfare State: Parties and Policies in Global Markets*. Chicago, IL: University of Chicago Press.

Huber, E. & Stephens, J. D. (2012). *Democracy and the Left: Social Policy and Inequality in Latin America*. Chicago, IL: University of Chicago Press.

Hunter, W. (2010). *The Transformation of the Workers' Party in Brazil, 1989–2009*. Cambridge, UK: Cambridge University Press.

Hunter, W. & Sugiyama, N. B. (2009). Democracy and Social Policy in Brazil: Advancing Basic Needs, Preserving Privileged Interest. *Latin American Politics and Society*, 51(2), 29–58.

Hunter, W. & Sugiyama, N.B. (2014). Transforming Subjects into Citizens: Insights from Brazil's Bolsa Família. *Perspectives on Politics*, 12(4), 829–845.

Hunter, W. & Sugiyama, N. B. (2017). Making the Newest Citizens: Achieving Universal Birth Registration in Contemporary Brazil. *The Journal of Development Studies*, 1–16

Huntington, S. P. & Harrison, L. E. (2000). *Culture Matters: How Values Shape Human Progress*, New York, NY: Basic Books.

IBGE Cidades (2010). IBGE Cidades (Database). Retrieved from: https://cidades.ibge.gov.br/brasil/ba/amargosa/panorama.

IBGE MUNIC (2013). Perfil dos Municípios Brasileiros – 2013. Retrieved from: https://ww2.ibge.gov.br/home/estatistica/economia/perfilmunic/2013/default.shtm.

Instituto Nacional de Estudos e Pesquisas Educacionais Anísio Teixeira (2016). *Censo Escolar da Educação Básica. 2016*. Brasilia, DF: Ministerio da Educacao.

International Labor Organization (2018). *World Employment and Social Outlook: Trends for Women 2018 – Global Snapshot.* Geneva: International Labor Organization.

Interparliamentary Union (2016). Women in National Parliaments (PARLINE Database). Retrieved from: www.ipu.org/wmn-e/classif.htm.

Jaccoud, L, Hadjab, P. D. E., & Chaibub, J. R. (2010). *The Consolidation of Social Assistance in Brazil and Its Challenges, 1998–2008* (Working Paper No. 76). Brasilia, D.F.: International Policy Centre for Inclusive Growth.

Jacobi, P. (1989). *Movimentos Sociais e Políticas Públicas: Demands por Saneamento Básico e Saúde São Paulo 1974–84.* São Paulo, SP: Cortez Editora.

Jann, W. & Wegrich, K. (2007). Theories of the Policy Cycle in F. Fischer & G. J. Miller, eds., *Handbook of Public Policy Analysis: Theory, Politics and Methods.* Abingdon, UK: Routledge, 43–62.

Johnson, C. (1982). *MITI and the Japanese Miracle: The Growth of Industrial Policy: 1925–1975.* Palo Alto, CA: Stanford University Press.

Johnson, O. A. (1998). Racial Representation and Brazilian Politics: Black Members of the National Congress, 1983–1999. *Journal of Interamerican Studies and World Affairs,* 40(4), 97–118.

Kabeer, N. (2005). Gender Equality and Women's Empowerment: A Critical Analysis of the Third Millennium Development Goal. *Gender and Development,* 13(1), 13–24.

Kaufman, R. R., & Nelson, J. M. (2004). *Crucial Needs, Weak Incentives: Social Sector Reform, Democratization, and Globalization in Latin America.* Washington, DC: Woodrow Wilson Center Press.

Keck, M. (1995). *The Workers' Party and Democratization in Brazil,* New Haven, CT: Yale University Press.

Keefer, P. (1999). *When Do Special Interests Run Rampant? Disentangling the Role of Elections, Incomplete Information and Checks and Balances in Banking Crises* (World Bank Policy Research Working Paper No. 2543). Retrieved from: https://papers.ssrn.com/sol3/papers.cfm?abstract_id=632610

Keefer, P. (2007). The Poor Performance of Poor Democracies in C. Boix & S. C. Stokes, eds., *The Oxford Handbook of Comparative Politics.* Oxford, UK: Oxford University Press, 886–909.

Keefer, P., & Khemani, S. (2003). *Democracy, Public Expenditures, and the Poor.* Washington, D.C.: World Bank Publications.

Kerche, F. (2014). O Ministério Público no Brasil: Relevância, Características e Uma Agenda para o Futuro. *Revista USP,* (101), 113–120.

Khandker, S. R., Koolwal, G. B. & Samad, H. A. (2009). *Handbook on Impact Evaluation: Quantitative Methods and Practices.* Washington, DC: World Bank Publications.

King, G., Keohane, R. & Verba, S. (1994). *Designing Social Inquiry: Scientific Inference in Qualitative Research.* Princeton, NJ: Princeton University Press.

Kingstone, P., & Power, T. J. (eds.). (2017). *Democratic Brazil Divided.* Pittsburgh, PA: University of Pittsburgh Press.

Kitschelt, H. (2000). Linkages between Citizens and Politicians in Democratic Polities. *Comparative Political Studies,* 33(6–7), 845–879.

Kitschelt, H., Hawkins, K. A., Luna, J. P., Rosas, G., & Zechmeister, E. J. (2010). *Latin American Party System.*, New York, NY: Cambridge University Press.

Knobel, M. (2014, January 12). Brazil's Scary PISA Results. *Inside Higher Ed.* Retrieved from: www.insidehighered.com/blogs/world-view/brazils-scary-pisa-results.

Kohli, A. (2004). *State-Directed Development: Political Power and Industrialization in the Global Periphery.* Cambridge, UK: Cambridge University Press.

Kolehmainen-Aitken, R. L. (2004). Decentralization's Impact on the Health Workforce: Perspectives of Managers, Workers and National Leaders. *Human Resources for Health*, 2(5), 1–11.

Kosack, S. (2012). *The Education of Nations: How the Political Organization of the Poor, Not Democracy, Led Governments to Invest in Mass Education.* Oxford, UK: Oxford University Press.

Lake, D. & Baum, M. (2001). The Invisible Hand of Democracy Political Control and the Provision of Public Services. *Comparative Political Studies*, 34(6), 587–621.

Lasker, R. D., & Weiss, E. S. (2003). Broadening Participation in Community Problem Solving: A Multidisciplinary Model to Support Collaborative Practice and Research. *Journal of Urban Health*, 80(1), 14–47.

Laurell, A. C., & Giovanella, L. (2018). Health Policies and Systems in Latin America. *Oxford Encyclopedia of Global Public Health.* Retrieved from: http://oxfordre.com/publichealth/abstract/10.1093/acrefore/9780190632366.001.00 01/acrefore-9780190632366-e-60

Layton, M. L. (2019). Bolsa Familia: Historical, Popular and Electoral Perspectives in B. Ames, ed., *Routledge Handbook of Brazilian Politics*, New York, NY: Routledge.

Leal, V. N. (1997). *Coronelismo, Enxada e Voto: O Município e o Regime Representativo no Brasil*, 3rd ed. São Paulo, SP: Editora Nova Fronteira.

Leão Rego, A. & Pinzani, M. (2013). *Vozes do Bolsa Família: Autonomia, Dinheiro e Cidadania.* São Paulo, SP: Editora da Unesp.

Lei de Responsabilidade Fiscal (Lei Complementar n° 101). (2000). *Diario Oficial da Uniao.* Brasilia, DF: Government of Brazil.

Levine, D. H., & Molina, J. E. (eds.). (2011). *The Quality of Democracy in Latin America.* Boulder, CO: Lynne Rienner Publishers.

Lieberman, E. S. (2005). Nested Analysis as a Mixed-Method Strategy for Comparative Research. *American Political Science Review*, 99(3), 435–452.

Lim, S. S., Dandona, L., Hoisington, J. A., et al. (2010). India's Janani Suraksha Yojana, a Conditional Cash Transfer Programme to Increase Births in Health Facilities: An Impact Evaluation. *The Lancet*, 375(9730), 2009–2023.

Lima, I. M. (2011). *Os Conselhos Escolares e a Construção da Gestão Democrática no Município de Jaboatão dos Guararapes* (Unpublished master's thesis). Recife, PE: Universidade Federal de Pernambuco.

Lindberg, S. I., Coppedge, M., Gerring, J. & Teorell, J. (2014). V-Dem: A New Way to Measure Democracy. *Journal of Democracy*, 25(3), 159–169.

Lindert, K. (2005). Brazil: Bolsa Família Program – Scaling-Up Cash Transfers for the Poor in *Managing for Development Results Principles in Action:*

Sourcebook on Emerging Good Practices. Retrieved from: http://www .mfdr.org/Sourcebook/1stEdition/6-1Brazil-BolsaFamilia.pdf

Lindert, K., Linder, A., Hobbs J. & Brière, B. de la. (2007). *The Nuts and Bolts of Brazil's Bolsa Família Program: Implementing Conditional Cash Transfers in a Decentralized Context* (SP Discussion Paper No. 0709). Washington, D.C.: World Bank.

Lindert, P. H. (2004). *Growing Public: Volume 1, The Story: Social Spending and Economic Growth since the Eighteenth Century*. 2nd ed. Cambridge, UK: Cambridge University Press.

Linz, J. J., & Stepan, A. (1996). *Problems of Democratic Transition and Consolidation: Southern Europe, South America, and Post-Communist Europe*. Baltimore, Maryland: John Hopkins University Press.

Lopez-Calva, L. & Rocha, S. (2012). *Exiting Belindia? Lesson from the Recent Decline in Income Inequality in Brazil*. Washington, DC: World Bank.

Lüchmann, L. H., & Almeida, C. C. (2010). A Representação Política das Mulheres nos Conselhos Gestores de Políticas Públicas. *Revista Katálysis*, 13(1), 86–94.

Lüchmann, L. H. H., Almeida, C. & Gimenes, É. R. (2016). Gênero e Representação Política nos Conselhos Gestores no Brasil. *Dados*, 59(3), 789–822.

Lupu, N., & Riedl, R. B. (2013). Political Parties and Uncertainty in Developing Democracies. *Comparative Political Studies*, 46(11), 1339–1365.

Lustig, N., Lopez-Calva, L. & Ortiz-Juarez, E. (2013). Declining Inequality in Latin America in the 2000s: The Cases of Argentina, Brazil, and Mexico. *World Development*, 44, 129–141.

Machado, M. G. (2009). História e Memória na Formação de Identidades no Castainho: Busca de Significados aos Quilombolas em Garanhuns-PE. Retrieved from: www.snh2011.anpuh.org/resources/anais/anpuhnacional/S .25/ANPUH.S25.1500.pdf

Macinko, J., Guanais, F., & de Souza, M. (2006). Evaluation of the Impact of the Family Health Program on Infant Mortality in Brazil, 1990–2002. *Journal of Epidemiology and Community Health*, 60(1), 13–19.

Macinko, J. & Harris, M. (2015). Brazil's Family Health Strategy – Delivering Community-Based Primary Care in a Universal Health System. *New England Journal of Medicine*, 372(23), 2177–2181.

Maddison, A. (1992). *The Political Economy of Poverty, Equity, and Growth: Brazil and Mexico*. New York: Oxford University Press.

Madison, J. (1788). Federalist Paper No. 51, reprinted in *The Federalist Papers* (1987). New York, NY: Penguin Classics.

Madrid, R. (2003). *Retiring the State: The Politics of Pension Privatization in Latin America and Beyond*. Stanford, CA: Stanford University Press.

Mainwaring, S. (1986). *The Catholic Church and Politics in Brazil, 1916–1985*. Stanford, CA: Stanford University Press.

Mainwaring, S. (1999). *Rethinking Party Systems in the Third Wave of Democratization*. Stanford, CA: Stanford University Press.

Mainwaring, S., & Zoco, E. (2007). Political Sequences and the Stabilization of Interparty Competition: Electoral Volatility in Old and New Democracies. *Party Politics*, 13(2), 155–178.

Malloy, J. M. (1977). Social Security Policy and the Working Class in Twentieth-Century Brazil. *Journal of Interamerican Studies & World Affairs*, 19(1): 35–60.

Malloy, J. M. (1979). *The Politics of Social Security in Brazil*. Pittsburgh, PA: Pittsburgh University Press.

Malta, D. C., Santos, M. A. S., Stopa, S. R., et al. (2016). Family Health Strategy Coverage in Brazil, According to the National Health Survey, 2013. *Ciencia & Saude Coletiva*, 21(2), 327–338.

Mansbridge, J. (1999). Should Blacks Represent Blacks and Women Represent Women? A Contingent "Yes." *The Journal of Politics*, 61(3), 628–657.

Marshall, T. (1950). *Citizenship and Social Class, and Other Essays*. Cambridge, UK: Cambridge University Press.

Marteleto, L. J. (2012). Educational Inequality by Race in Brazil, 1982–2007: Structural Changes and Shifts in Racial Classification. *Demography*, 49(1): 337–358.

Marx, J., Borner, J. & Caminotti, M. (2009). Gender Quotas, Candidate Selection, and Electoral Campaign: Comparing Argentina and Brazil in J. S. Jaquette, ed., *Feminist Agendas and Democracy in Latin America*. Durham, NC: Duke University Press, 45–64.

Mason, K. O. (1987). The Impact of Women's Social Position on Fertility in Developing Countries. *Sociological Forum*, 2(4), 718–745.

Mayhew, D. R. (1974). *Congress: The Electoral Connection*, New Haven, CT: Yale University Press.

Mayka, L. (2019). *Building Participatory Institutions in Latin America: Reform Coalitions and Institutional Change*. New York (NY): Cambridge University Press.

McAdam, D., McCarthy, J. D. & Zald, M. N. (eds.) (1996). *Comparative Perspectives on Social Movements: Political Opportunities, Mobilizing Structures, and Cultural Framings*. Cambridge, UK: Cambridge University Press.

McGuire, J. W. (2006). Basic Health Care Provision and Under-5 Mortality: A Cross-National Study of Developing Countries. *World Development*, 34(3), 405–425.

McGuire, J. W. (2010). *Wealth, Health, and Democracy in East Asia and Latin America*. Cambridge, UK: Cambridge University Press.

McNulty, S. (2011). *Voice and Vote: Decentralization and Participation in Post-Fujimori Peru*. Stanford, CA: Stanford University Press,.

Medeiros, M., Britto, T. & Soares, F. V. (2008). *Targeted Cash Transfer Programmes in Brazil* (Working Paper No. 46). Brasilia, DF: International Poverty Centre.

Medeiros, M., Diniz, D. & Squinca, F. (2015). *Cash Benefits to Disabled Persons in Brazil: An Analysis of BPC-Continuous Cash Benefit Programme* (Discussion Paper No. 170). Brasilia, DF: Institute for Applied Economic Research.

Mesa-Lago, C. (1978). *Social Security in Latin America: Pressure Groups, Stratification, and Inequality*. Pittsburgh, PA: University of Pittsburgh Press.

Mettler, S. (2007). *Soldiers to Citizens*. New York, NY: Oxford University Press.

Mills A., Vaughan J.P., Smith D.L., Tabibzadeh I. (eds) (1990). *Health System Decentralization: Concepts, Issues and Country Experience*. Geneva: World Health Organization.

Ministry of Education (2013). *Primary Education in Brazil.* Brasilia, D.F.: Ministry of Education.

Ministry of Education (2017). Lei N° 13.415, de 16 de Fevereiro de 2017. Retrieved from: www.planalto.gov.br/ccivil_03/_ato2015-2018/2017/lei/L13415.htm.

Ministry of Education (2018). *Primary Education in Brazil.* Brasilia, D.F.: Ministry of Education.

Ministry of Health (2013). *Infant Mortality.* Brasilia, D.F.: Ministry of Health.

Ministry of Health (2016). Portal da Saude: Datasus (Database). Retrieved from: www2.datasus.gov.br/DATASUS/index.php?area=0205.

Ministry of Health (2017). Indicadores e Dados Brasicos: Brasil-2002 (Database). Retrieved from: http://tabnet.datasus.gov.br/cgi/idb2012/matriz.htm.

Ministry of Planning, Budget, and Management (2011). Orçamento Federal ao Alcance de Todos: Projeto de Lei Orçamentária Annual – PLOA. Retrieved from: www.planejamento.gov.br/secretarias/upload/Arquivos/sof/ploa2012/1 10831_orc_fed_alc_todos.pdf.

Ministry of Social Development (2013). *Poverty in Brazil.* Brasilia, D.F.: Ministry of Social Development.

Ministry of Social Development (2015). Bolsa Família e Cadastro Único no seu Município. Retrieved from: www.mds.gov.br/bolsafamilia.

Ministry of Social Development (2018). *Program Bolsa Familia.* Brasilia: Government of Brazil.

Mische, A. (2008). *Partisan Publics: Communication and Contention across Brazilian Youth Activist Networks*, Princeton, NJ: Princeton University Press.

Modesto, L. (2014). O Papel da Gestora na Política Pública. *RESPVBLICA,* 13 (1), 86–97.

Møller, J. & Skaaning, S. E. (2012). *Democracy and Democratization in Comparative Perspective: Conceptions, Conjunctures, Causes and Consequences.* New York, NY: Routledge.

Molyneux, M. (1985). Mobilization without Emancipation? Women's Interests, the State, and Revolution in Nicaragua. *Feminist Studies,* 11(2), 227–254.

Montalvo, J. G. & Ravallion, M. (2010). The Pattern of Growth and Poverty Reduction in China. *Journal of Comparative Economics,* 38(1), 2–16.

Montero, A. (2014). *Brazil: Reversal of Fortune.* Cambridge, UK: Polity Press.

Montero, A. & Samuels, D. (2004). *Decentralization and Democracy in Latin America.* Notre Dame, IN: University of Notre Dame Press.

Moore, J. D. & Donaldson, J. A. (2016). Human-Scale Economics: Economic Growth and Poverty Reduction in Northeastern Thailand. *World Development,* 85, 1–15.

Moura, J. E. D. (2009). *O Sentido da Participação na Construção da Política Urbana em Camaragibe* (Unpublished doctoral dissertation). Recife, PE: Universidade Federal de Pernambuco.

Mozaffar, S., & Scarritt, J. R. (2005). The Puzzle of African Party Systems. *Party Politics,* 11(4), 399–421.

Mullainathan, S., & Shafir, E. (2013). *Scarcity: Why Having Too Little Means So Much.* New York, NY: Times Books/Henry Holt and Co.

Nabatchi, T. (2012). Putting the "Public" Back in Public Values Research: Designing Participation to Identify and Respond to Values. *Public Administration Review,* 72(5), 699–708.

Narayan, D., Patel, R., Schafft, K., Rademacher, A., Koch-Schulte, S. (2000). *Voices of the Poor: Can Anyone Hear Us?* Washinton, D.C.: World Bank Group.

Negreiros, E. D. & da Fonte, E. M. (2003). Pacto Camaragibe: Experiência de Uma Pólis em Renovação. *Estudos de Sociologia*, 2(9), 97–118.

Niedzwiecki, S. (2015). Social Policy Commitment in South America: The Effect of Organized Labor on Social Spending from 1980 to 2010. *Journal of Politics in Latin America*, 7(2), 3–42.

North, D. C., & Weingast, B. R. (1989). Constitutions and Commitment: The Evolution of Institutions Governing Public Choice in Seventeenth-Century England. *The Journal of Economic History*, 49(4), 803–832.

Nussbaum, M. (2011). *Creating Capabilities*. Cambridge, MA: Harvard University Press.

O'Donnell, G. (1973). *Modernization and Bureaucratic-Authoritarianism: Studies in South American Politics*. Berkeley, CA: University of California Press.

O'Donnell, G. (1994). The State, Democratization and Some Conceptual Problems: A Latin American View with Glances at Some Post-Communist Countries in W. C. Smith, C. H. Acuma & E. A. Gamarra, eds., *Democracy, Markets, and Structural Reform in Latin America*. Miami, FL: University of Miami North-South Center.

O'Donnell, G. (1998). Horizontal Accountability in New Democracies. *Journal of Democracy*, 9(3), 112–126.

Oakes, J. M. & Kaufman, J. S. (2017). *Methods in Social Epidemiology* (V 16), Hoboken, NJ: John Wiley & Sons.

OECD (2011). *Report on the Gender Initiative: Gender Equality in Education, Employment and Entrepreneurship*. Retrieved from: www.oecd.org/social/48 111145.pdf.

OECD (2014). Population Who Attained Upper Secondary Education, by Sex and Age Group. Retrieved from: www.oecd.org/gender/data/populationwhoattaine duppersecondaryeducationbysexandagegroup.htm.

OECD (2016). *Education at a Glance 2016: OECD Indicators*. Paris, FR: OECD Publishing.

Oliveira, F. M. D. (2003). *Cidadania e Cultura Política no Poder Local: O Conselho da Administração Participativa de Camaragibe* (Unpublished masters' thesis). Recife, PE: Universidade Federal de Pernambuco.

Olken, B. A. (2010). Direct Democracy and Local Public Goods: Evidence from a Field Experiment in Indonesia. *American Political Science Review*, 104(2), 243–267.

Olson, M. (1965). *Logic of Collective Action: Public Goods and the Theory of Groups*. Cambridge, MA: Harvard University Press.

Olsson, L., Opondo, M., Tschakert, P. et al. (2014). Livelihoods and Poverty in C. Field, V. Barros, D. Dokken, et al., eds., *Climate Change 2014: Impacts, Adaptation, and Vulnerability*. Cambridge, UK: Cambridge University Press, 793–832.

Ostrom, E. (1990). *Governing the Commons: The Evolution of Institutions for Collective Action*. New York, NY: Cambridge University Press.

Ostrom, E. (1996). Crossing the Great Divide: Coproduction, Synergy, and Development. *World Development*, 24(6), 1073–1087.

Pateman, C. (1970). *Participation and Democratic Theory*. New York, NY: Cambridge University Press.

Pateman, C. (2012). Participatory Democracy Revisited. *Perspectives on Politics*, 10(1), 7–19.

Pereira, C., & Renno, L. (2003). Successful Re-Election Strategies in Brazil: The Electoral Impact of Distinct Institutional Incentives. *Electoral Studies*, 22(3), 425–448.

Pereira, O. L. C. B. & Spink, P. K. (2015). *Reforma do Estado e Administração Pública Gerencial*, Rio de Janeiro, RJ: Editora Fundação Getulio Vargas.

Peterson, M. A. (1993). Political Influence in the 1990s: From Iron Triangles to Policy Networks. *Journal of Health Politics, Policy and Law*, 18(2), 395–438.

Phillips, A. (1995). *The Politics of Presence*. New York, NY: Oxford University Press.

Pickett, K. E. & Wilkinson, R. G. (2015). Income Inequality and Health: A Causal Review. *Social Science & Medicine*, 128, 316–326.

Pierson, P. (1993). When Effect Becomes Cause: Policy Feedback and Political Change. *World Politics*, 45(4), 595–628.

Pierson, P. (2000). Increasing Returns, Path Dependence, and the Study of Politics. *American Political Science Review*, 94(2), 251–267.

Piovesan, F. (2009). Violence against Women in Brazil: Feminist Agendas and Democracy in Latin America in M. R. Tobar, J. Marx, J. Borner & M. Caminotti (2009), eds., *Feminist Agendas And Democracy in Latin America*. Durham, NC: Duke University Press, 113–128.

Piovesan, F. (2011). Lei de Anistia, Sistema Interamericano e o Caso Brasileiro in L. F. Gomes & V. O. Mazzuoli, eds., *Crimes da Ditadura Militar: Uma Análise à Luz da Jurisprudência Atual da Corte Interamericana de Direitos Humanos: Argentina, Brasil, Chile, Uruguai*. São Paulo, SP: Editora Revista dos Tribunais, 71–74.

Pires, R. (ed.) (2011). *Efetividade das Instituições Participativas no Brasil: Estratégias de Avaliação* (V 7). Brasilia, DF: Instituto de Pesquisa Econômica Aplicada.

Pires, R. & Vaz, A. (2012). *Participação Social como Método de Governo? Um Mapeamento das "Interfaces Socioestatais" nos Programas Federais* (TD No. 1707). Brasilia, DF: Instituto de Pesquisa Econômica Aplicada.

Pitkin, H. F. (1967). *The Concept of Representation*. Berkeley, CA: University of California Press.

Pitt, M. M. & Khandker, S. R. (1998). The Impact of Group-Based Credit Programs on Poor Households in Bangladesh: Does the Gender of Participants Matter? *Journal of Political Economy*, 106(5), 958–996.

Pogrebinschi, T. & Samuels, D. (2014). The Impact of Participatory Democracy: Evidence from Brazil's National Public Policy Conferences. *Comparative Politics*, 46(3), 313–332.

Polletta, F. (2015). Public Deliberation and Political Contention in C. W. Lee, M. McQuarrie & E. T. Walker, eds., *Democratizing Inequalities: Dilemmas of the New Public Participation*. New York, NY: New York University Press, 222–243.

Porter, D. (1999). The History of Public Health: Current Themes and Approaches. *Hygiea Internationalis*, 1(1), 9–21.

Power, T. J. (2010). *Political Right in Postauthoritarian Brazil: Elites, Institutions, and Democratization*. University Park, PA: Penn State Press.

Power, T. J. & Zucco Jr, C. (2009). Estimating Ideology of Brazilian Legislative Parties, 1990–2005: A Research Communication. *Latin American Research Review*, 44(1), 218–246.

Przeworski, A., Stokes, S. C. & Manin, B. (1999). *Democracy, Accountability, and Representation* (V 2). New York, NY: Cambridge University Press.

Putnam, R. D., Leonardi, R. & Nanetti, R. Y. (1994). *Making Democracy Work: Civic Traditions in Modern Italy*. Princeton, NJ: Princeton University Press.

Quibria, M. G. (2002). *Growth and Poverty: Lessons from the East Asian Miracle Revisited* (ADB Institute Research Paper 33). Tokyo, JP: Asian Development Bank Institute.

Raile, E. D., Pereira, C., & Power, T. J. (2011). The Executive Toolbox: Building Legislative Support in a Multiparty Presidential Regime. *Political Research Quarterly*, 64(2), 323–334.

Rakodi, C. (2014). *Urban Livelihoods: A People-Centred Approach to Reducing Poverty*, Abingdon, UK: Routledge.

Rasella, D., Aquino, R., Santos, C., Paes- Sousa, R. & Barreto. M. (2013). Effect of a Conditional Cash Transfer Programme on Childhood Mortality: A Nation-Wide Analysis of Brazilian Municipalities. *The Lancet*, 382(9886), 57–64.

Ravallion, M. (1997). Good and Bad Growth: The Human Development Reports. *World Development*, 25(5), 631–638.

Ravallion, M. & Chen, S. (2007). China's (Uneven) Progress against Poverty. *Journal of Development Economics*, 82(1), 1–42.

Reis, M. C. (2004). *O Projeto Camaragibe Conta, Canta e Encanta e a Relação Prática Pedagógica e Cultura Popular* (Unpublished master's thesis). Recife, PE: Universidade Federal de Pernambuco.

Riedl, R. B. (2014). *Authoritarian Origins of Democratic Party Systems in Africa*, New York, NY: Cambridge University Press.

Robinson, J. A., & Verdier, T. (2002). The Political Economy of Clientelism (CEPR Discussion Paper No. 3205). Retrieved from: https://papers.ssrn.com/s ol3/papers.cfm?abstract_id=303185.

Rocha, S. (2008). Transferências de Renda Federais: Focalização e Impactos Xobre Pobreza e Desigualdade. *Revista de Economia Contemporânea*, 12(1), 51–66.

Rodrigues, C. R. O. (1996). *Programa da Saúde da Família, Camaragibe-PE: Uma abordagem qualitativa*, Recife, PE: Fundação Oswaldo Cruz – Centro de Pesquisas Aggeu Magalhães (CPqAM).

Rodrik, D. (2000). Growth versus Poverty Reduction: A Hollow Debate. *Finance and Development*, 37(4), 8–9.

Rodrik, D. (2014). The Past, Present, and Future of Economic Growth. *Challenge*, 57(3), 5–39.

Roodman, D. (2014). How to Do Xtabond2: An Introduction to Difference and System GMM in Stata. *The Stata Journal*, 9(1), 86–136.

Ross, M. (2006). Is Democracy Good for the Poor? *American Journal of Political Science*, 50(4), 860–874.

Rowlands, J. (1997). *Questioning Empowerment: Working with Women in Honduras*. Oxford, UK: Oxfam.

Sabatier, P. A., & Weible, C. M. (eds.). (2014). *Theories of the Policy Process*. Boulder, CO: Westview Press.

Sachs, J. (2008). *Common Wealth: Economics for a Crowded Planet*. London, UK: Penguin.

Salles, F. C., & Vieira, S. G. S. (2017). The Capacity for Power of Local Governments in the Area Of Development: A Position Analysis of Minas Gerais, Brazil, Starting in 2003. *Apuntes*, 41(74), 163–189.

Samuels, D. (1999). Incentives to Cultivate a Party Vote in Candidate-Centric Electoral Systems Evidence from Brazil. *Comparative Political Studies*, 32(4), 487–518.

Samuels, D. J., & Zucco, C. (2018). *Partisans, Antipartisans, and Nonpartisans: Voting Behavior in Brazil*. New York, NY: Cambridge University Press.

Sánchez-Ancochea, D. & Mattei, L. (2011). Bolsa Família, Poverty and Inequality: Political and Economic Effects in the Short and Long Run. *Global Social Policy*, 11(2–3), 299–318.

Santos, B. (Ed.). (2005). *Democratizing Democracy: Beyond the Liberal Democratic Canon*. New York, NY: Verso.

Santos, D. B. (2011). Pesquisa de Informacoes Basicas in R. R. C. Pires, ed., *Efetividade das Instituições Participativas no Brasil: Estratégias de Avaliação*, Brasilia, D. F.: Ipea.

Santos, O., Ribeiro, L. C. D. Q., & Azevedo, S. D. (2004). *Governança Democrática e Poder Local: A Experiência dos Conselhos Municipais no Brasil*, Rio de Janeiro, RJ: Revan, Fase, 223–248.

Santos, T. (1970). The Structure of Dependence. *The American Economic Review*, 60(2), 231–236.

Santos, T. D. (1970). The Structure of Dependence. *The American Economic Review*, 60 (2), 231–236.

Santos, T. M. S. (2002). Desenvolvimento Local e Cidadania: Desafios e Estrategias de Comunicaaco da Gestao Participativa Popular da Prefeitura de Camaragibe/PE, paper presented at VI Congress of the Latin American Communications Associations (ALAIC), Santa Cruz de la Sierra, Bolivia, 5–7 June.

Sartori, G. (1970). Concept Misformation in Comparative Politics. *American Political Science Review*, 64(4), 1033–1053.

Schattschneider. E. E. (1960). *The Semisovereign People: A Realist's View of Democracy in America*. New York, NY: Holt, Rinehart and Winston.

Schell, S. F., Luke, D. A., Schooley, M. W., et al. (2013). Public Health Program Capacity for Sustainability: A New Framework. *Implementation Science*, 8(15), 1–9.

Schmitter, P., & Karl, T. L. (1991). What Democracy Is . . . and Is Not. *Journal of Democracy*, 2(3), 75–88.

Schneider, B. R. (2015). The Developmental State in Brazil: Comparative and Historical Perspectives. *Revista de Economia Política*, 35(1), 114–132.

Schramm, J. M. D. A. & Szwarcwald, C. L. (2000). Diferenciais nas Taxas de Mortalidade Neonatal e Natimortalidade Hospitalares no Brasil: Um Estudo com Base no Sistema de Informações Hospitalares do Sistema Único de Saúde (SIH/SUS). *Cadernos de Saúde Pública*, 16(4), 1031–1040.

Schumpeter, J. A. (1950). The March into Socialism. *The American Economic Review*, 40(2), 446–456.

Scott, J. C. (1998). *Seeing Like a State: How Certain Schemes to Improve the Human Condition Have Failed*. New Haven, CT: Yale University Press.

Scutchfield, F. D., Knight, E. A., Kelly, A. V., Bhandari, M. W., & Vasilescu, I. P. (2004). Local Public Health Agency Capacity and Its Relationship to Public Health System Performance. *Journal of Public Health Management and Practice*, 10(3), 204–215.

Secretaria Nacional de Políticas para as Mulheres (2014). *Guia para Criação e Implementação de Organismos Governamentais de Políticas para as Mulheres – OPM*. Retrieved from: www.google.com/url?sa=t&rct=j&q=&esrc=s&source=web&cd=2&ved=2ahUKEwj81pH7tvjhAhVQT6wKHdpHDIIQFjABegQIBBAC&url=http%3A%2F%2Fwww.consultaesic.cgu.gov.br%2Fbusca%2Fdados%2FLists%2FPedido%2FAttachments%2F444120%2FRESPOSTA_PEDIDO_Guia%2520para%2520a%2520criao%2520de%2520OPM%252021%252001%25202015%2520final.docx&usg=AOvVaw21VCjJkdCb_ZoVSdkWOvgf.

Sen, A. (1999). *Development as Freedom*. New York, NY: Alfred A. Knopf.

Shahidur, R., Koolwal, G. & Samad, H. (2010). *Handbook on Impact Evaluation: Quantitative Methods and Practices*. Washington, DC: World Bank Publications.

Silva, A. M. (2012). *Estrutura das Regionais de Saude do Municipio de Jaboatão dos Guararapes-PE* (Unpublished monograph). Recife, PE: Fundacao Oswaldo Cruz- Centro de Pesquisas Aggeu Magalhães (CPqAM).

Sintomer, Y. (2010). Random Selection, Republican Self-Government, and Deliberative Democracy. *Constellations*, 17(3), 472–487.

Skocpol, T. (1992). *Protecting Soldiers and Mothers*. Cambridge, MA: Harvard University Press.

Smith, G. (2009). *Democratic Innovations: Designing Institutions for Citizen Participation*. Cambridge, UK: Cambridge University Press.

Smulovitz, C. & Peruzzotti, E. (2000). Societal Accountability in Latin America. *Journal of Democracy*, 11(4), 147–158.

Snyder, R. (2001). Scaling Down: The Subnational Comparative Method. *Studies in Comparative International Development*, 36(1), 93–110.

Soares, F. V., Ribas, R. P. & Osório, R. G. (2010). Evaluating the Impact of Brazil's Bolsa Família: Cash Transfer Programs in Comparative Perspective. *Latin American Research Review*, 45(2), 174–190.

Soares, S. (2012). *Bolsa Família, Its Design, Its Impacts and Possibilities for the Future* (Working Paper No. 89). Brasília, DF: International Policy Center for Inclusive Growth.

Soares, S., Guerreiro Osorio, R., Veras Soares, F., Medeiros, M., & Zepeda, E. (2009). Conditional Cash Transfers in Brazil, Chile and Mexico: Impacts upon Inequality. *Estudios Económicos*, 207–224.

Somers, M. R. (2008). *Genealogies of Citizenship: Markets, Statelessness, and the Right to Have Rights*. Cambridge, UK: Cambridge University Press.

Sorj, B. & Gama, A. (2013). Family Policies in Brazil in M. Robila, ed., *Handbook of Family Policies across the Globe*. New York, NY: Springer, 459–471.

Soss, J and Weaver, V. (2017). Police Are Our Government: Politics, Political Science and the Policing of Race-Class Subjugated Communities. *Annual Review of Political Science* 20, 565–591.

Speck, B. W. (2011). Auditing Institutions in T. J. Power & M. M. Taylor, eds., *Corruption and Democracy in Brazil: The Struggle for Accountability*. Notre Dame, IN: University of Notre Dame Press.

Spink, P. (2000). The Rights Approach to Subnational Government: The Experience of the Public Management and Citizenship Program. *Cadernos Gestão Pública e Cidadania*, 17, 1–34.

Spink, P., & Clemente, R. A. D. S. (eds.) (1997). *20 Experiências de Gestão Pública e Cidadania*. Rio de Janeiro, RJ: Editora Fundação Getulio Vargas.

Starfield, B., Shi, L., & Macinko, J. (2005). Contribution of Primary Care to Health Systems and Health. *The Milbank Quarterly*, 83(3), 457–502.

Stigler, G. J. (1972). Economic Competition and Political Competition. *Public Choice*, 13(1), 91–106.

Stiglitz, J. E. (2002). *Globalization and Its Discontents* (V 500). New York, NY: W. W. Norton & Company.

Stiglitz, J. E. (2012). *The Price of Inequality: How Today's Divided Society Endangers Our Future*. New York, NY: W. W. Norton & Company.

Sugiyama, N. B. (2007). Theories of Policy Diffusion: Social Sector Reform in Brazil. *Comparative Political Studies*, 41(2), 193–216.

Sugiyama, N. B. (2011). The Diffusion of Conditional Cash Transfer Programs in the Americas. *Global Social Policy*, 11(2/3): 250–278.

Sugiyama, N. B. (2012). *Diffusion of Good Government: Social Sector Reforms in Brazil*. Notre Dame, IN: University of Notre Dame Press.

Sugiyama, N. B. & Hunter, W. (2013). Whither Clientelism? Good Governance and Brazil's Bolsa Família Program. *Comparative Politics*, 46(1), 43–62.

Superior Electoral Tribunal (2013). *Municipal Election Profiles*. Brasilia, D.F.: Superior Electoral Tribunal.

Superior Electoral Tribunal (2017). *Tribunal Superior Eleitoral* (Database). Brasilia, DF: Government of Brazil.

Tarrow, S. (1994). *Power in Movement: Social Movements, Collective Action and Mass Politics*. New York, NY: Cambridge University Press.

Teichman, J. (2004). The World Bank and Policy Reform in Mexico and Argentina. *Latin American Politics and Society*, 46(1), 39–74.

Teichman, J. (2008). Redistributive Conflict and Social Policy in Latin America. *World Development*, 36(3), 446–460.

Teixeira, A. C. C., & Tatagiba, L. (2005). *Movimentos Sociais e Sistema Político: Os Desafios da Participação*. São Paulo, SP: Instituto Polis/PUC-SP.

Telles, E., & Paschel, T. (2014). Who Is Black, White, Or Mixed Race? How Skin Color, Status, and Nation Shape Racial Classification in Latin America. *American Journal of Sociology*, 120(3), 864–907.

Tendler, J. (1997). *Good Government in the Tropics (The Johns Hopkins Studies in Development)*. Baltimore, MD: Johns Hopkins University Press.

Terreblanche, S. J. (2002). *A History of Inequality in South Africa: 1652–2002*, South Africa: University of Kwazulu Natal Press.

Thévenon, O. (2011). Family Policies in OECD countries: A Comparative Analysis. *Population and Development Review*, 37(1), 57–87.

Thompson, E. P. (1964). *The Making of the English Working Class*. New York, NY: Pantheon Books.

Touchton, M. (2016). The Benefits of Balance: Credibility, The Rule of Law, and Investment in Latin America. *Latin American Research Review*, 51(2), 195–216.

Touchton, M., Sugiyama, N. B. & Wampler, B. (2017). Democracy at Work: Moving beyond Elections to Improve Well-Being. *American Political Science Review*, 111(1), 68–82.

Touchton, M. & Wampler, B. (2014). Improving Social Well-Being through New Democratic Institutions. *Comparative Political Studies*, 47(10), 1442–1469.

Touchton, M., Wampler, B. & Peixoto, T. (2018). *Of Governance and Revenue: Participatory Institutions and Tax Compliance in Brazil*. Forthcoming. World Bank Working Paper.

Travis, P., Bennett, S., Haines, A., et al. (2004). Overcoming Health-Systems Constraints to Achieve the Millennium Development Goals. *The Lancet*, 364 (9437), 900–906.

True, J. & Mintrom, M. (2001). Transnational Networks and Policy Diffusion: The Case of Gender Mainstreaming. *International Studies Quarterly*, 45 (1):27–57.

Tsai, P. L. & Huang, C. H. (2007). Openness, Growth and Poverty: The Case of Taiwan. *World Development*, 35(11), 1858–1871.

Tsebelis, G. (2002). *Veto Players: How Political Institutions Work*. Princeton, NJ: Princeton University Press.

UN Women (2015). *Progress of the World's Women 2015–2016*. New York, NY: UN Women.

UN Women (2016). Women's Empowerment. Website. Retrieved from: www .undp.org/content/undp/en/home/gender-equality/women-s-economic-empow erment.html.

UNESCO (2017). UNESCO eAtlas of Literacy. Retrieved from: https://tellmaps .com/uis/literacy/#!/tellmap/-601865091.

United Nations (1948). Universal Declaration of Human Rights. Retrieved from: www.ohchr.org/EN/UDHR/Documents/UDHR_Translations/eng.pdf.

United Nations (1995a). *Report of the World Summit for Social Development*. Retrieved from: https://undocs.org/A/CONF.166/9.

United Nations (1995b). *Beijing Declaration and Platform for Action*. Retrieved from: www.un.org/womenwatch/daw/beijing/pdf/BDPfA%20E.pdf.

United Nations (1996). *Human Development Report 1996*. New York, NY: Oxford University Press.

United Nations (2000). United Nations Millennium Declaration. Retrieved from: www.un.org/millennium/declaration/ares552e.pdf.

United Nations (2018). *Under-5 Mortality*. New York, NY: United Nations' Childrens' Fund. Retrieved from: https://data.unicef.org/topic/child-survival/under-five-mortality/.

United Nations, Department of Economic and Social Affairs (2015). *Transforming Our World: The 2030 Agenda for Sustainable Development*. New York: United Nations.

Viana, A. L. & Poz, M. R. (1998). A Reforma do Sistema de Saúde no Brasil e o Programa de Saúde da Família. *PHYSIS: Revista Saúde Coletiva*, 8(2), 11–42.

Victora, C. G., Aquino, E. M., do Carmo Leal, M., et al. (2011).Maternal and Child Health in Brazil: Progress and Challenges. *The Lancet*, 377 (9780), 1863–1876.

Villas-Boas, R. & Telles, V. D. S. (1995). *Poder Local, Participação Popular e Construção da Cidadania*. Sao Paulo, SP: Fórum Nacional de Participação Popular nas Administrações Municipais.

Wade, R. (1990). *Governing the Market: Economic Theory and the Role of Government in East Asian Industrialization*. Princeton, NJ: Princeton University Press.

Wampler, B. (2007). *Participatory Budgeting in Brazil: Contestation, Cooperation, and Accountability*. University Park, PA: Penn State Press.

Wampler, B. (2012). Participation, representation, and social justice: Using participatory governance to transform representative democracy. *Polity*, 44 (4), 666–682.

Wampler, B. (2015). *Activating Democracy: Popular Participation, Social Justice and Interlocking Institutions in Brazil*. Notre Dame, IN: Notre Dame University Press.

Wampler, B. & Avritzer, L. (2004). Participatory Publics: Civil Society and New Institutions in Democratic Brazil. *Comparative Politics*, 36(3), 291–312.

Wampler, B., McNulty, S., & Touchton, M. (2018). *Participatory Budgeting: Spreading Across the Globe*. Retrieved from: www.transparency-initiative.org/wp-content/uploads/2018/03/spreading-pb-across-the-globe_jan-2018.pdf.

Warren, M. E. (1996). Deliberative Democracy and Authority. *The American Political Science Review*, 90(1), 46–60.

Warren, M. E. (2005). Communities and Schools: A New View of Urban Education Reform. *Harvard Educational Review*, 75(2), 133–173.

Weffort, F. (1984). *Porque Democracia?* São Paulo, SP: Editora Brasiliense.

Weitz-Shapiro, R. (2012). What Wins Votes: Why Some Politicians Opt out of Clientelism. *American Journal of Political Science*, 56(3), 568–583.

Weyland, K. (1996). *Democracy without Equity: Failures of Reform in Brazil*. Pittsburgh, PA: University of Pittsburgh Press.

Wolfe, J. (1993). *Working Women, Working Men: Sao Paulo and the Rise of Brazil's Industrial Working Class 1900–1955*. Durham, NC: Duke University Press.

Wolford, W. (2010). *This Land Is Ours Now: Social Mobilization and the Meanings of Land in Brazil*. Durham, NC: Duke University Press.

Wong, J. (2004). Democratization and the Left: Comparing East Asia and Latin America. *Comparative Political Studies*, 37(10), 1213–1237.

Wooldridge J. (2014). *Introductory Econometrics: A Modern Approach*, 5th ed. New York, NY: Cengage Learning.

World Bank. (2004). *World Development Report: Making Services Work for Poor People*. Washington, DC: World Bank.

World Bank (2013). *World Development Report: Jobs*. Washington, DC: The World Bank.

World Bank (2015). *Sustaining Employment and Wage Gains in Brazil: A Skills and Jobs Agenda*. Washington, DC: World Bank Group.

World Bank (2016). GINI Index (World Bank Estimate). Retrieved from: https://data.worldbank.org/indicator/SI.POV.GINI

World Bank (2017). *World Development Indicators 2017*. Washington, DC: World Bank.

World Bank (2018). World Development Indicators (Database). Retrieved from: http://databank.worldbank.org/data/source/world-development-indicators

World Education Forum (2000). *The Dakar Framework for Action, Education for All: Meeting Our Collective Commitments*. Adopted by the World Education Forum. Dakar, Senegal. Retrieved from http://unesdoc.unesco.org/images/0012/001211/121147e.pdf

World Health Organization (1978). *Declaration of Alma Ata: International Conference on Primary Health Care, Alma Ata, USSR, 6–12 September 1978*. Geneva: World Health Organization.

World Health Organization (2012). *Maternal Mortality Fact Sheet. No. 348. 2012*.

World Health Organization (2016). Global Health Observatory (GHO) Data: Neonatal Mortality. World Health Organization. Retrieved from: www.who.int/gho/child_health/mortality/neonatal/en/

Wylie, K. N. (in press). *Amplifying Women's Voices: Party Institutionalization and Leadership in Brazil*. New York, NY: Cambridge University Press.

Xue, J. (2012). *Growth with Inequality: An International Comparison on Income Distribution*. Singapore: World Scientific Press.

Yashar, D. J. (2005). *Contesting Citizenship in Latin America: The Rise of Indigenous Movements and the Postliberal Challenge*. Cambridge, UK: Cambridge University Press.

Zakocs, R. C., & Edwards, E. M. (2006). What Explains Community Coalition Effectiveness? A Review of the Literature. *American Journal of Preventive Medicine*, 30(4), 351–361.

Zucco Jr, C. (2013). When Payouts Pay Off: Conditional Cash Transfers and Voting Behavior in Brazil 2002–10. *American Journal of Political Science*, 57 (4), 810–822.

Index

Lightning Source UK Ltd.
Milton Keynes UK
UKHW011955080422
401328UK00002B/41